Academic Writing, Assessment, and Neurodiversity

The number of students with specific learning difficulties entering higher education has increased dramatically over the last decade, yet academic support for these students is often insufficient. This innovative book will equip teaching staff with the tools to support these students with learning and assessment, arming them with the skills they need to excel in higher education.

Combining a scholarly rationale for inclusive pedagogies with practical strategies for busy practitioners, the book uses accessible and meaningful inclusive techniques based on the principles of Universal Design for Learning (UDL), the theory of Complementary Cognition, and the author's own principles of compositional pictography to show how educators can harness students' differing cognitive strengths and help them to use them to their own advantage. The book demonstrates how the challenges associated with learning differences are manifested in student writing and assessment, with chapters covering such topics as:

- How to scaffold support to develop the areas students find challenging.
- How to deploy metaphorical and visual pedagogies to develop approaches to studying and writing.
- How to make assessment design more inclusive.

Presenting an inclusive, practical, and research-informed pedagogical approach to the teaching of academic writing, this practical guide is an essential read for anyone supporting higher education students with assessment, including tutors, lecturers, learning developers, and disability advisors.

Adrian J. Wallbank is an Associate Professor in Academic Development at the Oxford Centre for Academic Enhancement and Development, Oxford Brookes University, UK.

"If you're looking for ways to support diverse learners – especially when it comes to supporting assessment-related learning for students with dyslexia, autism, and ADHD – this book is essential reading. *Academic Writing, Assessment, and Neurodiversity: Pedagogies for Inclusion* is rich with research, insights, and personal experiences that have already made me reflect on my own practices and think about how I can incorporate its advice into my own practices. This invaluable resource offers practical guidance that educators can immediately apply to create more inclusive learning environments. A great addition to the reading lists of any academic interested in access, inclusion, and equity."

Kevin L. Merry, *Associate Dean of Curriculum and Assessment, Global Banking School, UK*

"Inclusive pedagogies are inherently good for everyone – this edited collection successfully grapples with the concepts of neurodiversity, disabilities, learning differences, and learning difficulties to argue that adopting a pedagogy of inclusion benefits all learners. The book is a thoughtful, considered authority on the topic, a must-read for anyone who teaches in HE today, with practical examples of how good design can influence successful student outcomes across the board."

Emily McIntosh, *Director of Student Success, University of the West of Scotland, UK*

"Our increasingly nuanced understanding of the interconnected nature of learning, cognition, and social interaction offers both opportunities and obligations for how we work with students in more flexible, responsive ways. *Academic Writing, Assessment, and Neurodiversity: Pedagogies for Inclusion* is a timely and deeply useful book that offers important resources to provide all students with more inclusive and effective teaching. This book combines a rich foundation of current theory and research with practical and adaptable approaches to writing pedagogy and assessment. Anyone interested in how to approach inclusive teaching in more creative and collaborative ways should be reading this book."

Bronwyn T. Williams, *Professor of English/Endowed Chair in Rhetoric and Composition, University of Louisville, USA*

"It's been exciting to read a book on a topic that is close to my heart, to 'educate the educators' in further and higher education, in awareness and supportive strategies for dyslexic and neurodiverse students, so the whole teaching body can offer some support, creating an environment of understanding and inclusivity that would benefit all students. This book gives crucial and evidenced guidance to help achieve this aim and in my view is essential reading for anyone working with neurodiverse students."

Sarah J. Myhill, *Dyslexia Specialist Tutor, Lecturer in Academic Skills, and Founder of the Dyslexia Hub, University of Buckingham, UK*

Academic Writing, Assessment, and Neurodiversity

Pedagogies for Inclusion

Edited by Adrian J. Wallbank

LONDON AND NEW YORK

Cover image: Getty Images

First published 2026
by Routledge
4 Park Square, Milton Park, Abingdon, Oxon OX14 4RN

and by Routledge
605 Third Avenue, New York, NY 10158

Routledge is an imprint of the Taylor & Francis Group, an informa business

© 2026 selection and editorial matter, Adrian J. Wallbank; individual chapters, the contributors

The right of Adrian J. Wallbank to be identified as the author of the editorial material, and of the authors for their individual chapters, has been asserted in accordance with sections 77 and 78 of the Copyright, Designs and Patents Act 1988.

All rights reserved. No part of this book may be reprinted or reproduced or utilised in any form or by any electronic, mechanical, or other means, now known or hereafter invented, including photocopying and recording, or in any information storage or retrieval system, without permission in writing from the publishers.

Trademark notice: Product or corporate names may be trademarks or registered trademarks, and are used only for identification and explanation without intent to infringe.

British Library Cataloguing-in-Publication Data
A catalogue record for this book is available from the British Library

Library of Congress Cataloging-in-Publication Data
Names: Wallbank, Adrian J. editor
Title: Academic writing, assessment and neurodiversity : pedagogies for inclusion / Edited by Adrian J. Wallbank.
Description: Abingdon, Oxon ; New York, NY : Routledge, 2026. | Includes bibliographical references and index.
Identifiers: LCCN 2025009052 (print) | LCCN 2025009053 (ebook) | ISBN 9781032505503 hardback | ISBN 9781032505497 paperback | ISBN 9781003398974 ebook
Subjects: LCSH: Academic writing--Evaluation | Neurodiversity | Educational tests and measurements | College students with disabilities | Inclusive education
Classification: LCC LB2369 .A234 2018 (print) | LCC LB2369 (ebook) |
DDC 808.06/6378--dc23/eng/20250523
LC record available at https://lccn.loc.gov/2025009052
LC ebook record available at https://lccn.loc.gov/2025009053

ISBN: 978-1-032-50550-3 (hbk)
ISBN: 978-1-032-50549-7 (pbk)
ISBN: 978-1-003-39897-4 (ebk)

DOI: 10.4324/9781003398974

Typeset in Bembo
by KnowledgeWorks Global Ltd.

Contents

List of Contributors		vii
Preface		ix
Acknowledgements		xi

1 Understanding Neurodiversity: How Learning Differences Affect Approaches to Assessment 1
Adrian J. Wallbank, Helen Taylor, Brock L. Eide, and Fernette F. Eide

2 The Need for Inclusive Pedagogies 45
Adrian J. Wallbank

3 Supporting Learning Differences for Assessments: Universal Design for Learning, GenAI, and Assessment *as* Learning 71
Adrian J. Wallbank

4 Navigators, Pilots, Conductors: Meta-roles as an Inclusive Pedagogical Strategy to Develop Metacognitive Awareness 100
David Channon

5 From Theory to Practice: Compositional Pictography for Academic Writing and Assessment 127
Adrian J. Wallbank and Mona Khatibshahidi

6 Designing Assessment Tasks to Be Inclusive and the Future of Assessment in an Age of GenAI 181
Adrian J. Wallbank

7 Conclusion 210
Chris Rust

Index 217

List of Contributors

David Channon is a Teaching Fellow at the Department of Health Studies, Royal Holloway, University of London, UK, where he teaches and develops specialised learning materials for Planetary Health Education (PHE). He previously worked at the Centre for the Development of Academic Skills (CeDAS) in the role of Learning Developer for the School of Life Sciences and the Environment and as lead of the RHUL Pre-Sessional programme. He has acted as an educational consultant for curriculum development projects in Myanmar and Sri Lanka and as a project leader and teacher trainer in several countries in Europe and Asia. He is a contributing member of the Planetary Health Alliance Education Sub-Group. Recent conference presentations include 'Education in Challenging Environments: Promoting Peace, Trust and Sustainable Development in ASEAN Countries', Asian Heritage Forum, Chulalongkorn University, Bangkok, 2022. His academic and research interests are in curriculum design, Education for Sustainable Development, teacher training, and inclusive pedagogies.

Brock L. Eide is CEO of Neurolearning.com, a social purpose corporation dedicated to accurate, affordable, and informative identification of dyslexia for children and adults. Brock is co-author of *The Dyslexic Advantage* (Hay House, 2011, 2023) and *The Mislabeled Child* (Hachette Books, 2006) and is an international authority on dyslexia and learning differences. Brock is a Phi Beta Kappa graduate of the University of Washington and University of Washington Medical School and has been a consultant to the President's Council of Bioethics and a visiting lecturer at the Stanford Graduate School of Education. He is the co-founder and CFO of DyslexicAdvantage.org.

Fernette F. Eide is co-author of *The Dyslexic Advantage* (2011, 2023) and *The Mislabeled Child* (2006) and is an international authority on dyslexia and learning differences. She is a Magna Cum Laude with the highest departmental honours graduate of Harvard-Radcliffe College and the University of California-San Francisco, and has been a consultant to the President's Council on Bioethics and visiting lecturer at the Stanford Graduate School of Education. She directs all teacher and parent training, positive dyslexia awareness, and student talent programmes in addition to being editor-in-chief for the Dyslexic Advantage newsletter and Premium magazine.

Mona Khatibshahidi is an Academic Advisor at Royal Holloway, University of London, UK. She specialises in providing bespoke academic literacies and skills support to students with dyslexia, ADHD, and autism as well as providing training to academic staff in the area of inclusion and inclusive pedagogies. Previously she was a

Learning Support Assistant at Ealing, Hammersmith and West London College and has also taught English as a Second Language. She is a Fellow of AdvanceHE, an Associate Member of the Dyslexia Guild, and has a PGCE in Post-Compulsory Education from the University of Wolverhampton, UK.

Chris Rust is Emeritus Professor of Higher Education at Oxford Brookes University, UK, where he worked for over 25 years. He was Head of the Oxford Centre for Staff and Learning Development, and Deputy Director of the Human Resource Directorate from 2001 to 2011. Between 2005 and 2010 he was also Deputy Director for two Centres for Excellence in Teaching and Learning – ASKe (Assessment Standards Knowledge Exchange) and the Reinvention Centre for Undergraduate Research (led by Warwick University). For his last three years he was Associate Dean (Academic Policy). He has researched and published on a wide range of pedagogical issues but most especially on assessment. He has been a Fellow of the RSA, a Senior Fellow of SEDA (Staff and Educational Development Association), and was one of the first 14 Senior Fellows of the UK Higher Education Academy. In 2015, he was a member of a group that reviewed external examining arrangements in the UK and between 2016 and 2021 was a member of the Advance HE *Degree standards* project team.

Helen Taylor is the originator of Complementary Cognition, a scientific theory proposing that humans evolved to specialise in different but complementary learning strategies that enable us to create the knowledge we need to adapt and prosper. She is working to unseat the long-held view that individuals with dyslexia have a learning 'disability', instead showing that their learning strategy is to learn through 'global' exploration, translating as an aptitude for understanding complex adaptive systems, with strengths in areas such as originality, discovery, and invention. Her work shows how forms of learning play a critical role in enabling human systems from business to society to adapt and prosper. Dr Taylor is a Research Fellow at the Hunter Centre for Entrepreneurship, University of Strathclyde, UK and is affiliated with the University of Cambridge, where she was awarded her doctorate. Her 2022 paper, 'Developmental Dyslexia: Disorder or Specialisation in Exploration?', ranks in the top 1% of *Frontiers* journals for views and downloads. Dr Taylor's research has gained global media coverage, appearing in over 100 news outlets, including BBC Science Focus, *Scientific American*, and *The Daily Telegraph*. She has presented keynotes at venues like the Swedish Royal Palace, Victoria and Albert Museum, and Imperial College London, reaching policymakers, academics, and business leaders worldwide.

Adrian J. Wallbank is an Associate Professor in Academic Development at the Oxford Centre for Academic Enhancement and Development, Oxford Brookes University, UK. He is a Senior Fellow of AdvanceHE, and author of *Academic Writing and Dyslexia: A Visual Guide to Writing at University* (Routledge, 2018, 2022). His research interests span multiple disciplines and encompass late eighteenth-century and Romantic-period literature and philosophy, educational development, learning differences and neurodiversity, academic and assessment literacies, inclusive pedagogies, transition pedagogies, and the philosophy of higher education. He writes regularly for *Times Higher Education* and the *Staff and Educational Development Association* (SEDA) on topics such as generative artificial intelligence, inclusive pedagogies, and the experiences of academic staff with learning differences.

Preface

This book is about learning differences, primarily dyslexia, ADHD, and autism, in so far as they affect students' abilities to engage with and succeed in assessment within higher education. Yet the title speaks of 'neurodiversity'. The reason for this is owing a) to confusion surrounding what neurodiversity is (and a great deal of mislabelling of individuals as being 'neurodiverse' or 'neurodivergent' when in reality we are all neurodiverse); b) to try and move us away from deficit discourses that associate learning differences as being a disability, an aberration from the norm, or primarily associated with disadvantages (all of which need remediating and even medicating); and c) a desire to advocate for the fact that inclusive pedagogies are inherently good for everyone and should be seen as a 'route to excellence'. The nomenclature and debates surrounding terminology will be discussed fully in Chapter 1, but for now, it is worth foregrounding the following principles that underpin and run throughout this book:

1) Learning differences such as dyslexia, ADHD, and autism are marked by distinct cognitive advantages and trade-offs that are an inherent part of the neurodiversity of the human species.

2) Learning differences are a life-long, inescapable part of the life of people with dyslexia, ADHD, and autism, and as such cannot be fundamentally altered or (to borrow the medical, deficit language we eschew), 'cured'. As such, in order to compete with their peers, individuals with learning differences need pedagogical interventions that a) harness their cognitive strengths and b) provide workarounds or compensatory mechanisms (scaffolding) that enable them to overcome their challenges.

3) University assessment (like any assessment, properly done) is not about the testing of knowledge. Rather, it should be seen as part and parcel of good teaching and pedagogy, and is a form of learning, discovery, and self-actualisation, in and of itself.

4) The act of writing is a key component of learning. Academic writing is not merely a mechanism for demonstrating knowledge and skills.

5) The most promising pedagogical approach for students with learning differences is Universal Design for Learning (UDL), especially when mediated via visual approaches.

6) Visual, UDL pedagogical approaches and scaffolding are inherently good for everyone, hence why the title of this book retains the term 'neurodiversity' in its fullest sense (meaning encompassing all the rich cognitive variations of humanity), and as originally intended by its originator, Judy Singer (1988).

Declaration:

Much of the research contained within this book is intertwined with several of the authors' identities and experiences of learning differences. As such, to ensure the academic integrity, value, worth, and authenticity of this research, and to do justice to the effort required to write and become academically successful despite the inherent challenges associated with those learning differences, the authors would like to assert that no generative artificial intelligence (GenAI) was used in the writing of this book.

Adrian J. Wallbank,
17 January 2025, Oxford Brookes University, UK

Acknowledgements

This book was first conceived in 2018 on the back of the publication of my student-facing textbook, *Academic Writing and Dyslexia: A Visual Guide to Writing*. I would like to thank the many individuals who have written to me over the years to express their thanks for this book and to tell me how much it helped them. However, one glaring flaw was obvious. Students were telling me that it worked, it helped them, and they were happy, and tutors were telling me that it worked, and it helped their students. But the latter were mystified as to *how* and *why* it worked. This is the piece of the jigsaw that has been missing for several years and hopefully this book provides that missing piece of the jigsaw.

The book would have been completed much earlier if it had not been for a catalogue of medical issues that beset me along the way, most notably my wife's illness and those of my baby daughter, Yasmine. However, both have been incredibly forbearing while I have utilised many weekends and evenings to get this book finished. I hope to spend more time with them now that it is finally finished, but for now, all I can do is thank them both from the bottom of my heart for putting up with my writing! Their support and encouragement have been invaluable, as has the patience of Sarah Hyde at Routledge who has been expecting delivery of this manuscript for all too long! Thank you, Sarah and her team for keeping the faith in the face of so many unforeseeable delays.

Finally, I would like to thank the contributors to this book, especially Helen Taylor, whose ideas continually inspire, and Chris Rust, who read all the drafts of this book and provided us all with invaluable feedback.

1 Understanding Neurodiversity

How Learning Differences Affect Approaches to Assessment

Adrian J. Wallbank, Helen Taylor, Brock L. Eide, and Fernette F. Eide

Disabilities, learning difficulties/differences, or neurodiversity?

As educators, many of us have students with dyslexia, ADHD, and autism in our classrooms, lecture theatres, one-to-ones, and personal tutorials, and as we have seen, increasing numbers of students with these learning differences are entering higher education. In the UK and elsewhere, there have been calls to adopt more of a social model of disability, not only as means of complying with external drivers such as legislation (e.g. the Equality Act [2010] in the UK, the Americans with Disabilities Act [2008] in the US, and the Disability Discrimination Act [1992] in Australia), changes to the Disabled Students' Allowance (in the UK), and to better shore up key metrics that feed into quality assurance (and in the UK, the Teaching Excellence Framework) but also as a pedagogical 'route to excellence' (Layer, 2017). However, in reality, a deficit model of support often persists, a situation compounded by the fact that 'study skills' are often seen as an optional 'bolt-on' mechanism of support (Lea and Street, 2006; Wingate, 2006; Dampier et al., 2019; Reynolds, 2019; Richards and Pilcher, 2020). In many respects, this is hardly surprising. With academics under enormous pressure to conduct teaching, research, leadership, and administration, often in the face of mounting budget constraints, it is often easier to see the support requirements of students with so-called disabilities as belonging 'over there' within specialist disability and/or study skills centres. It is this deficit, remedial, 'bolt-on' model of support that this book partly aims to reject. We view dyslexia, ADHD, and autism as very much part of the inherent diversity of the student body, and inclusive pedagogies as 'a route to excellence' in terms of providing *all* students with outstanding, accessible teaching, learning, and assessment experiences.

In your practice, you will undoubtedly see or hear four interchangeable terms bandied about, namely specific learning difficulties (SpLDs), disabilities, neurodiversity, and learning differences. SpLDs, strictly speaking, only cover dyslexia, dysgraphia, and dyscalculia, but autism and ADHD, for example, undoubtedly affect learning, are supported by neurodiversity/disability departments, and in the UK at least, are also covered by the Disabled Students Allowance (DSA). To what extent any of these terms denote a 'disability' is highly debatable, but they are all covered by the Equality Act (2010) (in the UK), and as such, individuals with learning differences are considered to have 'protected characteristics'. However problematic the disability model is, it is useful insofar as it opens the door to support and guarantees (in theory at least) and legal protection. Irrespective of debates about nomenclature, it is worth outlining the clusters of traits that coalesce around certain key 'disabilities' and learning differences, as you will

DOI: 10.4324/9781003398974-1

undoubtedly encounter these in your classrooms and tutorials. It is also worth outlining and clarifying these traits because there are not only similarities and co-occurrences but sometimes misunderstandings and misconceptions about what is or is not an indicator of each learning difference. This is not so that you can undertake a 'diagnosis' but merely so that you can understand and recognise some of the traits you may encounter, accommodate them with more skill, and (where the inclusive pedagogical interventions recommended in this book are insufficient or beyond your remit) signpost students to specialist support and assessments if required. Here are the most common learning differences and the associated traits you may encounter in your practice:

Learning difference	Prevalence	Key characteristics (strengths)	Key characteristics (challenges)
ADHD (often diagnosed alongside dyslexia)	5%, 3:1 prevalence in males (NICE, 2024).	Curiosity Multitasking Activity/energy Creativity Resilience Self-reliance 'Big picture' thinking Problem-solving Imagination Comfortable with change/chaos Divergent thinking Joining the dots to anticipate future issues/ideas/implications	Impulsivity Disorganisation Time management Narrow focus/mind wandering Planning/organisation Completing tasks Reading/writing Working memory Stress Restlessness Talking excessively Lack sense of danger Details Rules and procedures Long explanations Forgetfulness Sensitive to criticism
Dyslexia (often co-occurring with ADHD)	10–20%. 30–50% of individuals with dyslexia will have co-occurring ADHD (Houalla, 2023).	Highly intuitive Highly creative, particularly in terms of originality Generally highly intelligent Vivid imaginations Can see patterns and interconnected ideas that others cannot 'Big picture' thinkers Think in visuals better than in words Visual learning Problem-solving Joining the dots to anticipate future issues/ideas/implications	Easily distracted Difficulty remembering verbal instructions or directions Poor sequencing Slow reading Poor spelling and grammar Easily fatigued or stressed by reading or writing-related tasks Disorganisation Details Leave sentences incomplete Time management issues Difficulty with coordination (e.g. distinguishing between left and right) Reliance on calculators or finger counting Reliance on grammar and spell checkers Easily bored/tired when reading

Autism	1%. 4:2 prevalence in males (WHO, 2022).	Detailed thinkers, take things literally Fascination with isolated details Organised, like routines Highly focused Intelligent Detailed memory Direct, honest communication Punctual Rule oriented Logic Accuracy Specialist knowledge	Understanding abstract concepts Nuances and subtleties Need extra time to process information Repeating what others say to them (echolalia) 'Reading' or understanding people Social situations/cues Establishing friendships Can appear insensitive Repetitive/restrictive behaviours Change Sensitivity to certain lights, sounds, colours etc. Sensory overload Anxiety Eye contact/facial expressions Difficulty understanding instructions Expressing feelings/emotions Difficulty interpreting non-verbal cues 'Big picture' thinking and context/purpose/function Coordination

You will notice that both dysgraphia and dyscalculia are omitted from this list and are not covered in this book. This is because dysgraphia mainly affects writing in the form of syntax errors, illegible handwriting, erratic spelling, and inaccurate word production. These are undoubtedly problematic, but dysgraphia does not present the wider range of challenges associated with dyslexia, ADHD, and autism, and can be supported via word processing. Dyscalculia, meanwhile, mainly affects mathematics, whereas the focus of this book is primarily on reading and writing-related issues.

The characteristics summarised above are far from being an exhaustive list and as such are simply intended as a practical guide. There will undoubtedly be traits here that you recognise in yourself, even if you do not have a known learning difference, but this is precisely the point about seeing these so-called learning differences as part of a continuum. Everyone is different, learns differently, behaves differently, and experiences the world differently. This is normal – it is part of the rich tapestry of human life. Yet historically, traits associated with educational difficulties have been treated as an aberration or even 'mental retardation' (in the US) – a problem needing to be observed, managed, and even medicated. Partly, this is due to how the modern education system has developed in the West, with its emphasis on text-based learning. For the majority of human existence, people learnt through 'apprenticeship' and experience, not from books. The challenges some regularly encounter with these approaches have become labelled as 'disorders'. Known as the medical model approach, this emphasises an individual's deficits with a focus on diagnosis and treatment. The approach tends to place the burden of overcoming limitations on the person with said difficulties rather than acknowledging any issues with the system at play or considering that there may be countervailing advantages present. The emphasis on deficits also contributes to stigma. For example, individuals with dyslexia may perceive themselves as less intelligent or capable due to their difficulties with reading and writing. Importantly, Haft, de Magalhães, and Hoeft (2023) found that greater SpLD stigma scores are significantly correlated with lower self-esteem. More research in the area increasingly recognises that individuals with learning differences experience higher rates of negative socioemotional outcomes, such as lower self-esteem and increased mental health issues (Nelson and Harwood, 2011; Haft et al., 2016; Mammarella et al., 2016). Recent years have seen an increasing push-back against this medical model approach. The following sections will explore two new approaches that present an alternative.

Neurodiversity: the social model

Neurodiversity is a term coined by the sociologist Judy Singer in 1998. Her intention was to balance the medical deficit model of neurological 'disorders' with a social constructionist model that asked: 'what is it about our society that turns some differences into disabilities?' A social model perspective posits that societal barriers and lack of accommodations contribute significantly to the challenges faced by individuals with so-called conditions like autism and dyslexia. This model argues that disability is not just an inherent trait but is created and exacerbated by various environmental and social factors. It also advocates for changes in societal attitudes, policies, and practices to reduce these factors and support the inclusion and well-being of affected individuals (Kapp, 2019).

Singer's work grew out of her personal experiences with autism after her daughter was diagnosed with Asperger's syndrome, and Singer's subsequent recognition of autistic traits in her mother and herself. As such, her campaigning focused on people with high-functioning autism, and the neurodiversity movement was pioneered by autistic activists through communities on the then newly emerging internet.

Singer challenged the conception of autism as a medical syndrome defined by functional deficits. Instead, she viewed it as part of the variation in how human brains function, with the term neurodiversity encompassing the 'whole of humanity'. She likened it to biodiversity in nature, arguing that it was a beneficial and necessary aspect of the human species (Singer, 2017), and presented the neurodiversity movement as a political movement for human rights. Others have highlighted that dual views of autism can coexist. On the one hand, we can think of autism as existing on a continuum of population variation with both social and adaptive functioning traits, but this can exist alongside recognition of co-occurring disabilities and functional impairments in some autistic individuals, particularly those with the highest support needs (Chawner and Owen, 2022).

The shift in view advocated for by the neurodiversity movement has the potential to significantly change how autism is researched and how such individuals are valued in society. It offers an alternative to the medical model with its overfocus on deficits, which in turn constrains what can be understood about autism (Pellicano and Houting, 2022). Over time, the political movement was increasingly taken up by those who were also framed as having disorders from the perspective of the medical model approach, including those diagnosed with dyslexia and ADHD. That said, it should be noted that dyslexia has an even longer history when it comes to challenging the idea of a deficit-centric approach (e.g. Critchley, 1970; Geschwind, 1982).

As the neurodiversity movement developed, so too did the surrounding language. Theorists like Nick Walker suggest that 'neurodiversity' usually refers to two main groups: those labelled as 'neurodivergent', who are a minority because they differ from the dominant societal norms of what is considered typical neurocognitive functioning, and the majority who are referred to as 'neurotypical' (Walker, 2021). However, this dichotomy differs significantly from Singer's original idea. Indeed, Singer (2017) has spoken out against this framing, highlighting that it leads straight back to the old deficit model, with 'neurodivergent' essentially becoming a synonym for 'neurodevelopmental disorder'. Nevertheless, such language has proliferated in popular culture, and you are likely to hear it being used by students and even researchers.

You may also encounter very different definitions of what neurodiversity or neurodivergence mean. For example, NHS Foundation Trusts in the UK have various local definitions of 'neurodiversity' that do not necessarily align and can include autism, ADHD, Variable Attention Stimulus Trait (VAST), dyspraxia, dyslexia, dysgraphia, dyscalculia, and Tourette's syndrome (NHS, Cambridge University Hospitals, 2024), while other definitions are wider, including for example Down's syndrome, depression, or dementia (Cleveland Clinic, 2022; Children's Hospital Colorado, 2024).

In sum, the term 'neurodiversity' is primarily used as part of a *social justice movement*, with implications for research, that campaigns for the rights of individuals with certain diagnoses. In this book, we refer throughout to students with autism, ADHD, and dyslexia as having a 'learning difference' in order to a) counter the deficit-centric approach, b) counter the currently misaligned use of the words 'neurodiversity' and 'neurodivergence' in popular culture and some segments of academia, and c) in line with the idea (to be discussed below) that they reflect learning strategies that are simply not well catered for in the current educational system.

Complementary Cognition

In this section, we will discuss a new approach to understanding learning differences: Complementary Cognition. While the neurodiversity movement has significantly influenced social perceptions of cognitive differences, it was not intended to provide a scientific explanation for their existence beyond acknowledging natural diversity. In contrast, Complementary Cognition offers a scientific and evolutionary explanation, grounded in multidisciplinary evidence focusing on how humans learn. This theory posits that cognitive differences play a pivotal role in our species' ability to generate the knowledge needed to prosper and adapt (Taylor, Fernandes, and Wraight, 2021; Taylor and Vestergaard, 2022). Both perspectives view individuals diagnosed with dyslexia and autism as having cognitive differences rather than deficits, suggesting that modern environments contribute to the challenges they face. However, while the neurodiversity movement is broad in scope, Complementary Cognition, at present, specifically addresses dyslexia, autism, and some cases of ADHD.

A key difference to note is that Complementary Cognition, rather than seeing diversity as random, posits that humans are *specialised* in complementary learning strategies.

These strategies function together so that humans learn collaboratively, enhancing our collective capacity to generate knowledge. This specialisation implies that different learning strategies serve important, interdependent roles; their collaboration is crucial, and the absence of one can adversely affect group performance. Given that strengths and trade-offs are an inherent part of specialisation, this perspective also highlights that everyone in the population has strengths and weaknesses. As will be discussed in more detail below, however, current educational systems favour certain learning strategies over others, putting those with the learning strategies discussed in this book at a distinct disadvantage.

What is learning?

The essence of higher education lies in fostering learning and driving the continuous advancement of knowledge. Knowledge forms the foundation of all human endeavours, driving progress in every field, including science, technology, medicine, and the arts, and it is learning that generates knowledge. But what do we mean by learning, and what is meant by complementary learning strategies?

In education, we often think of learning in quite narrow terms, focusing on *exploitation*. That is, rote learning and memorisation of existing human knowledge, which we then utilise and exploit as needed. The ability to *exploit* existing knowledge is very important because it is a fast track to learning and building on what has often taken many generations to understand. However, this learning strategy has its limitations. What if you want to improve things, further knowledge, or critically evaluate pre-existing ideas, as increasingly becomes the case at university? Then you need to *explore*, interrogate existing knowledge and create new knowledge, often via experimentation, discovery, innovation, or what we call critical thinking. Indeed, most learning involves some level of exploration and at university, this is arguably what we want to encourage our students to do the most (and is often weighted most highly in assessment marking criteria and rubrics).

It is important to emphasise that learning strategies exist along a *continuum*. At one extreme, one could simply exploit or copy existing ideas or solutions. Or, exploring just locally, one might develop and refine an invention or idea. At the other extreme, one could explore entirely new terrain to arrive at fundamentally new knowledge by coming up with an unrefined but highly original solution that accounts for unusual discrepancies far from the current hypothesis or approach.

In academia, exploration is often captured by terms like experimentation, innovation, discovery, and critical thinking. Exploitation, on the other hand, encompasses terms like refinement, efficiency, and execution. In the dimension of time, you can think of this as the trade-off between making predictions about longer-term outcomes versus more short-term planning. Exploratory learning essentially encompasses those activities that in some way attempt to make the unknown known – developing new knowledge or understandings of the world.

Importantly, time and energy spent on exploratory activities come at a trade-off to that spent on activities more related to exploitation. Explore too much and you lose energy without gaining the benefits; over-exploit and you might not get to the correct answer. Every student encounters this exploration–exploitation dilemma first-hand.

For example, in attempting an assignment, when faced with inconclusive data, uncertainties, or ambiguities, a decision on how to proceed becomes necessary. One option is to continue with the current experiment, study, line of enquiry, or reading materials, hoping that additional effort and data will yield more promising results or answers. Alternatively, the student might abandon the experiment or line of enquiry in favour of modifying the experimental design, methodology, or hypothesis, adopting a new approach to the problem or even pursuing an entirely new assignment topic. This situation presents a trade-off between the benefits of exploitation and exploration, highlighting the importance of this issue in decision-making, critical thinking, and knowledge production. The key objective of exploration is to find the truth or generate new ideas and theoretical understanding, whereas exploitation is more concerned with utility (including getting things finished and handed in on time).

Appropriately balancing this trade-off is so fundamental to learning and decision-making that how we search for information and learn (which involves balancing the degree to which we explore and exploit) can be used as a common framework for understanding cognitive behaviour and the function of cognitive control across domains (Hills et al., 2015). In other words, we can also understand cognition – how our brain processes information – through this lens.

Complementary Cognition holds that humans are specialised in different strategies along this exploration–exploitation continuum. This confers humans with two important advantages. Firstly, by specialising and collaborating, it increases our overall capacity to learn. Secondly, specialising ensures that we are always exploring and exploiting to different degrees. This means that as a society/species, we are always globally (holistically) exploring *and* locally refining and exploiting knowledge - and so continually updating our understanding of the world and adapting to change (Taylor, Fernandes, and Wraight, 2021).

A student's learning strategy will significantly affect how they assimilate existing knowledge and the extent to which they can then use that knowledge, recalling it verbatim or generalising to entirely new solutions. You may have already noticed how students differ in their tendencies and abilities in exploration and exploitation. What is important to understand for the purposes of this book is where dyslexia, autism and ADHD fit into this framework, and why existing structures and approaches may be causing them difficulties.

Dyslexia and exploration

Since at least the 1960s, researchers have been interested in the notion that as well as the better-known deficits, dyslexia may be associated with certain strengths. Research published in the 1970s and 1980s already suggested that dyslexia may be associated with considerable advantages in mechanical, visual-spatial, and creative endeavours (Critchley, 1970; Geschwind, 1982). Critchley, for example, noted that children with dyslexia were often particularly adept in areas such as poetry, dance, model-making, and mechanical pursuits – an expertise which he emphasised 'cannot be regarded as merely a projection of unconscious channelling of their interests away from books' (Critchley and Critchley, 1978, p.92). Geschwind, meanwhile, described dyslexia as a 'pathology of superiority', suggesting that differences in the brain 'that have led to the disability of dyslexia in certain literate societies also determine superiority in the same brains' (Geschwind, 1982, p.23). Since that time, several articles and books have been written that build on these insights and describe various strengths in more detail (e.g. West, 2010, 2017; Nicolson, 2014; Taylor and Vestergaard, 2022; Eide and Eide, 2023).

By connecting discussions of higher-level strengths observed in people with dyslexia with research in cognitive neuroscience around search, and learning, Taylor, Fernandes, and Wraight (2021) propose that these strengths all emerge from an exploratory learning specialisation. We have already outlined multiple lines of evidence in support of this hypothesis (Taylor, Fernandes, and Wraight, 2021; Taylor and Vestergaard, 2022), and if correct this provides substantial insights into the likely neural underpinnings of dyslexia-associated cognition as already clarified through research on exploratory learning.

Exploration becomes much more efficient if you direct efforts towards areas that are likely to be more fruitful through prediction and inference. This can include inferring the most likely location of resources, the consequences of events and actions, or simulating different scenarios in your mind to discern what is most likely to work. Internal search enables you to try out an action in your mind first and so avoid expending unnecessary time and energy or potentially putting yourself in danger. Efficient exploration, therefore, relies on 'cognitive maps' – a concept introduced by Tolman (1948). Tolman was the first to recognise that to predict or infer, you need representations (models) of the structure of the world. As discussed in Taylor, Fernandes, and Wraight (2021), the kinds of internal models we create can be thought of as ranging from more global to local. Global features refer to the broader, more abstract structural forms of the environment, such as the overall layout or relational structure between different entities or states. These global representations are crucial for making broad inferences, such as finding shortcuts or inferring relationships that were never directly experienced. On the other hand, local representations involve more detailed, specific information about particular experiences or segments of the environment. These can include the exact sequence of steps required to navigate a known route or the precise attributes of a familiar object or location. In Taylor, Fernandes, and Wraight (2021), we argue that people are specialised in terms of a preference for different strategies along this global (exploration) to local (exploitation) continuum. In the case of dyslexia, we argued that they create more global-level internal models (see also Taylor and Vestergaard, 2022). Such models are primarily encoded in the hippocampus and the entorhinal cortex (O'Keefe and Nadel, 1978; Hafting et al., 2005); these provide the most complexity and flexibility but are also the most computationally demanding.

To explain very simply how we learn through exploration, you search your environment, for example, by moving through the landscape and by using your senses (e.g. visually searching) and you can also search through memory for relevant information. In combination, these different aspects of search enable you to construct internal representations or models of the world through experience, such as the physical layout of the landscape or the causal structure of how the world works. Once you are familiar with your environment, you can use your knowledge and internal models to make predictions about the consequences of different cues, events, and actions. If you are successful in finding the food, resource, or solution you need, you can exploit that. If your predictions are wrong – perhaps because your environment has changed and things are not what you expected – you will then need to explore further to update your internal models to adapt.

As these internal models become richer and better informed, you can become better at making predictions or inferences, enabling you to identify problems, invent, and discover more effectively. This ability enables individuals to respond flexibly and more quickly if there are changes in their environment, as they are better able to infer or generalise from past experiences to correctly predict the best course of action. Different internal representations may be used to construct 'meta-representations' that capture both commonalities and specific details across different environments. These meta-representations then enable more effective exploration and rapid adaptation to unfamiliar and uncertain environments. As anticipated by Tolman (1948), such models may not just represent physical space but be more domain general, for example, in organising temporal, conceptual and social information (Behrens et al., 2018). The strong exploratory/global bias observed in individuals with dyslexia across multiple areas of cognition (Taylor and Vestergaard, 2022), as well as corresponding weaknesses in local process/exploitation, suggest that they rely more on exploration, that is, model-based learning. This involves using a detailed mental model of the environment to simulate various actions and outcomes before making a decision, allowing for more flexible and strategic choices. In general, more exploratory strategies excel in domains where there is more complexity and uncertainty, and more exploitation-related or model-free strategies in contexts where there is less uncertainty and more is known.

The way individuals with dyslexia learn is reflected in how they search for and process information visually. In visual processing studies, individuals with dyslexia have been found to have a deficit in focal attention (Facoetti et al., 2008; Ruffino et al., 2010) but a better resolution for features in the periphery of the visual field (Geiger and Lettvin, 1987; Lorusso et al., 2004). Other studies of visual processing have shown that people with dyslexia can correctly detect impossible figures (like Escher's 'Waterfall' [1961]) faster than non-dyslexic participants without a loss of accuracy (von Károlyi, 2001; von Károlyi et al., 2003).

Detecting the impossibility of these figures relies on global processing; that is, they appear possible when looking at a small (local) area but their impossibility can only be detected when looking at the whole (global) figure. These studies indicate an enhanced ability in people with dyslexia to 'see the big picture' whereby there is a bias towards capturing visual-spatial information globally (holistically) rather than locally (part by part) (von Károlyi, 2001; von Károlyi et al., 2003). This enables connections, or discrepancies, between different pieces of information to be more easily identified.

Experiments also suggest that people with dyslexia are faster at building up these internal models of the structure of the world around them. For example, an experiment (Attree, Turner, and Cowell, 2009) involving adolescents with and without dyslexia asked participants to navigate through a 3D virtual environment and search through each room of a bungalow to locate a toy car. Afterwards, they were asked to create a plan of the virtual bungalow from memory. They were also given a task that tested two-dimensional spatial reasoning. On the standard 2D tests of spatial ability, both groups performed comparably. However, on the task involving recalling the 3D virtual environment, the performance of those adolescents with dyslexia was significantly better than those without dyslexia. Their ability to recreate the map of the rooms suggests that they are more reliant on exploratory search/learning (i.e. they had built up an internal model of their surroundings as they searched through the house).

In accordance with an exploratory learning specialisation, another area of strength seems to be in episodic memory. Episodic memory encodes the context of past experience, including information specific to the time and space of acquisition (Tulving, 2002). A key adaptive function of episodic memory is to also allow individuals to flexibly retrieve and recombine these building blocks of previous experiences to envisage future events (Schacter and Addis, 2007; Schacter, Benoit, and Szpunar, 2017). Hence, if one has a representation of the structure of the world (a cognitive model), one can use it to search through potential future possibilities to predict outcomes or consider the best course of action (Redish, 2012). This is referred to as episodic future thinking (Atance and O'Neill, 2001), and is even applicable to possibilities that have not been experienced previously (Buckner and Carroll, 2007; van der Meer, Kurth-Nelson and Redish, 2012; Schacter, Benoit and Szpunar, 2017). As such, it saves time and energy, avoiding the need to physically explore different possibilities and enabling an individual to anticipate and avoid problems. Greater divergent thinking ability is associated with a greater capacity to imagine more detailed episodic simulations (Addis et al., 2016; Duff et al., 2013). This finding is also consistent with fMRI evidence (Benedek et al., 2014) showing that divergent thinking engages regions of the default network that are also associated with imagining future scenarios (Addis et al., 2016, p.95). As discussed elsewhere (Taylor and Vestergaard, 2022), given that adults with dyslexia tend to perform higher on tests of divergent thinking, this provides indirect evidence that they have richer episodic future (and past) thinking.

Given that the brain has limited capacity, specialisation towards any particular strategy comes with corresponding trade-offs. In the case of individuals with dyslexia, strengths in more global (holistic) exploration will result in weaknesses in local search and exploitation. One example of this is regarding procedural memory. In this case, individuals with dyslexia have been shown to be less efficient at procedural learning than non-dyslexic individuals (Lum et al., 2013). Procedural memory is a long-term memory system that enables implicit learning and the automatic execution of motor and cognitive skills without conscious awareness. This includes activities like reading, writing, and playing instruments. It involves brain regions such as the frontal lobes, basal ganglia, parietal lobes, and cerebellum.

It has been proposed that many of the difficulties observed in individuals with dyslexia may be explained by a failure to automatise skills because of an impaired procedural memory system and underlying deficits thought to exist in the cortico-cerebellar circuit (Nicolson and Fawcett, 1990, 2007; Nicolson, Fawcett and Dean, 2001). This makes it challenging for them to automatise skills, leading to slower and more effortful task execution. However, because they retain conscious awareness of these processes, they can continually explore new strategies and integrate new information. While this approach requires more effort, it promotes innovative thinking and adaptability (Nicolson, 2014).

The trade-off between exploration and exploitation in learning parallels a similar concept within fuzzy-trace theory (FTT) concerning memory encoding and retrieval (Reyna, 2005). According to FTT, information is represented in the long-term memory via two distinct memory traces, verbatim and gist. Verbatim traces capture literal details for precise analysis, such as the order of letters in a word or digits in a number, while gist traces provide 'fuzzy', meaning-based representations related to context or category (Brust-Renck, Weldon, and Reyna, 2021). Verbatim processing prioritises analytical precision, while gist emphasises insightful intuition. This distinction between verbatim and gist trace memories aligns with the contrast between local and global cognitive search strategies. Local search identifies between-item similarity, while global search prioritises contextual or categorical relationships (Todd, Hills, and Robbins, 2012). Obidziński and Nieznański (2017) found that individuals with dyslexia display poorer verbatim trace memory than those without dyslexia but proposed that they possessed an enhanced gist memory. In particular, they reported a higher likelihood of gist trace retrieval when semantically similar stimuli were presented to individuals with dyslexia compared to controls. That is, as would be expected with a more global/explorative strategy, items are activated based on contextual or categorical relationships. In this case, deficits in the cognitive process that distinguishes orthographically similar items in dyslexia may coexist with an improved ability to recognise semantic *similarity*.

Differences in the degree of exploration and exploitation also exist with regard to how the two hemispheres of the brain process information – again reflecting how fundamental this trade-off is in information processing and successful adaptation. As with the other areas discussed, individuals also seem to differ in the degree to which they employ circuits involving their brain's right or left hemispheres when performing particular tasks. As a general rule, the brain's right hemisphere focuses on the large-scale or global features of objects or concepts (McGilchrist, 2021), that is, broad exploration. It is adept at spotting relationships or connections between these elements, important background context, larger systems they might be a part of, and their purposes, meaning, use, gist, or essence. The 'big picture' problem-solving circuits in the brain's right hemisphere are often heavily employed in settings that are new, unfamiliar and complex, or involve important background context that must be taken into account when trying to sort meaning. The brain's left hemisphere, by contrast, is more oriented towards fine-detail processing, that is, local exploration or exploitation. It precisely characterises and differentiates the component parts of ideas and objects, and pursues detailed rather than holistic approaches to analysis (McGilchrist, 2021).

Of particular importance to note is a tendency for the distribution of hemispheric processing to shift for particular cognitive tasks with increasing experience. Early attempts at processing a particular stimulus generally involve a larger proportion of right hemisphere processing, but this proportion typically declines with practice and increasing skill. Musically untrained individuals, for example, process music primarily with right hemisphere circuits because they tend to focus on identifying large-scale (global) features like melody. Skilled musicians, by contrast, employ more left hemisphere circuits because they focus more on fine-detail (local) technical features that reveal the quality of a performance (Ono et al., 2011). The act of reading provides another good example. Beginning readers tend to use both hemispheres quite heavily, but with experience, most readers come to use primarily left-sided circuits (Turkeltaub et al., 2003). However, this is not true of all readers. Individuals with dyslexia, for instance, tend persistently to employ right hemisphere circuits, even after considerable practice (Finn et al., 2014). As such, their reading typically shows greater than usual reliance on problem-solving strategies characteristic of the right hemisphere, such as trying to use contextual cues from the meaning of the passage as a whole to guess individual word meaning, rather than employing characteristic left hemisphere approaches like phonetic decoding or breaking whole words down into detailed components like morphemes, blends, or individual letters to determine their sounds (Eide and Eide, 2023, pp.34–41). This is what makes such tasks particularly effortful and can result in cognitive overload (Wallbank, 2022, pp.3–6).

Evidence suggesting possible dyslexia-associated strengths has led various experts to propose neural bases that might account for the presence of both strengths and challenges. Geschwind and Galaburda (1984) noted a tendency among the post-mortem brains of individuals with dyslexia to have relatively larger right hemispheres (that is, to show symmetrically sized hemispheres rather than the typical left hemisphere predominance). They speculated that this failure to develop dominance in the linguistically superior left hemisphere was a source of both dyslexic challenges and strengths in non-verbal reasoning. West (1997) drew upon this work as well as the work of researchers including Sperry (1982, 1983), Gazzaniga (1983, 1985), and Bogen (1986), whose studies of commisurectomised patients purported to show functional differences between the brain's right and left hemispheres. West proposed that a bias towards right hemispheric processing led both to dyslexic individuals' challenges and to visual and spatial strengths due to favouring more 'global and simultaneous' or 'gestalt' processing (traits purportedly more characteristic of the brain's right hemisphere), at the expense of the more 'verbal … analytical and sequential modes of thought that roughly characterise the left-hemisphere style of thinking' (1997, p.257).

Beyond cognitive and hemispheric distinctions, there is compelling evidence supporting neurophysiological differences in individuals with dyslexia and autism that are again intricately linked to the exploration–exploitation trade-off. Notably, variations in minicolumn circuitry, fundamental units in the neocortex of mammalian brains (Buxhoeveden and Casanova, 2002), contribute to these differences. Minicolumns play a crucial role in cortical information processing, and differences in connectivity within and between modular cortical circuits influence how information is processed (Casanova and Tillquist, 2008; Williams and Casanova, 2010). A study conducted by Williams and Casanova (2010) revealed that individuals with dyslexia exhibit stronger global connectivity in minicolumn circuitry at the expense of local connectivity compared to controls and individuals with autism. Specifically, increased minicolumnar width and spacing, coupled with a lower minicolumn count, result in diminished local connections. Consequently, reduced local connectivity in the cortex proves advantageous for long-range connectivity. Williams and Casanova (2010) propose that this gives rise to a more globally oriented, gestalt processing bias in dyslexia or, in other words, strengths in exploration. In essence, global search strengths may be said to partly derive from the greater distances in which computational networks in the brain travel. In travelling greater distances, the thought processes may be slower and less automatised but more able to intersect with other networks, thereby enhancing the likelihood of more global, gist-based, exploratory searching and 'joining the dots'.

Higher-level strengths of global explorers

In order to understand the strengths and difficulties that different learning strategies might confer at a higher level, it is useful to think of these strategies in terms of what a more global versus local view of the world enables us to understand.

Put simply, a global exploratory strategy encompasses a wide range of interconnected elements and their interactions in abstract space and time, while a local strategy associated with exploitation is narrower, focusing on specific components or aspects of a system. Moreover, local strategies can provide detailed, in-depth understandings of specific elements, whereas more global strategies emphasise integration and overall system dynamics.

A more global strategy might help in understanding a forest ecosystem, for example. This more broad, overarching view includes the various components like plants, animals, microorganisms, soil, and climate, and how these elements interact (e.g. how plants produce oxygen, how animals depend on plants for food, and how decomposers break down organic matter), helping to understand the entire ecosystem's balance and functionality. In contrast, a more local strategy might provide a detailed understanding of how a specific part of the broader forest ecosystem works without looking at how multiple parts interact, such as understanding the role of fungi in breaking down organic matter or the distribution of a single species in the forest.

In general, how broadly/globally we need to explore depends on how complex and multidimensional the environment is and how much we need to learn about that environment. The more diverse and complex the possibilities are, the more important exploration becomes. In individuals with dyslexia, as discussed, internal representations are reported as being particularly multidimensional, dynamic, and often visual. In this regard, the works of Thomas West, who spent decades interviewing and/or profiling dyslexic scientists, are particularly notable (see West, 1997, 2010, 2017).

This more global exploratory learning ability can also be understood as an aptitude for understanding complexity and the dynamics of complex adaptive systems and how they change over time (Taylor, Zaghi, and Rankin, 2023). Such systems consist of networks of interdependencies, are more than the sum of their parts and so need to be understood holistically and contextually. This can be reflected, for example, as an aptitude for exploring in imagination the dynamics and interactions in an ecosystem or inside a cell, recognition of fundamental (global) patterns between different complex systems enabling the translation of insights and solutions between fields, the ability to imagine an engineered system in multiple dimensions of space and time to simulate how it might behave in different contexts, or the ability of an entrepreneur to see a market opportunity and envisage the future of their business. The importance of this kind of systems thinking approach is increasingly recognised as critical to solving many modern-day problems in both the sciences and social sciences (Dominici, 2012; Arnold and Wade, 2015). Given that the entire natural world is made up of complex adaptive systems, it is perhaps unsurprising, from an evolutionary point of view, that at least a portion of the population has particularly strong aptitudes for understanding such system dynamics.

Learning approaches and how dyslexia manifests itself in student approaches to assessment

The idea that individuals with dyslexia are more exploratory, complex systems thinkers provides insights into how they learn best and where they can contribute most to academic problems. Given this learning strategy, it should be no surprise that they tend to revel in understanding complexity and are comfortable in situations with many unknowns. They tend to work across different domains of knowledge, easily making interdisciplinary connections – although this can mean that they inadvertently increase their workload in the context of assessments where their desire to connect everything can lead to their assignments becoming too unwieldy to complete in a particular time frame or within the parameters of an assignment brief. Indeed, traditional academic boundaries make little sense to individuals who view the world as an interconnected network. Rather than learning by rote, their brains are trying to create global internal mental models, partly through 'fuzzy' or gist-based memories. These then enable them to infer and generalise to achieve or propose new situations or solutions. This can be slow to do initially, but once they develop this understanding they can create a more complex understanding and develop highly original insights. For example, while studying the heart, they may feel they need to understand the rest of the organs and circulatory system and how everything interconnects first before going into detail. Given this learning strategy, learning through immersion or by doing, perhaps drawing or making diagrams or through practical strategies (e.g. experimental work, project-based learning, apprenticeship), may be more effective than simply reading and writing. In the context of assessment, then, students with dyslexia often focus on context and interrelationships at the expense of addressing the assignment title or generating marks, often to the extent that the points they make at the end of their assignment are the most productive and insightful.

The following are three examples of how the above traits might manifest themselves in assessment/academic writing:

Example 1: Is climate change the greatest threat to human security in the twenty-first century? 2000-word essay.

Here we have a typical example of an assignment that requires an argument, evaluation, and critical thinking, yet the relatively short word count (for such a huge topic) means that the student needs to be concise and focused – both of which immediately present challenges for a student with dyslexia (individuals with dyslexia invariably struggle with concision as they feel they need to examine all the interrelated parts of an issue rather than homing in on the core issues with brevity). As such, what is of interest in this example is how the student's struggle and discomfort with concision or focus manifests itself in resorting to excessive and unnecessary context (a key strength) – making links to the context and the big picture, setting the scene, explaining linkages and 'joining the dots' without getting to the point (in this case answering the question). The following passage is typical:

> A discussion of climate change at the International level is in Resolution 2349 of the UNSC in which it, 'Recognises the adverse effects of climate change and ecological changes among other factors on the stability of the Region, including through water scarcity, drought, desertification, land degradation, and food insecurity, and emphasises the need for adequate risk assessments and risk management strategies by governments and the United Nations relating to these factors' (United Nations

> Security Council, 2017). This evidence shows that at the international level, the United Nations, there are discussions of the effects of climate change and there is legal framework at the State level, the Climate Change Act 2008 by the United Kingdom Government, to combat climate change. The evidence shows that, especially that of the United Nations Security Council Resolution, that climate change is a great threat to human security. However, the argument of if climate change is the greatest threat to human security in the twenty-first century as climate change is a great threat as there are international discussion and state led legislation to combat climate change but the international resolutions and laws are not enforceable and thus states that choose not to or cannot, due to varying factors like economic, enact climate change legislation cannot be forced to do so. This factor brings a complexity to the issue as it could be argued that other states have to do more, whether that be higher and more unobtainable targets or more money invested in infrastructure, to offset the states that are not enacting anything in relation to climate change. Climate change is one of the great threats to human security in the twenty-first century as in the long term can have many effects on the 7 elements of Human Security but is not the greatest as there are more discussions and more legal frameworks to combat climate change.

Much of the above can quite easily be seen as 'waffle', padding, repetition, and wasting words, but what is happening here is the student is emphasising the context and the background because this is a key strength associated with their dyslexia and exploratory learning strategy. Often, individuals with dyslexia will struggle to 'get to the point' in conversations, or in seeking information, they will ask for the context before getting to the specific detail. The same is happening here. But note what also is happening. While the student is focusing on the big picture and the context, in places they rapidly shift in the opposite direction and make connections without fully introducing them or teasing out their implications. So we have, on the one hand, excessive context and definitions, but on the other, what seems like a very cursory and unexplored set of linkages to state-level interventions, 'economic' factors, targets, investment in infrastructure, and efforts to offset states that are 'not enacting anything', coupled with a very brief attempt to link the whole to the fact that the UN Resolution is evidence in and of itself that climate change is 'a great threat to human security' (note that the term 'greatest' in the title has been changed to 'great', thus missing the point that the essay requires an argument/evaluation in respect of whether it is the 'greatest' threat out of many threats). What sometimes happens is that students with dyslexia, when they are on more confident ground (i.e. in joining up the dots and making links to new ideas), assume that such links are obvious, so they are glossed over and remain unexplained. The speed and enthusiasm with which individuals with dyslexia make such connections comes across in their writing as haphazard or is dealt with via unexplained, seemingly cursory remarks, often because they 'have difficulty explaining to other people how I come up with the answers I do' (Eide and Eide, 2023, p.395). This tendency is exacerbated by their ability to think in non-linear ways and excel in 'gist' thinking rather than literal detail. These students will need support to enable them to structure and explain their thoughts in ways that conform to the requirements and conventions of academic writing if they are to attain the marks they are surely capable of.

Example 2: 'Development is a Western idea that has been imposed on the rest of the world with terrible consequences.' Discuss. 2000 words.

In this example, we see a typical case of the student's dyslexia causing them to struggle with focus and linearity in argumentation and coherence. The essay starts very strongly, and briefly teases out the fact that 'development' is a contested term with various meanings, ranging from ideas to services and even products. However, the student, instead of fully unpacking the ideas surrounding development, the imposition of such development, and the degree to which they have inflicted 'terrible consequences' (whatever that may mean), presents an array of points that do not fully address the task and only become clear at the end of each paragraph (by which time the key issues are left unexamined). The following paragraph is typical:

> Over-focussing resources on one particular country or region is one example of negative outcomes as a result of the west imposing development on developing countries. Song (2014) argued that NGOs often paint developing countries in a negative light because their agenda comes from Western state governments and the multi-national businesses which fund them. A clear example of this is when NGOs target areas of need which most closely conform to what the public expect to be done, and then neglect other areas which do receive as much media attention. For example, 'Africa'. A crucible and stage on which development work is expected to take place. Celebrities are so often seen in countries mainly in Africa and are surrounded by grateful looking children, creating a 'white saviour' mentality. This means that the images are broadcast across the world, to a global audience promoting what people think is development. By presenting Africa as underdeveloped, Africa is in fact privileged when it comes to developmental work. Although this is a hugely positive outcome for Africa, it leads to an over-focus of resources on one place, and therefore neglects other developing countries. The over-focus of resources on specific countries and continents, like Africa, was argued by Matthews (2017), when he stated that the number of registered non-profit organisations in South Africa alone is over 100,000. Furthermore, the number of NGOs in Kenya increased by over 400% from 1997 to 2006. As a result, rather than sharing development resources among the countries most in need, a bigger divide is created between countries receiving an abundance of this developmental help and the countries which are ignored. So, although this imposed development has a positive outcome for the countries it is concentrated in, the negative consequences of this is the fact that the rest of the developing world is deprived of this help and left behind. A more positive outcome of this imposed development would be if it could be shared between all developing nations.

What we have here is a rather confusing, vague statement about overfocusing, quite a lot of confusing (and unfocused) detail about NGOs painting developing countries in a negative light, the example of Africa, the involvement of celebrities, the 'white saviour' mentality, overfocusing again (with data), and then detail about how this exacerbates a divide between countries that get an abundance of help and those that are 'ignored'. This is then loosely related to 'imposed development'. Although it remains slightly unclear how this all equates to 'terrible consequences', the point of the paragraph, and the main thrust of the argument, only emerges at the end. This is a typical trait in assignments submitted by students with dyslexia, namely that the best points and the areas most worthy of scoring high marks often appear at the ends of either paragraphs or indeed the essay as a whole, but even then they are left unexamined (primarily because the student has reached the maximum word count afforded by the assignment task or because they think they have actually analysed the issue in sufficient depth by virtue of examining the interconnections via 'gist' thinking [to them it is obvious, but for the requirements of the assignment it needs to be detailed and explicit]). The good stuff (in terms of generating marks), unfortunately, is often prefaced by a lengthy focus on context (as in the example above) or unfocused, non-linear thoughts that seem to meander around the topic before finally getting to the point. Again, this is derived from the tendency for students with dyslexia to not quite know how they got to the conclusions or answers they did, as well as the speed with which they make links and join up the dots without properly explaining the logic behind them. In many essays by students with dyslexia, their concluding sentences or even paragraphs would make better topic sentences and opening paragraphs, as it takes them a long time to get to the point.

Example 3: Multiple-choice questions

Multiple-choice questions can be especially troubling and cognitively demanding or confusing for students with dyslexia. To illustrate just how problematic multiple-choice questions can be it is worth thinking about how websites often ask us to 'prove' that we are 'human' by selecting appropriate squares in a 'Captcha'. On the face of it, this seems straightforward enough. Often, we are faced with the task of, for example, selecting all the squares with traffic lights. However, this can cause issues for individuals with dyslexia, as although the 'correct answer' is to select the squares only containing the actual lights, there are often other squares that contain the posts and gantries carrying the lights. Someone with an exploratory, global search strength will inevitably then select the squares that also show the infrastructure. This seems entirely logical to them as surely these are an integral part of the traffic lights? But that is not the answer the computer is looking for. This is precisely the scenario in the case of multiple-choice academic tasks and assessments.

Example question and options

The study was flawed owing to the fact that:

a) The respondents were all female

b) The study was only conducted in and around Oxford

c) The authors did not declare that their research was privately funded

d) The tests only looked for candida as a source of the symptoms

In this case, owing to their propensity to search for overarching patterns or links, a student with dyslexia is likely to become sidetracked into questioning whether *all* the above options are valid. While students without dyslexia may choose the correct answer, the 'big picture' thinking skills of students with dyslexia mean that they will immediately think either 'all of these are relevant' or 'it depends', and thus overcomplicate the responses and question, possibly leading to an incorrect answer. What can be especially problematic in these scenarios is when the well-intentioned lecturer (or increasingly, a computer or artificial intelligence marking tool) marks this as incorrect and perhaps provides feedback along the lines that the student has a) not understood or b) not done the work or lacks the knowledge. This can be incredibly demotivating and upsetting, as often it is the case that the studying and revision have indeed been done. Rather, the matter is problematic owing to their learning difference. In essence, to borrow a common metaphor, the task is akin to asking them to put a square peg into a round hole. The problem is not an inherent deficit; the issue stems from the strengths associated with dyslexia and the necessary trade-off in not exploiting or understanding detail.

ADHD and global exploration

In 30–50% of cases, ADHD is diagnosed concurrently with dyslexia (Germanò et al., 2010). A genome-wide association study identified significant associations between dyslexia and ADHD, although no statistically significant genetic links were observed between dyslexia and autism (Gialluisi et al., 2021). Individuals with ADHD are often characterised as having impaired goal-directed control and are sometimes described as having an 'aberration' in search behaviour leading to excessive exploration (Hills, 2006; Todd, Hills, and Robbins, 2012). In line with the perspective that humans are specialised in complementary learning strategies, however, it can also be argued that people being diagnosed with ADHD, similar to those with dyslexia, are specialised in exploratory learning. Indeed, associated advantages in exploration have also been found in areas such as divergent thinking ability (White and Shah, 2006, 2011, 2016; Fugate, Zentall, and Gentry, 2013). Additionally, individuals with ADHD traits exhibit more explorative foraging behaviours in both visual and semantic searches (Van den Driessche et al., 2019).

The major caveat that should be noted, however, is that researchers are increasingly questioning whether diagnostic labels such as ADHD reflect unified groups of people (e.g. Syme and Hagen, 2020; Astle et al., 2022). For example, children are more likely to be diagnosed with ADHD if they are the youngest in their school class, suggesting that they are diagnosed due to their comparatively earlier developmental stage (Karlstad et al., 2017; Root et al., 2019; Caye et al., 2020). Individuals who have experienced childhood trauma may also be given an ADHD diagnosis (Szymanski, Sapanski, and Conway, 2011; Brown et al., 2017). Such examples highlight the problem of an overly broad catchment when using behavioural diagnostic criteria.

It has been argued that some problematic symptoms of ADHD may be best explained by stress. Stress is experienced when a person feels threatened because they conclude that they are ill-equipped for a task they must perform (Salas, Driskell, and Hughes, 1996). Cotton (2020) found a positive correlation between ADHD severity and a chronic stressor score, where nearly half of possible stressors related to school experiences. It may be that the real commonality we are seeing between many people diagnosed with ADHD is stress. Consequently, we suggest that *some* individuals receiving this label are likely to have a strong exploratory learning strategy and may well share the strengths (as well as difficulties) outlined above for dyslexia, but due to these diagnostic issues, this is unlikely to be the case for all those diagnosed with ADHD.

Learning approaches and how ADHD manifests itself in student approaches to assessment

The traits and strengths or trade-offs associated with ADHD have not been studied so comprehensively as those associated with dyslexia, and as Weyandt and Dupaul (2008) note, 'studies of ADHD in the college age group are few, preliminary in nature, or methodologically weak' (p.316). However, from the literature we have studied and the research we have undertaken, the following can be surmised in respect of ADHD strengths (although as mentioned, diagnostic criteria and debates rather muddy the waters).

Despite the lack of literature, especially in the area of academic interventions (Sedgwick-Müller et al., 2022), that which exists reinforces what we have said above in relation to academic challenges, barriers, areas of success/strengths/trade-offs and 'big-picture' thinking vs. a preference for detail/local processing. In the case of ADHD, difficulties tend to exist regarding organisational skills, executive function (cognitive processes that assist in task representation, planning, execution and self-evaluation [Zelazo and Jacques, 1997]), cognition and study skills, as well as discomfort or challenges with emails, internet searches, multitasking and academic writing (Parker and Banerjee, 2007; Weyandt and Dupaul, 2008, pp.313–314). Meanwhile, in research conducted by Kaminski et al. (2006), 68 participants ranging in age from 18 to 23 were recruited from a prominent university in the United States to examine strategies for managing ADHD, obstacles to academic achievement, and sources of motivation. The participants disclosed coping strategies such as working diligently (which seems not only ambiguous but again aligns with deficit models), seeking social support, employing effective organisational and time management skills, engaging in physical exercise, maintaining a positive mental attitude, incorporating spirituality/religion or meditation, practising self-awareness/therapy, utilising fidgeting, and accepting oneself. Reported obstacles to success included procrastination, neglecting organisational and time management skills, succumbing to peer pressure for socialising over studying, time constraints, and the pursuit of perfectionism. As for sources of motivation, participants cited making others proud, avoiding disappointment from others, striving towards long-term career goals, preventing self-disappointment, proving sceptics wrong, overcoming the fear of failure, competing with peers, managing stress associated with procrastination, and pursuing long-term financial objectives (Sedgwick, 2018). Emmers et al. (2016, p.440), also found that students with ADHD have poor conventional study skills and test strategies, and suggest that the available literature points convincingly towards students with ADHD being 'unable to prioritise and select main ideas from side issues' (see also Bradshaw and Salzer, 2003; Weyandt and Dupaul, 2008). As Weyandt and Dupaul (2008, p.313) summarise, it is 'especially in writing' that many of these challenges coalesce, and students with ADHD are at risk for lower achievement scores as a result of poor or compromised academic coping skills. However, more positively, Sedgwick (2018) identifies some literature on the 'giftedness' of students with ADHD, and scholars have written about how impulsivity, inattentiveness, and wide-ranging interests are typical of 'creative people' and often equate with being talented (e.g. Cramond, 1994).

More sobering, however, is the fact that, as Pope (2010) and Emmers et al. (2016) report, many students with ADHD fail to graduate or, owing to the stresses of secondary education, struggle to enter higher education in the first place. Weyandt and Dupaul (2008, p.315) postulate that those who do make it through the system and enter higher education represent a 'distinct subpopulation of individuals with ADHD' and suggest (along with Frazier et al., 2007), that this may be owing to their exhibiting 'more adaptive compensatory abilities (e.g. better time management and study skills)'. In other words, it is suggested that with sufficient 'adaptive compensatory' strategies, students with ADHD can excel, although they do not outline what these strategies might look like. In the research and literature reviews conducted by Emmers et al. (2016), they concur that much of the research into study skills for students with ADHD is either lacking or of poor quality. Indeed, they suggest that despite the fact that higher education institutions have 'developed a range of educational accommodations following the ratification of the UN Convention on the Rights of Persons with Disabilities (UN2006) … these efforts have not led to an increase in the academic success rate of students with disabilities (such as ADHD)' (p.442). Indeed, Soto et al. (2021), studying the writing skills of children with ADHD, found that underdeveloped working memory and executive functions negatively affected three areas of composition: written expression, spelling, and writing fluency. Intriguingly, however, they postulate that these writing challenges may be less attributable to the overt behavioural symptoms associated with ADHD (as outlined above) than low working memory capacity. Interestingly, they suggest that their findings 'may help explain why evidence-based treatments that target overt ADHD symptoms have minimal impact on writing skills' (p.792). Again, this is where this book comes in as we propose pedagogical techniques that help students with ADHD exploit their strengths through 'compensatory strategies'.

The following are two examples of how the above traits associated with ADHD might manifest themselves in assessment and academic writing:

Example 1: Report: reading and social cognition, 2–7 years

> This report will focus on the reading development and social cognition levels of children within the age range of two to seven years old. As all children from the age of five to 16 years old should attend an educational provision within the UK however, it is the commonly held assumption that many children under five will attend preschool around 2 years old, this report will discuss and highlight the reading abilities of those children attending preschool starting at two years old and their social cognition abilities up to the age of year 2 students aged 7. As 2 - 7 is a wide range for reading abilities it is important to emphasis that although the UK schooling system outlines progression levels this report wants to highlight that it has not been complied for comparing skills levels amongst children but rather strengthen the curriculum education providers use to enhance a child's ability to not only read well for their age bracket but also understand their own thought processes and create a foundation for further develop their social cognition whilst moving through the school.

Notable features of the sample above are the run-on sentences and their excessive length. Indeed, the paragraph comprises only three sentences of 24, 73, and 85 words, respectively. What is also noteworthy, however, is the 'busyness' of the sentences. In the second sentence, for example, instead of moving from the classic format of subject–verb–object (with varying options of clauses or subordinate clauses), in terms of sheer topic coverage we move swiftly from children aged 5–16, compulsory educational provision in the UK, preschool attendance from 2 years old, the remit of the report, preschool students aged 2, and then the social cognition abilities to the age of Year 2 students aged 7. This is a lot of detail (arguably six different facets of the issue at stake), and the flow and logical connections between them appear incoherent and confusing. Indeed, even at a micro level, there are inconsistencies in terms of the use of numerals or words (e.g. 'five to 16 years' and '2 years old' vs. 'two years old'). This is because the student's thought processes are simply going too fast, and because of their strength in explorative cognitive search and 'big picture' thinking, they are making links in their writing which are obvious to them (but not to the reader or marker). Indeed, the speed with which they transition from idea to idea is unproblematic for them but obviously highly problematic in terms of the conventions of writing and the marking criteria. For students with ADHD, trying to force such speed and linkages to the conventions of academic writing, logical sequencing, or grammar is problematic, as such conventions impede progress and slow them down (if they pause to concentrate on such issues, either the idea they were originally trying to voice would be forgotten owing to their short-term memory issues or they would suffer from cognitive overload owing to too many demands being placed on their working memory simultaneously). This is why the writing, at first glance, appears hurried, haphazard, and on occasion incoherent, but it is important to note that such traits are a result of the cognitive strengths associated with ADHD, not laziness or lack of effort/knowledge.

Example 2: Psychology essay, 3000 words – reviewing the literature on the subject of good and evil

The above example shows how ADHD can cause the student's ideas to become incoherent or intertwined within a sentence or paragraph, but the same applies across an assignment as a whole. Below is a 'map' of an overall essay structure from a student with ADHD.

Paragraph	Topics covered
1	Stanford Prison Experiment (no context), aims of the essay (no argument/thesis statement).
2	Milgram's study (1963) and obeying authority, situational influence, F-scale to measure authoritarian personalities, methodological problems, Milgram's study critiqued, destructive obedience.
3	Situational variables, Milgram's methodology critiqued, agentic state, emotionally detached behaviours, altered states of consciousness, anyone capable of committing acts of evil, not all people inherently good.
4	Milgram's study is not generalisable, obedience, disobedience, destructive obedience, infliction of pain.
5	Stanford Prison Experiment, line between good and evil is permeable, anonymity, legitimacy, authority, methodological problems, powerful situations.

Again, the first thing to note here is the length of the paragraphs and the sheer breadth of topics covered and intertwined. However, in terms of sequencing, the above exemplifies how the overall structure of the essay is somewhat muddled and in some cases repetitive or circular. If you were to read the whole essay you would find that the student does a decent job of trying to orientate the argument of the essay and paragraphs by including good topic sentences (e.g. paragraph 4 starts with the sentence 'despite the persuasive arguments to be made regarding the power of situations, Milgram's obedience studies face several validity and generalisation concerns which might undermine how strongly they support a situational approach to destructive obedience'). However, the rest of the paragraph does not support the key argument made in the topic sentence (owing to the sheer range of topics covered and their associated tangents and assumptions), veers off on tangents, and more generally the essay lacks a clear argument or 'thread' that knits the whole together. Again, this is owing to the inherent issues with planning, organisation, and attention spans associated with ADHD, and it manifests itself at both a macro and micro level. More positively, however, you can see that, at both a macro and micro level, the sheer range of topics and ideas in both of the examples are impressive. Again, this links to the idea of students with ADHD having particular strengths in exploratory learning and often having wide-ranging interests that they want to synthesise into their responses. The challenge for these students is trying to integrate such varied ideas into the parameters and conventions of an academic assignment, as this runs counter to their strengths. This often results in the incoherences, run-on points, confused structures and sequences and unfinished/unfocused points exemplified above.

Autism and local, depth-first search strategies

Individuals with autism are in many ways the opposite of those with dyslexia, having a learning strategy closer to exploitation. Given the negative connotations of the word 'exploitation' in other contexts, this might be better described as a depth-first (versus breadth-first) learning strategy.

As with ADHD, some types of autism involving stereotypies (repetitive movements or utterances) are framed as pathologies of goal-directed control, but in this case in terms of exploitation (Hills, 2006; Hills and Dukas, 2012). However, as before, viewed in the context of Complementary Cognition, that is, the idea that we are specialised in complementary learning strategies, individuals with autism could also be viewed as having a superiority in local, depth-first search. This is in line with early work also suggesting that many people with autism might instead be considered to have a processing bias rather than a deficit (Frith, 1989; Happé and Frith, 2006).

This local or depth-first processing superiority is reflected in different ways such as greater pitch sensitivity (Bonnel et al., 2003), a more detail-focused drawing style (Mottron et al., 1999; Booth et al., 2003), superior performance when identifying geometric shapes in larger complex images (Shah and Frith, 1983; Happé and Frith, 2006), strong memory for facts (Happé and Vital, 2009), and the ability to master systems that require the discovery of if-then rules and regularities (Baron-Cohen et al., 2002).

Again, opposite to individuals with dyslexia, those with autism tend to have better verbatim memory. For example, there is a high degree of literal, especially verbal, preservation of memories and less or even 'poor context processing' such as that seen in terms of 'gist' processing in the case of dyslexia (Desaunay et al., 2023). Indeed, tests requiring participants to make emotional connections based on stimuli revealed specific weaknesses and errors in favour of more literal memory encoding. The difficulties associated with the integration of cognition and emotion were found to be correlated with the 'compulsive, ritualistic, and sameness behaviours and stereotypic and restricted interests' often found in people with autism (Solomon et al., 2019, p.1).

In contrast to the more model-based strategy described for dyslexia, a depth-first strategy explains certain needs. For example, if one's learning strategy entails limited abilities in prediction, uncertainty represents an almost complete unknown. This may help to explain why people with this strategy become more anxious in the face of any uncertainty and prefer routine and predictability. A depth-first strategy is also in line with the preference for special interests.

A local learning strategy closer to exploitation is also reflected in reading and writing difficulties as well as strengths. Hyperlexia is a profile opposite to dyslexia, where reading skills are advanced relative to comprehension or general intelligence. Ostrolenk et al. (2017) found that over 80% of those with hyperlexia were also autistic. Conversely, some individuals with autism may also suffer reading-related difficulties but they appear to be opposite and complementary to those found in people with dyslexia. Whereas dyslexic readers may show superior processing for meaning relative to their decoding abilities, autistic readers on average show stronger decoding strategies on a word-to-word basis relative to their abilities in reading comprehension (Frith and Snowling, 1983; Henderson, Clarke, and Snowling, 2014; Snowling et al., 2020). That is, as would be expected, a more global exploratory strategy facilitates overall comprehension, whereas a more local strategy favours word-by-word decoding.

Individuals with autism, as identified by Williams and Casanova (2010), exhibit heightened local connectivity within the brain with regard to minicolumn circuitry. It has been suggested that so-called defects in minicolumn circuitry are responsible for the development of autism (Courchesne and Pierce, 2005). It should be noted that in our view the classification of such differences as 'defects' is erroneous, as such a difference may be functional and come with considerable benefits. In essence, however, there appear to be minicolumn microcircuitry differences owing to differently patterned connectivity in the frontal cortex. This results in reduced long-distance connectivity and 'aberrantly heightened local frontal excitability'. In other words, the frontal cortex 'talks to itself but fails to hear and respond to other brain systems' (Williams and Casanova, 2010, pp.228–229). Furthermore, this population displays a greater number of minicolumns characterised by reduced width and spacing, fostering hyperconnectivity in short-range connections within modular units compared to controls and individuals with dyslexia. Moreover, a concomitant reduction in the size of the gyral window imposes constraints on the development of commissural white matter, contributing to a decrease in long-range connectivity between modular units. All this means that there is significantly reduced connectivity throughout the brain, and while this manifests itself as a local processing bias and 'weak coherence … due to lack of synchronisation of neural activity necessary to bind parts to wholes' (Happé and Frith, 2006, p.20), the trade-off is 'brain specialisation' and strengths in detailed, local processing. In other words, despite all the language frequently found in the literature surrounding the deficit model of autism as 'defective' brain circuitry, autism may come with significant benefits, as highlighted in the section above.

Williams and Casanova (2010) propose that the differences in minicolumn circuitry highlighted above underpin a spectrum of cognitive styles, ranging from a holistically oriented, gestalt processing bias in dyslexia to a detail-oriented or local processing bias in autism. In essence, due to inherent physical constraints in the brain, individuals with dyslexia manifest a global processing bias, leading to enhanced abilities in exploring information, while individuals with autism exhibit a contrasting specialisation in local or depth-first search and learning.

Learning approaches and how autism manifests itself in student approaches to assessment

In common with ADHD, there is little research on autism and academic study or cognitive strengths. As Cox et al. (2020, p.253) suggest, 'the literature on college students with autism, and the institutional initiatives designed to support them, is remarkably thin' – so much so that the first mention of autism in any of the top four journals in the field of higher education did not appear until 2017.

In terms of learning approaches, what is key here is the trade-off between breadth-first (exploration) and depth-first learning (exploitation), so while a focus on detail and exploitation often manifests itself as a talent, problems often arise in an 'inability to experience parts as wholes without full attention to the constituent parts' (Kanner, 1943, p.246). Indeed, as Happé and Frith (2006) affirm, 'a persistent preoccupation with parts of objects' is one of the diagnostic criteria for autistic disorder in current practice' (p.5). This 'processing bias for featural and local information, and relative failure to extract gist or see the big picture' (p.6) poses problems for autistic students when it comes to assessment, as while they may excel in recall of facts and details, articulating that detail with reference to its overarching meaning, nuances, debates, implications, context, and the bigger picture is problematic.

The following are two examples of how the traits associated with autism might manifest themselves in assessmentandacademic writing:

Example 1: Primary source analysis: Painting by Grigorii Soroka, View of the Dam in Spasskoe (1840s). 1,000 words.

In this assignment, the task is to provide a critical analysis of the above painting, which depicts a dam on an estate in Russia prior to the Great Reforms of 1861. In the foreground there is a small group of labourers with agricultural tools, and in the background, there is an array of trees, an extensive landscaped garden, and a large house, which looks like it belongs to the gentry. The dam effectively divides the two and acts as a division between the gentry and the serfs. The task is essentially to subject the scene to critical analysis. This particular student's response was to divide the essay into three clear parts labelled 'context', 'content', and 'significance' (which reveals a desire to deal with each part in relative isolation, thus aligning with local, depth-first learning strategies). The latter section is where the only real analysis of the painting takes place, but it only consists of 173 words. The rest of the essay is equally divided between 'context' and 'content'. This in itself immediately shows how the student's autistic traits and strengths have made them gravitate towards detailed description rather than analysis – local detail rather than bigger-picture implications and analysis. But what is most noteworthy is the sheer level of minute detail in these sections. Here is a sample from the 'context' section:

> The Gentry consisted of Serf owners along with landowners among other influential groups. By this point through the minor reforms made by Nicholas which allowed peasants to have a limited number of freedoms including the granting of a piece of land by the landlord who owns the peasant in question in exchange for returns. This created a new type of peasants known as obligated peasants. However very few landlords took advantage of this after the law was passed in 1842. Although Nicholas did bring in certain measures regarding serfdom to state peasants who had been under his control by giving them autonomy by organising serfs into councils with an elder leading the council along with their own judicial system. Although following poor harvests between 1839 and 1840 and after intervention by the Tsar the potato uprising occurred which saw officials and priests among others killed and beaten by the angry peasants which saw the government crackdown through reprisals. This was known as the potato uprising and occurred in 1842. [1] This source was created by Grigorii Soroka who was a serf who had been given permission to paint this painting of the estate by the landowner who owned Soroka.

Here we have 216 words (nearly a quarter of the allocated word count) dedicated to a detailed description of the historical context of the painting, none of which is explicitly related to the task of subjecting the artwork to critical analysis and thus contributes little, if anything, to generating marks. As a detailed description of the historical context though, it is superb. Indeed, within the extract the student talks in detail about how Nicholas the First granted a small number of freedoms and some land, notes that few landlords took advantage of this after the law was passed in 1842, provides details about peasant ownership, poor harvests (with dates), the potato uprising, reprisals – including who was targeted – and then finally the context of how the painting came into existence. The level of detail is extremely impressive and illustrates the student's clear strengths in processing local detail. Where the student does turn to analysis, by contrast, they have more difficulties, and they again often lapse into detailed description. Take the following extract as an example:

> In terms of the significance of the source itself I argue it is very significant as the source shows an accurate interpretation of Serfdom within Russia prior to the Great Reforms in 1861. It is also arguably very significant as the source itself also shows how European Culture and society began to have a considerable impact on Russian society due to the architecture and elements seen within the actual source itself including the style of the house seen within the source itself along with the gazebo

> and the pillars seen within the source. I also argue how it shows the level of inequality and division within 1840s Russia as we can see how there is poor maintenance of the land itself on the peasantry side and the high maintenance and development which we can see of the land on the other side of the divide. Overall I argue this source provides a valuable insight and interpretation of Serfdom era Russia due to the elements of the source itself along with it providing an insight in how Russia began to change significantly in the European era due to the influence of European culture and society.

Here we can see that the student is markedly less confident (as evidenced by the frequent 'padding', 'waffle', and unnecessary boosting, such as 'it is also arguably very significant …', 'it is very significant', 'significantly', and the repetition of 'seen within'), and the extract offers little in the way of analysis in favour of trying to force a 'significance' which is not teased out or subjected to analysis. We can also see how the student lapses into description and detail by referencing the level of maintenance on both sides of the dam and the architectural elements of the building. These details are undoubtedly important, but they are largely descriptive rather than analytical. All in all, it is significant that at no point in the essay does the student refer to the fact that the dam acts as a metaphor for the divisions in society and that the water itself all comes from the same source (it is seen on both sides of the dam yet interestingly is seemingly at the same level), irrespective of the laws and social hierarchies, and, as such, could act as a metaphor for how life (and water as the wellspring from which all life is dependent) is shared and not hierarchical. What we see, as Happé and Frith (2006, p.5) suggest, is 'a persistent preoccupation with parts of objects' at the expense of making connections to the bigger picture, relating context to implications, hidden meanings, subtlety, metaphors, analogies, and the figurative – something very much affirmed by the research on autism and impaired metaphor processing (Morsanyi, Stamenković, and Holyoak, 2020).

Example 2: Essay: 'A success that failed' (Joseph Gill). Is this a fair description of the Council and Union of Florence? 2,500 words.

This example needs far less elaboration than the previous one as it suffers from the same focus on detail. Take this passage as an example:

> The Union was a product of many theological discussions between the Greeks and the Latin delegates and in the end the Decree of Union was an agreement between the two sides. The Byzantines were able to keep traditions, such as their own rites and using leavened, rather than unleavened bread for the Eucharist. In addition, via the 'agreement of the saints', which meant that although the Western and Eastern Church Fathers used different expressions to describe the Procession of the Holy Spirit they all were talking of the same Truth, adding 'filioque' (and from the Son) to the Creed was to be regarded as a valid clarification but not necessary, allowing both East asolomanto use their versions of the Creed.

Here we see a similarly impressive focus on detail, but of the 124 words, very little of this passage contributes to answering the question. Elsewhere in the essay, however, the student does direct their response more towards the question, but here again there is a preference for local detail rather than teasing out the wider implications. For example, there are paragraphs discussing how compromise, military aid, and improved perceptions of the Byzantines might be considered successes, and how the alienation of Russia and the Turks might point towards its failure. In this sense, if we wade through the dense detail, the essay follows a 'block' structure, arguing roughly in the first two-thirds that the Union was a success and for the last third that it was a failure, before briefly concluding that it was, on balance, a success. This reliance upon the block structure is very rigid and logical but does not allow for combined, comparative synthesis and analysis of ideas, again illustrating how the strengths associated with autism manifest themselves in writing. Complex comparative analysis is sacrificed in favour of predictability, argumentative symmetry, detail, and local logic.

Furthermore, at no point in the essay does the student tackle the paradox within the quotation, and at no point do they address the extent to which it is a '*fair* description'. The keyword within the essay question is the adjective 'fair', which requires the student to not simply lay out the successes and failures but to evaluate the contention. Indeed, the contention itself is a paradox; it is seemingly contradictory, and as such the student needed to tease out the nuances and subtleties within the contradiction, as well as assess to what extent it is 'fair'. In other words, there are two areas within this essay question that require a keen eye for nuances and subtleties - areas that are particularly problematic for students with autism owing to their preference for the literal. This student has answered the question by either a) not seeing or appreciating the nuances within the question, or b) avoiding them entirely by preferring to focus on detail and successes or failures. Either way, the student did not properly answer the question and thus was unable to achieve the mark they could have done with appropriate scaffolding and guidance.

The role of working memory in learning differences

Working memory is a cognitive system that temporarily holds and manipulates information for active use in mental tasks (Fang et al., 2016). It plays a crucial role in various cognitive processes, including learning, comprehension, reasoning, and problem-solving. The capacity of working memory is a key factor in determining an individual's ability to perform complex cognitive tasks and is predictive of academic performance (Fang et al., 2016; Emch, von Bastian and Koch, 2019). The structure of working memory is typically described using Baddeley's (2007) multi-element model, which consists of the visuospatial sketchpad (which stores and processes visual and spatial information), the phonological loop (which holds verbal and auditory information and maintains information through subvocal rehearsal), and the central executive (which allocates attentional resources, organises information, and coordinates the other components) (Emch, von Bastian, and Koch, 2019). The capacity and efficiency of the working memory have significant implications for cognitive development, learning, and academic achievement. Individual differences in working memory capacity can explain variations in performance across various mental tasks and learning outcomes.

Individuals with dyslexia typically exhibit diminished working memory capacity in the central executive, phonological loop (Ghani and Gathercole, 2013), and visuospatial sketch pad (Lipowska, Czaplewska, and Wysocka, 2011). Individuals with ADHD are also predisposed to so-called working memory deficits (Al-Saad, Al-Jabri, and Almarzouki, 2021). In particular, research consistently demonstrates that children with ADHD exhibit issues with the central executive, with estimates suggesting that 62–85% of children with ADHD show impairments in working memory, which are associated with core ADHD symptoms and functional impairments across academic, social, and family domains (Al-Saad, Al-Jabri, and Almarzouki, 2021). Autistic individuals, meanwhile, also display diminished working memories, but primarily in the area of spatial working memory, and this often results in poor performance in tasks requiring variance, flexibility and dual tasks (Kercood et al., 2014; Habib et al., 2019). Typically, all individuals with reduced working memory suffer from 'cognitive overload' (Sweller, 1988), which is essentially a 'bottle-neck' within the ability of the working memory to cope with the demands placed upon it by external or internal stimuli – something that obviously occurs much sooner in individuals with dyslexia, ADHD and autism, and especially in academic scenarios.

It is worth noting, however, that emerging evidence suggests that low working memory capacity may have distinct advantages in certain contexts. Several studies note a negative correlation between working memory capacity and divergent thinking ability, with working memory training improving capacity but diminishing divergent thinking performance (Takeuchi et al., 2011). Fugate, Zentall, and Gentry (2013) found that the lower the working memory capacity in students with ADHD and with high fluid intelligence, the higher their ability in divergent thinking.

Lower working memory capacity is also associated with enhanced insight-based reasoning (DeCaro, Van Stockum, and Wieth, 2016), where insight involves a sudden reinterpretation of stimuli to produce a non-obvious solution or comprehension (Kounios and Beeman, 2014). While there are no formal studies on reasoning style in dyslexia, clinical observations and later experimental work suggest a potential area of enhanced ability in insight-based reasoning for individuals with dyslexia (Eide and Eide, 2011; DeCaro, Van Stockum, and Wieth, 2016). Lower working memory capacity is also associated with enhanced insight-based reasoning (DeCaro et al., 2016). Insight refers to the sudden reinterpretation of a stimulus, situation, or event to produce a non-obvious interpretation, seemingly disconnected from the stream of conscious thought, that finds a solution to a problem or the comprehension of a joke or metaphor (Kounios and Beeman, 2014). High working memory capacity has a negative impact on the ability to perform the problem-restructuring and solving processes necessary for insight (DeCaro et al., 2016). This is thought to be because insight problem-solving relies on 'associative processes that operate outside of close attentional control' (DeCaro et al., 2016). Given this, it may be that low working memory capacity facilitates insight in some individuals.

Typically, individuals with high working memory capacity show less frequent transitions between local and global cues compared to those with low working memory capacity, indicating superior exploitation of local information during long-term memory searches (Rosen and Engle, 1997; Hills and Pachur, 2012). In contrast, individuals with lower working memory capacity, such as those with dyslexia, tend to transition more readily from local information patches to global exploration (Todd, Hills, and Robbins, 2012). These findings align with observations of individuals with dyslexia excelling in recognising relationships, connections, and global patterns, showcasing heightened abilities in detecting gist, context, and relevance (Eide and Eide, 2011). However, it seems at odds with the tendency of individuals with autism to focus on local search and exploitation. It would seem that in the case of autism, low working memory capacity acts differently (and is domain-specific), and mainly affects variance, flexibility, and dual tasks, but as we shall see, we still need to consider the role of diminished working memory in our pedagogical approaches for everyone with a learning difference.

In summary, then, despite lower working memory capacity often being viewed as a limitation, in individuals with dyslexia and ADHD at least, evidence indicates compensatory advantages in divergent thinking and insight-based reasoning, both related to explorative search. The interventions in the following chapters of this book are in part designed to alleviate the issues associated with reduced working memory ('cognitive overload') while harnessing the compensatory advantages.

Recent developments and debates: the rise of ADHD and the emergence of AuDHD

Dyslexia and autism have been recognised diagnoses since the late nineteenth and early twentieth centuries, respectively, and ADHD-like behaviours began to be documented as far back the late eighteenth century. Recently, debates have been reinvigorated by the increasing numbers of previously undiagnosed and/or undeclared cases of possible ADHD coming forward and, in higher education, students seeking a formal diagnosis of ADHD by an educational psychologist. Indeed, Danielson et al. (2023) recently reported that prescriptions for ADHD medications increased by 10% during 2020–2021, especially among young adults, while the incidence of ADHD in the US is reported to have surged by 123% between 2007 and 2016, leading to claims of services being 'swamped' (Topping, 2023). What accounts for this relatively recent uptick in cases, and is our bid to make education ever more digitally 'enabled' making it worse?

It has been suggested that ADHD has only been rising since around 2000 (CDC, 2024), the date Will Self associates with the inception of the age of bi-directional digital media. For Self (2016), young people are now 'in the larval stage of a new form of human'. It is striking that the proliferation of bi-directional digital media maps closely to increases in the diagnosis of ADHD, and alterations in brain structure resulting from our increasingly digital lives may well be a possibility (Greenfield, 2014). Indeed, interestingly, the Oxford 'Word of the Year for 2024' is 'brain rot', meaning 'the supposed deterioration of a person's mental or intellectual state, especially viewed as the result of overconsumption of material (now particularly online content) considered to be trivial or unchallenging'. The word captures both 'the impact of consuming excessive amounts of low-quality online content, especially on social media' and the 'somewhat cheeky self-awareness in the younger generations about the harmful impact of social media that they've inherited' (Oxford University Press, 2024).

Smartphones, tablets, laptops, and social media interactions largely revolve around rapid swiping and skim reading – headlines or 'clickbait' are the key anchors into our consciousness and long-term memory rather than slow, deep, and considered thinking. More recently, with the advent of generative artificial intelligence (GenAI), not only has the pace and diversity of our interactions with digital media increased, but what we now view is not necessarily reliable or even true. Deepfakes and examples of 'fake news' are proliferating, and AI-powered algorithms are becoming ever more powerful. Take Facebook for example. Prior to 2024, Facebook's algorithms tracked users' activity and tried to tailor (often very successfully) content to the user's preferences and viewing habits, much like YouTube. In other words, if you wanted a reel about cooking eggs, the chances are you would soon see other suggested reels or posts about cooking (usually with eggs). However, the new 2024 algorithm uses AI to monitor users' habits, even to the level of scrolling time, to tailor content based on not only interests but intention, engagement, and predictions (Kieu, 2024). This means that if the user pauses on an image or story while scrolling, even only momentarily, the AI-powered algorithm thinks they are interested in this topic, and so more such posts appear – not the next time Facebook is opened but during the same session. The user could have paused while scrolling merely to look out of the window or take a sip of tea, but by then it is too late – the algorithm then bombards the user with that content, even if it was accidental. Such 'predictions' and assumptions about the user's 'intention' can be useful if they correctly predict what they are interested in, but it can very soon seem like things are spinning out of control, especially if what the user is viewing is not even real.

What is at stake here, Hern (2024) argues, is not emotions but our attention. 'Emotions, after all, are rarely under our control at the best of times. Attention is supposed to be different. It's something we have conscious control over …. The idea of tech attacking our attention isn't new, and there's a whole concept of the "attention economy" underpinning that barrage.' For Hern, however, technology, with its constant bombardment of notifications and predictions, has 'crossed the line to become real cognitohazards'. In an age of rapid knowledge consumption and searching, 'fragmented by push notifications and digital dopamine hits', Korducki (2022) has recently asked, 'who doesn't have trouble multitasking or following through with tasks?' But with AI, Hern now asks, what does it even mean 'to be wary of what' we 'even *look* at?' Interestingly, at the time of writing, the Australian government has passed a law effectively banning social media for children below the age of 16 – one of the core reasons being given is that based on academic studies, it has been shown to 'interfere with health brain development, sleep and academic performance' (AHRC, 2024).

Bi-directional digital media, by definition, is multifaceted, and as such problems often occur in relation to multitasking or when there are simultaneous cognitive demands that overwhelm the brain's ability to make connections. In the world of studying and academia, typical triggers can include unscaffolded, disorganised information, cognitive overload via file sharing, hopping from one login to another – often on different devices (e.g. Mentimeter), moving transcripts in recordings, and the rapid switching of individuals in meetings without being able to see the class as a whole (e.g. Zoom/Teams classes or recordings). The movement of the video sections at the bottom of recordings (e.g. Panopto) is also problematic, as is having multiple tabs open or having to switch between tabs as part of a session, chat occurring simultaneously with other inputs, and mind mapping or collaborative online tools (e.g. Google docs, Padlet, Miro Board), particularly in cases where panes move around as others contribute or text that others are writing can be read synchronously. Additionally, with the advent and increasing promotion or absorption of AI in higher education, students can now access a dizzying plethora of tools (upwards of 137 productivity apps alone at the time of writing) to help with summarising and research through to GenAI tools such as ChatGPT or scheduling assistants such as Clara.

Hopping between all these apps and platforms, students with ADHD (and indeed dyslexia) can become overwhelmed by trying to make sense of these multiple cognitive burdens. In addition, the speed of switching between different apps and the multifaceted nature of their delivery exacerbates students' pre-existing difficulties in concentration and focus. At the same time, it feeds the propensity of our digital native students without previously undiagnosed ADHD to learn and consume information in heavily fragmented, multifaceted, often superficial forms. This leads them to seek ADHD diagnoses that often come back as negative, or they are diagnosed as positive simply because the student's inattention (owing to their interactions with digital media) has developed into full-blown ADHD-like symptoms without actually being ADHD in the truest sense. With the advent of GenAI to assist with both searching and writing, the ADHD 'epidemic' is only likely to get worse as focus and concentration become increasingly unnecessary and outsourced, and information becomes ever more pre-digested and summarised for us. We are obviously yet to witness the full effects of GenAI, but the evidence in relation to bi-directional digital media suggests a further 'negative cascade effect' in respect of attention spans. In an age of GenAI, maybe sustained attention and focus are seldom needed, but we can hardly claim to be surprised when we are confronted with increasing numbers of students with ADHD (or students pathologising themselves as having ADHD) when they come up against tasks requiring deep, sustained concentration. The question remains, therefore, to what extent the recent proliferation in cases of ADHD may be attributable to an actual rise, increased awareness, or perhaps merely our addiction to what Korducki (2022) calls our 'digital dopamine hits'. At present, there are no clear answers, but it is worth considering to what extent, by promoting digital tools and GenAI in education, we may be making the problem even worse.

As discussed above, ADHD and autism are at opposite ends of the spectrum when it comes to viewing academic and cognitive challenges and strengths through the perspective of cognitive search, divergent thinking and learning strategies, and until around a decade ago, it was a widespread belief that ADHD and autism were 'mutually exclusive' (Boyle, 2024) and seemingly a 'paradox' (Craddock, 2024). However, the notion that autism and ADHD can coexist is gaining traction, and recent research has suggested that up to 50% of individuals diagnosed with autism also display symptoms of ADHD, while characteristics associated with autism exist in 30–80% of individuals with ADHD (Craddock, 2024). In addition, Brimo et al. (2021) report that in their sample of 128 dyslexic individuals, 11.7% showed significant symptoms consistent with autism spectrum disorder versus only 0.9% of the non-dyslexic control group.

Yet there are reasons to question whether the lens of co-occurrence is the appropriate one through which to view individuals who show traits that bear features of both autism and ADHD and/or dyslexia. In the Brimo et al. (2021) study cited above, for example, autism spectrum symptoms were measured using three subscales that examined behaviours in the domains of flexibility, language, and social interaction. While higher scores in autism-associated behaviours in the domains of language and social interaction correlated with a higher risk of dyslexia, there was a negative correlation in the domain of flexibility, such that the more autism-like signs of inflexibility an individual showed, the lower their risk of dyslexia (Brimo et al., 2021). In addition, studies have shown that compared with non-dyslexic children, children with dyslexia showed enhanced signs of emotional reactivity, including emotional facial behaviour, skin conductance, and respiration rate when viewing emotion-inducing film clips (Sturm et al., 2020). In light of such findings, we should pause to consider whether interpreting similar symptoms as signs of co-occurring learning differences is either useful or reliable, or whether we are, to borrow a distinction from comparative anatomy, mistaking merely analogous or superficially similar symptoms or behaviours for homologous ones with identical origins.

When considering whether similar behaviours should be considered signs of true co-occurrence, several things should be kept in mind. The first relates to the nature of clinical syndromes. Syndromes are combinations of symptoms that can be produced either by a single discrete cause or, as is the apparent case with dyslexia, ADHD, and autism, by symptoms which occur together so commonly that they constitute a distinct clinical picture (Miller-Keane, 2003). In clinical medicine, syndrome diagnoses are of immense practical value, as certain common symptoms often lend themselves to similar interventions, irrespective of cause; but it is equally recognised in medicine that a misattribution of similar causes to situations with superficially similar symptoms can lead to disastrous mistakes if dissimilarities in the clinical situations are not noted.

This touches on the second consideration, which is the behavioural nature of these diagnoses and particularly their lack of exclusionary symptoms. What we mean here is illustrated by our earlier discussion of flexibility in Brimo et al. (2021), and emotional reactivity in Sturm et al. (2020). These large differences in the dyslexic group would certainly be expected to produce differences in the nature of the social interaction challenges dyslexic students experience versus those of autistic students who meet all criteria. We have written previously (Eide and Eide, 2006) about the problematic nature of the diagnostic criteria for autism, which places a heavy emphasis on social fluency or the ability to display socially appropriate responses in real time in busy social environments. The problem with social fluency as a diagnostic criterion is that difficulties in this area can have many sources besides problems with theory of mind or cognitive empathy, which have historically been considered the core of the autism diagnosis. Often, individuals with certain forms of dyslexia or ADHD, particularly those impacting procedural learning and processing speed, will be dysfluent or 'dyspraxic' in their social interactions; this is because social interactive skills are implicitly learned habits or skills just like many other types of academic basic skills or routine motor skills, so individuals who struggle with such skills will look socially obtuse in many busy or complex situations. Yet if you read these individuals a story or show them a film with important social interactive content, they will typically 'get' the relevant social details in a way a truly autistic child will not. Indeed, such individuals are often extremely emotionally sensitive (Sturm et al., 2020; Palser et al., 2021). In this way, similar processing features among these broadly different conditions may result in similar or analogous symptoms but against a backdrop of broad differences that make them more properly approached as mere similarities rather than signs of an identical or homologous source. As a result, it might be more useful to say that individuals with autism can share certain features with individuals with dyslexia or ADHD rather than saying that these conditions are often co-occurring. Over time, perhaps the best thing we can do is simply become better observers and recorders of what we see, so that we can develop better phenotypes and more reliable diagnostic criteria containing core, secondary, and exclusionary features.

Cognitive strengths and challenges in academic study and assessment: a summary

In summary, and to use a common metaphor, we may characterise dyslexia (and in some cases, ADHD) as having the ability to see the wood/forest (and even comprehend where it sits within the context of the world) but struggle with the trees, and autism as being the ability to see the trees (and their precise details and systems) but having difficulty seeing the wood/forest and how the trees are interconnected within that forest. As we have seen, this has significant implications for how such students approach assessments and writing, as well as pedagogies to support them.

In essence, rather than having learning deficits, individuals diagnosed with dyslexia, ADHD, and autism can instead be understood as having learning strategies that are important but simply not well catered for in current educational contexts. In the case of dyslexia, they excel at exploration, which involves more global or holistic strategies and the ability to understand the dynamics of complex adaptive systems. These abilities add the most value in contexts characterised by complexity and uncertainty. This is in contrast to autism where strengths lie in local or depth-first learning, adding particular value where in-depth, specialised knowledge is required and in systems with greater predictability. In the case of ADHD, given the broad diagnostic criteria, one may be presented with a student who lies at either end of this continuum or is experiencing other kinds of difficulties. Often any co-occurring diagnosis may provide more insight, although be aware that a label of 'dyslexia' may be given to a student with autism experiencing some of the autism-related reading challenges described above.

Some further, general observations may be made. Firstly, individuals with a more explorative learning strategy may encounter particular difficulties in academic environments. Most educational and academic systems strongly favour less exploration, assessing primarily the ability to reproduce known information rather than utilising information for novel solutions and the exploration of the unknown. Western academic systems, in particular, reward written outputs, traditionally favouring narrowly specialised local search over interdisciplinary global search (Taylor and Vestergaard, 2022). The prevalent dependence on reading and writing in the realms of learning and communication poses particular challenges for individuals whose strategy leans towards exploration. The utilisation of writing technology appears to align more favourably with individuals exhibiting lower exploratory tendencies (Taylor and Vestergaard, 2022). Difficulties associated with dyslexia, for example, are, in part, linked to procedural memory, facilitating knowledge exploitation. These challenges manifest themselves particularly in adapting phonological information and automating skills crucial for reading (Nicolson et al., 2001; Nicolson and Fawcett, 2007). In other words, activities valued in assessments in particular tend to highlight the weaknesses of both exploratory and exploitative, depth-first learners while providing limited opportunities to express and develop their strengths, leading to frustration, stress, and anxiety (Taylor and Vestergaard, 2022) and the types of responses shown in the assessment scripts analysed above.

To conclude this chapter, then, there is still much we do not know about the precise causes of dyslexia, ADHD, and autism, but their impact upon the way students approach learning and, in particular, assessment is profound. What is needed is a pedagogical intervention and/or toolkit to help students tie in what they know (and what they are good at) to the 'bigger picture' or context. Students with autism need scaffolded assistance to help them make sense of detail in relation to the bigger picture and context in their assignments, and students with dyslexia and ADHD need a mechanism to support them in linking bigger ideas to structure and detail. This is precisely what this book aims to set out in the following chapters.

Having examined the various strengths and challenges associated with learning differences, Chapter 2 examines why inclusion is so important, why it matters to all of us as educators, and why much of the literature on the subject of academic literacies hitherto has little to say (often at a practical level) to help us render our practice more inclusive. Chapter 3 provides an overarching pedagogical explanation for, and rationale behind, inclusive pedagogies and UDL and considers the role of AI in this area. The emphasis then shifts more to practical advice and strategies. Chapter 4 outlines Dr David Channon's work on metacognition and meta-roles as means of demystifying and rendering more accessible approaches to academic study and assessment, while Chapter 5 outlines the theory and practice of compositional pictography as a means of teaching the components of academic writing and presenting evidence of its effectiveness. Chapter 6 offers insights and principles for making other types of assessment more inclusive, before Chris Rust's conclusion draws the book to a close via a summary examining the wider implications of inclusive approaches to teaching assessment literacies for contemporary higher education with a particular emphasis on feedback.

References

Addis, D. R., Pan, L., Musicaro, R., and Schacter, D. L., (2016) 'Divergent Thinking and Constructing Episodic Simulations', *Memory*, 24, pp.89–97. Available from: www.tandfonline.com/doi/full/10.1080/09658211.2014.985591 (Accessed: 3 June 2023).

Australian Human Rights Commission (AHRC), (2024) 'Proposed Social Media Ban for Under-16s in Australia'. Available from: https://humanrights.gov.au/about/news/proposed-social-media-ban-under-16s-australia (Accessed: 30 November 2024).

Al-Saad, M. S. H., Al-Jabri, B., and Almarzouki, A. F., (2021) 'A Review of Working Memory Training in the Management of Attention Deficit Hyperactivity Disorder', *Frontiers in Behavioral Neuroscience*, 15. Available from: www.frontiersin.org/journals/behavioral-neuroscience/articles/10.3389/fnbeh.2021.686873 (Accessed: 7 June 2023).

Arnold, R. D., and Wade, J. P., (2015) 'A Definition of Systems Thinking: A Systems Approach', *Procedia Computer Science*, 44, pp.669–678 https://www.sciencedirect.com/science/article/pii/S1877050915002860 (Accessed: 14 June 2025).

Astle, D. E., Holmes, J., Kievit, R., and Gathercole, S. E., (2022) 'Annual Research Review: The Transdiagnostic Revolution in Neurodevelopmental Disorders', *The Journal of Child Psychology and Psychiatry*, 63, pp.397–417. Available from: https://acamh.onlinelibrary.wiley.com/doi/10.1111/jcpp.13481 (Accessed: 5 June 2023).

Atance, C. M., and O'Neill, D. K., (2001) 'Episodic Future Thinking', *Trends in Cognitive Sciences*, 5, pp.533–539. Available from: www.cell.com/trends/cognitive-sciences/abstract/S1364-6613(00)01804-0 (Accessed: 25 June 2023).

Attree, E. A., Turner, M. J., and Cowell, N., (2009) 'A Virtual Reality Test Identifies the Visuospatial Strengths of Adolescents with Dyslexia', *Cyberpsychology and Behavior*, 12, pp.163–168. Available from: https://doi.org/10.1089/cpb.2008.0204 (Accessed: 26 June 2023).

Baddeley, A., (2007) *Working Memory, Thought, and Action*, Vol. 45 Oxford: Oxford University Press.

Baron-Cohen, S., Wheelwright, S., Griffin, S., Lawson, J., and Hill, J., (2002) 'The Exact Mind: Empathising and Systemising in Autism Spectrum Conditions', in Goswami, U. C. (ed.), *Handbook of Cognitive Development*. Hoboken, NJ: Blackwell Publishers, pp.491–508.

Behrens, T. E. J., Muller, T. H., Whittington, J. C. R., Baram, A., Stachenfield, K. L., and Kurth-Nelson, Z., (2018) 'What Is a Cognitive Map? Organizing Knowledge for Flexible Behavior', *Perspective*, 100:2, pp.490–509. Available from: https://doi.org/10.1016/j.neuron.2018.10.002 (Accessed: 14 June 2025).

Benedek, M., Jauk E., Fink A., Koschutnig K., Reishofer G., Ebner F., and Neubauer A. C., (2014) 'To Create or to Recall? Neural Mechanisms Underlying the Generation of Creative New Ideas', *Neuroimage*, 88:100, pp.125–133. Available from: https://pubmed.ncbi.nlm.nih.gov/24269573/ (Accessed: 13 June 2024).

Bogen, G. M., (1986) 'On the Relationship of Cerebral Duality to Creativity', *Bulletin of Clinical Neurosciences*, 51, pp.30–32.

Bonnel, A., Mottron, L., Peretz, I., Trudel, M., Gallun, E., and Bonnel, A.-M., (2003) 'Enhanced Pitch Sensitivity in Individuals with Autism: A Signal Detection Analysis', *Journal of Cognitive Neuroscience*, 15, pp.226–235. Available from: https://direct.mit.edu/jocn/article-abstract/15/2/226/3730/Enhanced-Pitch-Sensitivity-in-Individuals-with?redirectedFrom=fulltext (Accessed: 13 June 2023).

Booth, R., Charlton, R., Hughes, C., and Happé, F., (2003) 'Disentangling Weak Coherence and Executive Dysfunction: Planning Drawing in Autism and Attention-deficit/hyperactivity Disorder', *Philosophical Transactions of the Royal Society B*, pp.358, 387–392. Available from: https://royalsocietypublishing.org/doi/10.1098/rstb.2002.1204 (Accessed: 4 July 2023).

Boyle, S., (2024) 'The Sudden Rise of AuDHD: What is Behind the Rocketing Rates of this Life-changing Diagnosis?' *The Guardian*, 4 April 2024. Available from: www.theguardian.com/lifeandstyle/2024/apr/04/audhd-what-is-behind-rocketing-rates-life-changing-diagnosis (Accessed: 22 November, 2024).

Bradshaw, M. J., and Salzer, J. S., (2003) 'The Nursing Student with Attention Deficit Hyperactivity Disorder', *Nurse Educator*, 28:4, pp.161–165. Available from: https://pubmed.ncbi.nlm.nih.gov/12878893/ (Accessed: 4 January 2023).

Brimo, K., Dinkler, L., Gillberg, C., Lichtenstein, P., Lundström, S., and Åsberg Johnels, J., (2021) 'The Co-occurrence of Neurodevelopmental Problems in Dyslexia', *Dyslexia*, 27, pp.277–293. Available from: https://doi.org/10.1002/dys.1681 (Accessed: 5 January 2024).

Brown, N. M., Brown, S. N., Briggs, R. D., Germán, M., Belamarich, P. F., and Oyeku, S. O., (2017). 'Associations between Adverse Childhood Experiences and ADHD Diagnosis and Severity', *Academic Pediatrics*, 17, pp.349–355. Available from: www.academicpedsjnl.net/article/S1876-2859(16)30416-8/abstract (Accessed: 5 November 2025).

Brust-Renck, P. G., Weldon, R. B., and Reyna, V. F., (2021) 'Judgment and Decision Making', in Knight, B. J. (ed.), *Oxford Research Encyclopedia of Psychology*. Oxford: Oxford University Press. Available from: https://oxfordre.com/psychology/view/10.1093/acrefore/9780190236557.001.0001/acrefore-9780190236557-e-536 (Accessed: 9 November, 2023).

Buckner, R. L., and Carroll, D. C., (2007) 'Self-projection and the Brain'. *Trends in Cognitive Science*, 11, pp.49–57. Available from: www.cell.com/trends/cognitive-sciences/abstract/S1364-6613(06)00327-5 (Accessed: 6 November, 2024).

Buxhoeveden, D. P., and Casanova, M. F., (2002) 'The Minicolumn Hypothesis in Neuroscience', *Brain: A Journal of Neurology*, 125, pp.935–951. Available from: https://academic.oup.com/brain/article-abstract/125/5/935/328135 (Accessed: 23 November 2023).

Casanova, M. F., and Tillquist, C. R., (2008) 'Encephalization, Emergent Properties, and Psychiatry: A Minicolumnar Perspective', *The Neuroscientist*, 14, pp.101–118. Available from: https://journals.sagepub.com/doi/10.1177/1073858407309091 (Accessed: 22 November, 2024).

Caye, A., Petresco, S., de Barros, A. J. D., Bressan, R. A., Gadelha, A., Gonçalves, H., et al., (2020) 'Relative Age and Attention-Deficit/Hyperactivity Disorder: Data from Three Epidemiological Cohorts and a Meta-analysis', *Journal of the American Academy of Child and Adolescent Psychiatry*, 59, pp.990–997. Available from: www.jaacap.org/article/S0890-8567(19)31432-7/abstract (Accessed: 11 September 2023).

Centre for Disease Control (CDC), (2024) 'Facts about ADHD Throughout the Years'. Available from: www.cdc.gov/adhd/data/adhd-throughout-the-years.html?CDC_AAref_Val=www.cdc.gov/ncbddd/adhd/timeline.html (Accessed: 9 September 2024).

Chawner, S. J. R. A., and Owen, M. J., (2022) 'Autism: A Model of Neurodevelopmental Diversity Informed by Genomics', *Frontiers in Psychiatry*, 13, 981691. Available from: www.frontiersin.org/journals/psychiatry/articles/10.3389/fpsyt.2022.981691/full (Accessed: 24 October 2023).

Children's Hospital Colorado, (2024) 'A Parent's Guide to Neurodiversity'. Available from: www.childrenscolorado.org/conditions-and-advice/parenting/parenting-articles/neurodiversity/ (Accessed: 22 November 2024).

Cleveland Clinic, (2022) 'Neurodivergent'. Available from: https://my.clevelandclinic.org/health/symptoms/23154-neurodivergent (Accessed: 22 November 2024).

Cotton, J., (2020) *How Do Childhood ADHD and Stress Relate to Adult Wellbeing and Educational Attainment? A Data Science Investigation Using the 1970 British Cohort Study*. Pleasanton, CA: Baishideng Publishing Group.

Courchesne, E., and Pierce, K., (2005) 'Why the Frontal Cortex in Autism Might be Talking Only to Itself: Local Over-connectivity but Long-distance Disconnection'. *Current Opinion in Neurobiology*, 15:2, pp.225–230. Available from: www.sciencedirect.com/science/article/pii/S0959438805000334?via%3Dihub (Accessed: 23 November 2023).

Cox, B. E., Edelstein, J., Brogdon, B., and Roy, A., (2020) 'Navigating Challenges to Facilitate Success for College Students with Autism'. *The Journal of Higher Education*, 92:2, pp.252–278. Available from: https://doi.org/10.1080/00221546.2020.1798203 (Accessed: 12 April 2023).

Craddock, E., (2024) 'Raising the Voices of AuDHD Women and Girls: Exploring the Co-occurring Conditions of Autism and ADHD', *Disability and Society*, 39:8, pp. 2161–2165. Available from: https://doi.org/10.1080/09687599.2023.2299342 (Accessed: 12 August 2024).

Cramond, B., (1994) 'Attention-Deficit Hyperactivity Disorder and Creativity — What Is the Connection?' *The Journal of Creative Behavior*, 28, pp.193–210. Available from: https://doi.org/10.1002/j.2162-6057.1994.tb01191.x (Accessed: 12 August 2023).

Critchley, M., (1970) *The Dyslexic Child*. London: Heinemann Medical.

Critchley, M., and Critchley, E. A., (1978) *Dyslexia Defined*. London: W. Heinemann Medical Books.

Dampier, G., Baker, L. A., Spencely, C., Edwards, N. J., White, E., and Taylor, A. M., (2019) 'Avoiding the Deficit Model and Defining Student Success: Perspectives from a New Foundation Year Context', *Journal of the Foundation Year Network*, 2, pp.41–52. Available from: https://jfyn.co.uk/index.php/ukfyn/article/view/32 (Accessed: 23 November 2024).

Danielson, M. L., Bohm, M. K., Newsome, K., Claussen, A. H., Kaminski, J. W., Grosse, S. D., et al., (2023) 'Trends in Stimulant Prescription Fills Among Commercially Insured Children and Adults — United States, 2016–2021', *Morbidity and Mortality Weekly Report*, 72, pp.327–332. Available from: http://dx.doi.org/10.15585/mmwr.mm7213a1 (Accessed: 23 September 2024).

DeCaro, M. S., Van Stockum, C. A., Jr., and Wieth, M. B., (2016) 'When Higher Working Memory Capacity Hinders Insight', *Journal of Experimental Psychology: Learning, Memory, and Cognition*, 42:1, pp.39–49. Available from: https://psycnet.apa.org/doiLanding?doi=10.1037%2Fxlm0000152 (Accessed: 23 July 2024).

Desaunay, P., Guillery, B., Moussaoui, E., Eustache, F., Bowler, D. M., and Guénolé F., (2023) 'Brain Correlates of Declarative Memory Atypicalities in Autism: A Systematic Review of Functional Neuroimaging Findings', *Molecular Autism*, 14:1. Available from: https://molecularautism.biomedcentral.com/articles/10.1186/s13229-022-00525-2#citeas (Accessed: 23 July 2024).

Dominici, G., (2012) 'Why Does Systems Thinking Matter?' *Business Systems Review*, 1:1, 1–2. Available from: https://papers.ssrn.com/sol3/papers.cfm?abstract_id=2046736 (Accessed: 22 July 2024).

Duff, M. C., Kurczek, J., Rubin, R., Cohen, N. J., and Tranel, D., (2013) Hippocampal Amnesia Disrupts Creative Thinking'. *Hippocampus*, 23, pp.1143–1149. Available from: https://doi.org/10.1002/hipo.22208 (Accessed: 16 July 2024).

Eide, B. L., and Eide, F. F., (2006) *The Mislabeled Child: How Understanding your Child's Unique Learning Style Can Open the Door to Success*. New York: Hachette Book Group.

Eide, B. L., and Eide, F. F., (2011) *The Dyslexic Advantage: Unlocking the Hidden Potential of the Dyslexic Brain*. First Edition. London: Hay House.

Eide, B. L., and Eide, F. F., (2023) *The Dyslexic Advantage: Unlocking the Hidden Potential of the Dyslexic Brain*. Second Edition. London: Hay House.

Emmers, E., Jansen, D., Petry, K., van der Oord, S., and Baeyens, D., (2016) 'Functioning and Participation of Students with ADHD in Higher Education According to the ICF-framework', *Journal of Further and Higher Education*, 41:4, pp.435–447. Available from: https://doi.org/10.1080/0309877X.2015.1117600 (Accessed: 1 August 2023).

Emch, M, von Bastian, C. C., and Koch, K., (2019) 'Neural Correlates of Verbal Working Memory: An fMRI Meta-Analysis', *Frontiers in Human Neuroscience*, 13, Article 180. Available from: https://doi.org/10.3389/fnhum.2019.00180 (Accessed: 14 June 2025).

Facoetti, A., Ruffino, M., Peru, A., Paganoni, P., and Chelazzi, L., (2008) 'Sluggish Engagement and Disengagement of Non-spatial Attention in Dyslexic Children', *Cortex*, 44:9, pp.1221–1233. Available from: www.sciencedirect.com/science/article/pii/S0010945207001402?via%3Dihub (Accessed: 25 July 2024).

Fang, X., Zhang, Y., Zhou, Y., Cheng, L., Li, J., Wang, Y., et al., (2016) 'Resting-state Coupling between Core Regions within the Central-executive and Salience Networks Contributes to Working Memory Performance', *Frontiers in Behavioral Neuroscience*, 10:27. Available from: www.frontiersin.org/journals/behavioral-neuroscience/articles/10.3389/fnbeh.2016.00027/full (Accessed: 25 October 2024).

Finn, E. S., Shen, X., Holahan, J. M., Scheinost, D., Lacadie, C., Papademetris, X., Shaywitz, S. E., Shaywitz, B. A., and Constable, R. T., (2014) 'Disruption of Functional Networks in Dyslexia: A Whole-brain, Data-driven Analysis of Connectivity', *Biological Psychiatry*, 76:5, pp.397–404. Available from: www.biologicalpsychiatryjournal.com/article/S0006-3223(13)00813-5/fulltext (Accessed: 15 January 2023).

Frazier, T. W., Youngstrom, E. A., Glutting, J. J., and Watkins, M. W., (2007) 'ADHD and Achievement: Meta-analysis of the Child, Adolescent, and Adult Literatures and a Concomitant Study with College Students', *Journal of Learning Disabilities*, 40:1, pp.49–65. Available from: https://journals.sagepub.com/doi/10.1177/00222194070400010401 (Accessed: 23 February 2024).

Frith, U., and Snowling, M., (1983) 'Reading for Meaning and Reading for Sound in Autistic and Dyslexic Children', *British Journal of Developmental Psychology*, 1, pp.329–342. Available from: https://bpspsychub.onlinelibrary.wiley.com/doi/10.1111/j.2044-835X.1983.tb00906.x (Accessed: 14 March 2023).

Frith, U., (1989) *Autism: Explaining the Enigma*. Oxford: Basil Blackwell.

Fugate, C. M., Zentall, S. S., and Gentry, M., (2013) 'Creativity and Working Memory in Gifted Students with and without Characteristics of Attention Deficit Hyperactive Disorder: Lifting the Mask', *Gifted Child Quarterly*, 57:4, pp.234–246. Available from: https://doi.org/10.1177/0016986213500069 (Accessed: 23 September 2023).

Gazzaniga, M., (1983) 'Right Hemisphere Language Following Brain Bisection: A 20-Year Perspective', *American Psychologist*, 38, pp.525–537. Available from: https://psycnet.apa.org/doiLanding?doi=10.1037%2F0003-066X.38.5.525 (Accessed: 24 November 2024).

Gazzaniga, M., (1985) *The Social Brain*. New York: Basic.

Geiger, G., and Lettvin, J. Y., (1987) 'Peripheral Vision in Persons with Dyslexia', *New England Journal of Medicine*, 316, pp.1238–1243. Available from: www.nejm.org/doi/abs/10.1056/NEJM198705143162003 (Accessed: 13 April 2024).

Germanò, E, Gagliano, A, and Curatolo, P., (2010) 'Comorbidity of ADHD and Dyslexia', *Developmental Neuropsychology*, 35:5, pp.475–493. Available from: https://pubmed.ncbi.nlm.nih.gov/20721770/ (Accessed: 14 June 2025).

Geschwind, N., (1982) 'Why Orton Was Right', *Annals of Dyslexia*, 32, pp.13–30. Available from: www.jstor.org/stable/23769838 (Accessed: 16 April 2023).

Geschwind, N., and Galaburda, A. M. (eds), (1984) *Cerebral Dominance: The Biological Foundations*. Cambridge, MA: Harvard University Press.

Ghani, S. K. A., and Gathercole, S. E., (2013) 'Working Memory and Study Skills: A Comparison between Dyslexic and Non-dyslexic Adult Learners', *Procedia – Social and Behavioral Sciences*, 97, pp.271–277. Available from: www.sciencedirect.com/science/article/pii/S1877042813036781 (Accessed: 20 December 2023).

Gialluisi, A., Andlauer, T. F. M., Mirza-Schreiber, N., Moll, K., Becker, J., Hoffmann, P., et al., (2021) 'Genome-wide Association Study Reveals New Insights into the Heritability and Genetic Correlates of Developmental Dyslexia'. *Molecular Psychiatry*, 26, pp.3004–3017. Available from: www.nature.com/articles/s41380-020-00898-x (Accessed: 23 August 2023).

Greenfield, S., (2014) *Mind Change: How Digital Technologies Are Leaving Their Mark on Our Brains*. London: Rider.

Habib, A., Harris, L., Pollick, F., and Melville, C. A., (2019) 'Meta-analysis of Working Memory in Individuals with Autism Spectrum Disorders', *PLoS One*, 14:4. Available from: https://journals.plos.org/plosone/article?id=10.1371/journal.pone.0216198 (Accessed: 12 May 2014).

Haft, S. L., Greiner de Magalhães, C., and Hoeft, F. A., (2023) 'Systematic Review of the Consequences of Stigma and Stereotype Threat for Individuals with Specific Learning Disabilities', *Journal of Learning Disabilities*, 56:3, pp.193–209. Available from: https://journals.sagepub.com/doi/10.1177/00222194221087383 (Accessed: 15 May 2024).

Haft, S. L., Myers, C. A., and Hoeft, F., (2016) 'Socio-emotional and Cognitive Resilience in Children with Reading Disabilities: Current Opinion in Behavioral Sciences', *Neuroscience of Education*, 10, pp.133–141. Available from: https://doi.org/10.1016/j.cobeha.2016.06.005 (Accessed: 5 May 2024).

Hafting, T., Fyhn, M., Molden, S., Moser, M-B., and Moser, E. I., (2005) 'Microstructure of a Spatial Map in the Entorhinal Cortex', *Nature*, 436, pp.801–806. Available from: https://doi.org/10.1038/nature03721 (Accessed: 10 May 2023).

Happé, F., and Frith, U., (2006). 'The Weak Coherence Account: Detail-focused Cognitive Style in Autism Spectrum Disorders', *Journal of Autism Developmental Disorders*, 36, pp.5–25. Available from: https://link.springer.com/article/10.1007/s10803-005-0039-0 (Accessed: 17 May 2022).

Happé F., and Vital P., (2009) 'What Aspects of Autism Predispose to Talent?' *Philosophical Transactions of the Royal Society B*, 364, pp.1369–1375. Available from: https://royalsocietypublishing.org/doi/10.1098/rstb.2008.0332 (Accessed: 13 May 2023).

Henderson, L. M., Clarke, P. J., and Snowling, M. J., (2014) 'Reading Comprehension Impairments in Autism Spectrum Disorders', *L'Année psychologique*, 114, pp.779–797. Available from: https://shs.cairn.info/revue-l-annee-psychologique1-2014-4-page-779?lang=fr (Accessed: 15 May 2023).

Hern, Alex, (2024) 'TechScape: Could AI-generated Content be Dangerous for Our Health?' *The Guardian*, 9 April 2024. Available from: www.theguardian.com/technology/2024/apr/09/techscape-deepfakes-cognitohazards-science-fiction (Accessed: 3 June 2024).

Hills, T. T., (2006) 'Animal Foraging and the Evolution of Goal-directed Cognition', *Cognitive Science*, 30, pp.3–41. Available from: https://onlinelibrary.wiley.com/doi/10.1207/s15516709cog0000_50 (Accessed: 5 December 2023).

Hills, T. T., and Dukas, R., (2012) 'The Evolution of Cognitive Search', in Todd, P. M., Hills, T. T., and Robbins, T. W. (eds), *Cognitive Search: Evolution, Algorithms, and the Brain (Strungmann Forum Reports)*. Cambridge, MA: MIT Press, pp.11–28.

Hills, T. T., and Pachur, T., (2012) 'Dynamic Search and Working Memory in Social Recall', *Journal of Experimental Psychology, Learning, Memory, and Cognition*, 38, pp.218–228. Available from: https://psycnet.apa.org/doiLanding?doi=10.1037%2Fa0025161 (Accessed: 5 March 2023).

Hills, T. T., Todd, P. M., Lazer, D., Redish, A. D., and Couzin, I. D., (2015) 'Exploration versus Exploitation in Space, Mind, and Society', *Trends in Cognitive Sciences*, 19, pp.46–54. Available from: https://doi.org/10.1016/j.tics.2014.10.004 (Accessed: 23 June 2023).

Houalla, N., (2023) 'The Prevalence of Dyslexia', *Dyslexia Action*. Available from: https://dyslexiaaction.org.uk/2023/10/the-prevalence-of-dyslexia/ (Accessed: 22 November 2024).

Kaminski, P. L., Turnock, P. M., Rosén, L. A., and Laster, S. A., (2006) 'Predictors of Academic Success Among College Students with Attention Disorders', *Journal of College Counselling*, 9, pp.60–71. Available from: https://doi.org/10.1002/j.2161-1882.2006.tb00093.x (Accessed: 12 March 2023).

Kanner, L., (1943) 'Autistic Disturbances of Affective Contact', *Nervous Child*, 2, pp.217–250.

Kapp, S., (2019) 'How Social Deficit Models Exacerbate the Medical Model: Autism as Case in Point', *Autism Policy and Practice*, 2, pp.3–28. Available from: https://openaccessautism.org/index.php/app/article/view/16 (Accessed: 5 November 2023).

Karlstad, Ø., Furu, K., Stoltenberg, C., Håberg, S. E., and Bakken, I. J., (2017) 'ADHD Treatment and Diagnosis in Relation to Children's Birth Month: Nationwide Cohort Study from Norway', *Scandinavian Journal of Public Health*, 45, pp.343–349. Available from: https://journals.sagepub.com/doi/10.1177/1403494817708080 (Accessed: 12 March 2023).

Kercood, S., Grskovic, J. A., Banda, D., and Begeske, J., (2014) 'Working Memory and Autism: A Review of Literature', *Research in Autism Spectrum Disorders*, 8:10, pp.1316–1332. Available from: https://doi.org/10.1016/j.rasd.2014.06.011 (Accessed: 2 March 2023).

Kieu, H., (2024) 'Facebook Algorithm Explained: How Does It Work in 2024?' *Megadigital Blog*. Available from: https://megadigital.ai/en/blog/facebook-algorithm/ (Accessed: 10 November 2024).

Korducki, K. M., (2022) 'TikTok Trends or the Pandemic? What's Behind the Rise in ADHD Diagnoses', *The Guardian*, 2 June 2022. Available from: www.theguardian.com/society/2022/jun/02/tiktok-trends-or-the-pandemic-whats-behind-the-rise-in-adhd-diagnoses (Accessed: 14 June 2025).

Kounios, J., and Beeman, M., (2014) 'The Cognitive Neuroscience of Insight', *Annual Review of Psychology*, 65, pp.71–93. Available from: www.annualreviews.org/content/journals/10.1146/annurev-psych-010213-115154 (Accessed: 19 March 2023).

Layer, G., (2017). *Inclusive Teaching and Learning in Higher education as a Route to Excellence*. London: Department for Education. Available from: www.gov.uk/government/publications/inclusive-teaching-and-learning-in-higher-education (Accessed: 24 September 2023).

Lea, M. R., and Street, B. V., (2006) 'The "Academic Literacies" Model: Theory and Applications', *Theory Into Practice*, 45:4, pp.368–377. Available from: www.tandfonline.com/doi/abs/10.1207/s15430421tip4504_11 (Accessed: 23 May 2023).

Lipowska, M., Czaplewska, E., and Wysocka, A., (2011) 'Visuospatial Deficits of Dyslexic Children', *Medical Science Monitor*, 17:4, pp.216–221. Available from: https://medscimonit.com/abstract/index/idArt/881718 (Accessed: 23 May 2023).

Lorusso, M. L., Facoetti, A., Pesenti, S., Cattaneo, C., Molteni, M., and Geiger, G., (2004) 'Wider Recognition in Peripheral Vision Common to Different Subtypes of Dyslexia', *Vision Research*, 44, pp.2413–2424. Available from: www.sciencedirect.com/science/article/pii/S0042698904002342?via%3Dihub (Accessed: 23 May 2023).

Lum, J. A. G., Ullman, M. T., and Conti-Ramsden, G., (2013) 'Procedural Learning Is Impaired in Dyslexia: Evidence from a Meta-analysis of Serial Reaction Time Studies', *Research in Developmental Disabilities*, 34:10, pp.3460–3476. Available from: www.sciencedirect.com/science/article/pii/S0891422213003107?via%3Dihub (Accessed: 23 May 2024).

Mammarella, I. C., Ghisi, M., Bomba, M., Bottesi, G., Caviola, S., Broggi, F., and Nacinovich, R., (2016). 'Anxiety and Depression in Children with Nonverbal Learning Disabilities, Reading Disabilities, or Typical Development', *Journal of Learning Disabilities*, 49:1, pp.130–139. Available from: https://doi.org/10.1177/0022219414529336 (Accessed: 23 July 2023).

McGilchrist, I., (2021) *The Matter with Things: Our Brains, Our Delusions, and Unmaking of the World*. London: Perspectiva.

Miller-Keane Encyclopedia and Dictionary of Medicine, Nursing, and Allied Health. Seventh Edition, (2003). Available from: https://medical-dictionary.thefreedictionary.com/syndrome (Accessed: 5 November 2023).

Morsanyi, K., Stamenković, D., and Holyoak, K. J., (2020) 'Metaphor Processing in Autism: A Systematic Review and Meta-analysis', *Developmental Review*, 57. Available from: https://doi.org/10.1016/j.dr.2020.100925 (Accessed: 23 November 2024).

Mottron, L., Belleville, S., and Ménard, E., (1999) 'Local Bias in Autistic Subjects as Evidenced by Graphic Tasks: Perceptual Hierarchization or Working Memory Deficit?', *Journal of Child Psychology and Psychiatry*, 40, pp.743–755. Available from: https://pubmed.ncbi.nlm.nih.gov/10433408/ (Accessed: 3 July 2024).

Nelson, J. M., and Harwood, H., (2011) 'Learning Disabilities and Anxiety: A Meta-Analysis', *Journal of Learning Disabilities*, 44, pp.3–17. Available from: https://doi.org/10.1177/0022219409359939 (Accessed: 5 June 2024).

NHS, Cambridge University Hospitals, (2024) 'What Is Neurodiversity?' Available from: www.cuh.nhs.uk/our-people/neurodiversity-at-cuh/what-is-neurodiversity/ (Accessed: 11 November 2024).

NICE, (2024) 'Attention Deficit Hyperactivity Disorder: How Common Is It?' Available from: https://cks.nice.org.uk/topics/attention-deficit-hyperactivity-disorder/background-information/prevalence/ (Accessed: 22 November 2024).

Nicolson, R. I., (2014) *Positive Dyslexia*. Paris: Rodin Books.

Nicolson, R. I., and Fawcett, A. J., (1990) 'Automaticity: A New Framework for Dyslexia Research?', *Cognition*, 35, pp.159–182. Available from: www.sciencedirect.com/science/article/abs/pii/001002779090013A?via%3Dihub (Accessed: 16 June 2023).

Nicolson, R. I., and Fawcett, A. J., (2007) 'Procedural Learning Difficulties: Reuniting the Developmental Disorders?', *Trends in Neurosciences*, 30, pp.135–141. Available from: www.cell.com/trends/neurosciences/abstract/S0166-2236(07)00041-0 (Accessed: 23 July 2023).

Nicolson, R. I., Fawcett, A. J., and Dean, P., (2001) 'Developmental Dyslexia: The Cerebellar Deficit Hypothesis', *Trends in Neurosciences*, 24, pp.508–511. Available from: www.cell.com/trends/neurosciences/abstract/S0166-2236(00)01896-8 (Accessed: 23 July 2024).

Obidziński, M., and Nieznański, M., (2017) 'False Memory for Orthographically versus Semantically Similar Words in Adolescents with Dyslexia: A Fuzzy-trace Theory Perspective', *Annuals of Dyslexia*, 67, pp.318–332. Available from: https://link.springer.com/article/10.1007/s11881-017-0146-6 (Accessed: 23 July 2024).

O'Keefe, J., and Nadel, L., (1978) *The Hippocampus as a Cognitive Map*. Oxford: Clarendon Press.

Ono, K., Nakamura, A., Yoshiyama, K., Kinkori, T., Bundo, M., Kato, T., and Ito, K., (2011) 'The Effect of Musical Experience on Hemispheric Lateralization in Musical Feature Processing', *Neuroscience Letters*, 496:2, pp.141–145. Available from: www.sciencedirect.com/science/article/pii/S030439401100368 (Accessed: 3 July 2023).

Ostrolenk, A., Forgeot d'Arc, B., Jelenic, P., Samson, F., and Mottron, L., (2017) 'Hyperlexia: Systematic Review, Neurocognitive Modelling, and Outcome', *Neuroscience and Biobehavioral Review*, 79, pp.134–149. Available from: www.sciencedirect.com/science/article/pii/S014976341630639X (Accessed: 3 July 2023).

Oxford University Press, (2024) '"Brain Rot" Named Oxford Word of the Year 2024'. Available from: https://corp.oup.com/news/brain-rot-named-oxford-word-of-the-year-2024/ (Accessed: 2 December 2024).

Palser, E. R., Morris, N. A., Roy, A. R. K., Holley, S. R., Veziris, C. R., Watson, C., et al., (2021) 'Children with Developmental Dyslexia Show Elevated Parasympathetic Nervous System Activity at Rest and Greater Cardiac Deceleration During an Empathy Task', *Biological Psychology*, 166. Available from: https://doi.org/10.1016/j.biopsycho.2021.108203 (Accessed: 3 June 2024).

Parker, D., and Banerjee, M., (2007) 'Levelling the Digital Playing Field: Assessing the Learning Technology Needs of College-Bound Students with LD and/or ADHD', *Assessment for Effective Intervention*, 33, pp.5–14. Available from: https://journals.sagepub.com/doi/10.1177/15345084070330010201 (Accessed: 23 November 2024).

Pellicano, E., and Houting, J. den, (2022) 'Annual Research Review: Shifting from "Normal Science" to Neurodiversity in Autism Science', *Journal of Child Psychology and Psychiatry, and Allied Disciplines*, 63, pp.381–396. Available from: https://doi.org/10.1111/jcpp.13534 (Accessed: 3 July 2023).

Pope, D. J., (2010) 'The Impact of Inattention, Hyperactivity and Impulsivity on Academic Achievement in UK University Students', *Journal of Further and Higher Education*, 34:3, pp.335–345. Available from: https://doi.org/10.1080/0309877X.2010.484053 (Accessed: 5 July 2023).

Redish, A. D., (2012) 'Search Processes and Hippocampus', in Todd, P. M., Hills, T., and Robbins, T. W. (eds), *Cognitive Search: Evolution, Algorithms, and the Brain (Strungmann Forum Reports)*. Cambridge, MA: MIT Press, pp.81–95.

Reyna, V. F. (2005) 'Fuzzy-Trace Theory, Judgment, and Decision-making: A Dual-Processes Approach', in Izawa, C. and Ohta, N. (eds), *Human Learning and Memory: Advances in Theory and Application: The 4th Tsukuba International Conference on Memory*. Mahwah, NJ: Lawrence Erlbaum Associates Publishers, pp. 239–256.

Reynolds, C., (2019) 'A Brief Reflection on the Implication of "Deficit Model" Considerations within Foundation Year Provision', *Journal of the Foundation Year Network*, 2, pp.53–58. Available from: https://jfyn.co.uk/index.php/ukfyn/article/view/39/35 (Accessed: 12 July 2023).

Richards, K., and Pilcher, N., (2020) 'Study Skills: Neoliberalism's Perfect Tinkerbell', *Teaching in Higher Education*, pp.1–17. Available from: https://doi.org/10.1080/13562517.2020.1839745 (Accessed: 3 November 2023).

Root, A., Brown, J. P., Forbes, H. J., Bhaskaran, K., Hayes, J., Smeeth, L., et al., (2019) 'Association of Relative Age in the School Year with Diagnosis of Intellectual Disability, Attention-deficit/hyperactivity Disorder, and Depression', *JAMA Pediatrics*, 173, pp.1068–1075. Available from: https://jamanetwork.com/journals/jamapediatrics/fullarticle/2751331 (Accessed 4 July 2024).

Rosen, V. M., and Engle, R. W., (1997) 'The Role of Working Memory Capacity in Retrieval', *Journal of Experimental Psychology General*, 126, pp.211–227. Available from: https://psycnet.apa.org/doiLanding?doi=10.1037%2F0096-3445.126.3.211 (Accessed: 12 December 2023)

Ruffino, M., Trussardi, A. N., Gori, S., Finzi, A., Giovagnoli, S., Menghini, D., et al., (2010). 'Attentional Engagement Deficits in Dyslexic Children', *Neuropsychologia*, 48:13, pp.3793–3801. Available from: www.sciencedirect.com/science/article/pii/S0028393210003829 (Accessed: 23 June 2023).

Salas, E., Driskell, J. E., and Hughes, S., (1996) 'Introduction: The Study of Stress and Human Performance', in Driskell, J. E. and Salas, E. (eds), *Stress and Human Performance*. Mahwah, NJ: Lawrence Erlbaum Associates Inc., pp.1–47.

Schacter, D. L., and Addis, D. R., (2007) 'On the Constructive Episodic Simulation of Past and Future Events', *Behavioral and Brain Sciences*, 30:3, pp.331–332. Available from: www.cambridge.org/core/journals/behavioral-and-brain-sciences/article/abs/on-the-constructive-episodic-simulation-of-past-and-future-events/4857CCE46631D0DBC017B7F45AB4028A (Accessed: 3 July 2023).

Schacter, D. L., Benoit, R. G., and Szpunar, K. K., (2017) 'Episodic Future Thinking: Mechanisms and Functions', *Current Opinion in Behavioral Sciences*, 17, pp.41–50. Available from: www.sciencedirect.com/science/article/pii/S2352154616302753?via%3Dihub (Accessed: 24 July 2023).

Sedgwick, J., (2018) 'University Students with Attention Deficit Hyperactivity Disorder (ADHD): A Literature Review', *Irish Journal of Psychological Medicine*, 35, pp.221–235. Available from: www.cambridge.org/core/journals/irish-journal-of-psychological-medicine/article/abs/university-students-with-attention-deficit-hyperactivity-disorder-adhd-a-literature-review/1C27638C01D24833BD9163EAAD00262A (Accessed: 14 July 2024).

Sedgwick-Müller, J. A., Müller-Sedgwick, U., Adamou, M., Catani, M., Champ, R., Gudjónsson, G., et al. (2022) 'University Students with Attention Deficit Hyperactivity Disorder (ADHD): A Consensus Statement from the UK Adult ADHD Network (UKAAN)', *BMC Psychiatry*, 22:1, 292. Available at: https://doi.org/10.1186/s12888-022-03898-z (Accessed: 23 November 2024).

Self, W., (2016) 'Will Self: Are Humans Evolving Beyond the Need to Tell Stories?' *The Guardian*, 25 November 2016. Available from: www.theguardian.com/books/2016/nov/25/will-self-humans-evolving-need-stories (Accessed: 23 July 2023).

Shah, A., and Frith, U., (1983) 'An Islet of Ability in Autistic Children: A Research Note', *The Journal of Child Psychology and Psychiatry*, 24:4, pp.613–620. Available from: https://acamh.onlinelibrary.wiley.com/doi/10.1111/j.1469-7610.1983.tb00137.x (Accessed: 23 November 2023).

Singer, J., (2017) *NeuroDiversity: The Birth of an Idea.* Lexington, KY: Judy Singer.

Snowling, M. J., Hayiou-Thomas, M. E., Nash, H. M., and Hulme, C., (2020) 'Dyslexia and Developmental Language Disorder: Comorbid Disorders with Distinct Effects on Reading Comprehension', *The Journal of Child Psychology and Psychiatry*, 61:6, pp.672–680. Available from: https://acamh.onlinelibrary.wiley.com/doi/10.1111/jcpp.13140 (Accessed: 23 November 2024).

Solomon, M., Iosif, A. M., Krug, M. K., Nordahl, C. W., Adler, E., Mirandola, C., and Ghetti, S., (2019) 'Emotional False Memory in Autism Spectrum Disorder: More than Spared', *Journal of Psychopathology and Clinical Science*, 128:4, pp.352–363. Available from: https://psycnet.apa.org/doiLanding?doi=10.1037%2Fabn0000418 (Accessed: 23 November 2024).

Soto, E. F., Irwin, L. N., Chan, E. S. M., Spiegel, J. A., and Kofler, M. J., (2021) 'Executive Functions and Writing Skills in Children with and without ADHD', *Neuropsychology*, 35:8, pp.792–808. Available from: https://psycnet.apa.org/record/2021-88901-001 (Accessed: 23 November 2023).

Sperry, R. W., (1982) 'Some Effects of Disconnecting the Cerebral Hemispheres', *Science*, 217, pp.1223–1226.

Sperry, R. W., (1983) *Science and Moral Priority: Merging Mind, Brain and Human Values.* New York: Columbia University.

Sturm, V. E., Roy, A. R. K., Datta, S., Wang, C., Sible, I. J., Holley, S., R., et al., (2020) 'Enhanced Visceromotor Emotional Reactivity in Dyslexia and its Relation to Salience Network Connectivity', *Cortex*, 134, pp.278–295. Available from: https://doi.org/10.1016/j.cortex.2020.10.022 (Accessed: 1 August 2024).

Sweller, J. (1988) 'Cognitive Load During Problem Solving: Effects on Learning', *Cognitive Science*, 12, pp.257–285.

Syme, K. L., and Hagen, E. H., (2020) 'Mental Health Is Biological Health: Why Tackling "Diseases of the Mind" Is an Imperative for Biological Anthropology in the 21st Century', *American Journal of Biological Anthropology*, 171:70, pp.87–117. Available from: https://onlinelibrary.wiley.com/doi/10.1002/ajpa.23965 (Accessed: 24 November 2024).

Szymanski, K., Sapanski, L., and Conway, F., (2011) 'Trauma and ADHD – Association or Diagnostic Confusion? A Clinical Perspective', *Journal of Infant, Child, and Adolescent Psychotherapy*, 10, 51–59. Available from: www.tandfonline.com/doi/abs/10.1080/15289168.2011.575704 (Accessed: 24 August 2023).

Takeuchi, H., Taki, Y., Sassa, Y., Hashizume, H., Sekiguchi, A., Fukushima, A., et al., (2011) 'Working Memory Training Using Mental Calculation Impacts Regional Gray Matter of the Frontal and Parietal Regions', *PLoS One*, 6, e23175. Available from: https://journals.plos.org/plosone/article?id=10.1371/journal.pone.0023175 (Accessed: 24 August 2024).

Taylor, H., Fernandes, B., and Wraight, S., (2021) 'The Evolution of Complementary Cognition: Humans Cooperatively Adapt and Evolve through a System of Collective Cognitive Search', *Cambridge Archaeological Journal*, 32, pp.61–77.Available from: https://doi.org/10.1017/S0959774321000329 (Accessed: 23 August 2023).

Taylor, H., and Vestergaard, M. D., (2022) 'Developmental Dyslexia: Disorder or Specialisation in Exploration?' *Frontiers in Psychology*. Available at: https://pubmed.ncbi.nlm.nih.gov/35814102/ (Accessed: 4 July 2024).

Taylor, H., Zaghi, A., and Rankin, S., (2023) 'Marginalising Dyslexic Researchers Is Bad for Science', *eLife*, 12, e93980. Available from: https://doi.org/10.7554/eLife.93980 (Accessed: 5 August 2024).

Todd, P. M., Hills, T. T., and Robbins, T. W., (2012) 'Building a Foundation for Cognitive Search', in Todd, P. M., Hills, T., and Robbins, T. W. (eds), *Cognitive Search: Evolution, Algorithms, and the*

Brain (Strungmann Forum Reports). Cambridge, MA: MIT Press. Available from: https://direct.mit.edu/books/edited-volume/4000/Cognitive-SearchEvolution-Algorithms-and-the-Brain (Accessed: 23 November 2024).

Tolman, E. C., (1948) 'Cognitive Maps in Rats and Men', *Psychological Review*, 55, 189–208. Available from: https://doi.org/10.1037/h0061626 (Accessed: 12 December 2023).

Topping, A., (2023) 'ADHD Services "Swamped", Say Experts as More UK Women Seek Diagnosis', *The Guardian*, 13 January 2023. Available from: www.theguardian.com/society/2023/jan/13/adhd-services-swamped-say-experts-as-more-uk-women-seek-diagnosis (Accessed: 30 November 2024).

Tulving, E., (2002) 'Episodic Memory: From Mind to Brain', *Annual Review of Psychology*, 53, pp.1–25. Available from: www.annualreviews.org/content/journals/10.1146/annurev.psych.53.100901.135114 (Accessed: 12 December 2023).

Turkeltaub, P. E., Gareau, L., Flowers, D. L., Zeffiro, T. A., and Eden, G. F., (2003) 'Development of Neural Mechanisms for Reading', *Nature Neuroscience*, 6, pp.767–773. Available from: www.nature.com/articles/nn1065 (Accessed: 23 July 2023).

Van den Driessche, C., Chevrier, F., Cleeremans, A., and Sackur, J., (2019) 'Lower Attentional Skills Predict Increased Exploratory Foraging Patterns', *Scientific Reports*, 9, 10948. Available from: www.nature.com/articles/s41598-019-46761-0 (Accessed: 12 November 2024).

van der Meer, M, Kurth-Nelson, Z, and Redish, A. D., (2012) 'Information Processing in Decision-making Systems', *Neuroscientist*, 18:4, pp. 342–359. Available from: https://doi.org/10.1177/1073858411435128 (Accessed: 14 June 2025).

von Károlyi, C., (2001) 'Visual-spatial Strength in Dyslexia: Rapid Discrimination of Impossible Figures', *Journal of Learning Disabilities*, 34, pp.380–391. Available from: https://journals.sagepub.com/doi/10.1177/002221940103400413 (Accessed: 25 September 2024).

von Károlyi, C., Winner, E., Gray, W., and Sherman, G. F., (2003) 'Dyslexia Linked to Talent: Global Visual-spatial Ability', *Brain and Language*, 85:3, pp.427–431. Available from: www.sciencedirect.com/science/article/pii/S0093934X0300052X?via%3Dihub (Accessed: 25 September 2024).

Walker, N., (2021) *Neuroqueer Heresies: Notes on the Neurodiversity Paradigm, Autistic Empowerment, and Postnormal Possibilities*. Fort Worth, TX: Autonomous Press.

Wallbank, A. J., (2022) *Academic Writing and Dyslexia: A Visual Guide to Writing at University*. Second Edition. London: Routledge.

West, T. G., (1997) *In the Mind's Eye: Visual Thinkers, Gifted People with Dyslexia and Other Learning Difficulties, Computer Images and the Ironies of Creativity*. Amherst, NY: Prometheus Books.

West, T. G., (2010) *Thinking Like Einstein: Returning to Our Visual Roots with the Emerging Revolution in Computer Information Visualisation*. London: Prometheus.

West, T. G., (2017) *Seeing What Others Cannot See: The Hidden Advantages of Visual Thinkers and Differently Wired Brains*. London: Prometheus.

Weyandt, L. L., and Dupaul, G. J., (2008) 'ADHD in College Students: Developmental Findings', *Developmental Disabilities Research Reviews*, 14:4, pp.311–319. Available from: https://onlinelibrary.wiley.com/doi/10.1002/ddrr.38 (Accessed: 25 August 2024).

White, H. A., and Shah, P., (2006) 'Uninhibited Imaginations: Creativity in Adults with Attention-deficit/hyperactivity Disorder', *Personality and Individual Differences*, 40:1, pp.1121–1131. Available from: https://psycnet.apa.org/record/2006-03090-006 (Accessed: 12 August 2024).

White, H. A., and Shah, P., (2011) 'Creative Style and Achievement in Adults with Attention-deficit/hyperactivity Disorder', *Personality and Individual Differences*, 50, pp.673–677. Available from: www.sciencedirect.com/science/article/pii/S019188691000601X (Accessed: 24 August, 2024).

White, H. A., and Shah, P., (2016) 'Scope of Semantic Activation and Innovative Thinking in College Students with ADHD', *Creativity Research Journal*, 28, pp.275–282. Available from: www.tandfonline.com/doi/full/10.1080/10400419.2016.1195655 (Accessed: 24 August 2024).

Williams, E. L., and Casanova, M. F., (2010) 'Autism and Dyslexia: A Spectrum of Cognitive Styles as Defined by Minicolumnar Morphometry', *Medical Hypotheses*, 74:1, pp.59–62. Available from: www.sciencedirect.com/science/article/pii/S0306987709005490?via%3Dihub (Accessed: 26 August 2024).

Wingate, U., (2006) 'Doing Away with "Study Skills"', *Teaching in Higher Education*, 11:4, pp.457–469. Available from: www.tandfonline.com/doi/abs/10.1080/13562510600874268 (Accessed: 24 November 2023).

World Health Organization (WHO), (2022) 'Autism'. Available from: www.who.int/news-room/questions-and-answers/item/autism-spectrum-disorders-(asd) (Accessed: 11 November 2024).

Zelazo, P. D., and Jacques, S., (1997) 'Children's Rule Use: Representation, Reflection, and Cognitive Control', in Vasta, R. (ed.), *Annals of Child Development*, Vol. 12. London: Jessica Kingsley Press, pp.119–176.

2 The Need for Inclusive Pedagogies

Adrian J. Wallbank

The case for inclusive practice in supporting the development of students' academic literacies

Inclusion has been high on the agenda of many higher education institutions (HEIs) for at least a decade, but it is often misunderstood, remains an 'elusive concept', or attracts the application of 'superficial solutions in the name of valuing diversity' that do not do justice to the complexity of the issues at stake (Stentiford and Koutsouris, 2021, p.2245). Coupled with these issues is the fact that the development of students' academic and assessment literacies (broadly defined as the social, cultural, and contextualised nature of writing, assessment, and approaches to studying within higher education [Lea, 2017]) is often misunderstood, seen as peripheral, or viewed through a deficit lens. It is no wonder then that the terms inclusion and academic literacies need unpacking and justifying and the case made for their promotion and adaptation.

Inclusion, unfortunately, remains a 'hazy and under-examined concept', often covering a 'disparate array of policies' (Stentiford and Koutsouris, 2020, p.2246). In over ten years of practice as a learning and educational developer, I have seen first-hand how this manifests itself in teaching practices. While there is undoubtedly excellent practice throughout the sector, I have frequently encountered colleagues variously citing inclusive practice as consisting of putting materials onto a virtual learning space (e.g. Moodle, Canvas, or Blackboard), learning the students' names, or even making sure the heating is on so that the students are comfortable.

In my experience, one of the most essential aspects of inclusion – the pedagogy – is often neglected in favour of more eye-catching (but no less essential), tangible deliverables such as diversifying and decolonising the curriculum. Inclusion should be two sides of the same coin. On the one hand, we have content. Often, especially in the West, canons of knowledge and scholarship have been built up over centuries which either downplay or entirely neglect the work and achievements of women, ethnic minorities, and other cultures. Literature is a case in point. The Romantic period in the UK is often thought of as comprising the 'big six' poets, namely William Blake, Samuel Taylor Coleridge, William Wordsworth, John Keats, Percy Bysshe Shelley, and Lord Byron. Not a single female writer among them, let alone writers of colour. Byron is often thought of as the first 'celebrity' poet and is a name synonymous with the Romantic period in Britain. Yet Felicia Hemans, a contemporary female poet, vastly outsold Byron at the time, but how many people today have even heard of her, let alone studied her writing? Indeed, how many people are familiar with the pioneering and immensely popular *Memoirs* (1789) of Olaudah Equiano, the first African writer to be widely read in England (his *Memoirs* became a bestseller, went through nine editions, and was also published in Russia, Germany, Holland, and the United States)? How many people appreciate that the spark plug, a key component of the internal combustion engine, was invented by the African enslaved person and mechanic, Edmond Berger, in 1839? History has often preferred, until recently, to credit the German engineers Gottlob Holnold and Robert Bosch with such an invention. One side of inclusion, then, is the teaching of appropriately diverse content; uncovering and promoting the work of previously marginalised or unappreciated authors, thinkers, inventors, histories, and narratives to more accurately represent knowledge holistically; and providing students with a wider, more inclusive curriculum. This is often driven by the fact that the student body itself is more diverse than ever.

Unfortunately, this aspect of inclusion has often become a site where wider culture wars are played out. Recently in the UK, the Quality Assurance Agency (QAA) incorporated 'equality, diversity and inclusion' into its subject benchmark statements – a drive which the then higher education minister, Robert Halfon, branded 'decolonising nonsense' (Morgan, 2022) and which the *Daily Mail* newspaper suggested in 2022 was a demand for universities to 'go woke' as a result of 'the left-wing ideology of student activists' (Harding, 2022). This initiative is nothing of the sort, of course, but one thing that is often either overlooked or misconstrued here is the fact that decolonising and diversifying a curriculum, while offering relatively quick fixes and tangible actions, does not of itself make a module, lecture, seminar, or workshop inclusive. Inclusion is not just about decolonisation, diversity, and celebrating individual backgrounds and experiences. It is also about inclusive pedagogical *delivery* – the adoption of teaching strategies which, as Hockings (2010) defines, 'engage students in learning which is meaningful, relevant and accessible to all, embracing a view of the individual and of individual difference as a source of diversity that can enrich the lives and learning of others' (p.32). Innovative, accessible teaching is skilful, adaptive, and vastly different to the 'talk and chalk' approach many academics may have encountered during their time in education. As Brabazon (2018, p.52) notes, there is often a tendency, however well meaning, for tutors and lecturers to teach as they were taught, even though higher education and our students are markedly different from when many of us progressed through the system. Indeed, as French (2018) rightly observes, gone are the days when 'undergraduates (if not postgraduates) were part of a … homogenous, socially elite group who entered university via the successful completion of common educational qualifications' for which a fairly standardised 'autonomous approach to academic writing and writing development' has dominated (p.205).

Pedagogical innovation and adaptation can be challenging, and as such can easily be overlooked. Take, for instance, the Oxford Brookes Inclusive Curriculum Model (IDEAS) in the UK. The model espouses an approach that encourages 'inclusive, digitally enabled curriculum development' through a consideration of 1) inclusive learning, 2) digital inclusivity, 3) employability learning, 4) assessment for, as and of learning, and 5) a sustainability mindset. Yet its definition of inclusive learning is 'the design and delivery of teaching, learning and assessment that celebrates diversity and enables students to achieve their full potential by drawing on the strengths afforded by their individual backgrounds and experiences'. This is excellent but mentions nothing about accessibility, reasonable adjustments, or pedagogical accommodations or innovations.

Furthermore, while students from ethnic majority backgrounds can certainly have their 'backgrounds and experiences' accommodated and celebrated, it is unclear how learning differences such as autism or dyslexia constitute a 'background' or 'experience', or indeed how this can be leveraged to help students fulfil their potential. Irrespective of the rights or wrongs of medical/deficit models of neurodiversity, learning difference (the semantics of which we will discuss in the next chapter) diagnoses such as dyslexia or autism are legally defined as a 'disability' and thus constitute a 'protected characteristic' under the Equality Act (2010) in the UK. Similar legislation and provisions exist across the globe (such as the Individuals with Disabilities in Education Act [2015] in the United States and the Disability Discrimination Act [1992] in Australia). Learning differences, then, are patently not merely an 'experience' or 'background' but a significant neurological difference (often with considerable challenges) that require not just 'celebrating' but specific pedagogical, inclusive interventions to help these individuals to succeed. Even the most thoroughly decolonised and diverse curriculum can be delivered in a non-inclusive way, and this applies equally to the teaching of academic writing and the supporting of students with their assessment and feedback as it does to the delivery of subject content. Accommodations are often readily made for students with physical disabilities, and immense progress has been made to render buildings, classrooms, and timetables (to name a few examples) accessible. But what about so-called hidden disabilities such as dyslexia, ADHD, or autism? You might not be able to see them, but legally they are still a 'protected characteristic', and these students are legally entitled to 'reasonable adjustments'. Indeed, in light of the recent *Abrahart* case in the UK, even these 'reasonable adjustments' have come under scrutiny. Recently the Equality and Human Rights Commission (EHRC), in light of a High Court judgment against the University of Bristol, has stated that 'the duty to make reasonable adjustments is *anticipatory*' (my emphasis), and universities should 'further consider how assessments can be adjusted to accommodate different disabilities' (Rowsell, 2024).

Hitherto, most 'reasonable adjustments' are provided to students in the form of extra time in examinations (typically around 25%) or some form of 'sticker' which asks markers to refrain from applying penalties for poor spelling, grammar, and punctuation unless these are core to the learning outcomes and understanding. However, none of these 'adjustments' address how tutors and practitioners may go about teaching academic writing skills, exam skills, academic/assessment literacies, or even scaffolding feedback. Extra time is no doubt helpful, especially as it has been suggested that individuals with dyslexia, for instance, take twice as long to learn as non-dyslexic individuals (Nicolson and Fawcett, 2019; Eide and Eide, 2023, p.52), but it goes nowhere near far enough in rendering academic and assessment literacies pedagogically accessible for students with learning differences. Similarly, generic or indeed embedded academic skills classes and one-to-one tutorials, while again undoubtedly helpful and better than nothing, do little for the cause of inclusion if the principles and processes associated with, say, academic writing are taught in a non-inclusive manner.

What is needed is a more inclusive pedagogical approach, and this is what this book is fundamentally about. It is both a textbook for busy practitioners who want to make their delivery more pedagogically inclusive and a scholarly rationale for why and how this is desirable and effective. The book prioritises the genre of academic writing, primarily because it is currently (rightly or wrongly) the predominant mode of assessment within higher education (according to a study by Heuboeck, Holmes, and Nesi

[2007], essays account for around 43% of student writing [in the case of the humanities this figure is 83%, and for the social sciences, 56%]). Indeed, academic writing is an umbrella term for a host of subgenres that involve the written word such as case studies, critiques, and explanations through to exams, posters, reflective writing, and empathy writing, while academic literacies covers not only writing but other forms of assessment such as presentations, blogs, and podcasts, all of which are mediated via language and as such require similar structuring techniques to their more textual counterparts. As such, this book focuses on writing and language as the primary means of assessment, not least as even recent innovations to assessment in the light of the advent of generative artificial intelligence (GenAI) often involve the written word, and of course, the text-centric nature of the modern world (again, rightly or wrongly) means that literacy remains a cornerstone of civic participation and employability (employers continue to bemoan the lack of literacy skills among graduates, especially in the UK and USA [Fain, 2021; Kotsko, 2024]).

Irrespective of wider arguments about whether the genres associated with assessment are in themselves inclusive and perhaps ought to be rethought or further accommodations instigated, (Nieminen, 2022; Nieminen, Morina, and Biagiotti, 2024), a recurring question is often posed regarding why inclusion ought to be considered at all by most educators given that specialist staff in variously named disability, neurodiversity, and dyslexia departments often see the majority of students with learning differences. On the face of it, this is a legitimate question. Writing tutors, learning developers, lecturers, and personal tutors are often ill-equipped to deal with the specific pedagogical and cognitive challenges and strengths students with learning differences or specific learning difficulties (SpLDs) often present. Furthermore, they cannot necessarily be expected to have an in-depth knowledge of inclusive pedagogies, reasonable adjustments, Disabled Students Allowances (DSAs), or even specialist assistive technologies (Kioko and Makoelle, 2014, p.110). Even in the case of specialist academic skills practitioners, most are either from academic backgrounds, English for Academic Purposes (EAP)/language tutors who have increasingly taken on the role of supporting 'home' students, or learning developers, all of whom have a necessarily wider remit in terms of academic skills development (Caldwell, Stapleford, and Tinker, 2018, p.128). Indeed, in the UK, supporting students in receipt of the DSA usually requires a unique set of qualifications, membership of the Dyslexia Guild/British Dyslexia Association, and ongoing commitments to continuing professional development as a condition of registration, which most tutors in writing or academic skills centres, or indeed academics in the faculties, do not possess. However, inclusion is something that we need to embrace, even if we never become fully qualified to support such students. There are three principal reasons for this.

Firstly, it is incumbent upon all of us to make our practice inclusive. As the UNESCO definition illustrates, inclusion ought to be seen as:

> a process of addressing and responding to the diversity of needs of all learners through increasing participation in learning, cultures and communities, and reducing exclusion within and from education. It involves changes and modifications in content, approaches, structures and strategies, with a common vision ... Inclusion is concerned with providing appropriate responses to the broad spectrum of learning needs in formal and non-formal educational settings. Rather than being a

marginal issue on how some learners can be integrated in mainstream education, inclusive education is an approach that looks into how to transform education systems and other learning environments in order to respond to the diversity and to see it as a challenge and enrichment of the learning environment, rather than a problem. Inclusion emphasises providing opportunities for equal participation of persons with disabilities (physical, social and/or emotional) whenever possible into general education, but leaves open the possibility of personal choice and options for special assistance and facilities for those who need it.

(UNESCO, 2017, pp.13–15)

In other words, inclusive pedagogy and catering to the needs of *all* learners is part and parcel of our identities as educators (or ought to be so), providing it is within the realm of what constitutes 'reasonable adjustments' (preferably anticipatory) under legal frameworks such as the Equality Act (2010) in the UK. Providing such support and opportunities falls within what Layer (2017, pp.9–10) identify as the 'power' and remit of universities to 'transform lives' (p.3), and it can have a positive impact on institutions in the areas of external scrutiny (e.g. in the UK, the Teaching Excellence Framework and Quality Assurance Agency/Office for Students expectations), legislative adherence (e.g. the Public Sector Equality Duty, 2011, and the Equality Act 2010), cost savings (an 'anticipatory approach' saves money in the long run), and reputation. Indeed, Lawrence (2022) goes as far as to argue that inclusive education is not just a 'moral duty' and facilitative of significant league table improvements but constitutes 'pedagogic competence ... good pedagogic practice is inherently inclusive after all'. As Layer (2017) argues, an inclusive approach ought to be seen as a 'route to excellence' and can 'facilitate the deliverability' of institutional missions 'by forging the link between excellence and enabling all students to deliver to their full potential. This is after all the core purpose of higher education' (p.14).

There are further reasons to be inclusive though. Increasingly, external drivers are focusing minds on pedagogical inclusion. In the UK, for instance, the Office for Students (OfS) established the Disabled Students' Commission, which has just published its formal consultation on the production of a Disabled Student Commitment (DSC). The DSC is intended as a 'self-regulatory tool' and is a call for all HEIs to make a 'step change' in creating more inclusive environments. Part of the Commitment is to put in place better support for disabled students from induction, but more significantly, as we have seen in light of the *Abrahart* case, there is a call for institutions to embed inclusive practice and *anticipatory* reasonable adjustments into curriculum design and delivery, and for staff to understand the barriers facing disabled students. In addition, AdvanceHE (2023), through the launch of the new Professional Standards Framework (PSF) – the 'globally-recognised framework for benchmarking success within HE teaching and learning' – has prioritised inclusion. Hitherto, in the 2011 UKPSF, inclusive pedagogies were somewhat arbitrarily and vaguely encompassed within its 'Professional Values', namely V1: 'respect individual learners and diverse learning communities' (what 'respect' means on a practical level remains open to interpretation) and V2: 'promote participation in higher education and equality of opportunity for learners'. Given that these were all couched merely as 'values', it was not explicit how this ought to translate into practice. In the new PSF, 'effective and inclusive practice' is both more explicit and actionable but has been moved into the preface for the dimension of 'Areas of Activity', thus putting inclusion front and central if not integral to 'pedagogic competence'. This makes the pedagogical principles outlined in this book ideally aligned to both the emerging Disabled Students' Commission guidelines (in the UK) and, more globally, the 2023 PSF benchmarking standards/framework.

The second, and perhaps more pressing, practical driver for adopting inclusive, anticipatory practice, however, is the fact that the variously named disability, dyslexia and/or neurodiversity departments and services within HEIs are increasingly stretched. The sector has witnessed a year-on-year increase in the number of students with learning differences accessing and entering higher education, with 19% of all full-time students and 25% of part-time students in the UK now having a declared disability (OfS, 2024). Data from the UK Higher Education Statistics Agency show that the number of students with a 'known disability' rose from 221,145 in 2012/13 to 484,270 in 2022/23 – an increase of 118% (overall student numbers for the same period increased by 25%). According to Hubble and Bolton (2020), the most common disability type in 2018–19 was a SpLD (36% of all declared disabilities). Within Royal Holloway, University of London, for example, the number of students with a SpLD increased from 476 in 2017/18 to 747 in 2023/24 (an increase of 56%), while staffing levels within its disability and neurodiversity department remained constant. Of the 747 students with a declared SpLD, 189 are not in receipt of specialist support, which means they are either accessing more generic support or none at all. Similarly, in the United States, the American College Health Association reports that in 2022, of 54,000 undergraduates surveyed, 15% reported having ADHD, 5% had a learning disability, and 3% were autistic (together comprising 23% of those surveyed – slightly higher than the average in the UK). Of those with learning disabilities, dyslexia, according to the Yale Center for Dyslexia and Creativity, accounts for 80–90% of cases (Welding, 2023).

In the UK, the percentage of students in receipt of the DSA varies enormously across institutions, with the University of Oxford only having 5.6% of their student body receiving a DSA whereas for Plymouth College of Art that figure is 30.9%. The average across the UK higher education sector is 7.86% (HESA, 2024). At Royal Holloway, the disability and neurodiversity department provided 945 hours of DSA-funded study skills support across two terms (24 weeks), thus illustrating the amount of staff time involved, with most tutors providing five 1-hour appointments per day. All of these increases mean that a) writing tutors, learning developers, lecturers, and personal tutors are more likely to encounter students with learning differences than ever before; and b) already stretched disability, dyslexia and/or neurodiversity departments are likely to send increasing numbers of their students to the 'open to all' provision as a means of bolstering student support or merely as an overspill mechanism – all this at a time when academic skills departments are often subject to cost-cutting exercises to help institutions balance their books, frequently because senior management fail to see their pivotal role in supporting student learning and bolstering student attainment, retention, and progression. Most troubling is the fact that completion rates for disabled students are lower, as is the number graduating with a 'good degree'; in the UK, this is counted as a first or upper-second-class degree (OfS, 2024). Indeed, in the US, completion rates for students with disabilities was only around 49.5%, which stands in marked contrast to the 68% for students without disabilities (Welding, 2023).

Interestingly, the data above obscures the extent to which students are diagnosed with a SpLD only after arriving at university and seeking a diagnosis once they encounter difficulties. This number is increasing, and during the 2023–24 academic year at Royal Holloway, a total of 82 such students were screened for a SpLD. Of those, 72 went on to have a full diagnostic assessment at a total cost of £25,200, so the issue has not only resource but serious financial implications. One of the reasons for diagnosis at university may be the fact that some students are unwittingly adept at developing their own compensatory strategies for overcoming their difficulties at school or college and those strategies become less effective once at university, thus leading them to suspect that an underlying issue may be at play. This phenomenon may well be compounded by the fact that owing to widening participation agendas and the general lowering of entry tariffs (in the UK at least), more students are entering university who may not otherwise have done so in the past. This is undoubtedly a good thing, but it may be resulting in more students entering higher education who then need to have their underlying learning difficulties investigated, diagnosed, and supported, whereas in the past they may have either quit education earlier in their academic journey or entered other careers or made life choices that may not have had a direct bearing on their learning difficulties.

Another reason why increasing numbers of students may be seeking a diagnosis once at university is because of cuts to budgets for such support and interventions at the school level. Globally, many Western economies responded to the global financial crisis of 2008 by implementing deficit reduction policies. While cuts often fell most heavily across the health and social care sector (Malli et al., 2018), education and support for SpLDs also bore some of the brunt of these agendas. Indeed, the Covid-19 pandemic exacerbated this trend and has created what the World Bank, UNESCO, and UNICEF (2021) have described as 'a global education crisis'. The financial after-effects are likely to be just as detrimental. As Yamini Aiyar wrote for the International Monetary Fund (2022), 'spending demands are becoming critical at a time when countries are looking to scale down pandemic-induced expenditure stimulus and reimpose fiscal discipline'. Citing India as an example, Aiyar (2022) warns that 'education budgets, slashed at the peak of the pandemic' have fallen 'victim to fiscal deficit targets and have not been increased'. The UK, for instance, has witnessed the effects of more than 13 years of an 'austerity' agenda implemented by the then Conservative government, which has resulted in schools cutting budgets and making difficult decisions, especially in the area of special educational needs and disabilities (SEND). A *Guardian* survey in 2021 found that almost a third of the 1,500 headteachers in England who responded to their survey said they had cut overall budgets for SEND, with 35% saying they planned to make further cuts in 2021–22 and one in four saying that their budget would be in deficit (Hall, 2021). Despite the Department for Education claiming that funding was increasing, SEND funding has dropped by 17% across England since 2015, and the Institute for Fiscal Studies reported that government spending on schools overall had dropped by 9% in real terms for 2022/23 – the largest drop in funding for more than 40 years (Parveen, 2019; Hall and Adams, 2021). This is likely to translate into increasing numbers of students not receiving the support they need and deserve at school and thus seeking out support at university.

Finally, the third reason why it is incumbent upon us all to adopt inclusive pedagogies is intertwined with, on the one hand, an increasing realisation (in some quarters at least) that academic skills/literacies development is key to unlocking student achievement and, on the other, the increasing pressures facing the higher education sector and how this often translates into cutbacks in the field of learning development. Academic support, especially in the form of academic literacies and writing development, is proven to be effective in driving up student achievement and attainment, as well as making assessment more inclusive. A recent University Alliance-funded study (2024), conducted in six institutions across the UK, aimed to investigate 'what works' in terms of 'supporting student progression and attainment through sustainable inclusive assessment practices'. The study identified top-performing programmes (in terms of 'good degree outcomes' and retention) at the universities of Teesside, Birmingham City, University of the West of England, Bristol, Kingston, Brighton, Oxford Brookes, and Hertfordshire. The research (conducted with both staff and students) found that one of the key 'enablers' of both inclusion and student success was academic support in the form of one-to-one tutorials and workshops on essay writing, referencing, critical thinking, and planning, as well as in-class activities ahead of assignments. Academic literacies support, then, works, and it makes programmes inherently more inclusive as the practices associated with academic study are demystified and scaffolded (University Alliance, 2024). We shall also see later how such support translates into success in a detailed study of an Integrated Foundation Year programme.

In 2024, the Quality Assurance Agency (QAA) in the UK published a thematic analysis of 'features of excellence' in the 2023 Teaching Excellence Framework (TEF) to provide what it described as a 'treasure trove of information' about excellent practice. The report outlines seven 'features of excellence' via a graphic illustrating the features on which institutions performed most strongly. At the far end of the spectrum (strongest submissions/performances) they identified 'learning environment and academic support', followed in second place by 'staff professional development and academic practice', and in third place 'teaching, assessment and feedback'. Under 'learning environment and academic support', the QAA identified subthemes of course-specific and cross-discipline skills support such as 'essay writing, referencing and research' but also themes such as personal tutoring, equality, diversity, and inclusion interventions, and disability support (QAA, 2024). Again, this illustrates the importance and impact of academic literacies development, especially within an inclusive framework, along with staff CPD to enable such support to be given. Yet interestingly, it is precisely these two areas that are often subject to cuts when institutions have to make cost savings, often in favour of continuing to invest in estates (ironically, 'physical and virtual learning resources' is ranked seventh by the QAA in terms of features of excellence, indicating that often the priorities of senior management are entirely contrary to what is shown to achieve excellence [and inclusion]). Royal Holloway, University of London, for instance, invested £6.9 million in estates development and refurbishments in 2020–21, with total income being 7.5% higher in 2021/22 than 2020/21 (Royal Holloway, 2021) Yet despite student numbers and revenue increasing, staff numbers within its disability and neurodiversity department have remained static while staffing in their Centre for the Development of Academic Skills has been halved (mostly through staff turnover and not being replaced).

A corollary to this predicament is the need to support what has been dubbed the current 'Covid generation' of students. It has been argued (Roseneil, 2023) that 'for many years to come – perhaps a decade or more – our education system is going to be dealing with a generation whose learning, skills and personal development have been profoundly affected by the pandemic' (p.25). In the UK at least, the government recognised this fact in 2021 and launched the National Tutoring Programme following concerns about a 'lockdown illiteracy surge' and the suggestion that over 230,000 pupils would start secondary school without the requisite reading skills. The programme was intended to 'address the impact of COVID-19 school closures on pupil's learning' and help them 'catch up' with lost learning (Roseneil, 2023). Overall, this initiative was supported to the tune of over £1 billion in its first two years of operation and covered extra tuition in key subjects such as English, humanities, maths, languages, science, and literacy. All children were eligible for the support, including those with SEND, but by early 2022 the scheme was branded as having 'failed pupils and taxpayers' (Roseneil, 2023) as only 10% of the target had been achieved. The programme continues, despite the government's own report which found that, on the ground, phase 1 of the project was 'haphazard and poorly planned' (Ofsted, 2023). However, its continuation is again testimony to the fact that both educators and government acknowledge the scale of the challenge in terms of addressing missed learning and the associated educational deficits. This is now feeding through into universities. As Roseneil (2023) argues, there needs to be:

> the equivalent of the pupil premium for undergraduates – a COVID Generation Student Premium. This might be paid for every UK undergraduate, but with an enhanced level to support the academic skills and personal development of students from disadvantaged backgrounds. Tailoring the COVID Student Premium to each university's student profile would target the largest funding increases at the institutions with the greatest need to intervene to enable students to 'catch up', while ensuring that all universities receive additional funding to make good the lost learning opportunities of lockdown, and to embed the best changes in pedagogy and educational technologies that have emerged from the pandemic. (p.25)

Irrespective of the argument that all this feeds into and perpetuates the 'deficit' model of academic skills support, the evidence (e.g. Thonus, 2001, 2002; Durkin and Main, 2002; Baik and Greig, 2009; Yeats et al., 2010, Nzekwe-Excel, 2014, Wallbank and Le Hen, 2023) clearly suggests that academic literacies interventions within higher education, especially those that are contextualised, embedded and integrated into the disciplines, can have a hugely positive effect on delivering the type of 'catch up' support envisaged here. Unfortunately, however, the pandemic has ushered in (or perhaps merely accelerated) the trend for such support to come under increasing pressure. The issues pertaining to decreased funding discussed above do not merely apply to pre-university education but to universities as well. Decreased support for universities from central government, coupled with decreases – in the UK at least – in the number of international students (who pay higher fees and are a valuable source of revenue to help institutions balance their books and offset the costs of providing teaching and support to home students), the pressures of inflation, and the flatlining of undergraduate tuition fees have all combined to throw many HEIs into funding deficits. Indeed, according to the National Audit Office (2022), the number of higher education providers with an in-year deficit increased from 5% in 2015/16 to 32% in 2019/20. Weston's (2023) report for the House of Lords reported that the financial pressures being encountered by many providers translates (especially given the previously static tuition fee of £9,250) into spending on teaching and resources per student being 18% lower in 2022/23 than ten years previously. Unfortunately, learning development departments are often seen as easy targets for cuts, and given what Asher (2024) sees as the intensification of the 'worst ravages' of neoliberalism following the pandemic, learning development and its associated activities are being 'increasingly deprofessionalised, deskilled, and outsourced – diluted as to focus and ethos', endlessly restructured, and of course 'reconfigured' as 'professional services, low skilled support and administration rather than teaching' (p.147).

These trends often stand in sharp contrast to institutional provision and advertisement of high-profile equality, diversity, and inclusion (EDI) agendas and initiatives. However, as Langford and Kimberly (2024), Tate and Bagguley (2017), and Dhillon (2020) suggest, these can be seen largely as 'gestural approaches' that are part and parcel of 'policy statements' and 'marketing strategies … rather than engaging with the challenges faced by "diverse" students' (Langford and Kimberly, 2024, p.118). In other words, we have several things co-occurring here that create a set of complex contradictions. There is an increased emphasis (and need for) on inclusion but also an increase in gestural approaches to inclusion, marginalisation, or even cuts – cuts to precisely the areas of activity most ideally suited for delivering upon what is needed and what, in other areas, is explicitly promoted as being an area of activity needing expansion. As one of the learning developers in Langford and Kimberly's (2024) recent research neatly summarises, 'there are so many missed opportunities here'. Despite the unique, intermediary position of academic literacies work and its practitioners, and the huge potential such work has for enabling student success and facilitating and promoting inclusion, all too frequently 'learning development is poorly understood or not even known about in senior management' (p.123). Such sentiments are commonplace within the field and feed into learning development's ongoing struggle to position itself beyond being poorly understood, unappreciated, vulnerable, or merely part of the 'deficit model' of student support – a situation not helped by the field's own difficulties owing to being 'fragmented, underconfident, and inward-looking' (Webster, 2024, p.235; Wingate 2015).

Despite the clear rationale for adopting more inclusive, anticipatory practices and bolstering support for students with learning differences within higher education, unfortunately, the picture remains bleak. Research has shown that academic colleagues frequently lack training in assessment literacies (Kirby et al., 2008), and in general, 'students report poor treatment, lack of support, inflexibility from lecturers, and perceptions of discrimination and judgmental attitudes when they disclose their learning difficulties' (Clouder et al., 2020, p.771). Furthermore, owing to 'unbending' workloads, a reliance on traditional teaching and assessment methods, and a lack of knowledge and training in inclusive pedagogies or the outsourcing of assessment feedback to AI, the treatment of students with learning differences remains 'at best, mixed'. This situation, Clouder et al (2020, p.774), claim, is the 'primary challenge' going forward and is again where this book aims to help.

One-to-one support

When it comes to assessments, most students will encounter or access support in the form of either one-to-one interventions (from subject lecturers, personal tutors, academic advisors, writing centre specialists, study skills advisors, learning developers [open to all], or disability support advisors) or larger-scale workshops, lectures, and seminars (provided by either academic literacies/study skills specialists or subject lecturers). However, very little literature or practical advice exists that can help practitioners render such modes of support inclusive. Indeed, it often has little to say at a practical level to help us meet the expectations and learning differences exhibited by our increasingly diverse student cohorts. The remainder of this chapter provides an overview and evaluation of the existing literature on one-to-one writing tutorials and embedded 'bolt-on' academic literacies support for assessment in respect of inclusion.

The reason for the focus on one-to-one scenarios is the fact that the majority of academic writing and assessment support comes in the form of one-to-one tutorials, either by specialist academic writing/skills tutors and learning developers, specialist SpLD tutors, or by subject lecturers in office hours or via academic advising appointments. Additionally, however, research strongly indicates that one-to-one oral feedback is the most effective and valuable type of feedback (Murtagh and Baker, 2009).

A great deal of ink has been spilt during the last few decades on the topic of one-to-one academic writing tutorials and such provision appears to be coming under increasing scrutiny. Much of this scrutiny stems not so much from concerns about the efficacy of the pedagogy but owing to the increased emphasis on value for money, the ongoing metricitisation, marketisation, and bureaucratisation of higher education and, more recently, the financial squeeze as a result of the Covid-19 pandemic. The age of massification has ushered in not only a vogue for metrics and accountability but also the harsh realisation that one-to-one modes of delivery are costly to provide, pedagogically limited within specific time constraints, a heavy burden on both staff and departments in terms of workload, and are unable to deliver value for money given the number of students who can be seen per hour of staff allocation. This all makes one-to-one writing and assessment support provision increasingly difficult to justify, even though most one-to-one writing tutors, learning developers, study skills tutors, writing development researchers, personal tutors, and the research attest to their value in helping students to fulfil their academic potential. Given the increasing importance of widening participation agendas, the lowering of entry tariffs, concerns about retention and attainment gaps, the provision of foundation year programmes, and disruptions to pre-university educational experiences as a result of the pandemic, it would seem that the pressures (if not opportunities) facing one-to-one provision across the global higher education spectrum are likely to increase. Despite the exponential diversification of the student body (French, 2018, p.205), however, much of the literature on one-to-one writing tutorials (while incredibly valuable in terms of exploring, appraising, and dissecting processes and pedagogical techniques) has not kept pace with the increasing need for pedagogical inclusion.

Before looking specifically at the role of writing tutors and tutorials vis-à-vis inclusion, it is worth taking a step back to consider student experiences before they even seek one-to-one writing support. Often, guidance on their writing and approaches to assessment, especially in the case of undergraduates, is rarely inclusive or even developmental when it comes to feedback and support from subject lecturers. As Tuck's (2018) research has revealed, this is not because subject lecturers have no interest in inclusion or writing development but because of competing pressures on their time, a focus on research outputs, and an increase in managerialist target setting. In addition, a lack of recognition of marking and feedback often means that marking is endured rather than seen as an integral part of teaching and professional practice. As Sword (2017) notes, while many academics devote considerable 'air and light and time and space' to the research and writing aspects of their profession, by contrast, marking student writing is often conducted at unsociable hours, squeezed in between meetings or conferences, and in less-than-ideal places such as bedrooms, hotel rooms, and even on trains (pp.64–66). Tuck (2018) also shows the worrying extent to which, despite widespread advances in academic literacies pedagogies and its champions, writing support is still seen as not only 'over there' but as too remedial to be worthy of a lecturer's attention. Many of Tuck's case studies evince the extent to which the practices and attitudes of academics perpetuate the 'deficit discourse' associated with writing and academic literacies development (Coleman, 2016; O'Shea et al., 2016; Horner and Lu, 1999) by 'grumbling' that students 'can't write anymore' (Tuck, 2018, p.5). These issues render personalised, inclusive feedback and writing development increasingly difficult in the current climate. Indeed, as controversial as it may sound, the fact that subject academics are seldom inclusive or provide quality feedback is often the reason why writing support is needed in the first place, and as a study of the UK Royal Literary Fund Fellows has found, problems often lie 'in a student's complete inability to fathom the meaning of the tutor's comments … occasionally indeed to read them' (Davies, Swinburne, and Williams, 2006, p.85). As Tuck (2018, p.129) notes, while academics might be dismissive of the work of writing specialists (being 'flavour of the month upstairs' and entailing 'teaching a grandmother to suck eggs' were two of the more charming indictments of such work in Tuck's research), the patent lack of capacity and in some cases professional diligence to provide adequate writing support is frequently what forms the basis of the writing tutor's profession and the work of writing and learning development centres generally.

The situation outlined above presents considerable challenges, not least from a pedagogical perspective. One particularly troublesome issue that renders inclusive teaching in one-to-one writing tutorials challenging is the tendency, however well meaning, for tutors to teach as they were taught, even though higher education and our students are markedly different from when many of us progressed through the system (Brabazon, 2018, p.52). As French (2018) rightly observes, gone are the days when 'undergraduates (if not postgraduates) were part of a … homogenous, socially elite group who entered university via the successful completion of common educational qualifications' for which a fairly standardised 'autonomous approach to academic writing and writing development' has dominated (p.205). As such, more research and continuing professional development is needed to support writing tutors and academics since the difficulties, characteristics, symptoms, and strengths associated with learning differences are mapped directly onto the process of learning and the assignments our students submit. Given that student writing is necessarily both a measure of student learning (the product) and an inescapable part of learning itself (the process), the essays we read, as we have already seen in the previous chapter (especially in their developmental/draft stages), are inescapably both a microcosm and barometer of these students' learning differences.

In many respects, we should embrace Clughen and Connell's (2015) notion (adapted from Laing [1965]) that 'schizophrenese' or 'word salads' ought to be seen as inextricable from students' learning differences, and as such, rather than submitting such texts to the 'pathologizing gaze' (p.49), we need to invest time, knowledge, and skill in dissecting them as though they were a map of the student's learning differences. This is especially important because the inherent issues associated with the complexity and artificiality of writing are intensified when we deal with writing produced by students with learning differences. As Game and Metcalfe (1996) suggest, 'everything about writing is deliberately fabricated'. Its 'linearity', which of course is particularly prized in coherent, convincing argumentation, is especially problematic because:

> neither experience nor contemplative thought comes naturally in linear form … Writing … is not the report of thought, but the production of a specific type of thought and a specific account of life. It is important not to lose sight of linearity's artifice and cultural specificity … Writing is nothing but an invention, a concoction, an illusion. (p.109)

As we have seen, such a situation, is of course specifically exclusive, since students with dyslexia or ADHD, for example, typically have profound difficulties trying to force their thought into conventional linear form. As writing tutors, markers, or subject lecturers, when we encounter an assignment that seems to be almost wilfully defying such conventions, our reaction can often be unguarded (which can be highly problematic given that in one-to-ones 'unguarded statements' and 'reactions under pressure … are all magnified' [Gordon, 2003, p.543]). Unwittingly, we can not only 'pathologise' the student but misdiagnose their writing problems and misdirect them in terms of what strategies they ought to deploy to get their writing to conform more accurately to what might constitute a 'good essay'. We clearly need to invest time in working with such 'word salads', 'schizophreneze', and lack of conventional linearity, but we need to do so using pedagogically inclusive techniques. As we shall see, merely teaching grammar, sentence structure, or essay structures using the tried-and-tested strategies derived from EAP – whether attempting to inculcate 'essayist literacy' via Socratic dialogue (Lillis, 2006), using mitigation strategies (Thonus, 1999), or 'modelling' (Macbeth, 2010), to name but a few conventional approaches – is unlikely to work without tweaking, diversification, and differentiation. Indeed, it has even been suggested that dyslexia, for example, can be 'resistant to conventional teaching methods' (BDA, 2007).

On the face of it, one-to-one writing tutorials provide an unrivalled opportunity for providing bespoke, personalised learning that will be infinitely more beneficial to the student than the often rather more perfunctory, impersonal, didactic mediums of the lecture or seminar, and is, by its very nature, already student centred and inclusive. As Gordon (2003) has argued, 'one-to-one teaching is perhaps one of the most powerful ways of "influencing students"' and offers, as Scott and Davis (1979) originally proposed, 'exceptional but often unrealised potential' (Gordon, 2003, p.543). Gordon, and Scott and Davis were referring specifically to learning and teaching in medicine, but the phrase 'unrealised potential' is especially worth interrogating as it seems, however obliquely, to be suggesting that notwithstanding the acknowledged drawbacks of such modes of delivery in terms of 'efficiency' (Gordon, 2003, p.543), there is a fundamental, underlying problem associated with one-to-one teaching which is holding back the achievement of excellence. This is never elaborated upon by these authors, and one assumes that whatever is 'unrealised' could apply to either students or tutors (or perhaps both). Notwithstanding the effusive language, the problem of 'unrealised potential' remains a niggling one and seems to have nothing to do with the overarching medium of delivery but with its pedagogical actualisation. Indeed, as Phillips and Fok (2017) have observed, while there has been extensive research on feedback processes (Lillis and Swann, 2003), the effectiveness of one-to-one tutoring across student levels (Eckstein, 2013), discourse analysis (Thonus, 1999), feedback (Ferris 2003; Hyland and Hyland, 2006), and even what constitutes a 'successful' tutorial (Thonus, 2002), 'there is surprisingly little research work on academic writing conferencing techniques', and research on the issue of 'what … writing tutors actually DO during the conferencing process is minimal' (Phillips and Fok, 2017, p.212). Indeed, to date, there is virtually no literature on inclusive practice within one-to-one writing tutorials, which again seems surprising given increasing student diversity, the acknowledgement that such pedagogical scenarios offer 'exceptional but unrealised potential', and what has been rightly described as the 'dearth of academic literature and practical training guides for one-to-one writing tutorial situations' (Caldwell, Stapleford, and Tinker, 2018, p.125; Webster, 2017).

I conducted a meta-analysis of seventeen of the most seminal and often-cited articles on one-to-one writing tutorials dating from 1986 to the present, finding that the terms inclusion or inclusive are only mentioned by five publications (Harris, 1986; Wooton, 2013; Phillips and Fok, 2017; Caldwell, Stapleford, and Tinker, 2018) and often only cited briefly in regard to creating a 'positive environment' (Wooton, 2013, p.11) or in relation to bringing the realm of English Language Teaching (ELT) into the mainstream work of writing centres (Phillips and Fok, 2017). Even Caldwell, Stapleford, and Tinker's (2018) ostensibly more promising contribution to the literature on academic writing tutorials has little to say in this regard. Although they explicitly acknowledge the extent to which inclusive provision has increased in response to widening participation agendas, and although they acknowledge the interesting parallels which exist between the 'talk' in academic writing tutorials and 'counselling … medical and psychotherapy sessions' (p.125), there is little acknowledgement of the need to cater for the concomitant increase in students with learning differences. Their research and advice, especially in relation to evaluating the efficacy and use of cycling through 'tight evaluation-suggestion sequences' (following Thonus, 1999), and the quest to enable students to take ownership of their learning and academic acculturation through such activities as questioning, reformulation, suggesting, modelling, and directives (Caldwell, Stapleford, and Tinker, 2018, p.129) is undoubtedly useful and effective. However, these techniques remain unexplored in regard to the specific pedagogical requirements of students with learning differences. Indeed, the advice not only pertains (in many respects quite rightly) to what French has characterised as the academy's deeply entrenched view of what constitutes 'good writing' but directs itself exclusively towards the predominance of 'essayist' forms of writing (Lillis, 2001; French, 2018). As such, while one-to-one writing tutorials undoubtedly offer 'perhaps one of the most powerful ways of "influencing students"', their potential for embedding inclusive practice is largely 'unrealised' in the literature published hitherto (Gordon, 2003, p.543).

The 'schizophrenic' tutorial and the quest for inclusion

The writing tutor's mode of delivery is often fraught with irresolvable tensions and is inherently complex and multifaceted. Academic writing support is at the forefront when dealing with issues that are integral to the student's acquisition, exploration, synthesis, or demonstration of core subject knowledge (and this can be particular to an assignment task or even marker), yet often neither the subject expertise nor the subject lecturer are actually present (or vice versa) – a problematic scenario Thonus calls 'triangulation' (2001). Additionally, not only is time, 'value for time' (Stevenson and Kokkinn, 2009, p.42), and scope an issue (a 30-minute tutorial discussing a 2,000-word assignment from a perhaps unfamiliar discipline, for instance, is necessarily a compromise and often limited in its ability to cover all the ground thought desirable), but the necessarily hybrid nature of the teaching style is deeply problematic and may also account for much of the scenario's 'unrealised potential'. One of the best accounts of this problem is Leki's (1990) conception of the writing tutor's role as 'schizophrenic', owing to the complex blend of roles it entails, often encompassing reader, assessor, advisor, tutor, teacher, coach, mentor, counsellor, auxiliary marker, and, increasingly, customer service provider and e-learning practitioner. Indeed, the complex questions of whether feedback ought to be 'prescriptive' or 'reactive', 'holistic' or preoccupied with 'lower-order concerns' (such as grammar) complicate the picture still further (Phillips and Fok, 2017, p.214). More recently, the Covid-19 pandemic has also required tutors to be something of e-learning gurus and IT troubleshooters, and the advent of GenAI has shifted some of the focus to developing information and digital literacy skills (searching, prompt engineering, and deciphering fact from fiction [so-called AI hallucinations]). The inherent hybridity of the role thus often makes it difficult to be inclusive, irrespective of the lack of research or advice pertaining to writing tutorials and inclusion.

A particular area of critical enquiry within the research hitherto has centred around the structure of the sessions, but again, however invaluable, much of this work is not explicitly geared towards learning differences and inclusion and there remains a significant gap in the literature. At a macro level, Gordon (2003) suggests a 'sandwich' approach, which encompasses asking students to reflect on their writing and what they want from the session, followed by a period of feedback, and concluding with positive, actionable ways forward and reflection. Similarly, Thonus (1999) suggests four key stages encompassing the evaluation of problems, student acceptance or rejection of feedback, tutor suggestions, and student acceptance or rejection. Caldwell, Stapleford, and Tinker (2018, p.128), meanwhile, describe how most tutorials follow a 'three-part organisation' encompassing 'openings', 'responding to the problem/task', and 'closings', and they explore the various strategies deployed therein via a conversational analysis approach. Again, although these writers do an excellent job of elaborating upon the inherent complexities of negotiating meaning through suggestions and turn-taking, this does not necessarily help us to render our exchanges pedagogically suitable for students with learning differences.

Similarly, at a micro level, the key points or ingredients for successful tutorials have been exhaustively explored in relation to the centrality of dialogue (North, 1984, p.444), but again there has been little research on how to optimise such exchanges to suit the needs of students with learning differences. Thonus (2002), for example, discusses the usefulness and effectiveness of directive evaluation–suggestion sequences and the 'conversational difficulty' of unsymmetrical tutor–student interactions before usefully recommending nine attributes for successful writing tutorials. Lillis (2006) quite rightly champions the key role of dialogue with a view to 'talking writers into essayist literacy' while considering how collaborative and 'talkback' dialogue can empower students (p.34). Harris (1992, pp.375–377) proposes three key questions for facilitating dialogue (Why did you do that? How did you write this paper? And how are you going to get from here to there?), while elsewhere, Thonus (1999, 2001) exhaustively examines mitigation strategies, coaching and dominance, directives, the use of subjectivisers, hedging, and overlaps, as well as pronoun use (2001, p.64). Woodward-Kron (2007), meanwhile, suggests that the key ingredients of a good one-to-one writing tutorial ought to consist of seeking information and clarification, clarifying meanings (including supervisors' comments), directives, making suggestions and negotiating changes, jointly constructing and scaffolding text, investigating how to represent evidence and establish logical relations, and helping with textual organisation. Similarly, Wooton (2013) articulates a set of 'golden rules' for tutoring success, Park (2015) examines request forms, questioning, and 'advice resistance', and Merkel (2018) investigates the utility of role balance and role reversals as a way of going beyond scaffolding to foster more incisive, meaningful, dialogic interactions. Much has been made of the need to 'scaffold' learning via dialogic interactions (Merkel, 2018) and thus work with the student within what Vygotsky (1978) called the 'Zone of Proximal Development' (Woodward-Kron, 2007, p.254). This is self-evidently sound advice, and a great deal of research has been undertaken which explores the various ways in which this can be achieved (e.g. clarification requests, comprehension checks and negotiation [Ewert, 2009], dialogue [Craswell, 1995; Clerehan, 1996; Chanock, 1999; Williams, 2004], and 'mutual scaffolding' [De Guerrero and Villamil, 2002; Woodward-Kron, 2007]) – all of it pointing to and concerning itself with the 'asymmetrical ... hallmark of scaffolding' (Merkel, 2018, p.17). But while many of the benefits and drawbacks of scaffolding (Merkel, 2018) and dialogue are obvious and well documented (e.g. increased audience awareness, facilitative and confidence-building interaction, uncovering poorly articulated intentions, and the dangers of appropriation), there is again little in the way of advice in respect of how to adopt such practices for students with learning differences.

Undoubtedly, many of the above suggestions, caveats, and 'golden rules' are inherently student centred and thus likely to be useful, but many students with learning differences do not fit the mould and may even be 'resistant' to such techniques. Lillis's reference to teaching students as apprentices using socialisation strategies, for example, is not only deeply rooted within the language associated with the deficit model (and thus potentially subjects students to the 'pathologising gaze' [Clughen and Connell, 2015, p.49]) but does nothing to render academic socialisation and the pedagogies associated with an academic literacies approach inclusive. Indeed, the recommendation of using extensive hedging may make the pedagogy less overtly directive, but students who have issues with information processing (e.g. dyslexia, ADHD, and autism) often need direction, precision in meaning, and very careful use of words to leave minimal room for ambiguities. Indeed, dialogue itself might be difficult for autistic students, and students with cognitive overload (as a result of their slower processing and working memory) might find dialogue not only inhibiting but also stressful. As we have seen, often the type of dialogue recommended is quasi-interrogative, but for students with learning differences, working memory is often a significant inhibiting factor. Take Harris's (1992, p.375) advice to seek answers to the question 'why did you do that?' and Woodward-Kron's (2007) similar suggestion of seeking information and clarification. As we have already seen, dyslexic students in particular, but also students with ADHD, have notorious difficulties with sequencing, short-term memory, and cognitive overload when writing (Grant, 2010; Ghani and Gathercole, 2013; McLaren, 2019). Consequently, they may not remember why they did what they did (Eide and Eide, 2023) or remember what they meant by what they had written (which could inadvertently arouse either suspicions about plagiarism or lead to the 'pathologising gaze'). Woodward-Kron's (2007) suggestion of jointly constructing and scaffolding text on the face of it sounds like an excellent idea, but given that a hallmark of dyslexia is difficulty in writing and listening simultaneously, this can be problematic, lead to anxiety, and possibly cognitive overload. With ADHD, meanwhile, both inattention and an inability to concentrate might be problematic, and the characteristic of having difficulty with foresight or hindsight can lead to issues pertaining to learning from errors or even feedback.

Many writing tutors adopt their pedagogical strategies from tried-and-tested techniques espoused in seminal academic writing and study skills textbooks. However, these do not necessarily get us very far with students with learning differences. Let us take paragraph structure, for instance. Most tutors will rightly point out the centrality of the 'topic sentence' as a means of framing and signposting the subject and argument, and in what follows the standard evidence – evaluation/analysis sequence is usually taught. However, the analysis and evaluation section can prove especially problematic for students with learning differences, and the advice is not especially helpful. For instance, the bestselling author Stella Cottrell states that 'if you have difficulties with paragraphing', try dividing a page into columns comprising of 1) arguments, 2) main information, and 3) supporting detail, with each paragraph containing 'one, two or three items from column 2,' and 'several items from column 3' (Cottrell, 2013, p.299). However, as we saw in the extracts in the previous chapter, given that dyslexia and ADHD affect logical sequencing, working memory or cognitive overload impedes clarity and focus, and autism often prevents students from organising ideas effectively and ensnares them in a preference for precision, depth, and focus, how are these students to know which of the 'one, two, or three items from column 2' to include, and, more particularly, in what order they should occur? What might seem like a logical order to a dyslexic student might not seem so to a non-dyslexic student. A student with ADHD, meanwhile, might be too easily distracted to even listen to, remember, or heed such advice effectively. Yet there is little in the literature to help us assist these students.

Even most dyslexia-specific academic writing guides offer little in the way of differentiation or innovation to get around the above issues. For instance, Monica Gribben's *The Study Skills Toolkit for Students with Dyslexia* (2012), despite receiving critical acclaim from dyslexia specialists and having been written by a specialist dyslexia consultant and advisor, simply presents the font in larger than normal size and makes limited use of tables and visual black and white thought bubbles as a means of rendering the ideas and writing processes accessible (much in the same way as Stella Cottrell). Sandra Hargreaves's *Study Skills for Students with Dyslexia* (2012), meanwhile, is also marketed specifically at dyslexic students, but even for non-dyslexic students the text appears to be very dense. Like Gribben's book, there seems little to differentiate it from most other study skills guides in terms of pedagogical techniques and approaches. Neither the SQ3R reading method nor the Cornell System for note-taking, for instance, are adapted for the dyslexic student. Equally, there are no diagrams, exercises, or worked examples and as such, it seems somewhat detached, from a pedagogical perspective, from what students with dyslexia, ADHD, or autism have been shown to prefer and need (Cooper, 2019). The situation is better in respect of textbooks for supporting students with autism, and Geither and Meeks' *Helping Students with Autism Spectrum Disorder Express Their Thoughts and Knowledge in Writing* (2014) is especially useful, but for the most part, tutors attempting to use these 'textbook' strategies will find that students with learning differences are unlikely to find the techniques helpful, as the scaffolding is simply insufficiently bespoke.

There is clearly a wealth of pedagogical approaches and recommendations in the literature that seek to help tutors understand how to organise their tutorials from the moment students enter the door right through to when they leave (encompassing seemingly every dialogic and scaffolded interaction in between), but few of these articles contain anything which pertains to inclusive pedagogies for students with learning differences. Of all the literature currently available on one-to-one academic writing tutorials, French (2018) sails the closest to acknowledging issues pertaining to inclusion but only from the perspective of emotion and the vexed notion of learners expressing 'identities and feelings' (p.203). This is undoubtedly inclusive in the sense that situating our pedagogical perspectives in relation to the increasingly diverse writing backgrounds of our students (e.g. 'portfolio-based literacies' or vocational backgrounds) moves the debate towards a greater acknowledgement of diversity (pp.205–206). However, the question of how we might tutor those students with dyslexia, ADHD, or autism persists. Brabazon (2018) offers the most comprehensive solution to the issues relating to inclusion and diversity by proposing a 'universally designed ... programme' which scaffolds mentoring and academic supervision from the perspective of multimodality. This is undoubtedly excellent work but is entirely geared towards doctoral students, whereas the bulk of the students encountered in writing centres, learning development centres, and in office hours or personal tutorials are undergraduates or masters-level students. The most recent contribution to the field (Ker and van Gorp, 2024) is far more promising, as the authors do suggest the need for adopting 'multi-modal learning approaches' and 'providing clear and concise instructions' (p.7), but again there is little advice in terms of how to do this in practice.

Intersecting one-to-one and more cohort-based learning environments (which will be discussed below) is the notion of Self-Regulated Strategy Development (SRSD) espoused by the likes of Graham and Harris (2005). Unlike the recommendations above, SRSD is an overarching pedagogical strategy specifically designed for students with learning differences, and consists of modelling strategies along a five-step process consisting of 1) discuss it, 2) model it, 3) make it your own, 4) support it, and 5) independent performance. Graham and Harris describe the model as 'scientifically validated' (p.5), and it works by modelling strategies used by successful writers in ways that are 'purposeful, procedural, wilful, and effortful ... they must also be deliberately activated and require commitment and effort to be effective' (p.9). The evidence seems to suggest that such strategies are effective (Ellis and Scanlon, 1996; Mellard and Scanlon, 2006; Berry and Mason, 2012). However, because the techniques are modelled on what successful writers do (which means they are not bespoke to the needs of students with learning differences), I would argue that they are only effective by virtue of the effort required to learn and practise them, and it is significant that Graham and Harris use language associated with sheer wilfulness and persistence to promote their effectiveness (by implication, if they are not effective the student has not been sufficiently 'committed'). Arguably, any strategy, if enough dedication is put into it, will produce results and improvements, but the key thing that is missing here is that the system is not pedagogically meaningful. As we shall see in Chapters 3, 4, and 5, this is where Universal Design for Learning (UDL) and the pedagogies outlined in this book differ, as they are grounded in techniques that not only align with the specific exploratory learning and search strengths associated with dyslexia, ADHD, and autism but they are meaningful in the direct correlation the visual pedagogies have with what they are modelling, describing, or explaining. In other words, the strategies advocated by Graham and Harris are akin to hammering a square peg into a round hole. It is not necessarily the pedagogy that is doing the job; it is the hammering.

Models of embedded, generic, and cohort-based provision

Finally, there are the challenges associated with embedding academic literacies support (of whatever pedagogical creed) within the curriculum in an inclusive manner. Again, a great deal of ink has been spilt on this subject, including different named approaches such as Writing Across the Curriculum (WAC) and Writing in the Discipline (WID) – neither of which have garnered a great deal of traction in the UK. Aside from the one-to-one support discussed above, there are two predominant models of supporting students' academic literacies development at scale. The first is generic, 'bolt-on' support (often termed 'study skills'). This is decontextualised and often sits in study skills departments or writing centres. Students are often either signposted to such support by their subject lecturers or enrol on their courses, workshops, or even one-to-ones autonomously. Needless to say, the generic, centralised nature of such support often means that the general principles of essay writing, decoding and answering assignment questions, preparing for exams, critical thinking, referencing, and the like are taught but with little or necessarily limited reference to the actual subject and its disciplinary contexts or communities of practice. The second model is embedded support, where often colleagues from centralised centres or departments teach alongside subject specialists within core modules or courses, teaching the core principles of academic literacies but with specific reference to disciplinary conventions or even specific texts, assignments, or subject content. This approach is predicated upon the integrated 'academic literacies' and 'academic socialisation' models advocated by Lea and Street (2006), Hyland (2002), Ivanic (2004), Wingate (2006, 2015), and Ingle (2016), in which academic skills development aligns with contextualised 'experiential learning theories' (Wingate, 2006, p.458; Kolb and Fry, 1975). However, controversially, this model has recently been contested. For Richards and Pilcher (2020), claims that 'study skills' are 'valuable for every subject', 'can be embedded', and help students 'succeed in their subjects' are a 'constitutive fantasy' of neoliberal universality, marketisation and expansionism (pp.1, 8–9) that, ideally, should 'cease to exist' (p.13). In particular, Richards and Pilcher claim that any espousal of an 'embedded' model is 'misplaced' because rather than 'study skills' being developed, 'instead, students are being taught the subject' (p.7). This depiction is misguided, as the subject is indeed taught, but the subject-specialist knowledge is scaffolded through, and integrated within, the development of academic literacies. This renders the necessarily advanced nature of the topic more accessible and learnable within a framework of academic socialisation and its associated assessment and academic literacies are socialised alongside, and with direct relevance to, the discipline.

Many of the studies Richards and Pilcher cite as evidence that embedded 'study skills' are both 'ineffective' and not actually embedded in the first place prove the opposite – that 'students value a highly discipline-specific approach to language and academic skills support' (Baik and Greig, 2009, p.401) and embeddedness is 'the key factor in determining their effectiveness' (Durkin and Main, 2002, p.26). Richards and Pilcher fail to appreciate that, in Bloom's taxonomy (1956), 'subject mastery' is inseparable from higher-order skills such as application, analysis, and synthesis, precisely the skills often taught in academic writing, academic literacies, and critical thinking workshops. Knowledge alone, however masterful, is merely facts (a lower-order skill in Bloom's schema). Furthermore, research has shown that academic literacies development is a key to success, and various studies have revealed that attendance at academic writing workshops translates into increases in performance of 10–12% (Thonus, 2001, 2002; Yeats et al., 2010; Nzekwe-Excel, 2014; Wallbank and Le Hen, 2023). The question remains, however, how do we render the techniques and approaches to teaching academic literacies (in either embedded or generic scenarios) pedagogically inclusive for students with learning differences?

This is precisely where this book comes in. As either subject lecturers delivering tutorials and feedback on assessments, or writing tutors, learning developers, or specialist SpLD tutors, this book aims to equip you with not only a deeper understanding of learning differences but the inclusive pedagogical tools you need to enable students with the most common learning differences to excel in their assessments. To start with you need an overarching pedagogical framework that aligns with the cognitive strengths associated with learning differences while providing scaffolding for their challenges and trade-offs. As we shall see in the next chapter, this is where the principles of UDL can help.

References

AdvanceHE, (2023) 'Professional Standards Framework (PSF 2023)'. Available from: www.advance-he.ac.uk/teaching-and-learning/psf (Accessed: 23 June 2024).

Aiyar, Y., (2022) 'The Education Pandemic', *International Monetary Fund: Finance and Development Magazine*. Available from: www.imf.org/en/Publications/fandd/issues/2022/03/Education-pandemic-Aiyar (Accessed: 23 July 2023).

Asher, G., (2024) 'Learning Development in, Against, and Beyond the Neoliberal University: Critical Learning Development and Critical Academic Literacies', in Syska, A. and Buckley, C. (eds), *How to be a Learning Developer in Higher Education: Critical Perspectives, Community and Practice*. London: Routledge, pp.144–152.

Baik, C., and Greig, J., (2009) 'Improving the Academic Outcomes of Undergraduate ESL Students: The Case for Discipline-Based Academic Skills Programs', *Higher Education Research and Development*, 28, pp.401–416. Available from: www.tandfonline.com/doi/abs/10.1080/07294360903067005 (Accessed: 12 June 2024).

Berry, A. B., and Mason, L. H., (2012) 'The Effects of Self-regulated Strategy Development on the Writing of Expository Essays for Adults with Written Expression Difficulties: Preparing for the GED', *Remedial and Special Education*, 33:2, pp.124–136. Available from: https://psycnet.apa.org/record/2012-07077-006 (Accessed: 23 September 2024).

Bloom, B. S., Engelhart, M. D., Furst, E. J., Hill, W. H., and Krathwohl, D. R., (1956) *Taxonomy of Educational Objectives: The Classification of Educational Goals*. New York: David McKay Company.

Brabazon, T., (2018) 'The Deficit Doctorate: Multimodal Solutions to Enable Differentiated Learning', *International Journal of Social Sciences and Educational Studies*, 4:5, pp.52–69. Available from: https://ijsses.tiu.edu.iq/index.php/ijsses/article/view/364 (Accessed: 23 October 2023).

British Dyslexia Association (BDA), (2007) 'Definition of Dyslexia'. Available from: www.actiondyslexia.co.uk/view-article/Defining-Dyslexia (Accessed: 19 September, 2024).

Caldwell, E., Stapleford, K., and Tinker, A., (2018) 'Talking Academic Writing: A Conversation Analysis of One-to-one Learning Development Tutorials', *Journal of Academic Writing*, 8:2, pp.124–136. Available from: https://publications.coventry.ac.uk/index.php/joaw/article/view/464 (Accessed: 12 July 2023).

Chanock, K., (1999) '"You Get Me to Explain Myself More Better": Supporting Diversity through Dialogic Learning', *Cornerstones*. Proceedings of the HERDSA Conference held at the University of Melbourne, July 1999.

Clerehan, R., (1996) 'How Does Dialogic Learning Work?' in Chanock, K., Burley, V., and Davies, S. (eds), *What Do We Learn from Teaching One-to-one That Informs Our Work with Larger Numbers?* Proceedings of the Language and Academic Skills Conference held at La Trobe University, November, 1996, pp.69–81.

Clouder, L., Karakus, M., Cinotti, A., Virginia Ferreyra, M., Amador Fierros, G., and Rojo, P., (2020) 'Neurodiversity in Higher Education: A Narrative Synthesis', *Higher Education*, 80, pp.757–778. Available from: https://doi.org/10.1007/s10734-020-00513-6 (Accessed: 14 September 2024).

Clughen, L., and Connell, M., (2015) 'Working with Power: A Dialogue about Writing Support Using Insights from Psychotherapy', in Lillis, T., Harrington, K., Lea, M. R., and Mitchell, S. (eds), *Working with Academic Literacies: Case Studies Towards Transformative Practice*. Fort Collins, CO: The WAC Clearinghouse, pp.45–53.

Coleman, L., (2016) 'Offsetting Deficit Conceptualisations: Methodological Considerations for Higher Education Research', *Critical Studies in Teaching and Learning*, 4:1, pp.16–38. Available from: https://journals.co.za/doi/abs/10.14426/cristal.v4i1.59 (Accessed: 3 July 2019).

Cooper, R., (2019) 'Specific Learning Difficulties', in Krčmář, K. (ed.), *The Inclusivity Gap*. Aberdeen: Inspired by Learning, pp.80–95.

Cottrell, S., (2013) *The Study Skills Handbook*. Fourth Edition. Basingstoke: Palgrave Macmillan.

Craswell, G., (1995) 'To Integrate or Not? Interests, Practice and the Dialogic Development of Graduate Students' Discourse Skills', in Chanock, K. (ed.), *Integrating the Teaching of Academic Discourses into the Disciplines*. Proceedings of the Language and Academic Skills Conference held at La Trobe University, November 1996, pp.1–29.

Davies, S., Swinburne, D., and Williams, G., (2006) *Writing Matters*. London: Royal Literary Fund.

De Guerrero, M., and Villamil, O. S., (2002) 'Activating the ZPD: Mutual Scaffolding in L2 Peer Revision', *The Modern Language Journal*, 84:1, pp.51–68. Available from: https://onlinelibrary.wiley.com/doi/abs/10.1111/0026-7902.00052 (Accessed: 13 October 2023).

Dhillon, S., (2020) 'An Immanent Critique of Decolonisation Projects', *LD Theory*. Available at: https://ldtheory.wordpress.com/ (Accessed 12 September 2024).

Durkin, K., and Main, A., (2002) 'Discipline-based Study Skills Support for First-year Undergraduate Students', *Active Learning in Higher Education*, 3:1, pp.24–39. Available from: https://journals.sagepub.com/doi/abs/10.1177/1469787402003001003 (Accessed: 16 July 2023).

Eckstein, G., (2013) 'Implementing and Evaluating a Writing Conference Program for International L2 Writers across Language Proficiency Levels', *Journal of Second Language Writing*, 22, pp.231–239. Available from: www.sciencedirect.com/science/article/pii/S1060374313000155 (Accessed: 23 June 2023).

Eide, B. L., and Eide, F. F., (2023) *The Dyslexic Advantage: Unlocking the Hidden Potential of the Dyslexic Brain*. London: Hay House.

Ellis, E. S., and Scanlon, D., (1996) *Teaching Learning Strategies to Adolescents and Adults with Learning Disabilities*. Austin, TX: Pro-Ed, Inc.

Ewert, D. E., (2009) 'L2 Writing Conferences: Investigating Teacher Talk', *Journal of Second Language Writing*, 18:4, pp.251–269. Available from: www.sciencedirect.com/science/article/pii/S1060374309000332 (Accessed: 23 June 2023)

Fain, P., (2021) 'A Troubling Lack of Skills in Literacy and Numeracy', *Open Campus*. Available from: www.opencampusmedia.org/2021/06/10/a-troubling-lack-of-skills-in-literacy-and-numeracy/ (Accessed: 30 November 2024).

Ferris, D., (2003) 'Responding to Writing', in Kroll, B. (ed.), *Exploring the Dynamic of Second Language Writing*. Cambridge: Cambridge University Press, pp.119–140.

French, A., (2018) 'Academic Writing: Anxiety, Confusion and the Affective Domain: Why Should Subject Lecturers Acknowledge the Social and Emotional Aspects of Writing Development Processes', *Journal of Academic Writing*, 8:2, pp.202–211.

Game, A., and Metcalfe, A., (1996) *Passionate Sociology*. London: Sage.

Geither, E., and Meeks, L., (2014) *Helping Students with Autism Spectrum Disorder Express Their Thoughts and Knowledge in Writing: Tips and Exercises for Developing Writing Skills*. London: Jessica Kingsley Publishers.

Ghani, K. A., and Gathercole, S. E., (2013) 'Working Memory and Study Skills: A Comparison between Dyslexic and Non-dyslexic Adult Learners', *Procedia – Social and Behavioral Sciences*, 97. Available at: www.sciencedirect.com/science/article/pii/S1877042813036781 (Accessed: 13 September 2019).

Gordon, J., (2003) 'ABC of Learning and Teaching in Medicine: One-to-One Teaching and Feedback', *British Medical Journal*, 326:7388, pp.543–545. Available from: https://pubmed.ncbi.nlm.nih.gov/12623919/ (Accessed: 16 July 2023).

Graham, S., and Harris, K. R., (2005) *Writing Better: Effective Strategies for Teaching Students with Learning Difficulties*. Baltimore, MD: Paul H. Brookes Publishing Co.

Grant, D., (2010) *That's the Way I Think: Dyslexia, Dyspraxia and ADHD Explained*. London: Routledge.

Gribben, M., (2012) *The Study Skills Toolkit for Students with Dyslexia*. London: Sage.

Hall, R., (2021) 'Schools in England Forced to Cut Support for Special Needs Pupils', *The Guardian*, 8 September 2021. Available from: www.theguardian.com/education/2021/sep/08/schools-in-england-forced-to-cut-support-for-special-needs-pupils (Accessed: 14 September 2023).

Hall, R., and Adams, R., (2021) 'Per Pupil Spending in English Schools to Fall to Under 2009-10 Levels – IFS', *The Guardian*, 2 September 2021. Available from: www.theguardian.com/education/2021/sep/02/per-pupil-spending-in-english-schools-to-fall-to-under-2009-10-levels-ifs (Accessed: 15 December 2023).

Harding, E., (2022) 'Universities are Ordered to Go Woke: Courses from Computing to Classics are Told to 'Decolonise' by Degrees Watchdog and Teach about Impact of Colonialism and "White Supremacy"'. *MailOnline*, 16 November 2022. Available from: www.dailymail.co.uk/news/article-11431449/Universities-courses-computing-classics-told-decolonise-degrees-watchdog.html (Accessed: 12 September 2022).

Hargreaves, S., (2012) *Study Skills for Students with Dyslexia*. London: Sage.

Harris, M., (1986) *Teaching One-to-One: The Writing Conference*. Urbana, IL: National Council of Teachers of English.

Harris, M., (1992) 'Collaboration Is not Collaboration Is not Collaboration: Writing Center Tutorials vs. Peer-Response Groups', *College Composition and Communication*, 43:3, pp.369–383. Available from: www.jstor.org/stable/358228 (Accessed: 23 June 2023).

HESA, (2024) 'Who's Studying in HE?' HE Student Data. Available from: www.hesa.ac.uk/data-and-analysis/students/whos-in-he (Accessed: 3 July 2024).

Heuboeck, A., Holmes, J., and Nesi, H., (2007) *The BAWE Corpus Manual: An Investigation of Genres of Assessed Writing in British Higher Education*. ESRC, Project RES-000-23-0800.

Hockings, C., (2010) 'Inclusive Learning and Teaching in Higher Education: A Synthesis of Research', Higher Education Academy. Available from: www.advance-he.ac.uk/knowledge-hub/inclusive-learning-and-teaching-higher-education-synthesis-research (Accessed: 13 July 2024).

Horner, B., and Lu, M. Z., (1999) *Representing the 'Other': Basic Writers and the Teaching of Basic Writing*. Urbana, IL: National Council of Teachers of English.

Hubble, S., and Bolton, P., (2020) *Support for Disabled Students in Higher Education in England*. Available from: https://commonslibrary.parliament.uk/research-briefings/cbp-8716/ (Accessed: 27 November 2020).

Hyland, K., (2002) 'Options of Identity in Academic Writing', *ELT Journal*, 56:4, pp.351–358. Available from: https://academic.oup.com/eltj/article-abstract/56/4/351/410117?redirectedFrom=fulltext (Accessed: 23 June 2023).

Hyland, K., and Hyland, F., (2006) *Feedback in Second Language Writing: Contexts and Issues*. Cambridge: Cambridge University Press.

Ingle, J., (2016) 'Engaging with Academic Writing and Discourse', in Pokorny, H. and Warren, D. (eds), *Enhancing Teaching Practice in Higher Education*. London: Sage, pp.144–164.

Ivanic, R., (2004) 'Discourses of Writing and Learning to Write', *Language and Education*, 18:3, pp.220–245. Available from: www.tandfonline.com/doi/abs/10.1080/09500780408666877 (Accessed: 23 June 2023).

Ker, G., and van Gorp, R., (2024) 'Effective Learning Advisor Strategies for Neurodiversity: Time to Get it Right', *ATLAANZ Journal*, 7:1, pp.1–13. Available from: https://journal.atlaanz.org/atlaanz/article/view/75/55 (Accessed: 12 December 2024).

Kioko, V., and Makoelle, T. M., (2014) 'Inclusion in Higher Education: Learning Experiences of Disabled Students at Winchester University', *International Education Studies*, 7:6, pp.106–116. Available from: www.ccsenet.org/journal/index.php/ies/article/view/37419 (Accessed: 24 August 2024).

Kirby, A., Sugden, D., Beveridge, S., and Edwards, R., (2008) 'Dyslexia and Developmental Co-ordination Disorder in Further and Higher Education – Similarities and Differences. Does the 'Label' Influence the Support Given?' *Dyslexia*, 14:3, pp.197–213. Available from: https://doi.org/10.1002/dys.367 (Accessed 14 September 2024).

Kolb, D. A., and Fry, R., (1975) 'Toward an Applied Theory of Experiential Learning', in Cooper, G. (ed.), *Theories of Group Processes*. New York: Wiley, pp.33–57.

Kotsko, A., (2024) 'The Loss of Things I Took for Granted', *Slate*. Available from: https://slate.com/human-interest/2024/02/literacy-crisis-reading-comprehension-college.html (Accessed: 30 November 2024).

Langford, A-M., and Kimberly, E., (2024) 'Practice versus Policy: Learning Development's Role in Supporting, Developing, and Challenging Equality, Diversity, and Inclusion in the Higher Education Sector', in Syska, A. and Buckley, C., (eds), *How to Be a Learning Developer in Higher Education: Critical Perspectives, Community and Practice*. London: Routledge, pp.118–125.

Lawrence, J., (2022) 'Inclusive Academic Practice as Pedagogic Competence', *The SEDA Blog*. Available from: https://thesedablog.wordpress.com/2022/05/12/inclusive-academic-practice-as-pedagogic-competence/comment-page-1/ (Accessed: 12 September 2024).

Layer, G., (2017) *Inclusive Teaching and Learning in Higher Education as a Route to Excellence*. London: Department for Education. Available from: www.gov.uk/government/publications/inclusive-teaching-and-learning-in-higher-education (Accessed: 24 September 2023).

Lea, M. R., (2017) 'Academic Literacies in Theory and Practice', in Street, B. and May, S. (eds), *Literacies and Language Education: Encyclopedia of Language and Education*. Cham: Springer. Available from: https://doi.org/10.1007/978-3-319-02252-9_19 (Accessed: 1 November 2024).

Lea, M. R., and Street, B. V., (2006) 'The "Academic Literacies" Model: Theory and Applications', *Theory Into Practice*, 45:4, pp.368–377. Available from: www.tandfonline.com/doi/abs/10.1207/s15430421tip4504_11 (Accessed: 23 June 2023).

Leki, I., (1990) 'Coaching from the Margins: Issues in Written Response', in Kroll, B. (ed.), *Second Language Writing: Research Insights for the Classroom*. Cambridge: Cambridge University Press, pp.57–68.

Lillis, T. M., (2001) *Student Writing: Access, Regulation, Desire*. London and New York: Routledge.

Lillis, T. M., (2006) 'Moving Towards an "Academic Literacies" Pedagogy: Dialogues of Participation', in Ganobcsik-Williams, L. (ed.), *Teaching Academic Writing in UK Higher Education: Theories, Practices and Models*. Basingstoke: Palgrave Macmillan, pp.30–43.

Lillis, T. M., and Swann, J., (2003) 'Giving Feedback on Student Writing', in Coffin, C., Curry, M. J., Goodman, S., Hewings, A., Lillis, T., and Swann, J. (eds), *Teaching Academic Writing: A Toolkit for Higher Education*. London: Routledge, pp.101–129.

Macbeth, K. P., (2010) 'Deliberate False Provisions: The Use and Usefulness of Models in Learning Academic Writing', *Journal of Second Language Writing*, 19, pp.33–48. Available from: www.sciencedirect.com/science/article/pii/S1060374309000393 (Accessed: 13 June 2023).

Malli, M. A., Sams, L., Forrester-Jones, R., Murphy, G., and Henwood, M., (2018) 'Austerity and the Lives of People with Learning Disabilities: A Thematic Synthesis of Current Literature', *Disability and Society*, 33:9, pp.1412–1435. Available from: https://doi.org/10.1080/09687599.2018.1497950 (Accessed: 24 August 2024).

McLaren, R., (2019) 'Inclusivity and Academic Writing: Drawing on Practice in American Higher Education', in Krčmář, K. (ed.), *The Inclusivity Gap*. Aberdeen: Inspired by Learning, pp.216–229.

Mellard, D., and Scanlon, D., (2006) 'Feasibility of Explicit Instruction in Adult Basic Education: Instructor–Learner Interaction Patterns', *Adult Basic Education: An Interdisciplinary Journal for Adult Literacy Educational Planning*, 16:1, pp.21–37. Available from: https://eric.ed.gov/?id=EJ744170 (Accessed: 16 June 2023).

Merkel, W., (2018) 'Role Reversals: A Case Study of Dialogic Interactions and Feedback on L2 Writing', *Journal of Second Language Writing*, 39, pp.16–28. Available from: www.sciencedirect.com/science/article/pii/S1060374317301893 (Accessed 13 June 2023).

Morgan, J., (2022) 'New Minister Halfon Criticises QAA's "Decolonisation Nonsense"', *Times Higher Education*, 16 November 2022. Available from: www.timeshighereducation.com/news/new-minister-halfon-criticises-qaas-decolonisation-nonsense (Accessed: 13 March 2024).

Murtagh, L., and Baker, N., (2009) 'Feedback to Feed Forward: Student Response to Tutors' Written Comments on Assignments', *Practitioner Research in Higher Education*, 3:1, pp.20–28.

National Audit Office, (2022) 'Regulating the Financial Sustainability of Higher Education Providers in England'. NAO Press Release, 9 March 2022. Available from: www.nao.org.uk/press-releases/regulating-the-financial-sustainability-of-higher-education-providers-in-england/ (Accessed: 1 August 2024).

Nicolson, R. L., and Fawcett, A. J., (2019) 'Development of Dyslexia: The Delayed Neural Commitment Framework', *Frontiers in Behavioral Neuroscience*, 13:112, pp.1–16. Available from: https://pubmed.ncbi.nlm.nih.gov/31178705/ (Accessed: 11 September 2024).

Nieminen, J. H., (2022) 'Assessment for Inclusion: Rethinking Inclusive Assessment in Higher Education', *Teaching in Higher Education*, 29:4, pp.841–859. Available from: www.tandfonline.com/doi/full/10.1080/13562517.2021.2021395 (Accessed: 12 August 2024).

Nieminen, J. H., Morina, A., and Biagiotti, G., (2024) 'Assessment as a Matter of Inclusion: A Meta-ethnographic Review of the Assessment Experiences of Students with Disabilities in Higher Education', *Educational Research Review*, 42. Available at: www.sciencedirect.com/science/article/pii/S1747938X23000751 (Accessed: 12 August 2024).

North, S. M., (1984) 'The Idea of a Writing Center', *College English*, 46, pp. 433–446.

Nzekwe-Excel, C., (2014) 'Academic Writing Workshops: Impact of Attendance on Performance', *Journal of Academic Writing*, 4:1, pp.12–25. Available from: https://publications.coventry.ac.uk/index.php/joaw/article/view/139 (Accessed: 24 June 2023).

O'Shea, S., Lysaght, P., Roberts, J., and Harwood, V., (2016) 'Shifting the Blame in Higher Education: Social Inclusion and Deficit Discourses', *Higher Education Research and Development*, 35:2, pp.322–336. Available from: www.tandfonline.com/doi/full/10.1080/07294360.2015.1087388 (Accessed: 23 June 2023).

Office for Students (OfS), (2024) 'Student Characteristics Data: Population Data'. Available from: www.officeforstudents.org.uk/data-and-analysis/student-characteristics-data/population-data-dashboard/ (Accessed: 13 September 2024).

Ofsted, (2023) 'Independent Review of Tutoring in Schools: Phase 1 Findings'. Available from: www.gov.uk/government/publications/independent-review-of-tutoring-in-schools-and-16-to-19-providers/independent-review-of-tutoring-in-schools-phase-1-findings (Accessed: 12 September 2024).

Oxford Brookes University, (n.d.) *IDEAS: The Brookes Inclusive Curriculum Model*. Available from: www.brookes.ac.uk/staff/student-support/ideas-model (Accessed: 16 May 2024).

Park, I., (2015) 'Requests: Knowledge and Entitlement in Writing Tutoring', *Language and Communication*, 43, pp.1–10. Available from: www.sciencedirect.com/science/article/pii/S0271530915000282 (Accessed: 15 June 2023).

Parveen, N., (2019) 'Funding for Pupils with Special Educational Needs Drops 17%', *The Guardian*, 4 April 2019. Available from: www.theguardian.com/education/2019/apr/04/funding-pupils-special-educational-needs-send-drops-north-england (Accessed: 23 December 2023).

Phillips, J., and Fok, H., (2017) 'Armies of Two: Effective One-to-one Writing Tutorials', *Online Proceedings of the International Conference*, DRAL 3/19th ESEA, pp.212–224. Available from: https://sola.kmutt.ac.th/dral2017/proceedings/5-6Additional/212-224_Armies%20of%20two%20effective%20one-to-one%20writing%20tutorials_Jeremy%20Phillips%20and%20Hilda%20Fok.pdf (Accessed: 27 June 2023).

QAA, (2024) 'Evaluating Excellence: TEF 2023 Submission and Panel Statement Analysis'. Available from: www.qaa.ac.uk/docs/qaa/news/evaluating-excellence-tef-2023-submission-and-panel-statement-analysis.pdf?sfvrsn=4da3b781_10 (Accessed: 23 August 2024).

Richards, K., and Pilcher, N., (2020) 'Study Skills: Neoliberalism's Perfect Tinkerbell', *Teaching in Higher Education*, pp.1–17. https://doi.org/10.1080/13562517.2020.1839745

Roseneil, S., (2023) 'Investing in Our Future: Higher Education as a Public Good', in Day, N., Husbands, C., Roseneil, S., and Tickell, A., *Election 2024: Three Vice-Chancellors' Manifestos. HEPI Report 164*. Available from: www.hepi.ac.uk/wp-content/uploads/2023/10/ELECTION-2024-Three-Vice-Chancellor-Manfiestos.pdf (Accessed: 24 September 2024).

Rowsell, J., (2024) 'Natasha Abrahart's Parents Back New Assessment Adjustment Rules', *Times Higher Education*, 25 September, 2024. Available from: www.timeshighereducation.com/news/natasha-abraharts-parents-back-new-assessment-adjustment-rules (Accessed: 4 October 2024).

Royal Holloway, University of London, (2021) 'Financial Statements 2021'. Available from: www.royalholloway.ac.uk/about-us/more/financial-information/ (Accessed: 4 September 2024).

Scott, N., and Davis, R., (1979) 'The Exceptional Potential in Each Primary Care Consultation', *The British Journal of General Practice*, 29, pp.201–205.

Stentiford, L., and Koutsouris, G., (2020) 'What Are Inclusive Pedagogies in Higher Education? A Systematic Scoping Review', *Studies in Higher Education*, 46:11, pp.2245–2261, Available from: www.tandfonline.com/doi/full/10.1080/03075079.2020.1716322 (Accessed: 13 July 2024).

Stevenson, M. D., and Kokkinn, B. A., (2009) 'Evaluating One-to-One Sessions of Academic Language and Learning', *Journal of Academic Language and Learning*, 3:2, pp.36–50. Available from: https://journal.aall.org.au/index.php/jall/article/download/86/66/ (Accessed: 27 June 2023).

Sword, H., (2017) *Air & Light & Time & Space: How Successful Academics Write*. Cambridge, MA: Harvard University Press.

Tate, S. A., and Bagguley, P., (2017) 'Building the Anti-racist University: Next Steps', *Race, Ethnicity and Education*, 20, pp.289–299. Available from: www.tandfonline.com/doi/full/10.1080/13613324.2016.1260227 (Accessed: 23 September 2023).

The World Bank, UNESCO, and UNICEF, (2021) 'The State of the Global Education Crisis: A Path to Recovery', Washington DC, Paris, and New York: The World Bank, UNESCO, and UNICEF. Available from: https://documents1.worldbank.org/curated/en/416991638768297704/pdf/The-State-of-the-Global-Education-Crisis-A-Path-to-Recovery.pdf?_gl=1*i3dk7t*_gcl_au*MTk2MDU0NDMzNy4xNzI2MTQ4OTQ4 (Accessed: 12 July 2023).

Thonus, T., (1999) 'Dominance in Academic Writing Tutorials: Gender, Language Proficiency, and the Offering of Suggestions', *Discourse and Society*, 10:2, pp.225–248. Available from: www.jstor.org/stable/42888250 (Accessed: 15 July 2023).

Thonus, T., (2001) 'Triangulation in the Writing Center: Tutor, Tutee, and Instructor Perceptions of the Tutor's Role', *The Writing Center Journal*, 22:1, pp.59–82. Available from: https://docs.lib.purdue.edu/wcj/vol22/iss1/5/ (Accessed: 22 July 2023).

Thonus, T., (2002) 'Tutor and Student Assessments of Academic Writing Tutorials: What Is 'Success'?' *Assessing Writing*, 8, pp.110–134. Available from: www.sciencedirect.com/science/article/pii/S1075293503000023 (Accessed: 14 June 2023).

Tuck, J., (2018) *Academics Engaging with Student Writing: Working at the Higher Education Textface*. London and New York: Routledge.

UNESCO, (2017) *A Guide for Ensuring Inclusion and Equity in Education*. Paris: UNESCO. Available from: https://unesdoc.unesco.org/ark:/48223/pf0000248254 (Accessed: 16 June 2023).

University Alliance, (2024) 'Supporting Student Progression and Attainment Through Sustainable Inclusive Assessment Practices: What Works?'. Available from: www.unialliance.ac.uk/wp-content/uploads/2023/10/Project-Progression-Report-Public-Facing-UA.pdf (Accessed: 12 June 2024).

Vygotsky, L. S., (1978) *Mind in Society: The Development of Higher Psychological Processes*. Cambridge, MA: Harvard University Press.

Wallbank, A. J., and Le Hen, P., (2023) 'The Politics of Integration: The Opportunities, Challenges and Successes of Embedding Academic Skills and Literacies Development into an Interdisciplinary, "Integrated" Foundation Year Programme', *Journal of University Teaching & Learning Practice*, 20:4, pp.1–21. Available from: https://doi.org/10.53761/1.20.4.05 (Accessed: 16 August 2024).

Webster, H., (2017) 'Developing the Developers'. *ALDinHE 2017: The Learning Development Conference*, 10–12 April 2017, University of Hull, UK.

Webster, H., (2024) 'Raising the Profile of Learning Development in Higher Education: Institutional and Sector Perspectives', in Syska, A. and Buckley, C. (eds), *How to Be a Learning Developer in Higher Education: Critical Perspectives, Community and Practice*. London: Routledge, pp.230–237.

Welding, L., (2023) 'Students with Disabilities in Higher Education: Facts and Statistics', *Best Colleges*. Available from: www.bestcolleges.com/research/students-with-disabilities-higher-education-statistics/#common-disabilities (Accessed: 17 July 2024).

Weston, T., (2023) 'In Focus: Financial Pressures on Higher Education'. House of Lords Library. Available from: https://lordslibrary.parliament.uk/financial-pressures-on-higher-education/ (Accessed: 13 September 2024).

Williams, J., (2004) 'Tutoring and Revision: Second Language Writers in the Writing Center', *Journal of Second Language Writing*, 13:3, pp.173–201. Available from: www.sciencedirect.com/science/article/pii/S1060374304000128 (Accessed: 23 September 2023).

Wingate, U., (2006) 'Doing Away with 'Study Skills', *Teaching in Higher Education*, 11:4, pp.457–469. Available from: www.tandfonline.com/doi/full/10.1080/13562510600874268 (Accessed: 13 June 2023).

Wingate, U., (2015) *Academic Literacy and Student Diversity: The Case for Inclusive Practice*. Bristol: Multilingual Matters.

Woodward-Kron, R., (2007) 'Negotiating Meanings and Scaffolding Learning: Writing Support for Non-English Speaking Background Postgraduate Students', *Higher Education Research and Development*, 26:3, pp.253–268. Available from: www.tandfonline.com/doi/full/10.1080/07294360701494286 (Accessed: 13 June 2023).

Wooton, S., (2013) *Personal Tutoring for the 21st Century*. Further Education Tutorial Network.

Yeats, R., Reddy, P., Wheeler, A., Senior, C., and Murray, J., (2010) 'What a Difference a Writing Centre Makes: A Small-scale Study', *Education and Training*, 52:6/7, pp.499–507. Available from: www.emerald.com/insight/content/doi/10.1108/00400911011068450/full/html (Accessed: 17 June 2023).

3 Supporting Learning Differences for Assessments

Universal Design for Learning, GenAI, and Assessment *as* Learning

Adrian J. Wallbank

Assessment and cognition

The main challenges students with learning differences face often coalesce around assessment, not least because of the additional pressures of high-stakes assessments which count towards overall degree results. Assessment within higher education comes in a variety of guises and genres and is currently undergoing rapid transformation as a result of the ease with which assignments can be undertaken by or outsourced to GenAI (the traditional essay being the most vulnerable in this regard). However, written assignments still predominate. At my own institution, for example, during the academic year 2024/25, the university will set 6,604 separate pieces of assessment, 3,520 (53%) of which will be either an essay, a written examination, or a dissertation. Overall, research into student work submitted to the Universities of Warwick, Reading, and Oxford Brookes in 2007 has shown that the most popular written genres are:

1) Essays – 43%
2) Methodology recounts – 12%
3) Critiques – 11%
4) Explanations – 7%
5) Case studies – 7%

The traditional essay is by far the most popular genre students are asked to use; in the case of humanities subjects, essays account for 83% of student writing and in the social sciences 56% (Heuboeck, Holmes, and Nesi, 2007, pp.7–10). Exams are often deployed (either online or in person, seen or unseen), but other assignment types are becoming increasingly popular, including blogs, podcasts, mock Wikipedia entries, oral presentations, posters, mini vivas (often being touted as a possible mechanism for testing students' academic integrity and knowledge if they are suspected of using GenAI), reflective writing, report writing, design specifications, and of course lab reports and literature reviews. What all these genres and innovations require is some degree of writing and composition and, underpinning this, an organisation and structuring of ideas, knowledge, arguments, and criticality. It does not matter if the assignment is a vlog, a podcast, an oral presentation, a critical dissection of a ChatGPT output, or even a relatively unstructured mini viva – all these assessment tasks require students to retrieve, process, organise, and then articulate knowledge and what they have learnt via some sort of linear, logical composition that adheres to academic conventions. The fact that this requires a) considerable mental effort in respect of the working memory, b) structuring and navigating between disparate pieces of information to find patterns and coherence, and c) articulating what is known or discovered into a reasonably coherent, structured, language-based output puts to the test all of the inherent challenges/trade-offs and strengths of students with learning differences – hence the need for the support proposed in this book, regardless of the direction assessment takes in response to GenAI.

As we can see, one of the main issues posed by writing in particular, and articulating one's thoughts and learning via language and academic conventions more generally, is the need for sequencing, coherence, and linearity. As we saw earlier in regard to Game and Metcalfe's (1996) suggestion that because of the need for 'linearity … everything about writing is deliberately fabricated', composition is not easy and is in many respects unnatural (language itself being a fairly late acquisition of *homo sapiens* [Poulos, 2022]). However, students with dyslexia or ADHD, for example, typically have profound difficulties trying to force thought into conventional, linear form, and as Taylor and Vestergaard (2022) note, writing technology 'appears to align more favourably with individuals who are less exploratory' (p.13). Dyslexia, ADHD, and autism all affect writing in the areas of sequencing, logic, structure, details, mechanics (e.g. grammar), and composition/expression (Molitor, Langberg, and Evans, 2016; Wallbank, 2022), hence why writing is so especially problematic for students with learning differences.

One of the best ways of understanding and thinking about the challenges faced by students with learning differences is to consider the mental effort required to force naturally incoherent thoughts (with their unique basis in either 'big picture', holistic, or detailed, local search specialisations and discrepancies/trade-offs) into a linear and sequential form. Dyslexia, for example, mainly affects how the working memory receives and processes information. As we have seen, in individuals with dyslexia the brain's right hemisphere (known for its role in visual processing and holistic thinking) is bigger and more active than in non-dyslexic brains, whereas in non-dyslexic brains, the left hemisphere and its language processing operations are more active and developed. With dyslexia, ADHD, and autism, when receiving or presenting information through language, mental activities are more effortful, and students can quickly become overwhelmed – a scenario called 'cognitive overload'. 'Cognitive overload' can happen with anyone of course, but if someone has a learning difference, this happens much sooner because of how inefficiently the brain processes language.

In individuals with dyslexia, ADHD, and autism, the episodic buffer, which brings together and puts into order the inputs from the visual and language functions of the working memory, has to route language to the visual side of the brain for processing because of a) the brain's preference for the visual and b) the language side (in the left hemisphere) is impaired. When working with language, this reliance upon the regions of the brain usually involved in visual processing is known as 'reversed functional lateralisation of language' and acts, in essence, as a 'compensatory mechanism' (Herringshaw et al., 2016). Indeed, the more the information being received or communicated is based in language, the more restrictions there are (owing to the working memory and processing deficits associated with the learning difference) and the more mental effort is required to find workarounds or compensatory strategies (Helland and Morken, 2015, p.20). In the case of dyslexia and autism, most information has to be decoded via the visual, right hemisphere because the left, language-based phonological loop is less effective and efficient. Any information that does reach the left hemisphere has to be routed back towards the visuospatial sketchpad to be decoded, thus taking up yet more valuable energy and again increasing the likelihood of forgetting information. Indeed, brain imaging (Waldie et al., 2013) has shown 'overactivation' of the right hemisphere as a result of this, which can again lead to tiredness. This 'overactivation' not only increases the likelihood of information being forgotten, but research has suggested that automaticity (for example, when writing) takes considerably longer, so the working memory has to work incredibly hard and is inherently inefficient (Nicolson and Fawcett, 1990, 2008). Reading and writing also entail the working memory handling various tasks simultaneously (decoding words or images, putting together sequences to piece together meaning, blending visual or language-based inputs, maintaining concentration, processing inputs, combining them with both 'gist' and literal inputs from the memory, and turning them into various outputs). Given that in individuals with dyslexia, ADHD, and autism the whole operation is inefficient, cognitive overload quickly occurs. Put another way, in individuals with learning differences, the brain is like a computer with limited RAM – the more demands you place on it (browsers, applications, etc.) the slower it gets. As such, it is no wonder that writing essays and responding to assignment tasks is so problematic.

The position taken in this book: assessment *as* learning, inclusion, and the centrality of language-based assessment literacies

One of the core tenets of this book is that assessment, as primarily conducted via the medium of language (predominantly through essayist genres but also via oral routes [presentations] and more diverse forms of assessment such as multiple-choice questions, posters, blogs, and vlogs), is a form of learning. Student writing is necessarily both a measure of student learning (the product) and an inescapable part of learning itself (the process). As such, the essays we read, especially in their developmental and draft stages, are inescapably a microcosm of these students' learning differences and a barometer of their challenges and strengths. Pedagogical approaches to, and understanding of, assessment frequently classify assessment as conducting three interrelated tasks – assessment *of* learning (the testing and measurement of knowledge acquisition and/or competency), assessment *for* learning (feedback on assessment as a vehicle for the promotion of learning via the encouragement and facilitation of feedback loops [Kolb, 1984]), and assessment *as* learning (the participation in assessment being in and of itself a form of learning, not just a regurgitation and testing of knowledge).

The National Forum for the Enhancement of Teaching and Learning in Higher Education (2020) usefully distil these principles into the following model, which also maps the degrees of student responsibility, the extent to which the assessment is 'high' or 'low stakes', and whether the assessment is summative or formative. As a whole, the model sees *learning* as central to the three main components or purposes of assessment.

74 *Academic Writing, Assessment, and Neurodiversity*

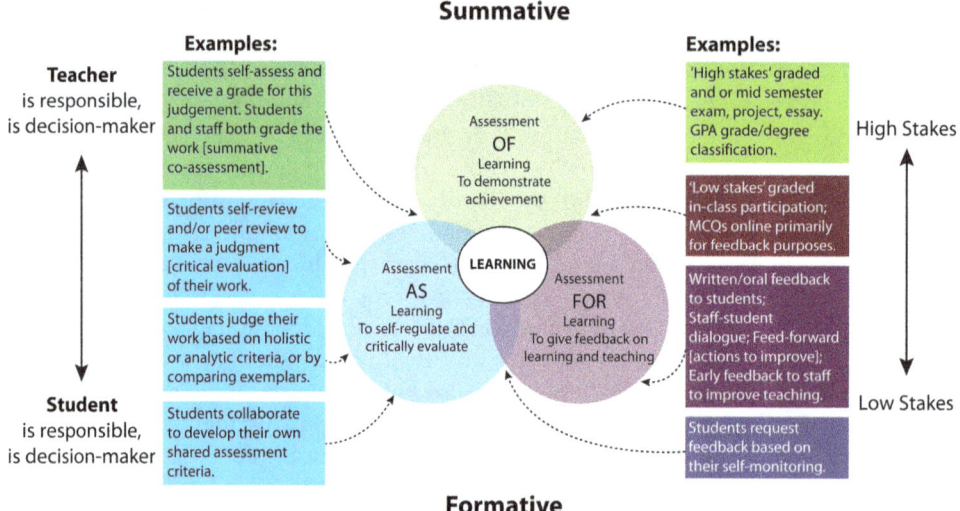

(National Forum for the Enhancement of Teaching and Learning in Higher Education, 2020)

Several issues need to be addressed at this point before we go any further. Firstly, since the onset of the Covid-19 pandemic, the average number of assignments per term/semester in UK higher education institutions has increased by 29% (formative) and 14% (summative) – an increase also attributed to modularisation (Elkington, 2020, p.5; Neves and Hewitt, 2021). When combined with other pressures, this has led to students and staff encountering difficulties with workloads and subsequent student dissatisfaction with assessment and feedback (Aristovnik et al., 2021; Neves and Hewitt, 2021, pp.46–47). Higher education should facilitate critical thinking, independence, and problem-solving (Biggs, 2003); however, excessive assessment can result in 'teaching to the test' or students focusing their limited energies only on assignment topics. Why might the assessment load have increased during this period? Intriguingly, the increase in assessment can be mapped, inversely, onto the decrease in student engagement during the same period. In the 2022 AdvanceHE UK Engagement Survey, 76% of academics questioned suggested that attendance is now lower than before the pandemic, 53% said that engagement was lower, and 54% said that of those students who do attend, they are less engaged (Holden, 2022). Similarly, an AdvanceHE/HEPI UK Engagement Survey from 2021 showed that overall student engagement had declined from 62.57% in 2018 to 56.28% in 2021 (Neves and Hewitt, 2021). There is often a sense among academics that, as Gibbs and Simpson (2005) so aptly put it, 'you have to assess everything that moves in order to capture students' time and energy', and that if you remove or reduce assessment loads, 'students simply do not do the associated studying' (p.8). It is easy to see where the recent increase in assessment has come from, then, as academics have merely responded to decreases in engagement with the simplest and most convenient tool in their arsenal in an attempt to drive up engagement. This is not assessment *as* or *for* learning, however, even if that was the intended outcome – it has merely placed students more firmly on the treadmill of engaging with assessment merely as a means to an end. In this scenario, assessment merely becomes another hurdle to jump through to get to the desired goal or product – the degree and its capacity to open up employment opportunities. Obviously, this instrumentalist approach to learning has been fostered elsewhere and often well before university. In the UK, the 'assessment objective' driven nature of A level and BTEC/Access curriculums produces students who are past masters at achieving the desired assessment objectives, but in the case of, say, a literature student, they might not have even read the entire text they are being assessed on. However, the recent increase in assessment loads has entrenched the instrumentalist view of assessment even further.

The second issue we need to unpack is the tendency to focus on assessment *of* learning as the key function of assessment. This issue exists in part owing to the historical use of assessment as a means of validating the acquisition of knowledge (unseen exams, for instance, were once commonplace, whereas today the emphasis in both tertiary and higher education is on coursework). Yet the core tenet of examining and testing students persists, and in many respects rightfully so. In disciplines allied to the professions, for instance, certain competencies need to be exhibited not only for the purposes of validation and professional recognition but for health and safety reasons. In nursing, for example, an incorrect understanding of a procedure could be life-threatening, and as such the demonstration of core competencies is at the heart of assessment protocols. But increasingly, with the massification, marketisation, and corporatisation of higher education, along with the introduction of tuition fees, results matter (as does impact). These results, often in the form of 'good degree outcomes', frequently have a direct bearing on the sustainability of courses, their attractiveness to students, league table results, and the career progression or even continued employment of academic staff. Given the concomitant focus on results fostered at school – often emanating either from the focus on 'assessment objectives' set by (in the UK) the Office of Qualifications and Examinations Regulation (Ofqual) and central government or from school league table results – and the increasing demand for both 'value for money' for degree courses and employability, it is easy to see why there is so much focus on assessment of learning, as opposed to considering it as an equal partner in the triage of assessment *of, for,* and *as* learning. Indeed, in some respects, it is almost as though the *learning* part of this equation has been forgotten entirely, as students are increasingly configured as, and often perceive themselves to be, customers buying their degrees rather than paying for their learning experience (Wallbank, 2021).

The third issue is the fact that assessment *as* learning often seems to be increasingly overlooked. As seen above, the key driver of assessment often seems to pivot around engagement or the drive for results, but even where assessment is explicitly aligned to the testing of or attainment of learning outcomes, the potential for assessment to be integral to the learning process itself seems to get lost. Essays, exams, oral presentations, and the like often seem designed to test whether the student has achieved the desired learning outcomes – as if the learning has happened before the student puts pen to paper and all that is required is proof and a written record of that proof (Docherty, 2011).

Nowhere has this trend been more noticeable than in recent debates about the advent of artificial intelligence. Much of the debate has centred around the issue of academic misconduct and misuse. Indeed, one of the most recent interventions in the debate proposes that 'cultivating a sense of moral character in students is an imperative', and that critical thinking skills ought to be fostered to create students with a 'firm moral compass' (Crawford, Cowling, and Allen, 2023, p.7). In days gone by, students' work could be checked for plagiarism using software such as Turnitin. The issue with GenAI is that it generates original text (albeit garnered from sources all over the internet) and as such it does not have a clear source, so it is almost impossible to prove whether or not it was used by the student. Universities have scrambled to update their policies and guidance for students, but most of these centre around issues of academic misconduct and the need to engage with such resources critically. However, they often do not tackle the issue that GenAI essentially 'de-authors' the student writer – a concept proposed by Wrigley (2019) in regard to 'de-plagiarism', which pre-dated the advent of GenAI) – and severely curtails the learning process itself. Even ChatGPT itself seems to have missed the point. In a 2023 blog, Phil Anthony asked ChatGPT 'what might the impact of ChatGPT-3 be on assessment?'. The response was as follows:

> There is no doubt that GPT-3 and similar technologies could make it easier for students to produce written work that appears to be of high quality. However, it is important to note that simply generating text does not guarantee that a student has actually learned the material. In order to assess whether a student has truly understood a subject, it is necessary to go beyond just evaluating their written work. Teachers could use a variety of assessment techniques, such as quizzes, exams, presentations and group projects, to ensure that students have a deep understanding of the material.
> (Anthony, 2023)

The emphasis here is clearly on the question as to whether assessment guarantees (or not) whether the student 'has actually learnt the material'. There is no mention of the fact that writing, in and of itself, is a form of learning. Writing is not just a product but a process. Indeed, as Rudolph, Tan, and Tan (2023, p.353) note, this is often echoed in faculty – 'most of the time, assessments are perceived and utilised by instructors for the assessment of students' learning. The majority of instructors ... may not possess the skills to use assessment both for learning (Wiliam, 2011) and as learning' (Earl, 2012). Others (e.g. McMurtrie, 2022) suggest that large language models such as ChatGPT will become a part of writing (or more accurately, hybrid writing) and are merely akin to the use of calculators in the field of maths and science. However, this again misses the point. The sum 2 + 2 = 4 is pure fact and logic, and the only creativity that can be derived from it is in its further applications. Writing, on the other hand, is not just the production of a product or a result like a mathematical sum or equation; it is integral to the process of critical thinking, evaluation, and innovation and can have a significant impact on one's audience. As Nietzsche is alleged to have argued in an often-misattributed quotation, 'all I need is a sheet of paper and something to write with, and then I can turn the world upside down' (Wallace, 2021). Writing and language, as Chomsky (2003) argues, 'is a process of free creation; its laws and principles are fixed, but the manner in which the principles of generation are used is free and infinitely varied. Even the interpretation and use of words involves a process of free creation' (p.402). Indeed, Chomsky contends that 'the most striking aspect of linguistic competence is what we may call the "creativity of language," that is, the speaker's ability to produce new sentences, sentences that are immediately UNDERSTOOD by other speakers although they bear no physical resemblance to sentences which are "familiar"' (2012, p.8). The use of a calculator cannot do all of this. Irrespective of the advent of GenAI, the notion of assessment as predominantly a measure of learning, not as a process of learning in and of itself (assessment *as* learning), seriously undermines the potential of assessment as a driver of learning and indeed engagement. That is why this book aims to reinforce the notion of assessment *as* learning through the particular power and affordances of writing.

Intertwined with this book's commitment to assessment *as* learning is our commitment to 'Writing to Learn' (WTL) pedagogies. WTL pedagogies and approaches do not have much traction in the UK, but elsewhere they are seen as very much part and parcel of the spectrum of writing instruction approaches (especially within the US model of writing and composition traditions and programmes), and often WTL intersects with Writing Across the Curriculum (WAC) and Writing in the Disciplines (WID) approaches. Understanding the nuances of these writing approaches is not strictly necessary; the important thing here is to highlight and appreciate the central role language and writing have in the learning process. As summarised by Fulwiler and Young (1982), there is a distinct contrast between 'writing to communicate' (or 'transactional writing'), which entails perfunctory roles such as informing, instructing, presenting, or persuading (much like the view that assignments are a means of demonstrating learning – assessment *of* learning), and writing to *learn*. 'Writing to learn is different', Fulwiler and Young (1982) claim, 'we write to ourselves as well as talk with others to objectify our perceptions of reality; the primary function of this "expressive" language is not to communicate, but to order and represent experience to our own understanding. In this sense language provides us with a unique way of knowing and becomes a tool for discovering, for shaping meaning, and for reaching understanding' (p. x). As Zinsser (1988) has argued,

> we write to find out what we know and what we want to say. I thought of how often as a writer I had made clear to myself some subject I had previously known nothing about by just putting one sentence after another—by reasoning my way in sequential steps to its meaning. I thought of how often the act of writing even the simplest document—a letter, for instance—had clarified my half-formed ideas. Writing, thinking and learning were the same process. (p.40)

Pedagogically, for Zinsser (1988), 'writing could get into corners that other teaching tools couldn't reach' (p.40), primarily because 'writing is how we think our way into a discipline, organise our thoughts about it and generate new ideas' (p.162).

In an age of GenAI, where writing and cognition can effectively be semi or wholly outsourced or 'offloaded' (Dickinson, 2024), this book seeks, in part, to reaffirm the potential of assessment and writing to engender learning itself, rather than it merely being a product and a means to an end. The main question, though, and the preoccupation of this book, is, how can we support students with learning differences more inclusively while helping them tap into the inherent strengths associated with their learning differences at the same time as putting in place scaffolding to enable them to overcome their difficulties?

Cognitive maps and conceptual frameworks: tying everything together within an inclusive pedagogical framework

Education is predicated upon notions of learning, knowledge, and intelligence, and as Cremin (1976) has proposed, 'is the deliberate, systematic, and sustained effort to transmit, provoke or acquire knowledge, values, attitudes, skills or sensibilities as well as any learning that results from the effort' (p.27). As educators, one of our central aims is to increase learning, skills, and the store of knowledge our students possess; enable and empower them to subject it to critical evaluation; and assess that they have acquired this knowledge and criticality to a requisite level to maintain standards. Knowledge is a contested term and multifaceted (Blackler, 1995; Krathwohl, 2002), is deployed in different ways, and presents various challenges and opportunities for students with learning differences, not least because certain types of knowledge are more easily assimilated or exploited depending on the students' search, divergent thinking, or exploitation strengths and internal models discussed in Chapter 1. But knowledge is nothing, of course, without intelligence – itself a contested term, as has been shown in reactions to Gardner's (2000) theory of multiple intelligences. This is where we need to return to, expand, and utilise the notion of cognitive maps, models, and 'meta-representations' discussed in Chapter 1 before we can harness their potential for supporting students with learning differences.

For Greenfield (2014), intelligence is 'a synthesis between facts, context and meaning' (p.250). Each of these three elements is obtained via learning and education, whether it be through parenting, school or, in our case, higher education. Crucially, however, what enables this synthesis to develop is not merely learning information. As Greenfield puts it,

> facts on their own are not enough! While collecting information is gathering dots, knowledge is joining them up, seeing one thing in terms of another and thereby understanding each component as part of a whole. The more connections you can make across an ever wider and disparate range of knowledge, the more deeply you will understand something. (p.250)

This 'synthesis' of facts, context, and meaning is unique to each individual and their experiences, and this is what constitutes their 'personal conceptual framework', 'meta-representations', and cognitive models or learning specialisations. It is only through these elements interacting and merging within our conceptual framework, Greenfield argues, that we understand, interpret, evaluate, and analyse what we see or learn (p.250). Indeed, the more we make connections between the world and our personal conceptual frameworks (through what we might loosely term thinking), the more that framework and its system of meta-representations grows and develops, resulting in ever deeper, richer, and more meaningful understanding and intelligence. This is why Greenfield quotes Arvid Carlsson's famous line,'thinking is movement confined to the brain' (p.253). In other words, the brain is a little like a muscle – use it, challenge it, and it becomes stronger, more supple, and more able to overcome challenges; neglect it and it will degrade.

While everyone's personal conceptual framework, cognitive models, and 'meta-representations' are unique and, like a muscle, are capable of getting stronger, 'gathering dots' and making links and connections between 'facts, context and meaning' are precisely what is affected by autism, ADHD, or dyslexia. As we have seen, for individuals with autism, it can be difficult to make links and connections to the 'bigger picture' context (whereas local links are enhanced), and for individuals with dyslexia or ADHD, their conceptual frameworks are able to make the links between disparate 'bigger picture' 'dots' and contextual factors, but they struggle to understand or process more local connections. What is needed in the case of students with learning differences is a pedagogical approach that strengthens their personal conceptual frameworks or meta-representations in a way that exploits the strengths of their learning differences while scaffolding the development of their challenges and trade-offs. Often the concepts (ideas, knowledge) are there; it is the framework (exploratory vs. exploitative) that causes issues owing to the inherent trade-offs of having a search specialisation and global or local learning strategy.

One of the core beliefs articulated in this book is that the accommodations, techniques, and inclusive visual pedagogies outlined here will perhaps never make such conceptual frameworks as effortlessly efficient as they are for someone who does not have a learning difference. This is primarily because the learning differences we examine here cannot be fundamentally altered. They are, after all, an inbuilt, inescapable learning difference or difficulty (hence the 'disability' label that is often applied to them) with corresponding structural or chemical differences in the brain. However, inclusive pedagogical scaffolding, while initially time-consuming to put in place, learn, and become habitual, allows these individuals to use workarounds and support frameworks that enable them to harness their inbuilt search strengths and trade-offs to construct personal conceptual frameworks that allow them to excel – in our case in the field of higher education through its mechanisms of assessment. Irrespective of the pedagogy, however, an individual with dyslexia, ADHD, or autism will always have a learning difference; it is just a case of trying to level the playing field to academic success.

One of the ways that we can harness the strengths of learning differences (while scaffolding the trade-offs) is by deploying principles from Universal Design for Learning (UDL). The core tenet of UDL is to facilitate inclusion via access, support, and exploiting executive function (essentially the management system of the brain). A key element of these strategies is to expedite the traffic of information into the brain and its retention via 'multiple means' of engagement, representation, and action and expression to maximise a) the opportunities for information to travel into the brain and be processed via the individual's personal conceptual frameworks, internal models, and cognitive strengths, and b) cater for as many individuals as possible, irrespective of where their strengths or learning preferences and differences may lie. As such, UDL advocates variability throughout the ways that information is presented, processed, and expressed as follows:

	Design multiple means of engagement (affective networks/the 'WHY' of learning)	*Design multiple means of representation (recognition networks/ the 'WHAT' of learning)*	*Design multiple means of action and expression (strategic networks/the 'HOW' of learning)*
Access:	**Design options for recruiting interest:** • Optimise choice and autonomy • Optimise relevance, value, and authenticity • Nurture joy and play • Address biases, threats, and distractions	**Design options for perception** • Support opportunities to customise the display of information • Support multiple ways to perceive information • Represent a diversity of perspectives and identities in authentic ways	**Design options for interaction:** • Vary and honour the methods for response, navigation, and movement • Optimise access to accessible materials and assistive or accessible technologies and tools

(Continued)

Support:	**Design options for sustaining effort and persistence:**	**Design options for language and symbols:**	**Design options for expression and communication:**
	• Clarify and heighten the salience of meaning, objectives, and the purpose of goals • Optimise challenge and support • Foster collaboration, interdependence, and collective learning • Foster belonging and community • Offer action-oriented or mastery-oriented feedback	• Clarify vocabulary, symbols, and language structures • Support decoding of text, mathematical notation, and symbols • Illustrate through multiple media	• Use multiple media for communication • Use multiple tools for construction, composition, and creativity • Build fluencies with graduated support for practise and performance • Address biases related to modes of expression and communication
Executive function:	**Design options for self-regulation:**	**Design options for comprehension and building knowledge:**	**Design options for strategy development:**
	• Recognise and promote expectations, beliefs, and motivations • Facilitate personal coping skills and strategies • Develop self-assessment and reflection	• Connect prior knowledge to new learning or activate/supply background knowledge • Highlight and explore patterns, critical features, big ideas, and relationships • Guide information processing and visualisation • Cultivate multiple ways of knowing and making meaning • Maximise transfer and generalisation	• Set meaningful goals • Anticipate and plan for challenges • Support planning and strategy development • Facilitate managing information and resources • Enhance capacity for monitoring progress • Challenge exclusionary practices

(Adapted from CAST, 2018, 2024)

Guides and literature advocating UDL often focus on the 'multiple means' of 'engagement', 'representation', and 'action and expression' to advocate for 'flexibility' (see, for example, Merry, 2023). What is less well understood about UDL, however, is the way these pedagogical avenues intersect with the 'why' of learning (aligned with affective networks and engagement), the 'what' of learning (aligned with recognition networks and representation), and the 'how' of learning (aligned with strategic networks and multiple means of action and expression), as well as the effective use of the executive function of the brain. UDL is conceived as a multidimensional pedagogical framework that provides sufficient variation to cater for neuro-variability, different conceptual frameworks, and internal models by aiming to harness how sensory information is processed by different areas of the brain. Three areas are targeted:

1) The back of the brain (classified as 'recognition networks' – the areas of the brain associated with processing what we see and hear and collecting information and processing it into meaningful categories).
2) The centre of the brain (classified as 'affective networks' – the core part of the brain responsible for creating meaning).
3) The front of the brain (classified as 'strategic networks' – the area of the brain associated with responses, planning, and action).

It is easy to get confused between these three categories of networks, learning strategies, and their various means of deployment, but for our purposes it is important to a) understand the importance of the 'why', 'what', and 'how' of learning and how the brain's executive function works, and b) how this book taps into and encourages students to exploit certain aspects of the framework strategically to facilitate the exploitation of their inherent search strengths while scaffolding the development of their trade-offs.

A key part of the UDL model we need to tap into is the 'what' of learning via the recognition networks. Notice that the recognition networks and the 'what' of learning are activated and supported by providing and emphasising visual information, clarifying structure, supporting the decoding of text, using multiple media, supplying background information, highlighting patterns and relationships, utilising visualisation, and harnessing generalisations. Additionally, note how UDL also focuses (particularly through the 'how' of learning for the strategic networks) on strategy development and multiple media for communication, while the 'why' of learning underpins it all by helping to develop means of engagement through emphasising relevance, value, and authenticity.

The strategies associated with the 'why', 'what', and 'how' of learning align with the strengths and support needs of students with learning differences. For example, in 2011 and 2023, Eide and Eide combined data from many of the studies on the brain and cognition discussed in Chapter 1, along with clinical examinations and interviews with cohorts of dyslexic individuals, to find patterns in the abilities of dyslexic people that appeared to be supported by data. They identified four potential functional strength patterns which were termed MIND strengths: M strength or material reasoning refers to three-dimensional spatial reasoning; I strength or interconnected reasoning refers to the ability to see connections, patterns, and relationships, and includes things like analogical reasoning, systems thinking, and interdisciplinary reasoning; N strength or narrative reasoning is the bias towards personal rather than semantic memory, as reflected in preferences for cases, stories, and examples rather than definitions or abstractions and an ability to use the reconstructive faculties of episodic memory for imaginative and creative purposes; and D strength or dynamic reasoning is the ability to mentally simulate patterns and processes across multiple iterations to predict either subsequent or previous states, often using insight-based and simulative approaches rather than analytic reasoning.

In the second edition of *The Dyslexic Advantage* (2023), Eide and Eide presented the results of a comprehensive survey (in all, 2,293 adults completed 5,070 questionnaires) comparing the responses from dyslexic and non-dyslexic individuals. The results validate and clarify the MIND strengths as constructs and show that these constructs may be measured with a high degree of reliability using these questionnaires. The data provide evidence that there is a relationship between being dyslexic and higher scores on the MIND strengths questionnaires. In particular, they support the observations of strengths in holistic processing, three-dimensional spatial reasoning, and mental simulation, and are consistent with the features attributed to exploratory specialisation discussed in Chapter 1. The dyslexic participants in the questionnaire endorsed to a much higher degree than their non-dyslexic counterparts preferences for learning through non-verbal means such as imagery, visuals, diagrams, metaphors, relationships, analogies, gist, and experience; beginning holistically with the 'big picture' rather than building up from details; learning through cases, examples, and stories rather than through generalisations and abstractions; and a bias towards reasoning processes like analogical reasoning, perspective shifting, insight, and mental simulation rather than rule-based or deductive approaches.

What we have here is a synergy between the principles of UDL and the evidence of how individuals with dyslexia like to learn and approach topics or assignments. But what about autism? As we saw in Chapter 1, there is less evidence concerning autism and academic study, but the above 'strengths' associated with dyslexia (and indeed ADHD) are *precisely* the areas students with autism need support with. Furthermore, research into visual pedagogical approaches with children with autism is compelling. Kluth and Darmody-Latham (2003) have suggested that visuals such as graphic organisers, flow charts, and Venn diagrams can be effective, Grandin (1995) promotes the idea of autism as 'thinking in pictures', while Janzen (1996) suggests that visual support for students with autism can help them to process whole messages. Cohen (1998) states that children with autism are visual rather than hearing/auditory learners and prefer alternative modes of communication, such as pictures, rather than written words, and visual supports have been successfully used to teach literacy skills to children with autism (Kluth and Darmody-Latham, 2003; Broun, 2004). Although much of the literature has focused on behaviours rather than academic literacies (Rao and Gagie, 2006), clearly there is sufficient evidence to suggest that the visual pedagogical techniques outlined in this book are likely to be effective in scaffolding support for the inherent strengths, challenges and trade-offs of students with autism.

In essence, we are back to our original metaphor from Chapter 1. Namely, our task is to help students with learning differences to 'see the wood for the trees' or 'the trees for the wood', depending on whether they are exploratory learners (dyslexia and ADHD) or exploitative, depth-first learners (autism). This is where the system of compositional pictography and metaphorical approaches outlined in this book become important and align with the key tenets of the UDL framework. The shape, structure, and underlying meaning of pictographic images, diagrams, icons, templates, and metaphors outlined in the subsequent chapters provide a *meaningful* connection between the concept under consideration and how it ought to be achieved via a strategic use of the 'what', 'why', and 'how' framework and its associated brain networks.

Compositional pictography

Compositional pictography (and as we shall see in Chapter 4, metaphors) provides an ideal framework for providing this support for two primary reasons. Firstly, the support is bi-directional. In other words, by utilising 'big picture' frameworks, images, and diagrams that display and model patterns, associations, and meaning, we can scaffold students who are exploratory learners to relate the 'big picture' to detail and support students who prefer depth-first detail to relate that detail to the 'bigger picture' context. Secondly, the principles of UDL – with their focus on developing strategic and recognition networks via emphasising the 'why', 'what', and 'how' of learning – are optimised for developing students' cognitive models, conceptual frameworks, and meta-representations. However, as alluded to earlier, we need to be mindful that UDL is not merely about providing 'multiple means' of engagement, representation, and action and expression. The framework goes deeper than that, and aligns with affective, recognition, and strategic networks of the brain that need to be harnessed strategically within our pedagogy to have the desired effect. In other words, the 'multiple means' of engagement, representation, and action and expression need to be *meaningful* and meaningfully deployed to fully harness the potential of the brain's executive function – variability in and of itself is not enough, and was never the main intention behind UDL, even though this is the message often associated with it.

Compositional pictography is derived from the pioneering work undertaken by Brown and Brown (2009) at the Maple Hayes Hall Dyslexia School and Research Centre. The core tenet of Brown and Brown's method is that spelling (one of the primary initial difficulties encountered by children with dyslexia) can be taught word segments via meaningful icons. In this way, the meaning of segments of each word is taught through morphemes. An example is the word segment 'vis'. The Latinate root morpheme of 'vis' means to see, look at, or observe, which in Brown and Brown's method is thus taught via an icon that represents eyes with a hand over them to denote looking. In other words, there is a *meaningful* correlation between the meaning and its associated visual representation. This is in stark contrast to the traditional phonics route in which words are taught through sound, which for individuals with dyslexia can be unreliable and confusing (for example, 'vis' is pronounced very differently in words such as *visit*, *revise*, and *revision* yet the spelling and underlying meaning remains the same). Brown and Brown tap into the 'why', 'what', and 'how' of spelling (contradicting Saussure's [1959] notion that language is both arbitrary and conventional) through four stategies: 1) activating and supplying meaningful background information ('what' and 'why'); 2) exploiting the need students with dyslexia have to see and understand the 'point' of something ('what' and 'why'); 3) highlighting patterns and harnessing the propensity of dyslexic readers/writers to need support in decoding and clarifying meaning ('how' and 'why'); and 4) harnessing the relative strengths of individuals with dyslexia to identify meanings via visual imagery, 'big picture' thinking, connections, analogies, and metaphors ('what', 'why', and 'how').

While Brown and Brown harness simple but meaningful icons to make links between the meaning, contexts, and spelling of words, the purpose of compositional pictography is to take this principle to the next level in order to help students see the meaning, context, 'why', 'what', and 'how' of sentences, paragraphs, essays, and complete assignment responses via similar visual representations. This has two purposes and uses. Firstly, in the case of dyslexia and ADHD, the method taps into and exploits the key strengths associated with visuals, diagrams, and the 'bigger picture' meaning in order to scaffold their challenges and trade-offs (structures, details, sequencing). In the case of autism, it helps exploit and reinforce autistic individuals' talent for detail and depth while scaffolding its relevance for the 'bigger picture' and context (their challenges and trade-offs). Secondly, it builds and reinforces students' cognitive models, conceptual frameworks. and meta-representations (the executive function) by providing a visual framework that taps into the underlying 'why', 'what', and 'how' of the academic principle under consideration. For example, as we shall see in Chapter 5, a triangle can be used to denote the narrowing of a paragraph's focus from broad principles and argument (via a topic sentence – itself denoted as a narrowing triangle to represent the shift from point to argument) to a narrowing of focus and argument via evidence and analysis/evaluation, along with accompanying images such as a fingerprint to represent evidence, a magnifying glass to indicate analysis, and a set of scales to denote evaluation. This is pedagogically meaningful in the sense that it provides a visual map and structure/sequence to the paragraph. Similarly, in David Channon's work in Chapter 4, a metaphor/meta-role, such as a detective, provides a storyboard or structural and conceptual framework for the process of investigating evidence and information to uncover hidden truths and solving the puzzles that academic challenges and literature present. This is why metaphors are so useful and align so well with the principles of UDL as they work by resembling or being analogous to the desired aim using an authentic, accessible, and easily understood meaning. In terms of etymology, the word 'metaphor' itself is from the Latin *metaphora* and the Greek *metaphora*, meaning 'a transfer' (especially of the sense of one word to a different word), literally 'a carrying over'. Moreover, the prefix 'meta' denotes being about itself, the overarching principle of which again reinforces the idea of providing meaningful context. Thus, metaphors scaffold (through exploiting the affordances of the executive function) the acquisition of the academic literacy under consideration.

Students with learning differences often find that meaningful orientations and a 'roadmap' to their learning activities help develop their personal conceptual frameworks and cognitive models, thus enabling them to structure their ideas and to get a better, more holistic handle on what is going on (whether this be during the teaching of subject content in a lecture or the development of writing skills in a one-to-one tutorial). They often need to see how what they are doing or learning fits in with the 'big picture' (Eide and Eide, 2011; Cooper, 2019; Wallbank, 2022), and once they can see the map and overall aims, the requirement to present material in linear form becomes more easily managed and navigable (Cooper, 2019, p.90). By frequently referencing learning activities back to an overarching, preferably visual, 'roadmap' that crucially provides a '*meaningful* context' (Cooper, 2019, p.85, my emphasis), students are less inclined to lose focus and are likely to find their learning more productive. In other words, think of the 'what', 'why', and 'how' of learning as a little like providing students with a 'satnav' to the session, content, or assignment, but like a satnav, it needs to be '*meaningful*' – arbitrary signalling and scaffolding is unlikely to be effective. Again, this is where compositional pictography and meta-role approaches to supporting students' academic literacies and assessments align with key aspects of the UDL framework.

One of the key reasons why a 'meaningful context' is so critical is due to working memory overload. Crucially, as Cooper (2019, p.82) puts it, 'up to one in five learners is overwhelmed by sequences of information without a meaningful context'. Visual representations of the 'why', 'what', and 'how' framework provide a meaningful context by not only provide a structure but anchoring content into a meaningful framework that exploits the strengths of individuals with learning differences while scaffolding their appreciation and understanding of their challenges and trade-offs. In addition, however, by harnessing and catering for different networks of the brain simultaneously, this meaningful framework also provides important, *meaningful* 'hooks' to ease the passage of information both into and out of the working memory and long-term memory. Moreover, the existence of the roadmap and scaffolding itself helps orientate the information and thereby helps alleviate working memory overload. In essence, then, and to borrow the terminology from Krathwohl's (2002) and Blackler's (1995) descriptors of the facets of intelligence, what we are aiming to do here is to exploit and build upon dyslexic and ADHD strengths in conceptual, metacognitive, embrained, and encultured knowledge while using those strengths to develop areas such as factual, procedural, encoded, and embodied knowledge. In the case of students with autism, we are seeking the opposite.

Such approaches (as we shall see later) can lead to increased student learning and achievement in academic writing and assessments. This is primarily because students with learning differences often have particular strengths in visual learning (Cooper, 2019). It has been suggested (Eide and Eide, 2011, p.128) that in the case of dyslexic individuals, for instance, 'their conceptual knowledge is often stored in … images … rather than abstract principles and definitions', and that they are potentially better than non-dyslexic individuals at tasks which enable them to see the 'big picture' and thus 'identify new connections' (West, 1997; Cryer, 2013, p.8; Wallbank, 2022). Furthermore, as Roberts (2019) shows, multimedia learning, with its emphasis on the visual, helps mitigate against the processing difficulties students with learning differences encounter with 'text-centricity'. It also caters more appropriately to the 'pictorial turn' in contemporary, postmodern society (Roberts, 2019, pp.252–253) and as such is arguably more accessible than other modes of delivery. In addition, primarily visual pedagogies are highlighted owing to the extremely compelling results of Roberts' (2016, 2018, and 2019) studies into the pedagogical efficacy of meaningful visuals in lectures. Interestingly, in alignment with Layer's (2017) proposition that inclusive pedagogies are a 'route to excellence', Roberts (2016) found that visual pedagogies not only substantially increase learning in dyslexic students (especially in the areas known to be problematic such as memory, understanding, and attention) but also produced comparable results in 'neurostandard' students.

Learning technologies, GenAI, and the scaffolding of academic/assessment literacies

At this point, you might be wondering what role assistive learning technologies and GenAI might play in supporting students with learning differences. If writing and structuring thoughts pose so many difficulties, can technology either provide workarounds, alleviate the strain on working memory, or help scaffold students' writing development? Many institutions seem to be deploying ever greater levels of technology in a bid to be inclusive. In the UK, Coventry University, for instance, sees the success of their educational offering and their delivery of 'access, participation and inclusion' as being 'underpinned by the development and delivery at scale of blended and fully online learning ... and the exploitation of digital connectivity and educational technology' (2024, p.17). Similarly, the University of Leeds views digital education as playing 'a leading role in ... growing our provision of accessible, inclusive and inspirational digital education opportunities for all' (2021, p.5). Dettmer and Welton (2024), meanwhile, bemoan the fact that following the Covid-19 pandemic and the subsequent 'return to face-to-face teaching practices, disabled students may no longer receive access to more inclusive learning environments', a fact that they appear to suggest not only jeopardises progress to reduce attainment gaps between disabled and non-disabled students, but explicitly positions online instruction as being an inherently 'inclusive teaching practice' and 'environment' (pp.64–65). Such claims and statements are typical, and are often reinforced and perpetuated through the labelling of online platforms, apps, or educational software as 'assistive', 'enabled', or 'enhanced' – especially in respect of how it may help students with learning differences.

The evidence for the pedagogical effectiveness of embedding and harnessing digital technologies for teaching and learning, however, is debatable at best and mostly fairly negative. In respect of online learning (frequently harnessed during the lockdown but also now incorporated into 'blended' or 'hybrid' offerings), research suggests that certain types of students (e.g. those with learning differences) may be at a disadvantage in their ability to adapt to online teaching and learning (Xu and Smith, 2013; Dumford and Miller, 2018; Wallbank, 2022). Indeed, for Dumford and Miller (2018), online classes have a statistically significant negative effect on three of ten engagement indicators for first-year students (collaborative learning, discussions with others, and quality of interactions), and a negative effect on five of the ten for senior students (teaching practices, student–faculty interaction, discussions with others, quality of interactions, and collaborative learning). In a survey of 325 undergraduates, meanwhile, Peper et al. (2021) compared online (Zoom) sessions with face-to-face delivery. 94% reported that they had moderate to considerable difficulty with online learning. Only 6% preferred online to face-to-face learning. Particular issues reported were communication (e.g. lack of or impaired non-verbal communication), cognitive overload, visual stress and reduced physical movement, uncontrollable interruptions, social isolation, technical issues, and the encoding and consolidation of knowledge in the long-term memory. Paul and Jefferson (2019), meanwhile, found 'no significant difference in performance between online and traditional classroom students with respect to modality, gender, or class rank' (p.6), while Nguyen's (2015) meta-study of the literature shows that while '92% of all distance and online education studies find ... [it] to be as least as effective, if not better, than traditional education, 3% of the studies ... show the reverse ... and about 4% show mixed findings' (p.315).

The picture is thus mixed and far from compelling in view of the claim by the University of Leeds (2021) that online learning can facilitate or play a 'leading role' in 'access, participation and inclusion' 'for all'. Indeed, more recently, UNESCO (2023) released their *Global Education Monitoring Report: Technology in Education* and concluded that while the adoption of online learning has undoubtedly resulted in 'many changes', it remains 'debatable whether technology has transformed education as many claim' (p. v), not least because of the 'deep-rooted tendency to see technological solutions as a universal tool, suitable for all situations, an inevitable form of progress' (p. vii). In particular, there remains 1) 'little robust evidence on technology's added value in education'; 2) 'a lot of the evidence comes from those trying to sell it'; and 3) 'it can have a detrimental impact if inappropriate or excessive' (pp. xvi–xvii). Indeed, it is suggested that the risks or negative implications of deploying digital learning technologies 'are often ignored by research and evaluations' (p.81). The report does suggest that educational technologies can render education more inclusive, but the focus is on disabilities such as visual or hearing impairments and speech impairments, and only one mention is made of specific learning difficulties (the report merely states that 'not all technologies are applicable', and they need to be 'individualised' [p.36]). Learning differences such as dyslexia and ADHD are not mentioned, and autism is only mentioned twice. As such, there is arguably a distinct lack of 'robust' evidence that educational technologies have either a positive or negative effect on the learning of students with learning differences, although one notable study into ADHD did illustrate that there was a significant correlation between the frequent use of digital media and the symptoms of ADHD (Ra et al., 2018).

Individual institutions are increasingly launching and refining their own local policies on how much use of GenAI is permissible within the framework of their academic misconduct regulations, but usefully, Perkins et al. (2024) have devised the following 'Artificial Intelligence Assessment Scale' (AIAS):

No AI:	Students must not use AI at any point during the assessment
AI planning:	AI can be used for planning, idea development, and research
AI collaboration:	AI can be used for drafting, refining, and evaluating work
Full AI:	AI can be used extensively, either as the student wishes, or as directed in the assessment instructions
AI exploration:	Creative use of AI, potentially co-designing new approaches with the instructor

Students and instructors should obviously adhere to their institution's policies, but many of them, and indeed models of integration and use such as the AIAS, concern the ethical use of GenAI. From a pedagogical (and indeed philosophical) point of view, the advent and use of GenAI – in terms of inclusion, learning differences, and assessment at least – can be seen through three lenses. At the time of writing (given the fact that the technology and adoption is so new) there is simply insufficient evidence and literature to ascertain with any degree of certainty what the long-term effects of the current 'embrace and adapt' model will be, how effective GenAI will be in facilitating learning, or how useful or detrimental the above scale will be in terms of learning or scaffolding academic literacies. However, here are the three main issues that need to be considered:

Cognitive offloading

In this view, the new technologies are used primarily as a means of reducing the burden associated with studying and assessment by 'outsourcing' it to GenAI. As Dickinson (2024) recently summarised, under 'cognitive offloading', students use tools or tech to reduce the cognitive demand of tasks – which in turn allows them to focus their mental resources (or time) elsewhere, or engage in more complex thinking, or take another shift in the cafe.

In some respects, it is understandable how this might be helpful. Using GenAI to summarise a journal article can certainly get you to the core message and speed up the process of academic reading and research immeasurably, thus allowing the student to 'engage in more complex thinking'. Indeed, if we return to Bloom's (1956) seminal taxonomy of educational goals and cognitive processes, we can think of GenAI as helping to reduce the burden of expending mental energies and cognitive demands on 'lower-order' concerns such as knowledge and comprehension, thus allowing more time and energy for analysis, evaluation synthesis, and creation. This could be especially helpful for students with learning differences, as demands upon the working memory can be substantially reduced, thus leaving more mental energies for 'more complex thinking'. Indeed, it is easy to see how this could lead to greater student attainment, and certainly GenAI tools in the form of ChatGPT, for example, can help students check their work, reduce the likelihood of basic errors (e.g. grammar and sentence structure), and help students to structure and write their assignments in a more cogent, coherent manner. So far so good, but what if this cognitive 'offloading' has the effect of short-circuiting the learning process? The focus of this book, as discussed previously, is not just assessment *of* and *for* learning, but *as* learning – in particular, writing *as* learning. If students 'outsource' or 'offload' some or all of their writing to GenAI, what are they learning, aside from the effective use and manipulation of GenAI tools (e.g. prompt construction or engineering [Wallbank, 2023] and checking for accuracy and truthfulness [Rudolph, Tan, and Tan, 2023])? Maybe room for 'more complex thinking' is created by offloading certain aspects of cognition to GenAI, but to what extent is this 'more complex thinking' underpinned by the basics? And to what extent is the speed and immediacy with which GenAI can produce responses, texts, and imagery detrimental to learning?

Martin Heidegger's work on the intersections between technology and thought is pertinent here. For Heidegger, humans need to be in harmony with what they produce, a harmony he calls 'poiesis'. Poiesis is a complex conglomeration of 'revealing', truth, the entity of things, and 'unconcealment' (Wheeler, 2020), but for our purposes, his discussion of what it takes to become a 'true cabinetmaker' is particularly insightful for our consideration of assessment. For Heidegger, if one is to become genuinely in tune with one's craft (in this case cabinetmaking),

> he makes himself answer and respond above all to the different kinds of wood and to the shapes slumbering within wood—to wood as it enters into man's dwelling with all the hidden riches of its essence. In fact, this relatedness to wood is what maintains the whole craft. Without that relatedness, the craft will never be anything but empty busywork, any occupation with it will be determined exclusively by business concerns. Every handicraft, all human dealings, are constantly in that danger.
> (Heidegger, 1976, p.379)

For Heidegger, once technology comes into the equation, our understanding of, and relationship to, what we produce is reduced to what he calls a 'standing reserve' – an empty, meaningless, purely utilitarian relationship akin to Marx's understanding of commodification. As Walker (2017) effectively summarises, this relationship tends to reduce our 'ways of being in the world' to being merely 'technological', and 'by striving for ever more speed, efficiency and interchangeability, this technological worldview makes objects or resources out of things that have previously had meaning for us' (p. xiv). In our context, then, there is a danger that outsourcing or 'offloading' certain cognitive processes to GenAI while undertaking an assessment might get the task done much faster (it is noteworthy that adverts for GenAI writing tools and assistants often emphasise that they will enable essays and assignments to be written 'effortlessly' and 'in seconds' [e.g. aithor.com] – which underscores the notion of 'offloading'). Additionally, the tools might free up valuable working memory for deeper thinking, but this reduces the task's significance as a means of fostering and developing meaning and even the intersection between intelligence and knowledge – the 'synthesis', as Greenfield (2014) puts it, between 'facts, context and meaning' (p.250). By 'offloading' these processes to GenAI, the assignment becomes merely a product devoid of meaning, devoid of 'poiesis', and we become, to an even greater extent, conformist 'curators' of information (Docherty, 2011) rather than honing critically aware and perceptive intelligence. Indeed, linguists have even noted that language itself is under threat, with GenAI language representing 'the ultimate superficiality' and thus rendering human communication 'administrative and robotic', thereby robbing humanity of our 'voice' (Booth, 2024). In regard to assessment though, because the parts of the assignment 'offloaded' are done with a view to speeding up the process, the valuable 'dwelling with all the hidden richness' of the intellectual processes and 'essence' of the assignment/writing is short circuited or bypassed entirely and thus lost. This is especially important and potentially detrimental for students with learning differences owing to the importance of context and the development of their personal conceptual frameworks discussed earlier. Additionally, educators often highlight the importance of Kolb's experiential learning cycle (1984) as integral to learning, and if we think of writing and assessment *as* learning (especially in relation to the cognitive processes involved in reiteratively drafting, rethinking, editing, and redrafting), arguably GenAI curtails the cycle or learning process.

As discussed above, context, the 'bigger picture', and the relationships between detail and the 'big picture' via search strengths are especially important for students with learning differences, not only as a means of tapping into their strengths but also as a mechanism for scaffolding their challenges and trade-offs. What we need to develop and scaffold are the personal conceptual frameworks and coping/compensatory strategies of our students. Here we find ourselves back with the principles of UDL. While the use of GenAI undoubtedly enables students to undertake assessments via multiple means of engagement, representation, and action or expression, the extent to which it encourages students to use and develop their affective, recognition, and strategic brain networks (executive function) via the 'why', 'what', and 'how' of learning is less certain. For example, 'self-regulation', especially the development of self-assessment, reflection, and personal coping skills or strategies, is considered to be important for engagement, the affective brain networks, and the 'why' of learning. Cognitive 'offloading' surely does little to develop these skills. Similarly, developing understanding and comprehension through activating and supplying background information, highlighting patterns, big ideas, and relationships, as well as through visualisation and knowledge transfer or generalisation, are key facets of developing recognition networks of the brain – the 'what' of learning. These are the building blocks and foundations of constructing 'personal conceptual frameworks', without which the students may get to the end product (to use the language associated with the commodification of education we are witnessing) 'in seconds' and with far less 'effort'. But is this fostering learning, especially for individuals with learning differences who both need and excel at making links, drawing out patterns, and exploiting or searching for the 'bigger picture' or the detail in order to fulfil their full potential? In other words, is GenAI entirely compatible with the principles of UDL? Probably not. Indeed, irrespective of UDL and scaffolding for learning differences, GenAI can be said to bypass important aspects of the notion of assessment *as* a form of learning. A brief search through five current GenAI essay writing tools or 'assistants' (essaygenius.ai, textero.ai, jenni.ai, editpad, and justdone.ai) reveals plenty of language centring around speed, efficiency, saving time for 'important things', essay writing being 'effortless', and even one claim by jenni.ai that 'writing without an AI assistant is a waste of time and energy', but there is not one mention of *learning*. In other words, the marketing of GenAI essay writing generators or 'assistants' is purely pitched towards assignment writing and academic literacies in terms of achieving product via the path of least resistance – very little is geared towards helping to facilitate the process of learning (which presumably constitutes a 'waste of time and energy').

I conclude this section with some final thoughts regarding the speed and efficiency associated with GenAI. One oft-unconsidered or neglected aspect of studying is the benefits of slowing down and reflection. Claxton (1998) has suggested that 'slow learning' is essential for the development of understanding, skilful practice, metacognition, and self-actualisation, while more recently Walker (2017) has espoused the benefits of slowing down in terms of reading. For Walker, drawing on Heidegger's notion of poiesis, 'reading slowly and rereading, returning time and time again to read anew, we return ... to the world anew. Our slow and very local readings resist the all too familiar tone of those technological or instrumental readings that no longer share a relation with thought' (p. xv). 'Slow reading', Walker argues,

> means providing our students with experiences that can transform their often instrumental relations with the world around them. By encouraging our students to listen attentively to what they read, we offer them opportunities to slow their habitual tendencies to read without regard for the intricate possibilities that any text contains. (p. 123)

This approximates with some of the arguments made in Freire's seminal text, *Pedagogy of the Oppressed* (2017) concerning the possibilities of pedagogy for liberation as opposed to purely instrumentalist learning. But given what we have found about writing as learning pedagogies, then the same arguments Walker makes regarding reading may equally be said of writing (and, of course, in order to write, one has to read). By deploying GenAI writing 'assistants' to speed up the essay writing (and reading) process, we surely run the risk of more deeply entrenching precisely the instrumentalist, 'surface' approaches to learning most of us, as pedagogues, are actively trying to discourage. In other words, irrespective of whether GenAI writing generators and 'assistants' are of little use in supplying the necessary contextual and neurological scaffolding required by students with learning differences to learn and fulfil assignments effectively, it seems the speed inherent within GenAI is detrimental to learning itself. Indeed, as Fuchs (2023) argues, an 'over-reliance' on such technologies could undermine the development of important critical thinking skills, as well as encouraging a 'passivity' that could 'hinder achieving some learning outcomes' (Mennella and Quadros-Mennella, 2024, p.7). Mennella and Quadros-Mennella's (2024) study shows that even some students perceive the use of ChatGPT as 'undermining creativity, learning and skill development' (p.14), while Crawford et al. (2024) have shown that when considered within the broader context of social support, psychological wellbeing, loneliness, and sense of belonging, the use of GenAI has a 'net negative effect on achievement' (p.1).

Extended mind

With the advent of GenAI, one of the initial concerns focused on cheating and academic misconduct – the extent to which students' work 'must be your own' (Dickinson, 2024). Irrespective of Bakhtinian arguments regarding the extent to which, given the necessarily 'heteroglot' nature of language and discourse, we can ever truly appropriate language and make it our 'own' (Bakhtin, 1981), for Dickinson the use of GenAI as a form of 'assistance' raises interesting questions about the 'extended mind' – the idea that 'instead of offloading, cognition can extend beyond the brain to include tools and technologies'. Thus, one's 'cognitive environment' encompasses not only what is within the brain but whatever the brain interacts with on a cognitive level – originally conceived as 'active externalism, based on the active role of the environment in driving cognitive processes' (Clark and Chalmers, 1998, p.389). A crude version of this, which remains illuminating for our purposes, is an anecdote provided by Seneca in his *Moral Epistles* (c. 65 AD). In his discussion of slavery, Seneca relates the tale of a freedman who wanted to appear intelligent and cultured. He purchased educated slaves to recite Homer and Hesiod at dinner parties, the idea being that because he owned the slaves, what they had learnt, he had learnt too. By extension, because a student's interactions with GenAI are based on the individual's prompts, the generated responses not only form part of their extended mind but are part and parcel of the wider 'cognitive environment' of humanity, just in the same way as language is constructed and disseminated socially. In other words, just as language is 'heteroglot', part of shared understandings and discourses, and difficult to 'appropriate' for one's own ends (Bakhtin, 1981), what is generated by GenAI (particularly large language models) is no different. In this view, nothing ever was truly one's 'own' anyway, and GenAI is merely an extension of what has always been the case for language and discourse. Therefore, in terms of originality and student learning and assessment, the use of GenAI is inextricably bound up with 'shared cognitive processing' (Dickinson, 2024); it is the natural evolution of language and shared, socially constructed intelligence, and GenAI becomes merely a form of external memory, cognition, knowledge, and learning.

As a form of scaffolding, supporting and acting as a writing 'assistant' for students with learning differences, then, the advent of GenAI is not 'cognitive offloading' but merely the next logical step in modern-day cognition, and hybrid writing (combining human and machine) is likely the new norm. As we shall see below, for students with learning differences, GenAI 'assistance' can be merely embraced as the next logical step in the evolution of 'assistive technologies'. Also, to return, however briefly and unfortunately, to the deficit/medical/remedial model of learning differences as a 'disability', GenAI can be used as an extension of the mind 'just as a prosthetic limb can become part of a body' (Clark, 2024).

GenAI as assistive technology

There is one further, complementary way in which we can think of GenAI is as an 'assistive technology'. Large language models such as ChatGPT can effectively scaffold student assignments and the writing process by suggesting correct spellings, grammar and structure, providing writing prompts and models, and helping students improve drafts ready for submission. In addition, GenAI can help students decipher assignment questions and tasks, and can summarise and even simplify long or complex texts, thus aiding comprehension and assimilation. In this sense, we can think of GenAI as a personal writing assistant or study buddy. The main arguments in favour of doing this again relate to working memory. Cognitive load theory (Baddeley, 1986; Kirschner, 2002) proposes that cognitive load is not infinite (as in the case of long-term memory), and its capacity can become swiftly depleted or overloaded if too much information or instruction is imposed upon it. Therefore, instruction ought to be broken down into manageable chunks for cognition to remain at optimal capacity. This is especially important for students with learning differences, of course, owing to the inherent additional stressors and limitations placed on the working memory, hence the main benefits of 'assistance' in the form of GenAI. By 'outsourcing' or scaffolding some mental tasks to GenAI, it frees up valuable working memory capacity to enable students with learning differences to function at a similar level to their peers (on the face of it, ideal for rendering education and assessment more inclusive, as it facilitates wider and more equitable participation).

Importantly, GenAI can help students with learning differences structure their thoughts and articulate them in a more logical, coherent manner. For instance, the student could write to the best of their abilities, producing what might initially be considered the type of 'schizophreneze' or 'word salads' (Clughen and Connell, 2015) mentioned earlier, and then simply ask a GenAI tool to reconfigure it into a form acceptable for submission. In essence, the GenAI application is 'assisting' in this instance, merely polishing up the student's original work and rendering it more compliant with academic expectations and conventions. Again, it could be argued that this is inherently inclusive, as it renders access to success within higher education more equitable. It also makes the pedagogy more effective because by assisting with and ultimately modelling good practice, it renders academic conventions more transparent while easing access to knowledge and learning.

Finally, GenAI can make learning and assessment more personalised. By asking GenAI tools for feedback or clarifications, the students get personalised, instantaneous responses, thus demystifying academic conventions and tailoring feedback to their specific needs. In today's increasingly pressured, marketised higher education system where cost-cutting measures are increasingly being implemented, getting feedback or support from tutors can be delayed or difficult to come by, whereas GenAI tools can provide instant assistance. What is more, through the effective use of prompts, further clarifications can be sought, again rendering the feedback, scaffolding, or modelling even more bespoke. The only issue here is that the above all assumes that the students are sufficiently skilled in prompt engineering. Arguably, you only get out of GenAI what you put in, and thus prompt engineering is likely to become an increasingly important academic literacy.

However, while this all sounds very promising, arguably GenAI can actually *increase* cognitive load. Firstly, prompt engineering is not as easy as it might sound, and its essential elements are detail, accuracy, and concision. As we have already seen, none of these are entirely unproblematic for students with learning differences. Furthermore, however, checking the accuracy of the GenAI outputs is cognitively burdensome. Take the above three paragraphs as an example. As an experiment, I copied and pasted them into ChatGPT and asked it to improve the points by citing and embedding academic literature to support the arguments. This it did very efficiently. However, GenAI is prone to so-called hallucinations, and responses now come with the caveat, for example, that 'ChatGPT can make mistakes. Check important info.' So, I diligently checked each reference. To ChatGPT's credit, they were all legitimate academic sources and easily found; however, ChatGPT claimed the sources as evidence of the legitimacy of the arguments. For instance, the following claim (which is merely representative) is made: 'the tool can assist in organising thoughts and structuring assignments, helping students better manage their time and meet deadlines (Langberg et al., 2011)'. Notice, however, that while the academic source is legitimate, ChatGPT was not invented in 2011. Indeed, none of the many references it provided were more recent than 2017, still some six years before ChatGPT or other forms of GenAI came out. With this in mind, I then read each of the sources to see if there was anything within them that I could use to legitimise my arguments. Most were applicable only as general principles – none of them could be used to support the specific claims being made with any rigour or accuracy, and most of them were related to school-aged children and learning generally rather than higher education and assessment (despite both being terms I had included in my prompt).

Other GenAI writing tools such as perplexity.ai are considerably better at providing legitimate and relevant academic sources, but since the articles cited, like those cited by ChatGPT, need checking, this is an additional cognitive burden. Indeed, as discussed by Wallbank (2022), the very act of having multiple tabs or websites open, with all their many and varied distractions, notifications, alerts, adverts, and varying degrees of accessibility in terms of layout, is in and of itself cognitively overwhelming; unless a very clear picture is kept in mind of the navigation between tabs and websites, students can become lost.

It is easy to forget that the internet is a 'world wide *web*' (my emphasis), and it can be easy to get cognitively entangled (Wallbank, 2022). As such, the use of ChatGPT (or any form of GenAI) requires such a degree of fact-checking, cross-referencing, and navigation that it can potentially cause more cognitive overload than actually finding the sources in the first place and only reading those that are of use or that fit the argument. Furthermore, while the GenAI tool may help students find academic sources easily and quickly, the fact that they do not necessarily have to read them (slow reading) means that potentially important connections or 'big picture' links can simply be missed, thus bypassing the strengths of students with learning differences entirely, as their abilities to see interrelationships, connections, join the dots and/or detail (exploratory vs. depth-first search specialisations) are not needed or utilised. As such, while GenAI can be perceived as an 'assistive technology', the additional layer of checking and navigation required presents a huge barrier at the time of writing, which can only be remedied by improvements in the accuracy, clarity, or accessibility of the technology, or possibly by upgrading to paid-for versions, which then raises additional questions about digital poverty and accessibility/equity.

Summary

As suggested above, assistive technologies and AI can certainly help scaffold the writing and academic literacies of students with learning differences, and they can be particularly useful for modelling linearity and structure. However, the position taken in this book is that without a thorough understanding of the reasons 'why' certain pieces of information grouped in certain ways make a piece of work structured and linear, students with learning differences will a) lack the necessary context of what they are producing to instil deep understanding, b) foster superficial approaches to learning and skills development, c) be ill-equipped for the wider world and employability, d) have potentially increased rather than decreased cognitive load, and, crucially, e) effectively bypass some of the inbuilt strengths students with learning differences possess as a result of their exploratory or depth-first learning strategies. Ultimately, the goal of fulfilling the assessment can be achieved by harnessing bespoke scaffolding (the position taken in this book), using assistive technologies, or by outsourcing to GenAI. But assistive technologies, and in particular GenAI, do not develop the skills needed to produce cogent responses autonomously (thus fostering dependence) and do not provide the necessary framework and rationale (the 'what', 'why', and 'how' of learning) to create deep understanding and encoding of knowledge within the long-term memory. On the other hand, the inclusive, predominantly visual pedagogies espoused in this book, coupled with an emphasis on writing *as* learning, can help our students develop the skills needed to become autonomous learners and writers. As Zinsser put it back in 1988, it is only by 'writing about a subject we're trying to learn that we reason our way to what it means. Reasoning is a lost skill of the children of the TV generation, with their famously short attention span. Writing can help them get it back' (p.22).

References

Anthony, P., (2023) 'AI and Higher Education: Is it Time to Re-think Teaching and Assessment?' University of Kent. Available from: https://blogs.kent.ac.uk/learn-tech/2023/01/11/ai-and-higher-education-is-it-time-to-re-think-teaching-and-assessment/# (Accessed: 11 September 2024).

Aristovnik, A., Keržic, D., Ravšelj, D., Tomaževic, N., and Umek, L., (2021) 'Impacts of the Covid-19 Pandemic on Life of Higher Education Students: Global Survey Dataset from the First Wave', *Data in Brief*, 39, pp.1–11. Available from: https://doi.org/10.1016/j.dib.2021.107659 (Accessed: 24 August 2024).

Astleitner, H., (2018) 'Multidimensional Engagement in Learning – An Integrated Instructional Design Approach', *Journal of Instructional Research*, 7, pp.6–32. Available from: https://files.eric.ed.gov/fulltext/EJ1188334.pdf (Accessed: 14 July 2024).

Baddeley, A. D., (1986) *Working Memory*. Oxford: Clarendon Press.

Bakhtin, M. M., (1981) *The Dialogic Imagination: Four Essays*, translated by Emerson, C. and Holquist, M. Austin, TX and London: University of Texas Press.

Biggs, J., (2003) *Teaching for Quality Learning at University: What the Student Does*. Second Edition. Buckingham: Society for Research into Higher Education and Open University Press.

Blackler, F., (1995) 'Knowledge, Knowledge Work and Organizations: An Overview and Interpretation', *Organization Studies*, 16:6, pp.1021–1046. Available from: https://doi.org/10.1177/017084069501600605 (Accessed: 15 June 2024).

Bloom, B. S., Engelhart, M. D., Furst, E. J., Hill, W. H., and Krathwohl, D. R., (1956) *Taxonomy of Educational Objectives: The Classification of Educational Goals*. New York: David McKay Company.

Booth, R., (2024) 'Losing Our Voice? Fears AI Tone-shifting Tech Could Flatten Communication', *The Guardian*, 11 December 2024. Available from: www.theguardian.com/society/2024/dec/11/ai-tone-shifting-tech-could-flatten-communication-apple-intelligence? (Accessed: 11 December 2024).

British Dyslexia Association, (2007) 'Definition of Dyslexia'. Available from: www.actiondyslexia.co.uk/view-article/Defining-Dyslexia (Accessed: 19 September 2024).

Broun, T. L., (2004) 'Teaching Students with Autistic Spectrum Disorder to Read: A Visual Approach', *TEACHING Exceptional Children*, 36:4, pp.36–40.

Brown, E. N., and Brown, D. L., (2009) *Meaning, Morphemes and Literacy: Essays in the Morphology of Language and its Application to Literacy*. Brighton: The Book Guild Ltd.

CAST, (2024) 'The UDL Guidelines'. Available from: https://udlguidelines.cast.org/ (Accessed: 5 November 2024).

Chomsky, N., (2003) *For Reasons of State*. London: Random House.

Chomsky, N., (2012) *Selected Readings on Transformational Theory*, eds. Allen, J. P. B. and Van Buren, P. New York: Dover Publications.

Clark, A., (2024) 'The Extended Mind in Science and Society'. The University of Edinburgh. Available from: www.ed.ac.uk/ppls/philosophy/research/impact/the-extended-mind-in-science-and-society (Accessed: 12 September 2024).

Clark, A., and Chalmers, D., (1998) 'The Extended Mind', *Analysis*, 58:1, pp.7–19. Available from: www.jstor.org/stable/3328150 (Accessed: 12 June 2024).

Claxton, G., (1998) *Hare Brain, Tortoise Mind*. London: Fourth Estate.

Clughen, L., and Connell, M., (2015) 'Working with Power: A Dialogue about Writing Support Using Insights from Psychotherapy', in Lillis, T., Harrington, K., Lea, M. R., and Mitchell, S., (eds), *Working with Academic Literacies: Case Studies Towards Transformative Practice*. Fort Collins, CO: The WAC Clearinghouse, pp.45–53.

Cohen, S., (1998) *Targeting Autism: What We Know, Don't Know, and Can Do to Help Young Children with Autism*. Berkeley, CA: University of California Press.

Cooper, R., (2019) 'Specific Learning Difficulties', in Krčmář, K. (ed.), *The Inclusivity Gap* Aberdeen: Inspired by Learning, pp.80–95.

Coventry University, (2024) *2030 Group Strategy*. Available from: www.coventry.ac.uk/the-university/about-coventry-university/2030-group-strategy/ (Accessed: 12 July 2024).

Crawford, J., Allen, K. A., Pani, B., and Cowling, M., (2024) 'When Artificial Intelligence Substitutes Humans in Higher Education: The Cost of Loneliness, Student Success, and Retention', *Studies in Higher Education*, 49:5, pp.883–897. Available from: https://doi.org/10.1080/03075079.2024.2326956 (Accessed: 12 August 2024).

Crawford, J., Cowling, M., and Allen, K-A., (2023) 'Leadership Is Needed for Ethical ChatGPT: Character, Assessment, and Learning Using Artificial Intelligence (AI)', *Journal of University Teaching and Learning Practice*, 20:3, pp.1–19. Available from: https://doi.org/10.53761/1.20.3.02 (Accessed: 13 July 2024).

Cremin, L. A., (1976) *Public Education*. New York: Basic Books.

Cryer, H., (2013) *Exploring the Need for Accessible Images for People with Dyslexia*, Birmingham: Royal National Institute for the Blind.

Dettmer, J., and Welton, K., (2024) 'Diversity in Our Expertise: Empowering Neurodivergent Students within Learning Development', in Syska, A. and Buckley, C. (eds), *How to Be a Learning Developer in Higher Education: Critical Perspectives, Community and Practice*. London: Routledge, pp.62–70.

Dickinson, J., (2024) '"Your Work Must be Your Own": What Does That Mean?' *WONK Corner*, 12 February. Available from: https://wonkhe.com/wonk-corner/your-work-must-be-your-own-what-does-that-mean/ (Accessed: 13 August 2024).

Docherty, T., (2011) *For the University: Democracy and the Future of the Institution*. London: Bloomsbury Academic.

Dumford, A. D., and Miller, A. L., (2018) 'Online Learning in Higher Education: Exploring Advantages and Disadvantages for Engagement', *Journal of Computing in Higher Education*, 30, pp.452–465. Available from: https://link.springer.com/article/10.1007/s12528-018-9179-z#citeas (Accessed: 19 September 2024).

Earl, L. M., (2012). *Assessment as Learning: Using Classroom Assessment to Maximize Student Learning*. Second Edition. Toronto: University of Toronto Press.

Eide, B. L., and Eide, F. F., (2011) *The Dyslexic Advantage: Unlocking the Hidden Potential of the Dyslexic Brain*. First Edition. London: Hay House.

Eide, B. L., and Eide, F. F., (2023) *The Dyslexic Advantage: Unlocking the Hidden Potential of the Dyslexic Brain*. Second Edition. London: Hay House.

Elkington, S., (2020) 'Essential Frameworks for Enhancing Student Success: Transforming Assessment in Higher Education', *AdvanceHE*. Available from: www.advance-he.ac.uk/knowledge-hub/essential-frameworks-enhancing-student-success-transforming-assessment Accessed: 5 July 2024).

Freire, P., (2017) *Pedagogy of the Oppressed*. London: Penguin Classics.

Fuchs, K., (2023) 'Exploring the Opportunities and Challenges of NLP Models in Higher Education: Is Chat GPT a Blessing or a Curse?' *Frontiers in Education*, 8, 1166682. Available from: https://doi.org/10.3389/feduc.2023.1166682 (Accessed: 20 September 2024).

Fulwiler, T., and Young, A., (1982) 'Introduction', in Fulwiler, T., and Young, A. (eds), *Language Connections: Writing and Reading Across the Curriculum*. Urbana, IL: National Council of Teachers of English, pp. i, x–xiii.

Game, A., and Metcalfe, A., (1996) *Passionate Sociology*. London: Sage.

Gardner, H. E., (2000) *Intelligence Reframed: Multiple Intelligences for the 21st Century*. London: Hachette.

Gibbs, G., and Simpson, C., (2005) 'Conditions Under Which Assessment Supports Students' Learning', *Learning and Teaching in Higher Education*, 1, pp.3–31. Available from: https://eprints.glos.ac.uk/3609/1/LATHE%201.%20Conditions%20Under%20Which%20Assessment%20Supports%20Students%27%20Learning%20Gibbs_Simpson.pdf (Accessed: 23 September 2023).

Grandin, T., (1995) *Thinking in Pictures and Other Reports from My Life with Autism*. New York: Doubleday.

Greenfield, S., (2014) *Mind Change: How Digital Technologies Are Leaving Their Mark on Our Brains*. London: Rider.

Heidegger, M., (1976) *What Is Called Thinking?* Translated by Glenngray, J. London: Harper Perennial.

Helland T, and Morken F., (2015) 'Neurocognitive Development and Predictors of L1 and L2 Literacy Skills in Dyslexia: A Longitudinal Study of Children 5–11 Years Old', *Dyslexia*. 22:1, pp.3–26. Available from: https://onlinelibrary.wiley.com/doi/10.1002/dys.1515 (Accessed: 15 September 2023).

Herringshaw, A. J., Ammons, C. J., DeRamus, T. P., and Kana, R. K., (2016) 'Hemispheric Differences in Language Processing in Autism Spectrum Disorders: A Meta-analysis of Neuroimaging Studies', *Autism Research*, 9, pp.1046–1057. Available from: https://pubmed.ncbi.nlm.nih.gov/26751141/ (Accessed: 13 July 2023).

Heuboeck, A., Holmes, J., and Nesi, H., (2007) *The BAWE Corpus Manual: An Investigation of Genres of Assessed Writing in British Higher Education*. ESRC, Project RES-000-23-0800.

Holden, C., (2022) 'UK Engagement Survey 2022', *AdvanceHE/UKES*. Available from: www.advance-he.ac.uk/knowledge-hub/uk-engagement-survey-2022 (Accessed: 12 September 2023).

Janzen, J., (1996) *Understanding the Nature of Autism: A Practical Guide*. San Antonio, TX: Therapy Skill Builders.

Kirschner, Paul, A., (2002) 'Cognitive Load Theory: Implications of Cognitive Load Theory on the Design of Learning', *Learning and Instruction*, 12:1, pp.1–10. Available from: https://doi.org/10.1016/S0959-4752(01)00014-7 (Accessed: 12 December 2023).

Kluth, P., and Darmody-Latham, J., (2003) 'Beyond Sight Words: Literacy Opportunities for Students with Autism', *Reading Teacher*, 56:6, pp.532–535.

Kolb, D. A., (1984) *Experiential Learning: Experience as the Source of Learning and Development* (Vol. 1). Englewood Cliffs, NJ: Prentice-Hall.

Krathwohl, D. R., (2002) 'A Revision of Bloom's Taxonomy: An Overview', *Theory Into Practice*, 41:4, pp.212–218. Available from: www.jstor.org/stable/1477405 (Accessed: 5 November 2023).

Layer, G., (2017) *Inclusive Teaching and Learning in Higher Education as a Route to Excellence*. London: Department for Education. Available at: www.gov.uk/government/publications/inclusive-teaching-and-learning-in-higher-education (Accessed: 16 July 2023).

McMurtrie, B., (2022) 'AI and the Future of Undergraduate Writing', *The Chronicle of Higher Education*. Available from: www.chronicle.com/article/ai-and-the-future-of-undergraduate-writing (Accessed: 14 November 2024).

Mennella, T., and Quadros-Mennella, P., (2024) 'Student Use, Performance and Perceptions of ChatGPT on College Writing Assignments', *Journal of University Teaching and Learning Practice*, 21:1, pp.1–25. Available from: https://open-publishing.org/journals/index.php/jutlp/article/view/712 (Accessed: 15 September 2024).

Merry, K. L., (2023) *Delivering Inclusive and Impactful Instruction: Universal Design for Learning in Higher Education*. CASTInc.

Molitor, S. J., Langberg, J. M., and Evans, S. W., (2016) 'The Written Expression Abilities of Adolescents with Attention-Deficit/Hyperactivity Disorder', *Research in Developmental Disabilities*, 51–52, pp.49–59. Available from: https://pubmed.ncbi.nlm.nih.gov/26802631/ (Accessed: 19 September 2024).

National Forum for the Enhancement of Teaching and Learning in Higher Education, (2020) *Assessment of/for/as Learning*. Available from: https://hub.teachingandlearning.ie/resource/assessment-of-for-and-as-learning-continuing-the-debate-and-creating-a-focus/ (Accessed: 22 June 2022).

Neves, J., and Hewitt, R., (2021) 'Student Academic Experience Survey 2021'. *HEPI*. Available from: www.hepi.ac.uk/wp-content/uploads/2021/06/SAES_2021_FINAL.pdf (Accessed: 11 September 2024).

Nguyen, T., (2015) 'The Effectiveness of Online Learning: Beyond No Significant Difference and Future Horizons', *Journal of Online Learning and Teaching*, 11:2, pp.309–319. Available from: https://jolt.merlot.org/Vol11no2/Nguyen_0615.pdf (Accessed: 12 November 2024).

Nicolson, R. I., Fawcett, A. J., and Dean, P., (2001) 'Developmental Dyslexia: The Cerebellar Deficit Hypothesis', *Trends in Neurosciences*, 24, pp.508–511. Available from: www.cell.com/trends/neurosciences/abstract/S0166-2236(00)01896-8 (Accessed: 23 July 2024).

Paul, J., and Jefferson, F., (2019) 'A Comparative Analysis of Student Performance in an Online vs. Face-to-Face Environmental Science Course From 2009 to 2016', *Frontiers in Computer Science*, 1:7. Available from: www.frontiersin.org/journals/computer-science/articles/10.3389/fcomp.2019.00007/full (Accessed: 2 December 2024).

Peper, E., Wilson, V., Martin, M., Rosegard, E., and Harvey, R., (2021) 'Avoid Zoom Fatigue, Be Present and Learn', *NeuroRegulation*, 8:1, pp.47–56. Available from: www.neuroregulation.org/article/view/21206/13976 (Accessed: 12 February 2023).

Perkins, M., Furze, L., Roe, J., and MacVaugh, J., (2024) 'The Artificial Intelligence Assessment Scale (AIAS): A Framework for Ethical Integration of Generative AI in Educational Assessment', *Journal of University Teaching and Learning Practice*, 21:6. Available from: https://doi.org/10.53761/q3azde36 (Accessed: 12 December 2024).

Poulos, G., (2022) 'When Did Humans First Start to Speak? How Language Evolved in Africa', *The Conversation*. Available from: https://theconversation.com/when-did-humans-first-start-to-speak-how-language-evolved-in-africa-194372 (Accessed: 11 December 2024).

Ra, C. K., Cho, J., Stone, M. D., De La Cerda, J., Goldenson, N. I., Moroney, E., et al., (2018) 'Association of Digital Media Use with Subsequent Symptoms of Attention-Deficit/Hyperactivity Disorder Among Adolescents', *JAMA*, 17:320(3), pp.255–263. Available from: https://pubmed.ncbi.nlm.nih.gov/30027248/ (Accessed: 11 January 2023).

Rao, S. M., and Gagie, B., (2006) 'Learning Through Seeing and Doing: Visual Supports for Children with Autism', *Teaching Exceptional Children*, 38:6, pp.26–33. Available from: https://journals.sagepub.com/doi/epdf/10.1177/004005990603800604 (Accessed: 10 December 2024).

Roberts, D., (2016) 'Visual Feasts of the Mind: Matching How We Teach to How We Learn', *TEDxLoughboroughU*. Available at: www.youtube.com/watch?v=FJyhTg26w-A (Accessed: 15 November 2020).

Roberts, D., (2018) 'The Engagement Agenda, Multimedia Learning and the Use of Images in Higher Education Learning: or, How to End Death by Powerpoint', *Journal of Further and Higher Education*, 47:7, pp.969–984. Available from: www.tandfonline.com/doi/full/10.1080/0309877X.2017.1332356 (Accessed: 13 July 2023).

Roberts, D., (2018) *The Ultimate Guide to Visual Lectures*. Amazon: David Roberts.

Roberts, D., (2019) 'Visual Lectures', in Krčmář, K. (ed.), *The Inclusivity Gap*. Aberdeen: Inspired by Learning, pp.350–364.

Rudolph, J., Tan, S., and Tan, S., (2023) 'ChatGPT: Bullshit Spewer or the End of Traditional Assessments in Higher Education?' *Journal of Applied Learning and Teaching*, 6:1, pp.1–22. Available from: https://journals.sfu.ca/jalt/index.php/jalt/article/view/689 (Accessed: 12 June 2024).

Saussure, F. de, (1959) *Course in General Linguistics*, ed. Bally, C. and Reidlinger, A. New York: Philosophical Library.

Taylor, H., and Vestergaard, M. D., (2022) 'Developmental Dyslexia: Disorder or Specialisation in Exploration?' *Frontiers in Psychology*. Available at: https://pubmed.ncbi.nlm.nih.gov/35814102/ (Accessed: 4 July 2024).

UNESCO, (2023) *Technology in Education: A Tool on Whose Terms?* Available from: www.unesco.org/gem-report/en/technology (Accessed: 12 July 2024).

University of Leeds, (2021) *Digital Education Strategy*. Available from: https://digitaleducation.leeds.ac.uk/strategy/ (Accessed: 13 August 2024).

Waldie, K. E., Haigh, C. E., Badzakova-Trajkov, G., Buckley, J., and Kirk, I. J., (2013) 'Reading the Wrong Way with the Right Hemisphere', *Brain Sciences*, 3:3, pp.1060–1075. Available from: www.mdpi.com/2076-3425/3/3/1060 (Accessed: 15 August 2023).

Walker, M. B., (2017) *Slow Philosophy: Reading Against the Institution*. London: Bloomsbury.

Wallace, J., (2021) 'Five Commonly Misattributed Quotations', *MLA Style Center*. Available from: https://style.mla.org/five-commonly-misattributed-quotations/ (Accessed: 23 August 2024).

Wallbank, A. J., (2021) 'Writing Support and Student Identity – Can We Help Learners Write in an Age of Massification and Consumerism?' in Padró, F. F., Kek, M., and Huijser, H. (eds), *Student Support Services: Exploring Impact on Student Engagement, Experience and Learning*. Singapore: Springer, pp.1–20.

Wallbank, A. J., (2022) *Academic Writing and Dyslexia: A Visual Guide to Writing at University*. Second Edition. London: Routledge.

Wallbank, A. J., (2023) 'Prompt Engineering as Academic Skill: A Model for Effective ChatGPT Interactions', *Times Higher Education*, 28 April 2023. Available from: www.timeshighereducation.com/campus/prompt-engineering-academic-skill-model-effective-chatgpt-interactions (Accessed: 13 July 2023).

West, T., (1997) *In the Mind's Eye: Visual Thinkers, Gifted People with Dyslexia and Other Learning Difficulties, Computer Images and the Ironies of Creativity*. New York: Prometheus Books.

Wheeler, M., (2020) 'Martin Heidegger', in Zalta, E. N. (ed.), *The Stanford Encyclopedia of Philosophy*. Available from: https://plato.stanford.edu/archives/fall2020/entries/heidegger/ (Accessed: 15 June 2024).

Wiliam, D., (2011) 'What Is Assessment for Learning?' *Studies in Educational Evaluation*, 37:1, pp.3–14. Available from: www.sciencedirect.com/science/article/pii/S0191491X11000149 (Accessed: 12 December 2023).

Wrigley, S., (2019) 'Avoiding "De-plagiarism": Exploring the Affordances of Handwriting in the Essay-writing Process', *Active Learning in Higher Education*, 20:2, pp.167–179. Available from: https://doi.org/10.1177/1469787417735611 (Accessed: 16 August 2021).

Xu, D., and Smith Jaggars, S., (2013) *Adaptability to Online Learning: Differences Across Types of Students and Academic Subject Areas* (CCRC Working Paper). New York: Teachers College, Columbia University. Available from: http://ccrc.tc.columbia.edu/publications/adaptability-to-online-learning.html (Accessed: 19 August 2023).

Zinsser, W., (1988) *Writing to Learn*. London: Harper Perennial.

4 Navigators, Pilots, Conductors

Meta-roles as an Inclusive Pedagogical Strategy to Develop Metacognitive Awareness

David Channon

Introduction

So embedded is metaphor within language that it is difficult to talk about it at all without metaphorising. The root of the word – for words have roots – derives from the Greek *metaphora* (to carry over or transfer) – and is itself a metaphor. A related word in the family – for words have families – is amphora, those vessels filled with wine or oil so treasured by the ancient Greeks. For our purposes, it is meaning that is being carried over, using language as a vessel, as we attempt to communicate one idea or concept by comparing it to another with which it may share certain similar features. The source metaphor, sometimes referred to as the vehicle, offers a simplified visual representation of the more abstract concept, referred to as the target, or tenor. Their shared attributes, or ground, consists of the particular associations or entailments that are chosen to connect source and target. For example, since Darwin, we have used the image of a tree to represent the process of evolution; electricity is commonly visualised as a current and the brain as a computer. It goes deeper, to our experience of time which is universally communicated using spatial metaphors such as forward and back or even up and down or high and low – the differences reflecting our unique cultural perspectives (Cooperrider and Núñez, 2016). Indeed, metaphor, freed from its literary and figurative roots, is now considered fundamental to how we experience and conceptualise the world around us. In this, I include simile as a specific type of metaphor, using 'like' or 'as' in its construction.

For Lakoff and Johnson (1981), conceptual metaphors are pervasive in thought and in language, shaping how we view reality and generating the semantic and linguistic networks through which they are communicated. This generative potential is exemplified in the conceptual metaphor 'learning is a journey', which is expressed linguistically using terms such as 'embark', 'navigate', explore', and 'discover'. To be on a course, from the Latin 'to run', is to be on a path and heading in a particular direction. Kovecses (2017, p.13) neatly defines conceptual metaphor as 'the understanding of one domain of experience that is typically abstract in terms of another which is typically concrete'. So ingrained are these metaphors in our everyday thought and language that they tend to operate below the level of conscious awareness. This brief introduction already points to a key issue with which we will have to deal. How appropriate is any given metaphor to its purpose? How accurately is it able to represent the concept we wish to communicate? Is evolution best represented by a tree or would a network or a 'tree with reticulations' (Morrison, 2014, p.628) be a better one?

The focus of this chapter is on the process of academic study and, in particular, the relevance of conceptual metaphor theory (CMT) to the development of academic literacies in higher education settings. CMT aims to explain the many uses of conceptual metaphors, how they are formulated, the extent to which they are universal or culturally varied, and the emergence of novel metaphors. CMT is also a theory of learning which argues that mental processes are best understood and studied as embodied phenomena, rooted in sensorimotor experience and situated within a particular set of environmental constraints (Gibbs, Costa Lima, and Francozo, 2004). In this view, knowledge is de-centred from the neurological architecture of the brain and distributed throughout the body, including in the skeletal and muscular systems. This insight has profound implications for how we think about learning differences. For example, Rucińska et al. (2021) point to evidence demonstrating that autistic individuals differ significantly in sensory-motor coordination and the patterning of proprioceptive sensory feedback. They argue that this underlies variations not only in the way information is processed but that it also has a shaping influence on imagination and how information is visualised. Further evidence suggests variations in the manner with which attention is selectively deployed in the search for information (Stuurman et al., 2019), leading to differences, and potential difficulties, in how that information is eventually synthesised into a coherent whole, or *gestalt*. The embodied approach to learning contends that such attentional and cognitive processes are inseparable from sensory-motor experiences, grounded in the physical environment or, in a weaker version, as neural simulations of such experiences.

When it comes to the teaching of academic literacies then, how should we adjust our pedagogies to reflect this understanding? Lakoff and Johnson (1981) demonstrated that conceptual metaphors are embodied in physical actions and gestures. As such, they offer both a visual and a kinaesthetic means of representing what are otherwise abstract concepts. This is especially the case in academic writing. In fact, we are probably already using them when we ask students to '*carve* out a *niche*', 'take a *stance*', '*interrogate* a source', or 'apply a conceptual *lens*', all of which possess strong visual and kinaesthetic elements. This cross-modal view of learning resonates with the principles of Universal Design for Learning (UDL), which in its broadest sense seeks to adapt pedagogy to the needs of all learners by, for example, providing multiple ways to perceive information (CAST, consideration 1.2). What is lacking is the explicit acknowledgement of conceptual metaphor in our current pedagogical approaches and the development of a systematic way of employing it with our students, especially those with learning differences.

It would be tempting to bypass the thorny distinction between metaphor and analogy, which also dates from ancient Greece and to Aristotle who considered metaphor to be a special case of analogical reasoning that could equally well be applied to non-verbal subjects such as visual and mathematical problems (Morsanyi, Stamenković, and Holyoak, 2020). Indeed, the origin of the word (Greek – *analogos*) denotes proportionality or numerical ratio in preference to language. Metaphor, by contrast, has traditionally been viewed as a linguistic phenomenon, the expression of which can vary substantially in verbal complexity and idiomaticity. Common phrases such as 'I got cold feet' or 'I lost my nerve' are not typically subjected to analogical reasoning and we understand them relatively quickly as indicating a lack of confidence or resolve. This is not the case with more novel metaphors (Bowdle and Gentner, 2005) such as the simile proposed by a student of mine recently – 'academic learning is like routinely hitting a stone until the water gushes out' – which requires further scrutiny to be fully understood and appreciated. In other words, except in the case of novel metaphors or unless explicitly directed, students, like the rest of us, are unlikely to reflect on the metaphors which serve to shape our experience. Conceptual metaphors, such as the almost ubiquitous use of 'up' to denote a more positive state of mind or 'warm' to denote kindness, also tend to be used unconsciously and with an automaticity that belies their philosophical and psychological complexity. The importance of this will become evident when we consider claims that autistic and dyslexic students face particular challenges when encountering metaphor. In more recent times, many of these claims have been revised. Studies which have tested analogical reasoning alongside metaphorical processing find that autistic students demonstrate no differences from their typically developing peers in this type of reasoning and in some studies have been shown to have an advantage (Morsanyi, Stamenković, and Holyoak, 2020). I will, however, tiptoe past the academic debate for now and opt to use the term metaphor in place of analogy, situating this chapter within the broader field of metaphor studies and scholarship. A more pragmatic contention is that the application of analogical reasoning, or metaphorisation, has the potential to help all students reorient their relationship to the realities of the learning environment.

In making the case for the utility of metaphor in the teaching of academic literacies, I am referring to its use in both the one-to-one tutorial setting and in group settings such as lectures and seminars. It is important to clearly differentiate between metaphors presented as aids to learning and metaphors generated by learners themselves. The former includes those found in textbooks and used in lectures that aim to scaffold students' understanding of abstract concepts. There are classical examples such as the evolutionary tree and the personal computer that serve to frame whole disciplines. The latter can arise flexibly in response to a particular student's enquiry (Power, Carmichael, and Goldsmith, 2007) or be generated by a student as an expression of their thoughts, feelings, and emotions at the time. The dialogic nature of personal tutorials and small-group seminars allows a degree of negotiation in which existing metaphors can be adapted or discarded and new ones generated as appropriate. As will be discussed, this distinction is significant when considering claims of deficits in the understanding of metaphors by students with learning differences. Wan and Turner (2018) argue that the kind of critical dialogue, characteristic of one-to-one and small-group learning, can strengthen metacognitive awareness by encouraging students to consider the appropriacy of a metaphorical source to its target and by examining the tensions that exist between them, applying the kind of analogical reasoning mentioned earlier. This active use of the analogical facility stands in sharp contrast to the passive comprehension of metaphor used in many studies aimed at determining differences between so-called neurodivergent and typical individuals.

Metaphor and metacognition

The emphasis in this chapter is on metaphorisation – the process of (co) creating novel metaphors or adapting conventional metaphors for new purposes. The focus of much research up until now has been on the comprehension of metaphor as part of an evaluation of its role in cognitive development. Its pedagogical uses have generally received less attention, but there is some evidence that it can offer a powerful strategy for supporting students' learning (Willox et al., 2010) and, in particular, the core metacognitive strategies of planning, monitoring, and reflecting. This contrasts with conventional metaphors, many of which will already be familiar to teachers such as the commonly used example of studying as a journey in which students reflect on the challenges and obstacles they might face in reaching their goal or as a garden in which knowledge is cultivated, allowing the seeds of understanding to grow and flourish. Such metaphors must be approached critically as they also have the potential to mislead or misrepresent the experience of student writers. In many cases they could be considered as a starting rather than an ending point, requiring further exploration and elaboration before their eventual usefulness can be established. This chapter will put forward two interrelated arguments. Firstly, it will argue that metaphorisation can be used as a means to raise metacognitive awareness, enabling students to reflect on their own learning process. Several lines of evidence point to gains in attainment following explicit instruction in the use of metacognitive strategies (Ben-David and Zohar, 2009; Donker et al., 2014; Dent and Koenka, 2016; Muijs and Bokhove, 2020). Such strategies can offer several affordances to students with learning differences. The ability to reflect is empowering; raising students' awareness of how they learn allows them to choose between those methods of study that work for them and those that do not. This awareness has the potential to put students in control of their own learning, helping them to mitigate feelings of dependence and anxiety and increasing their sense of self-efficacy. Secondly, the chapter will propose that more attention should be given to the affective and embodied dimension of metaphor and its role in the regulation of emotions and motivation. The chapter will introduce the concept of *meta-roles* as a means to realise this in academic practice and will present evidence from a small-scale research project in which university students, half of whom were registered as dyslexic, autistic, or having ADHD, participated in a pedagogical intervention based on this concept.

It is useful at this stage to differentiate between cognition and metacognition. Flavell (1979, p.909) distinguishes between the two thus – 'cognitive strategies are invoked to make cognitive progress, metacognitive strategies to monitor it'. Dent and Koenka (2016) invoke the metaphor of a toolkit to represent this relationship, imagining cognitive strategies as the range of tools we have available to complete a task and metacognitive strategies as the ability to choose between them or to better adapt their use to the goal of the task. Metacognition can refer to both consciousness of one's own cognitive processes and to one's identity as a learner when it has been referred to as self-regulated learning (SRL) (Muijs and Bokhove, 2020). A question such as 'What kind of a learner am I?' exemplifies the idea of SRL in practice. The answers are likely to be diverse, interwoven with personal beliefs such as, 'I am no good at arithmetic' or 'I have a bad memory for …' or 'I understand something better if I can visualise it'. Flavell (1979, p.908) describes metacognition as 'opportunities for thoughts and feelings about your own thinking' – a definition which encompasses both cognitive and affective dimensions, describing the knowledge of what you know and do not yet know and, by extension, the awareness of what you can and cannot yet do. The benefit of metacognition for students with learning differences is explicitly recognised in the UDL framework in which the capacity to monitor progress towards set assessments is seen as a key factor in scaffolding higher-level executive skills and strategies (CAST, consideration 6.4).

This kind of self-diagnostic monitoring will be familiar to anyone embarked upon a programme of study such as, in the first instance, an undergraduate degree in which academic performance is shaped by regimes of testing and assessment which demand adherence to perceived standards of academic excellence – for example, in constructing an argument or critically interrogating a source. Implicit beliefs about ourselves as learners can shape our attitudes and motivation to engage in learning but can also be brought into question. The burgeoning literature on learning differences demonstrates how perceived limitations can be reimagined as abilities (Taylor and Vestergaard, 2022). By becoming more aware of their own unique ways of learning, students can identify their strengths as well as the challenges they may face.

Such reflection on learning is critical in helping learners to regulate their own learning process and is amenable to instructional approaches that stress the importance of 'assessment *for* learning' and 'assessment *as* learning' (Earl, 2012). Unlike summative assessment or assessment *of* learning which determines the final grades students will receive, formative assessment uses evidence of learning to provide feedback to students in order to help them improve (Swaffield, 2011). This can include feedback on the learning strategies they are currently employing. The success of such an approach depends heavily on teachers' ability to provide constructive feedback and feedforward, which can be easily understood by students and that is relevant to the assessment they are engaged in. However, teacher workloads often mitigate against the provision of individually tailored feedback, leading to the creation and use of more generalised, formulaic rubrics that standardise the process. This can prove disengaging for students. Assessment *as* learning addresses some of the limitations inherent in formative assessment by extending the paradigm to include a greater role for students in the assessment process. Providing opportunities for students to self-assess their own learning enables them to develop metacognitive awareness through the generation of internal feedback (Clark, 2012) as they come to understand the gap between where they are academically and where they need to be. For formative assessment to succeed, students need to be actively involved in self-monitoring (Gipps, 1994). This accords well with an approach that foregrounds conceptual metaphor.

Selecting, shaping, and sculpting a metaphor that accurately represents one's experience of a particular skill requires a high degree of metacognitive awareness and control, involving the ability to monitor and adjust thinking in the quest to find a fitting analogy. Wan and Turner (2018) discuss the use of metaphor as an intervention tool, used intentionally as a means of improving the teaching and learning of academic literacies. They provide several examples of the efficacy of conceptual metaphor in scaffolding students' understanding of critical cognitive skills such as taking a stance and developing a cohesive argument. Understanding students' conceptualisations through metaphor can also help teachers understand and address the particular issues they might be facing (Wan, 2014). Of particular interest is Hart's (2015) investigation into students' self-generated metaphors for writing. Analysis of student conversations and discussions revealed the multiple ways in which students metaphorised writing and, crucially, how recognition of this diversity helped reduce students' anxiety (Hart, 2015. cited in Wan and Turner, 2018).

Metaphor and embodied cognition

Cognitive science and, in particular, the notion of embodied cognition (EC) developed over the past 40 years has argued that cognition cannot be separated from our experience in the physical world, enacted through our bodies in space and in relationship to others (Gibbs, 2019; Gibbs, Costa Lima, and Francozo, 2004). Lakoff and Johnson (1981) came to regard the source of many everyday conceptual metaphors as grounded in actual bodily sensory-motor experience. Examples abound. Feeling good means feeling *up* and conversely, we can *fall* into a depression or into a bad mood. Understanding means *seeing* or *grasping*. We take *positions* and *hold* beliefs. People can be *warm* or *cold*, *dark* or *light*. We are *in* control or *out* of it. Desire is *hunger*. We have *gut feelings*. Neither need we conceive of metacognition in anything other than in embodied terms. The very idea of self-reflection is an example of embodied metaphorisation in which we hold up a mirror to ourselves. Maturana and Varela (1998, p.24), cited in Shapiro and Stoltz (2018, p.21) visualise the process of embodied learning as 'circular', as we 'reflect' on 'knowing how we know' through the 'act of turning back upon ourselves'. What they describe as a 'feedback loop' between mind and body is very similar to the definition of metacognition proposed by Flavell and others, except that it is no longer viewed as an executive function operating in some elevated sphere of the mind but is rather embedded in action and extended in relation to the learning environment. In a very real sense, we can observe a shift in the dominant metaphor of learning from an earlier information processing view of cognition, that is, the mind as a computer, to an ecological metaphor in which the mind is conceived as 'embodied, embedded, enacted and extended' (Gibbs, 2019, p.33).

A key feature of metaphors used to describe the process of learning is that they are strongly visual (*journey, garden, jigsaw, building, patchwork*) and embodied (*grasp, handle, survey, see, feel*). Such metaphors can act as '*bridges*' between initially abstract ideas, making them accessible via more familiar concepts (Muscari, 1988, cited in Thomas and McRobbie, 2001, p.225). This capacity to illuminate or embody abstract and seemingly unrelated ideas extends to practices such as academic reading and writing – hence the expressions to *build* an argument and to *scaffold* understanding which fall within constructivist metaphors. Such metaphors are linked together into systems of related analogies and associated vocabularies (Cook-Sather, 2003), many of which can be described as embodied, involving action. So, for example, we tend to use agrarian metaphors such as ideas being *planted*, minds being *cultivated*, the *roots* and *branches* of knowledge, or constructivist metaphors that refer to the *foundational* theories of a discipline – the *pillars* of wisdom around which competing arguments are *built*. Similarly, as we will discover in more detail later in the chapter, the metaphor of *mapping* a field of knowledge implicates related ideas such as *exploring, surveying, navigating*, and ultimately *positioning* oneself in relation to a wider *landscape* of ideas. These metaphors are so embedded in conventional language and academic discourse that, for the most part, they are not attended to directly, remaining an underutilised conceptual resource as well as a source of potential confusion if the underlying metaphor proves alien to and outside of one's own way of understanding. Reflecting on such terminology is important if we are to use metaphor in a principled manner to support students' learning.

A key question is precisely which features of a metaphor are perceived as salient. Lakoff and Johnson (1981) point out that metaphors, while capable of revealing a phenomenon in certain of its core elements, can just as easily hide others. They use the example of 'argument as a battle', which is commonly used to conceptualise the process of academic debate, together with the notion of participants attacking and defending their positions. This metaphor, they argue, can occlude the more cooperative features of academic debate. Similarly, if learning is a journey, which features of the source metaphor are chosen to carry the intended meaning? There are several possibilities: 1) a sense of progression, of a step-by-step movement from one place, or state, to another; 2) a sense of discovery, of actively exploring and searching for knowledge; 3) a sense of challenge when faced with difficulties and obstacles; 4) a sense of personal transformation, of gaining new perspectives and expanding or broadening one's horizons, and 5) a sense of moving towards and reaching a destination, of achieving one's goals. I use the term 'sense' deliberately to emphasise the embodied nature of the metaphor which draws on and, according to Jamrozik et al. (2016), simulates sensorimotor activity. One or more of these features could be selected and choices could differ between individuals, depending on their age, culture, and neurotype (Littlemore, 2019). It is also likely that features will be further adapted, rejected, or replaced by novel mappings that hold particular meaning for individuals and are therefore easier to relate to, remember, and communicate to others.

There is no such thing as a perfectly fitting metaphor, although metaphors can be adapted for different purposes. The interpretation of metaphor is contingent on cultural and linguistic contexts which are dynamic and changing (Cameron et al., 2009), and what is apt for one context can feel quite unsuitable for another. According to this view, metaphor use is embedded in dynamic systems of discourse and should always be understood in context. The metaphor of the teacher as a candle may be a familiar and conventionally acceptable metaphor in China but feel quite inappropriate to a German learner for whom the teacher is more likely to be compared to a shepherd (Zhou and Heineken, 2009). Their use as a teaching tool is therefore not unproblematic. Nevertheless, Cameron et al. (2009, p.2) describe 'the potential of metaphor to uncover people's ideas, attitudes and values'. Introducing metaphor in this way has the potential to yield important insights for students who struggle to frame their experiences within the wider academy. The elicitation and generation of novel metaphors to describe their experiences is a powerful vehicle, enabling students to reflect on themselves as learners. An approach that utilises metaphorisation can be empowering for students who are culturally diverse and, in our case, students with learning differences, if they have the freedom to choose and/or adapt source metaphors to aspects of their own experience.

Metaphor and motivation

There has been less discussion on the affective and motivational aspects of metaphor use and yet this may prove to be one of its most significant benefits. Dyllick, Dickhäuser, and Stahlberg (2021) point to its value in fostering a more resilient mindset in situations involving an 'unpleasant obligation', arguing that the process of creating personal metaphors, which they call 'Motto Goals', 'make activity-related incentives, such as positive affect, awareness of own resources and personal values more accessible' (p.4). The participants in their empirical study were university students who were first asked to identify an unpleasant obligation. These frequently consisted of academic tasks such as writing an assignment or time management. They were then shown a number of pictures and related verbal associations and asked to choose those they could positively identify with and use as a motivational resource to deal with the stated obligation. The pictures were taken from the Zurich Resource Model (ZRM) picture inventory by Krause and Storch (2010). The ZRM is a psychotherapeutic technique in which individuals learn to develop a positive mindset through the activation of conscious and unconscious mental resources. The pictures served as metaphorical vehicles used to target and trigger positive cognitive and emotional states in the students. Examples included a wolf, an eagle, a hammock on a beach, a hiker, a lotus flower, and a girl on a scooter. Dyllick, Dickhäuser, and Stahlberg's results demonstrated significant increases in students' motivation in the face of an unpleasant obligation compared to a control group who were given an unrelated transcription task. They hypothesise that this occurs as a result of the metaphor providing a 'guiding principle' (p.1), although it is not made clear precisely how this might operate. It is relevant to note that the experiment is conceptualised through the lens of embodied cognition, following on from Damasio (2006) who theorised and provided some empirical evidence for the presence of 'somatic markers' or bodily changes associated with motivational processes which are crucial in decision-making.

For Damasio and Carvalho (2013, p.143), 'feelings are mental experiences of body states'. The sense which mediates conscious awareness of such internal bodily states is called interoception and the related sense we have of our bodies in space is called proprioception. These internal senses are hypothesised to have a significant influence on emotional states and affective experiences, and it is no accident that they are often represented using metaphor, so, for example, we talk of 'stomachs churning' and 'hearts racing' and anxiety is correlated with bodily tension (Eccles et al., 2024). Differences in the regulation of these internal senses have been linked to learning differences, and it is important that they are included in any definition that alludes to multiple ways of knowing and making meaning, as is the case in the UDL framework (CAST, consideration 3.3). These theoretical considerations informed a small-scale pedagogical intervention that I conducted in 2023/24 to test the efficacy of metaphor, specifically meta-roles, as a motivational resource but also as an inclusive pedagogical strategy that students could use to reflect on themselves, become more interoceptively and proprioceptively aware, and apply this awareness in their approach to study and assessment.

Metaphor and learning differences

Autism

The long-held view that autistic individuals have a diminished ability to process figurative metaphor has recently been questioned and a more nuanced picture is emerging. Morsanyi, Stamenković, and Holyoak (2020) conclude that any empirical differences between autistic individuals and typically developing (TD) peers are dependent on factors such as age, language ability, and the type of task demands placed on participants. Kalandadze, Bambini, and Næss (2019), in a systematic review of studies investigating metaphor comprehension in autism, point to the determining influence of verbal complexity on how autistic and TD individuals perform relative to each other. Tasks that involve verbally explaining a metaphor tend to prove more challenging for autistic individuals. However, when matched on verbal ability, few differences in the ability to understand figurative metaphors have been detected (Kalandadze, 2018). Familiarity is another factor that can influence the understanding of figurative metaphor. Kalandadze, Bambini, and Næss (2019) hypothesised that autistic individuals should experience more problems processing novel metaphors than conventional ones given the greater cognitive demands involved in making inferences between a novel source metaphor and its target, which they refer to as 'inferential pragmatic ability' (p.1425). However, the results of their meta-analysis proved inconclusive. Indeed, quite the opposite picture emerges from a study by Kasirer and Mashal (2016), which suggests that although autistic children may experience greater difficulties in understanding the meaning of conventional metaphors than their TD peers, there are no differences in their ability to comprehend novel metaphors. Moreover, on a task requiring them to generate novel metaphors, autistic children were demonstrably more creative. The rather vague claim that this is due to their 'good associative abilities' (p.60) would benefit from more rigorous analysis in light of the research into analogical reasoning in autism mentioned earlier. Being able to infer relationships between two distinct domains or entities is a core feature of analogical reasoning. Few studies have gone beyond figurative metaphor to explore the understanding of conceptual metaphor. One study by Olofson et al. (2014) found no differences between autistic individuals and their TD peers in the comprehension of primary conceptual metaphors of the type 'more is up' or 'kind is warm'.

Three main hypotheses have been proposed to explain differences in the way in which autistic individuals process information: 1) 'weak central coherence', commonly described metaphorically as not being able to see the wood for the trees; 2) 'executive dysfunction', a deficit in higher-order thought processes such as planning and organising information; and 3) 'theory of mind', or difficulty in attributing mental states to others (Rajendran and Mitchell, 2007). These explanations tend towards a deficit perspective on autism, emphasising what is lacking in cognitive functioning relative to what is considered normal or typical. The concept of 'context blindness' (Vermeulen, 2015) is claimed to be a common feature linking all three hypotheses, manifesting as difficulties in integrating contextual information or seeing the 'big picture'. As a metaphor, however, 'blindness' can be limiting if it closes down investigation into the diverse ways in which autistic individuals perceive the particular contexts they are situated in. As is core to the message of this book, a less deficit-oriented perspective frames the perception of context not as an inability but as a preference for processing local rather than global information (Stuurman et al., 2019; Taylor and Vestergaard, 2022), which can be advantageous in certain circumstances and not in others. Critics point to the disembodied nature of such theories, arguing that learning is an inherently bodily, sensory-motor experience (De Jaegher, 2013; Jespersen and He, 2015). De Jaegher (2013) takes an enactive perspective, proposing that autism be conceptualised as a different form of embodiment in which autistic individuals literally *make sense* of the world and their interactions with others in non-typical ways. In this view, particular differences in autism such as restricted interests or preference for detail are grounded in perception and movement and what differs is how autistic individuals coordinate their actions and interactions with others. This calls forth the need for more first-hand phenomenological accounts of autistic experiences of being in the world. It also has pedagogical implications, as will be described later in the chapter.

Challenges will arise as a result of the situational demands placed on individuals as they negotiate real-world tasks; in the case of autistic students, this entails engaging with a variety of course assignments assessed against a set of pre-defined criteria that set the context of each assignment. Doing this successfully and avoiding the mental health issues that can beset autistic students in higher education (Gelbar, Smith, and Reichow, 2014) will inevitably require the deployment of top-down, global processing skills needed to manage and organise study time effectively, decide what is relevant, and plan to meet multiple deadlines. Autistic students may encounter difficulties if, as is likely, the learning environment has not been designed to account for and include a neurodiverse student body. Crucial to the argument put forward in this chapter, these are metacognitive skills that may be amenable to an approach utilising metaphorisation.

Dyslexia

As with autism, there are inconsistencies in the definition of dyslexia (Elliott and Grigorenko, 2014, cited in Knight, 2018) as well as a tendency to take a deficit approach, evident in the term itself. Stereotypical views centre around specific difficulties with reading often associated with deficiencies in the ability to map phonological (sound) to orthographic (written) features of language that occur unexpectedly and irrespective of general IQ (Warmington, Stothard, and Snowling, 2013; Snowling, Hulme, and Nation, 2020; Stevens, Hall, and Vaughn, 2022), leading to problems with word recognition and spelling. Potential causal factors have been discussed including weaknesses in executive functioning (EF) such as poor working memory or the ability to simultaneously hold and process temporarily stored phonological or visuo-spatial information, resulting in cognitive overload (Fischbach et al., 2014; Smith-Spark and Gordon, 2022).

Kasirer and Mashal (2016) argue that executive functioning is central to the comprehension and generation of metaphor and could underlie the difficulties dyslexic individuals experience, evidenced in a supposed tendency to take figurative language literally. On the contrary, their investigation into metaphor comprehension and generation in dyslexic adolescents and adults found no stable differences between dyslexic individuals and their TD peers in metaphor comprehension; indeed, dyslexic adults demonstrated greater creativity in the generation of novel metaphors, which the authors – cautiously, given the lack of research – link to a possible advantage in fluid intelligence and executive functioning (p.101). Although they were unable to ascertain which particular capacities underlie the creativity involved in generating novel connections between apparently unrelated concepts, we could surmise a role for the kinds of analogical reasoning abilities described by Morsanyi, Stamenković, and Holyoak (2020). The ability to comprehend metaphor is theorised to occur alongside parallel developments in verbal intelligence, working memory, and analogical reasoning which mature sequentially, depending on chronological and mental age. Beginning as early as age three, young children seem to understand action-based metaphors and this capacity increases until in early adolescence they are able to understand and explain the links between a complex source metaphor and its target (Willinger et al., 2019). Could analogical reasoning, or metaphorisation as I have referred to it, be an area of relative strength as it is for autistic individuals? It is important to note that much of the research in this area centres on the comprehension of figurative as opposed to conceptual metaphor, especially the types of ontological and orientational metaphor that Lakoff and Johnson (1981) argue shape our experience of being in the world.

A pedagogical intervention using 'meta-roles'

Metaphors shape the discourses and practices that take place within educational institutions and are a determining influence on their ethos. They frame our views of knowledge and learning and yet there is seldom any attempt to clearly delineate or map their associations; they often remain fuzzy unless brought under scrutiny, functioning as assumptions that are rarely questioned. Take, for example, the production metaphor of education which foregrounds economic growth, viewing knowledge as a commodity that can be traded in the marketplace and manifesting in an assembly line model of teaching that conceptualises students as products and assessment as quality control. Cook-Sather (2003, p.6) calls this a 'Root Metaphor' and contrasts it with another – 'education as cure' – which casts students as ill or in need of treatment, assessment as diagnosis, and the teacher as therapist. To these, she proposes an alternative – 'education as translation' – that gives prominence to the ability of students to continually remake themselves. More pointedly, she argues that students be given the analytical tools to reflect on their learning, extending an invitation to teachers to engage in dialogue with students to find and create new metaphors. The following section describes my attempt to do just this, using metaphorisation as a metacognitive strategy to unearth university students' understanding of themselves as learners, their approach to assessments, and the challenges to study they perceive. As discussed above, the visual and kinaesthetic properties of metaphor afford additional sensory scaffolding of otherwise abstract academic concepts. Used consciously and systematically, they can provide a meaningful framework that students are able to use to reflect upon and relate to these concepts. These have relevance for students with learning differences seeking a means to engage more fully with the academy. According to UDL, the provision of options for self-regulation and the development of self-assessment and reflection are necessary prerequisites for maintaining motivation (CAST, consideration 9.3).

There is a clear need for more qualitative research into the subjective experience of students as they progress through higher education, and the use of metaphor is, as I have argued, a powerful vehicle for understanding the diverse ways in which students conceptualise this. The intervention described here is adapted from Dyllick, Dickhäuser, and Stahlberg (2021) and their exploration into how the identification of personal metaphors can act to increase students' motivation and sense of personal autonomy. Unlike the 'motto goals' employed in their research, which are represented in visual symbols, the metaphors utilised in this study are represented in fully embodied roles or 'meta-roles', embedded in sensory-motor schemata, in the manner described by Gibbs (2019). The intervention aims to provide evidence for the argument put forward in this chapter that eliciting and interacting with such embodied metaphors has the potential to evoke metacognitive and self-regulated learning, and it offers some proof of the efficacy of this approach as an inclusive teaching and learning tool for students with learning differences.

The move from using metaphor represented by abstract symbols to metaphor embodied in a role or 'meta-role' is significant. Ontologically, one is positioned with**in** a role, with a perspective that is simultaneously inside-out and outside-in; one is both self and other. Occupying, inhabiting, and adjusting to a role – that is to say, playing a role – necessitates a degree of internal monitoring or self-regulation that scholars of early learning have argued is central to the development of social-emotional learning and metacognitive awareness (Robson, 2010; Bredikyte and Brandisauskiene, 2023). Performing a meta-role creates an additional space for self-reflection as the source role is applied to the target activity. Role-play has been used across disciplines as diverse as nursing and business and for a variety of purposes such as improving communication skills, appreciating different perspectives, and understanding complex concepts (Rao and Stupans, 2012).

The intervention encompassed two distinct groups of university students: five participants officially diagnosed with specific learning difficulties (SpLD), such as autism or dyslexia (LD), and five participants without a diagnosed learning difference (WLD). This intentional diversity in participant demographics was designed to capture a broad spectrum of perspectives and experiences. The intervention methodology comprised three distinct stages, intended to elicit participants' reflections on their academic practices through the lens of embodied metaphors. These acted as data collection points.

Stage One: Participants were initially prompted to articulate their approach to studying, their experience of being a student, and the main challenges they face through the creation of their own novel metaphors. They were given three days to complete written responses to the following questions and prompts.

Q1: When you think about your approach to study and how you prepare for your assignments, what would you compare it with?

Approaching and preparing for an assignment is like...

Q2: How would you describe your experience of being a student?

Being a student is like being a ...

Q3: What are the most challenging or unpleasant obligations that you associate with studying and learning?

Stage Two: Drawing upon visual representations of 11 different meta-roles, each accompanied by a brief text summarising key elements of the role, participants were invited to select one meta-role they positively associated with and to engage in a week-long reflection period, during which they contemplated the applicability of their chosen meta-role to academic study. They were encouraged to take notes on their experiences over the week and to send these to the lead investigator prior to taking part in a brief interview.

The meta-roles

Explorer: Embarking on an intellectual expedition venturing into uncharted territory to discover new knowledge and insights and charting your course through the academic landscape.

Navigator (sailor): Plotting a clear course of action, mapping out the main points and direction of your essay to reach your destination effectively. Charting your academic journey, discovering insights, and navigating through challenges.

Architect: Designing the blueprint of your academic work, meticulously planning and organising your ideas and arguments to construct a solid and coherent structure.

Detective: Investigating the mysteries of your subject matter, scrutinising evidence and information to uncover hidden truths, and solving the puzzles that academic challenges present.

Pilot: Navigating your academic journey like a skilled aviator ensuring a smooth flight through coursework assignments and exams and making necessary course corrections along the way.

Athlete: Approaching your studies like a dedicated athlete, setting goals, training regularly, and constantly striving to improve your academic performance and skills.

Gardener: Cultivating your intellectual garden, planting seeds of knowledge, nurturing your ideas, and witnessing the blossoming of your understanding over time.

Conductor: Orchestrating the elements of your academic work, harmonising research analysis and writing to create a cohesive and well-structured composition.

Explorer of the Inner Self: Delving into the depths of self-awareness, reflecting on your motivations, learning style, and personal growth to enhance your academic journey.

Sculptor: Shaping your ideas and arguments with artistic precision, moulding and refining your academic work until it becomes a polished and impactful creation.

Weaver: Interlacing your ideas and arguments, creating a tapestry of coherent and interconnected thoughts.

Stage Three: The reflection period culminated in a short interview wherein participants were given the opportunity to articulate their experiences and any insights gained through the metaphorical exploration. Guided by a series of open-ended questions, participants reflected on the impact of their chosen metaphor on their approach to studies, emotional experiences, and overall perspective on learning.

Results (Stage One)

Approaching an assignment is like …

The metaphors students used to describe their approach to assignments varied in novelty from the almost literal, 'a simple chore', to the more conventional 'following a recipe, gathering ingredients' to the highly novel:

> 'collecting silt and sand from across multiple rivers then sifting/washing it, picking out potential items of interest (metals, artifacts)' (WLD)

The target – 'preparing for an assignment' – evoked strongly embodied source metaphors, embedded in action scenarios such as 'getting ready for a performance' and 'diving and exploring the deep seas'. Metaphors differed substantially in the level of detail used to map their associations to the target, from the rather blunt 'preparing for war' to 'packing a suitcase' in which ideas are laid out like outfits before being packed neatly into the suitcase or essay, removing those that do not fit, with paragraphs becoming 'packing cubes' into which ideas are placed.

Students used metaphor to express their affective responses. Beginning an assignment or preparing for an exam is compared to 'exploring the bottom of the sea. It is quiet, peaceful and interesting' but as the deadline approaches,

> 'you start feeling like you are running out of oxygen so you start swimming upwards and for a few moments you get a feeling of intense anxiety' (WLD).

'Submitting an assignment feels like coming up for air ... there are a few seconds of pure joy and relief ... like breathing is the best feeling in the world ... but then life goes on and you forget all about it' (WLD).

Students with learning differences were more likely to emphasise the challenges associated with preparing for an assignment, evoking feelings of uncertainty and isolation, using metaphors such as 'being chased by a barking dog' and 'being on a secret mission'.

Being a student is like being a ...

The second prompt was framed in such a way that students were deliberately led to choose a role that they perceived to be analogous to their own and with which they could identify – what I refer to as a meta-role. This was in part to prepare them for the next stage of the intervention in which students were invited to select such a role from a pre-defined list. The range of metaphors that students expressed varied in novelty. Some of them, such as explorer, navigator (sailor), and conductor, can be more easily mapped to the process of studying. Indeed, they all featured in the next stage of the intervention, even though participants had no prior knowledge of this.

The process of studying and learning has conventionally been compared to a journey of some kind, and this was evident in students' use of the metaphor to describe the trajectory they were on. Students also used the prompt to reflect on their emotional responses which coalesced around the theme of success and failure and their attendant expectations and anxieties, expressed using spatial metaphors:

'A cliff walker. The journey is hard but the views are constantly beautiful. You are in awe of what you see all the time, but it is also dangerous and even though you know it is very unlikely that you will fall, there is still that fear, that you could fall or that the trail will end right back where it started' (WLD).

'A person sitting in a roller coaster. There are always going to be ups and downs. It is important to embrace all these twists and turns and make sure you enjoy with your hands in the air' (WLD).

'An explorer with no set destination and just a vague direction while constantly trying not to dwell at attractions along the way or going in circles accidentally' (LD).

Once again, there is a suggestion that students with learning differences are faced with a more challenging set of circumstances:

'Being on a boat out at sea. It can be fun and tranquil with many exciting things to see and enjoy, but it also changes drastically with a dangerous storm coming, being drowned with guilt and potential failure' (LD).

'In my perspective, it is a lifeline or a bridge between the life I want and survival. A safe haven of knowledge from past negative childhood experiences from home' (LD).

'Being a student is like being an alien on earth – always slightly unsure if you're doing things correctly/enough, but everyone else seems to know what they are doing' (LD).

What are the most challenging or unpleasant obligations that you associate with studying and learning?

The predominant challenge for most students is how to manage their time effectively. Students with learning differences tended to express this using more emotive terms. Timed assessments were perceived to be particularly stressful, as was the difficulty of concentrating for long periods of time, leading to feelings of guilt. There were also feelings of jealously and irritation towards students without learning differences who seem to be able to find time to relax. The fear of failure was strongly in evidence.

'Anything with a strict time limit capping your knowledge or creativity is both unnaturally stifling and causes a great deal of pressure' (LD).

'It comes with other emotions such as jealousy, and anger sometimes, when we compare our feelings to other people's successes and achievements … the constant rushing and needing to fill a certain image, creates pain in the heart, of what our lives would be if, we would be organising ourselves more, or know to use that precious time to get a step closer to our dreams' (LD).

'Sitting down and concentrating for long periods, I get very fidgety and uncomfortable. Feeling as though nothing is ever done – you could always be doing more so it makes it hard to relax/do other things without feeling guilty' (LD).

Results (Stage Two)

The navigator/mariner was the most popular choice, selected by three students. The pilot and the conductor were each chosen twice. The remaining three choices were the explorer, the sculptor, and the explorer of the inner self. I will restrict my analysis and evaluation to the former three meta-roles as these were the most commonly chosen. In each case, I will offer some practical suggestions for how each meta-role could be introduced into the classroom or into a tutorial setting.

The navigator

One student (LD), who disclosed that they had ADHD, chose to focus on the image of a sailing boat, positioning themselves as captain of the boat and the surrounding ocean as the mysterious and unpredictable situations they are faced with. Question arise about who to invite onto the boat, who the crew will be, and whether they can be trusted. The boat represents safety but also a sense of direction, of moving forward with their life.

'A boat is like our own little world and the mysteries that we encounter in the ocean, I feel it's endless … and being directed by different people gives us a sort of destination … having this kind of sense of direction is very important'.

'It's like our own personal place and some people might not understand it'.

'Who to invite to our boats are the ones who are going to also take care of it in a way, because they are the ones who are going to support it'.

This student chose to focus on the boat as a means of survival. They compared themselves to:

'Someone being stranded on an island who had to build her boat from scratch, without the help of her parents and leaving home to a safer place to be'.

The image offers a sense of self-validation, helping them to understand their ADHD:

'The disabilities of neurodiversity would be a sort of new technology in the boat, which no one can read, it would require an expert of myself to be able to manoeuvre this boat'.

'It's not fair to compare myself to other people and what's the point of me designing another boat … I just have this boat. I built it myself'.

Another student reflected in particular on the planning involved in navigating.

'I feel that the role of navigator describes the kind of work ethic that I have and how I cope with the, often intense, workloads at university … I plan out my routes quite meticulously … planning my days, planning my essay outlines' (WLD).

Interestingly, rather than focusing exclusively on the navigator metaphor, this student described how thinking metaphorically, or metaphorisation, had led to new, more productive ways of visualising their assessments – for example, through using the metaphor of a battle or a gladiatorial contest:

'I feel like if I think about it, like for example a battle, something to overcome … I have a lot more resilience … to win rather than to succumb to the lion of temptation, it's sort of rooting for the gladiator to win' (WLD).

Another student/navigator chose to focus on the parallels between the sea/ocean and the unpredictability of their living circumstances or study context. Reflecting on the metaphor was positive in that it gave them another perspective with which to view this relationship, one that offered a greater sense of autonomy or self-control. As with other participants, it did not appear to have materially changed their practice; rather, it enabled them to see more clearly what this practice consisted of, confirming its validity to them:

'If you're a navigator, if you're on the sea, you're very much controlled by the elements. Sometimes a navigator will get blown off course by strong winds or get stuck with no wind at all … You're pretty much subjected to what the weather is like. Looking at the forecast is like preparation' (WLD).

'It didn't change anything. It made me more aware of what I do now, actually putting in perspective how I study or how I approach all of my assignments and … it made me way more OK with it because it works for me. It felt more purposeful' (LD).

USING THE NAVIGATOR META-ROLE TO FURTHER ACADEMIC PRACTICE

The examples above illustrate how students, by inhabiting the role of a navigator, were able to gain fresh perspectives on themselves as learners and on their attitudes and approaches to studying and learning. Stepping into the navigator meta-role is inherently empowering and enabling, positing the user as in control, purposefully guiding their ship through a changing and uncertain landscape or carefully plotting a course through existing bodies of knowledge and research. This has therapeutic as well as academic value for students with learning differences who can feel *lost* when confronted by the often complex demands of assessments. Tutors could introduce the meta-role early in an undergraduate or graduate course, ideally during an *orientation* week, and invite students to begin applying the analogy to their studies. In particular, tutors can use the navigator meta-role to help students orientate themselves within the often unfamiliar conceptual landscape of a field or discipline.

Navigation is a powerful conceptual metaphor that is implicit whenever we encounter a new field of knowledge and are tasked with searching for information within it. So, for example, we talk of *surveying* literature, *locating* sources, and the *scope* and *breadth* of research. Tutors can point out that the process of *mapping* an environment – whether physical or informational – enables us to navigate purposefully through it, whether in search of food, shelter, or understanding. In doing so, we learn to distinguish differences and similarities between ecological, geological, or informational features of that environment.

Unpacking the analogy further, tutors can highlight the most significant features of the conceptual landscape – the big ideas, relationships, and patterns (CAST, consideration 3.2) that are key to classifying it, as well as pointing out the changing and often contested boundaries where opinion divides and territorial claims proliferate. The analogy with scale is crucial here as an oft-cited characteristic of both autism and dyslexia; it concerns differences in the way information is synthesised into coherent and meaningful wholes, and a map is a visual representation of the environment at different scales. Each increase in scale entails a corresponding decrease in detail but a gain in overall perspective. Focusing attention on these conceptual analogies can help raise awareness of how students with learning differences move from a 'big picture' understanding to one that is more detailed and vice versa.

One of the greatest challenges many students face in academic writing is to create a coherent *line* of argument that takes into account and discusses the views of a diverse range of sources. This is often referred to as 'academic *voice*' and serves to clarify the writer's position in relation to these sources. Assessments frequently require students to *develop a position* or to *take a stance* in relation to the wider literature on a subject. This is often met with consternation from students who find the concept difficult to grasp. Using metaphorisation, it is rendered immediate, concrete, and graspable since in navigating any environment, whether physical or informational, we position ourselves in relation to it and to the particular perspectives or views that are present or that are being expressed. Tutors can use the navigator meta-role to assist students in reflecting on the route that they are taking through the literature. Ask them to calculate how long it will take to travel a certain distance, what the challenges might be, and the best route to take. Perhaps they need to adjust the pace and volume of their reading so that it fits with the time that they have available. Remind them that, alongside this route, they need to lay down an argument that is easily navigable by others. This means accurately signposting the structure of their writing.

As in many other instances, these metaphors (line, route, steps, position, move, stance, signpost) are already present in the lexicon applied to academic literacies; the question becomes how to use them in a purposeful and principled fashion. The use of spatial and orientational metaphors is implicit in Swales and Feak's (1994) CARS (Creating a Research Space) model, which proposes a series of *steps* by which students can *arrive* at a good research question. It begins with 'establishing a research *territory*' – understanding the *background* to the topic and identifying *gaps* in knowledge before 'establishing a *niche*' – *positioning* oneself in relation to the topic The task is how to utilise students' visual and kinaesthetic skills in a coordinated and systematic fashion to help build knowledge and understanding. Inviting students to inhabit a meta-role and apply the analogy to their own academic practice in novel ways, what I have termed metaphorisation, is a pedagogical approach that operationalises Gibbs' (2019) view of conceptual metaphor as embodied, embedded, enacted, and extended. As a metacognitive strategy, it can be especially useful for students with learning differences, particularly those identifying as autistic, maximising the transfer and generalisation of knowledge as laid out in the UDL guidelines (CAST, consideration 3.4), which expressly recommend the use of metaphor and analogy.

ACTIVITY IDEAS

Academic map-making

Students could be provided with whiteboards or flipboard paper and asked to draw their essay plan as a journey, starting by identifying the main destination (their thesis or main argument) and mapping out key stops along the way, such as critical points from various sources. They mark these stops as places where they will engage with each source's viewpoint, noting their position on each. Other students could be encouraged to question them further.

Concept mapping

Students could be asked to create a map representing key concepts and ideas with lines between them representing their relationships. They could do this together using cards and string. I have used this activity to help students understand the concept of 'planetary health' by asking them to draw the relationships between environmental problems and health issues, represented as two concentric circles one inside the other.

Value lines

To make the concept of taking a stance or position in academic writing tangible, arrange the classroom to represent a continuum, where one end represents strong agreement and the other strong disagreement with a given source. Students stand along this continuum based on their stance in response to a specific claim and then explain their position aloud. They move as their views or interpretations evolve during the discussion.

The pilot

The pilot might be considered an aerial version of the navigator meta-role. The following quotes represent and embody the changing, often unpredictable circumstances to which one has to adapt and the resources one has available to do so successfully. Students who chose this meta-role described a sense of being *on top of things*. Monitoring progress is a key metacognitive strategy that is embodied in the pilot meta-role. In a novel twist of the metaphor, the guiding role played by academic staff, but also the external demands placed upon students, are represented by a control tower.

> 'I imagine turbulence and so then you say I can still stay on top of things. In other words, I can because pilots I think, go above the turbulence, don't they?'. (WLD)

> 'It represents well the limited control I have over certain variables (for a pilot, it would be the weather, visibility, mechanical issues with the plane, etc. For me and my studies, it would be multiple deadlines at once, choice of topics, my ability to focus on that specific day, energy levels etc.) but still making the most out of it, changing course of actions, prioritising different things, choosing to make sacrifices in order to make it through' (LD).

> 'Being a pilot is stressful, but if you're doing things right, if feels like you're in control and feels like you're actually managing and you're flying and not crashing … It feels like continuously monitoring how much progress I've been making and it feels like consistency' (LD).

> 'I guess it would be like trying to fly the plane, but also constantly having the tower asking you to do extra stuff on top. You're trying to not crash, but you also have someone else telling you things when you don't feel they're important' (LD).

USING THE PILOT META-ROLE TO FURTHER ACADEMIC PRACTICE

A key characteristic of the pilot meta-role is the aerial perspective it affords. This relates to the process of mapping and the analogy with scale discussed above. The pilot embodies the key metacognitive strategy of monitoring progress, and it does so in relation to others in the learning environment. The well-worn phrase 'a bird's eye view' describes this process of awareness raising. As a visual and kinaesthetic method of self-assessment, it will appeal to students with learning differences, offering a vehicle they can use to enhance reflection on their progress – for example, in successfully following the requirements of an assessment rubric. The need for differentiated models of self-assessment is outlined in the UDL (CAST, consideration 6.4).

Inviting students to engage in metaphorisation using the pilot meta-role is a good starting point when students are beginning a course. What do they need to prepare for take-off? For example, building momentum by establishing a study routine, checking the flight plan or course requirements, listening to the control tower or seeking feedback from tutors, checking altitude, or assessing their level of understanding. Tutors can use sentence prompts such as 'navigating turbulence is like …' or 'preparing for landing is like …' to encourage students to reason analogically using the meta-role.

This can have particular resonance for students with learning differences who may experience difficulties in visualising the full scope of a course. The metaphor affords a clear step-by-step sequence using a familiar concept that helps break down a course or assessment into manageable parts, ensuring that critical details are not missed. These can act as metacognitive prompts: for example, 'monitor fuel levels' means keep track of your energy and motivation, or 'listen to the control tower' reminds students to seek feedback. This can be particularly beneficial for those who struggle with organisation and consistency. Linking abstract academic concepts to tangible actions can aid memory and understanding. In addition, the meta-role creates a common language that can be used by tutors, students, and peers to facilitate communication and support.

Tutors can also introduce the pilot metaphor by exploring how completing a written assignment can be likened to piloting a flight from take-off to landing. They can emphasise how each stage of writing (planning, drafting, revising, rewriting) corresponds to specific phases of a flight. For example, setting the tone and direction for an assignment can be likened to reaching a cruising altitude, and preparing for landing to writing a conclusion and ensuring all parts of the assignment are complete and coherent. Tutors could set a group activity in which students share their flight plans with each other or conduct 'check-ins' during which they discuss their progress and any challenges they are facing. Transforming abstract concepts into concrete actions makes it easier for students with learning differences to visualise their progress, anticipate challenges, and stay focused on their goals.

ACTIVITY IDEAS

Flight plan creation

Provide each student with a *flight plan template* where they outline key stages for the assignment (take-off, cruising altitude, turbulence, descent, and landing). Each section includes action items such as *consult the control tower* (seek feedback), *monitor fuel levels* (manage energy), and *adjust altitude* (evaluate understanding). In groups, students share their flight plans, discussing any foreseeable *turbulence* they anticipate and how they might navigate it.

Progress tracking dashboard

Set up a digital or physical *dashboard* for students to track their progress. Sections of the dashboard might include *fuel levels* (energy and motivation), *altitude* (understanding), *turbulence* (challenges), and *feedback received* (input from tutors or peers). Students update the dashboard weekly or at key project stages, reflecting on where they stand and any adjustments needed, and then share this with others.

Control tower feedback exchange

Set up a *control tower* where peers or tutors act as air traffic controllers. Each student pilot checks in with the control tower during specific stages of an assignment to seek advice or reassurance. Peers can give feedback on each other's work or help problem-solve, simulating a real-time guidance experience.

The conductor

Two students with learning differences chose to take on the role of conductor. One student, who disclosed that they were autistic, applied it, quite specifically, to the writing of lab reports – a regular form of assessment on their course. Autism, as we have discussed, involves a preference for the processing of local rather than global information. This can be disadvantageous when planning and organising an assignment such as this one that requires students to balance the focus of their attention in order to achieve meaningful cohesion. Interacting with the conductor meta-role seemed to have helped this student to reflect metacognitively on how to arrange the sections of the report into a cohesive whole:

> 'It felt like I was more in control, because obviously a conductor can put everything together and choose what does what and the person who's overseeing everything … what sections of an assignment you add to or take away from.'

> 'I thought about how in order to get to the final composition (the report), I would need each part of the orchestra (the sections of the report), so applying the metaphor means thinking about how to get the different instrumentalists to work as a whole orchestra … it helped me to break down both the bigger things as well as see more of an overall bigger picture.'

A second student/conductor, who disclosed that they were dyslexic, expressed a similar idea, applying it, in particular, to their perceived responsibilities as a PhD candidate. Once again, interacting with the meta-role does not appear to have changed their existing practice but has helped them to reflect upon it. The switch to a metaphorical perspective has a direct impact on how they approach and engage affectively with their studies.

> 'The guiding aspect of it … the idea of taking a lot of different parts together to make a greater whole … the feeling of juggling a lot of different pieces and a lot of different parts and importantly working with a lot of different people.'

> 'Because I am doing my PhD, oftentimes I'm helping … giving advice to master's students or I'm demonstrating for undergraduates or invigilating … I think the conductor fits that guiding role.'

> 'I don't think it's made a huge difference with how I approach it as much as it does how I think about it … it did help me think about things in a different way which made it not feel as pressing or as intense'.

USING THE CONDUCTOR META-ROLE TO FURTHER ACADEMIC PRACTICE

To conduct – from the Latin *conductus*, meaning to lead and to bring together – points to both cognitive and social dimensions of learning: the synthesis of knowledge required to interpret a musical score as well as the collaboration with peers, exemplified in the leading of an orchestra. The conductor meta-role enacts and embodies the notion, hinted at in Dyllick, Dickhäuser, and Stahlberg's (2021) study, that the utility of metaphor lies in its potential as a guiding principle. As with the navigator and the pilot, it puts the user in control. The conductor must balance the dynamics of a musical performance just as a student must prioritise the various tasks involved in pursuing a course or completing an assessment. Students with learning differences, in particular, may struggle with seeing the 'big picture' or managing details. The conductor meta-role offers a clear, visual, and kinaesthetic framework that makes the abstract process of academic study more concrete and accessible, enabling them to direct their attention and orchestrate their efforts towards a successful outcome. Students in the study tended to meld the conductor with the related role of composer. Both are capable of mirroring the academic process of synthesising information and ideas into a meaningful whole but do so in different ways. The composer works alone to create a piece of music, while the conductor's role is to communicate it publicly.

Tutors can invite students to imagine themselves as the conductor of an orchestra, where their essay is the musical piece that they are directing. Each section of the essay represents a different instrument or section of the orchestra, and it is their task to bring them together harmoniously. In order to do so effectively, they will first need to carefully read and analyse the musical score or essay prompt. Students can be encouraged to reflect on the tempo or pace of their writing, ensuring that they do not fall behind or end up rushing. A key skill is balancing the dynamics of a piece, the loudness and softness of the music, or the emphasis placed on different points, arguments, or pieces of evidence. It will be important to avoid overemphasis, checking that no section of the orchestra overwhelms the rest and that the key themes or main arguments are emphasised.

Tutors can also point out the similarities between the tuning of instruments prior to a performance and the process of gathering and organising notes and sources, making sure that they are 'in tune'. Planning an essay usually consists of creating outlines, and this can be likened to rehearsing with each section of an orchestra separately before coordinating them together harmoniously. Preparing and conducting the final performance will involve 'fine-tuning', ensuring that every detail is attended to.

Students with learning differences may find it challenging to maintain focus and concentration and this can negatively impact their ability to manage their time effectively, leading to increased feelings of anxiety (Clouder et al., 2020). Inviting students to reflect on the conductor meta-role early in a course can encourage them to consider how they will deal with the various demands placed on their time while still maintaining a sense of well-being.

ACTIVITY IDEAS

Orchestral manoeuvres: synthesising sources

Students can form *chamber orchestras* of three or four members. Before meeting, each student should choose one source related to the topic under investigation. They should annotate the source, summarise it in one or two paragraphs, and outline how they intend to use it. In small groups, students gather their summaries and begin to *orchestrate them*. They can discuss how the different arguments, evidence, and perspectives can be woven together into a single coherent narrative for their project. Using a large poster or digital tool, they can visually map how each person's summary, or *score*, relates to the others, noting overlaps, or *harmonies*, and contrasting viewpoints, or *dissonances*.

Tuning sources

Students review their sources in pairs, acting as *tuning partners*. They assess the currency, relevance, authority, accuracy, and purpose of each source, using a checklist of questions that determine author credentials, publication date, peer review status, potential bias, and the relationship of the source to the research or assignment question. Each pair discusses their evaluations as if tuning an instrument.

Conducting presentations

When rehearsing for a group presentation, each student identifies their specific role for the presentation, such as introductory speaker, section 1, 2, 3 speaker, or concluding speaker. Together, they outline how each *section* of their presentation will flow from one speaker to the next. For each rehearsal, a group leader or conductor is appointed to coordinate their timing and transitions to ensure a smooth presentation.

Conclusion

This chapter has examined conceptual metaphor theory and proposed ways in which it can be used to develop the academic practice of students both with and without learning differences. It builds on the work of Wallbank (2022) and others who argue for more inclusive approaches to education, based on the principles of Universal Design for Learning (UDL) and of assessment *as* learning. These take into account the challenges faced by an increasingly neurodiverse community of learners while also recognising the strengths they bring to the learning environment. The use of visual and kinaesthetic pedagogies is one example in which metaphor, in both its figurative and conceptual forms, can play a crucial role. Indeed, it has been the contention of this chapter that the practice of metaphorisation, or the application of analogical reasoning to understand academic practices, can help to develop core metacognitive skills of planning, monitoring, and reflection. The chapter has introduced the concept of meta-roles, which offers a visual and embodied approach designed to scaffold students' learning. This can be particularly beneficial for students with learning differences.

References

Ben-David, A., and Zohar, A., (2009) 'Contribution of Meta-strategic Knowledge to Scientific Inquiry Learning', *International Journal of Science Education*, 31:12, pp.1657–1682. Available from: www.tandfonline.com/doi/full/10.1080/09500690802162762 (Accessed: 3 March 2024).

Bowdle, B. F., and Gentner, D., (2005) 'The Career of Metaphor', *Psychological Review*, 112:1, pp.193–216. Available from: www.jstor.org/stable/43904133 (Accessed: 2 February 2023).

Bredikyte, M., and Brandisauskiene, A., (2023) 'Pretend Play as the Space for Development of Self-regulation: Cultural-historical Perspective', *Frontiers in Psychology*, 14: 1186512. Available from: www.frontiersin.org/journals/psychology/articles/10.3389/fpsyg.2023.1186512/full (Accessed: 10 February 2023).

Cameron, L., Maslen, R., Todd, Z., Maule, J., Stretton, P., and Stanley, N., (2009) 'The Discourse Dynamics Approach to Metaphor and Metaphor-Led Discourse Analysis', *Metaphor and Symbol*, 24:2, pp.63–89. Available from: www.tandfonline.com/doi/full/10.1080/10926480902830821 (Accessed: 19 May 2022).

CAST, (2024) 'Universal Design for Learning Guidelines version 3.0'. Available from: https://udlguidelines.cast.org (Accessed: 2 July 2023).

Clark, I., (2012) 'Formative Assessment: Assessment Is for Self-regulated Learning', *Educational Psychology Review*, 24:2, pp.205–249. Available from: https://link.springer.com/article/10.1007/s10648-011-9191-6 (Accessed: 17 June 2024).

Clouder, L., Karakus, M., Cinotti, A., Ferreyra, M. V., Fierros, G. A., and Rojo, P., (2020) 'Neurodiversity in Higher Education: A Narrative Synthesis', *Higher Education*, 80:4, pp.757–778. Available from: https://link.springer.com/article/10.1007/s10734-020-00513-6 (Accessed 25 October 2024).

Cook-Sather, A., (2003) 'Movements of Mind: The Matrix, Metaphors, and Re-imagining Education', *Teachers College Record (1970)*, 105:6, pp.946–977. Available from: https://journals.sagepub.com/doi/10.1111/1467-9620.00274 (Assessed: 2 September 2023).

Cooperrider, K., and Núñez, R., (2016) 'How We Make Sense of Time', *Scientific American*, pp.38–43. Available from: www.scientificamerican.com/article/how-we-make-sense-of-time/ (Accessed: 15 July 2024).

Damasio, A. R., (2006) *Descartes' Error: Emotion, Reason and the Human Brain*. London: Vintage.

Damasio, A. R., and Carvalho, G. B., (2013) 'The Nature of Feelings: Evolutionary and Neurobiological Origins', *Nature Reviews. Neuroscience*, 14:2, pp.143–152. Available from: www.nature.com/articles/nrn3403 (Accessed: 12 May 2022).

De Jaegher, H., (2013) 'Embodiment and Sense-making in Autism', *Frontiers in Integrative Neuroscience*, 7, pp.15–15. Available from: www.frontiersin.org/journals/integrative-neuroscience/articles/10.3389/fnint.2013.00015/full (Accessed: 14 January 2022).

Dent, A. L., and Koenka, A. C., (2016) 'The Relation Between Self-Regulated Learning and Academic Achievement Across Childhood and Adolescence: A Meta-Analysis', *Educational Psychology Review*, 28:3, pp.425–474. Available from: https://link.springer.com/article/10.1007/s10648-015-9320-8 (Accessed: 3 October 2024).

Donker, A. S., de Boer, H., Kostons, D., van Ewijk, C. C. D., and van der Werf, M. P. C., (2014) 'Effectiveness of Learning Strategy Instruction on Academic Performance: A Meta-analysis', *Educational Research Review*, 11, pp.1–26. Available from: www.sciencedirect.com/science/article/pii/S1747938X13000420?via%3Dihub (Accessed: 27 November 2022).

Dyllick, T. H., Dickhäuser, O., and Stahlberg, D., (2021) 'Personal Metaphors as Motivational Resources: Boosting Anticipated Incentives and Feelings of Vitality Through a Personal Motto-Goal', *Frontiers in Psychology*, 12:566215. Available from: www.frontiersin.org/journals/psychology/articles/10.3389/fpsyg.2021.566215/full (Accessed: 22 December 2024).

Earl, L. M., (2012) 'Assessment of Learning, for Learning, and as Learning', in *Assessment as Learning: Using Classroom Assessment to Maximise Student Learning*. London: Sage.

Eccles, J. A., Quadt, L, Garfinkel, S. N., and Critchley, H. D., (2024) 'A Model Linking Emotional Dysregulation in Neurodivergent People to the Proprioceptive Impact of Joint Hypermobility', *Philosophical Transactions of the Royal Society of London. Series B. Biological Sciences*, 379:1908. Available from: https://royalsocietypublishing.org/doi/10.1098/rstb.2023.0247 (Accessed: 4 July 2024).

Fischbach, A., Konen, T., Rietz, C. S., and Hasselhorn, M., (2014) 'What Is Not Working in Working Memory of Children with Literacy Disorders? Evidence from a Three-Year-Longitudinal Study', *Reading and Writing*, 27:2, pp.267–286. Available from: https://link.springer.com/article/10.1007/s11145-013-9444-5 (Accessed: 15 June 2022).

Flavell, J. H., (1979) 'Metacognition and Cognitive Monitoring: A New Area of Cognitive-developmental Inquiry', *The American Psychologist*, 34:10, pp.906–911. Available from: https://psycnet.apa.org/doiLanding?doi=10.1037%2F0003-066X.34.10.906 (Accessed: 17 May 2024).

Gelbar, N. W., Smith, I., and Reichow, B., (2014) 'Systematic Review of Articles Describing Experience and Supports of Individuals with Autism Enrolled in College and University Programs', *Journal of Autism and Developmental Disorders*, 44:10, pp.2593–2601. Available from: https://link.springer.com/article/10.1007/s10803-014-2135-5 (Accessed: 18 November 2023).

Gibbs, R. W., Costa Lima, P. L., and Francozo, E., (2004) 'Metaphor Is Grounded in Embodied Experience', *Journal of Pragmatics*, 36:7, pp.1189–1210. Available from: www.sciencedirect.com/science/article/abs/pii/S0378216604000219?via%3Dihub (Accessed: 24 August 2021).

Gibbs, R. W., (2019) 'Metaphor as Dynamical-Ecological Performance', *Metaphor and Symbol*, 34:1, pp.33–44. Available from: www.tandfonline.com/doi/full/10.1080/10926488.2019.1591713 (Accessed: 2 May 2020).

Gipps, C. V., (1994) *Beyond Testing: Towards a Theory of Educational Assessment*. London and Washington, DC: The Falmer Press.

Jamrozik, A., McQuire, M., Cardillo, E. R., and Chatterjee, A., (2016) 'Metaphor: Bridging Embodiment to Abstraction', *Psychonomic Bulletin and Review*, 23:4, pp.1080–1089. Available from: https://link.springer.com/article/10.3758/s13423-015-0861-0 (Accessed: 3 June 2002).

Jespersen, E., and He, J., (2015) 'The Embodied Nature of Autistic Learning: Implications for Physical Education', *Physical Culture and Sport Studies and Research*, 65:1, pp.63–73. Available from: https://sciendo.com/article/10.1515/pcssr-2015-0012 (Accessed: 17 December 2020).

Kalandadze, T., Bambini, V., and Næss, K.-A.B., (2019) 'A Systematic Review and Meta-analysis of Studies on Metaphor Comprehension in Individuals with Autism Spectrum Disorder: Do Task Properties Matter?', *Applied Psycholinguistics*, 40:6, pp.1421–1454. Available from: www.cambridge.org/core/journals/applied-psycholinguistics/article/abs/systematic-review-and-metaanalysis-of-studies-on-metaphor-comprehension-in-individuals-with-autism-spectrum-disorder-do-task-properties-matter/8FE488D2EB7C227349CBA4E4D4D8BC2C (Accessed: 3 January 2024).

Kasirer, A., and Mashal, N., (2016) 'Comprehension and Generation of Metaphors by Children with Autism Spectrum Disorder', *Research in Autism Spectrum Disorders*, 32, pp.53–63. Available from: www.sciencedirect.com/science/article/abs/pii/S1750946716300939?via%3Dihub (Accessed: 12 February 2023).

Knight, C., (2018) 'What Is Dyslexia? An Exploration of the Relationship between Teachers' Understandings of Dyslexia and Their Training Experiences', *Dyslexia*, 24:3, pp.207–219. Available from: https://onlinelibrary.wiley.com/doi/10.1002/dys.1593 (Accessed: 9 July 2021).

Kovecses, Z., (2017) 'Conceptual Metaphor Theory', in Semino, E., and Demjén, Z., (eds), *The Routledge Handbook of Metaphor and Language*. London and New York: Routledge, pp.13–27.

Krause, F., and Storch, M., (2010) *Ressourcen Aktivieren mit dem Unbewussten: Manual und ZRM-Bildkartei* [Activating Resources with the Unconscious: Manual and ZRM Picture Inventory]. Bern: Huber.

Lakoff, G., and Johnson, M., (1981) *Metaphors we Live By*. Chicago, IL: University of Chicago Press.

Littlemore, J., (2019). *Metaphors in the Mind: Sources of Variation in Embodied Metaphor*. Cambridge: Cambridge University Press. Available from: www.cambridge.org/core/books/metaphors-in-the-mind/ED8CB6AFD3EB666A16FCDFE8EEC39840 (Accessed: 22 May 2023).

Morrison, D. A., (2014) 'Is the Tree of Life the Best Metaphor, Model, or Heuristic for Phylogenetics?', *Systematic Biology*, 63:4, pp.628–638. Available from: https://academic.oup.com/sysbio/article-abstract/63/4/628/2848838?redirectedFrom=fulltext (Accessed: 7 August 2020).

Morsanyi, K., Stamenković, D., and Holyoak, K. J., (2020) 'Metaphor Processing in Autism: A Systematic Review and Meta-analysis', *Developmental Review*, 57. Available from: www.sciencedirect.com/science/article/abs/pii/S0273229720300319?via%3Dihub (Accessed: 9 June 2023).

Muijs, D., and Bokhove, C., (2020) 'Metacognition and Self-Regulation: Evidence Review', *Education Endowment Foundation*. Available from: https://educationendowmentfoundation.org.uk/education-evidence/evidence-reviews/metacognition-and-self-regulation (Accessed: 12 September 2023).

Olofson, E. L., Casey, D., Oluyedun, O. A., Herwegen, J. V., Becerra, A., and Rundblad, G., (2014) 'Youth with Autism Spectrum Disorder Comprehend Lexicalised and Novel Primary Conceptual Metaphors', *Journal of Autism and Developmental Disorders*, 44:10, pp.2568–2583. Available from: https://link.springer.com/article/10.1007/s10803-014-2129-3 (Accessed: 22 February 2024).

Power, C., Carmichael, E., and Goldsmith, R., (2007) 'Parrot Poo on the Windscreen: Metaphor in Academic Skills Learning', *Journal of Academic Language and Learning*, 1:1, A18–A32. Available from: https://journal.aall.org.au/index.php/jall/article/view/31 (Accessed: 22 September 2020).

Rajendran, G., and Mitchell, P., (2007) 'Cognitive Theories of Autism', *Developmental Review*, 27:2, pp.224–260. Available from: www.sciencedirect.com/science/article/abs/pii/S0273229707000032?via%3Dihub (Accessed: 25 April 2024).

Rao, D., and Stupans, I., (2012) 'Exploring the Potential of Role Play in Higher Education: Development of a Typology and Teacher Guidelines', *Innovations in Education and Teaching International*, 49:4, pp.427–436. Available from: www.tandfonline.com/doi/full/10.1080/14703297.2012.728879 (Accessed: 19 April 2024).

Robson, S., (2010) 'Self-regulation and Metacognition in Young Children's Self-initiated Play and Reflective Dialogue', *International Journal of Early Years Education*, 18:3, pp.227–241. Available from: www.tandfonline.com/doi/full/10.1080/09669760.2010.521298 (Accessed: 1 January 2023).

Rucińska, Z., Fondelli, T., and Gallagher, S., (2021) 'Embodied Imagination and Metaphor Use in Autism Spectrum Disorder', *Healthcare*, 9:2. Available from: www.mdpi.com/2227-9032/9/2/200 (Accessed: 14 June 2024).

Shapiro, L., and Stolz, S. A., (2018) 'Embodied Cognition and Its Significance for Education', *Theory and Research in Education*, 17:1, pp.19–39. Available from: https://journals.sagepub.com/doi/10.1177/1477878518822149 (Accessed: 9 March 2023).

Smith-Spark, J. H., and Gordon, R., (2022) 'Automaticity and Executive Abilities in Developmental Dyslexia: A Theoretical Review', *Brain Sciences*, 12:4, p. 446. Available from: www.mdpi.com/2076-3425/12/4/446 (Accessed: 20 March 2024).

Snowling, M. J., Hulme, C., and Nation, K., (2020) 'Defining and Understanding Dyslexia: Past, Present and Future', *Oxford Review of Education*, 46:4, pp.501–513. Available from: www.tandfonline.com/doi/full/10.1080/03054985.2020.1765756 (Accessed: 2 February 2023).

Stevens, E. A., Hall, C., and Vaughn, S., (2022) 'Language and Reading Comprehension for Students with Dyslexia: An Introduction to the Special Issue', *Annals of Dyslexia*, 72:2, pp.197–203. Available at: https://link.springer.com/article/10.1007/s11881-022-00260-6 (Accessed: 26 November 2024).

Stuurman, S., Passier, H. J., Geven, F., and Barendsen, E., (2019) 'Autism: Implications for Inclusive Education with Respect to Software Engineering', in *Proceedings of the 8th Computer Science Education Research Conference*, pp.15–25. Available from: www.researchgate.net/publication/339778131_Autism_Implications_for_Inclusive_Education_with_respect_to_Software_Engineering (Accessed: 11 January 2021).

Swaffield, S., (2011) 'Getting to the Heart of Authentic Assessment for Learning', *Assessment in Education: Principles, Policy and Practice*, 18:4, pp.433–449. Available from: www.tandfonline.com/doi/full/10.1080/0969594X.2011.582838 (Accessed: 4 September 2023).

Swales, J., and Feak, C. B., (1994) *Academic Writing for Graduate Students: Essential Tasks and Skills*. Second Edition. Ann Arbor, MI: University of Michigan Press.

Taylor, H., and Vestergaard, M. D., (2022) 'Developmental Dyslexia: Disorder or Specialisation in Exploration?', *Frontiers in Psychology*, 13, pp.1–19. Available from: www.frontiersin.org/journals/psychology/articles/10.3389/fpsyg.2022.889245/full (Accessed: 16 April 2024).

Thomas, G. P., and McRobbie, C. J., (2001) 'Using a Metaphor for Learning to Improve Students' Metacognition in the Chemistry Classroom', *Journal of Research in Science Teaching*, 38:2, pp.222–259. Available from: https://onlinelibrary.wiley.com/doi/10.1002/1098-2736(200102)38:2%3C222::AID-TEA1004%3E3.0.CO;2-S (Accessed: 3 October 2022).

Vermeulen, P., (2015) 'Context Blindness in Autism Spectrum Disorder: Not Using the Forest to See the Trees as Trees', *Focus on Autism and other Developmental Disabilities*, 30:3, pp.182–192. Available from: https://journals.sagepub.com/doi/10.1177/1088357614528799 (Accessed: 13 October 2022).

Wallbank, A. J., (2022) *Academic Writing and Dyslexia: A Visual Guide to Writing at University*. Second Edition. London: Routledge.

Wan, W., (2014) 'Constructing and Developing ESL Students' Beliefs about Writing Through Metaphor: An Exploratory Study', *Journal of Second Language Writing*, 23, pp.53–73. Available from: www.sciencedirect.com/science/article/abs/pii/S1060374314000034?via%3Dihub (Accessed: 3 August 2022).

Wan, W., and Turner, S., (2018) 'Applying Metaphor Analysis to Academic Literacy Research: A Critical Review over 30 Years', *Metaphor and the Social World*, 8:2, pp.286–311. Available from: www.jbe-platform.com/content/journals/10.1075/msw.17012.wan (Accessed: 11 September 2021).

Warmington, M., Stothard, S. E., and Snowling, M. J., (2013) 'Assessing Dyslexia in Higher Education: The York Adult Assessment Battery-revised', *Journal of Research in Special Educational Needs*, 13:1, pp.48–56. Available from: https://nasenjournals.onlinelibrary.wiley.com/doi/10.1111/j.1471-3802.2012.01264.x (Accessed: 24 June 2024).

Willox, A. C., Harper, S. L., Bridger, D., Morton, S., Orbach, A., and Sarapura, S., (2010) 'Co-Creating Metaphor in the Classroom for Deeper Learning: Graduate Student Reflections', *International Journal of Teaching and Learning in Higher Education*, 22:1, pp.71–79. Available from: https://eric.ed.gov/?id=EJ913531 (Accessed: 20 June 2023).

Willinger, U., Deckert, M., Schmoger, M., Schaunig-Busch, I., Formann, A. K., and Auff, E., (2019) 'Developmental Steps in Metaphorical Language Abilities: The Influence of Age, Gender, Cognitive Flexibility, Information Processing Speed, and Analogical Reasoning', *Language and Speech*, 62:2, pp.207–228. Available from: https://journals.sagepub.com/doi/10.1177/0023830917746552 (Accessed: 24 July 2021).

Zhou, D., and Heineken, E., (2009) 'The Use of Metaphors in Academic Communication: Traps or Treasures', *Ibérica*, 18:18, pp.23–42.

5 From Theory to Practice

Compositional Pictography for Academic Writing and Assessment

Adrian J. Wallbank and Mona Khatibshahidi

Having discussed the theory behind the need for visual scaffolding in helping students with learning differences harness their strengths and succeed in learning, academic writing, and assessment, we now need to examine how to implement such ideas in our day-to-day practice with students. This chapter outlines how the core ideas in the student textbook written by one of the chapter authors, *Academic Writing and Dyslexia: A Visual Guide to Writing at University* (Wallbank, 2018, 2022), combined with the theory elaborated upon in Chapters 1 and 3, can be taught and deployed for all students with learning differences, not just those with dyslexia. It is envisaged that practitioners should use the student textbook alongside this chapter.

Approaching and structuring the tutorial/feedback session

Before delving into any pedagogical techniques concerning students' writing and assessment itself, it is worth considering how to structure support and feedback sessions in a manner that is as inclusive as possible. The following is intended as guide for structuring one-to-one scenarios, as this is the most common way of providing students with guidance and or feedback on their writing and assessments, but the core 'WH' question framework can be readily adopted as a framework for group scenarios.

Obviously, as a core tenet of student-centred learning, the student ought to set the agenda, but equally there are some structural considerations that students with learning differences can find helpful. A good starting point, as advocated here, is to map some of the activities elaborated upon in the literature in Chapter 2 onto a visual model of coaching questions. As already discussed, students with learning differences often find that orientation and a 'roadmap' to their learning activities help structure their ideas and enable them to get a better, more holistic handle on what is needed; they often need to see how what they are doing or learning fits in with the 'big picture' (Cooper, 2019; Wallbank, 2022; Eide and Eide, 2023). As discussed in Chapter 1, students with dyslexia, for instance, often need to learn the whole, the 'bigger picture', and the context to better understand a particular part. For students with autism, meanwhile, their depth-first search strategies and focus on detail will require careful scaffolding to enable them to understand how that detail relates to the 'big picture' and context. Once students with learning differences can see the overall map of where they are going, what they need to do, and crucially why they need to do it, what is taught becomes more easily assimilated with their personal conceptual frameworks and cognitive strengths; the requirement to present material in linear form in the actual assessment also becomes more easily, understood, managed, and navigable (Cooper, 2019, p.90).

DOI: 10.4324/9781003398974-5

Additionally, by frequently referencing learning activities in the sessions back to an overarching visual 'roadmap', students are less inclined to lose focus and are likely to find their learning more productive – something which is especially useful for students with ADHD or any scenario where cognitive overload and working memory issues are raising challenges. It also saves on staff having to repeat content due to students losing focus.

Models of coaching advocate the use of open questions (which align with the 'what', 'how', and 'why' principles of UDL) to facilitate engagement, self-reflection, and learning. The basic framework of such questions can provide a convenient and flexible framework through which *all* learning can be scaffolded, structured, and represented within the writing tutorial. Almost any aspect of academic writing and assessment feedback within a one-to-one scenario can be scaffolded and taught using the following frameworks of 'WH question' words that can be adopted as a means of orientating students and building an easily navigable 'roadmap' into the tutorial and learning.

What is paramount is that for students with dyslexia and/or ADHD, the 'what' of the session needs to be covered first, followed by the 'why', as these learners need the context before dealing with the 'how'. Students with dyslexia and ADHD can become confused and cognitively overloaded if this sequence is not followed. The following is an example of how placing the 'how' before the 'what' and 'why' can cause confusion:

> Teaching summarising techniques or skills, or pointing out where students could have effectively deployed summarising skills without framing this in terms of 'what' summarising is and 'why' it is important within that particular context. This will be cognitively bewildering. Even worse is a scenario whereby you might teach summarising skills in detail but then only later explain what it is and why it is important. In this scenario, the student will not only spend all of the time you are explaining summarising trying to align the detail to the 'bigger picture' context (the 'what' and the 'why') and struggle to do so, but they will expend so much valuable cognitive resource doing so that they will not be able to fully assimilate what you are teaching. Furthermore, when they do get to the context, they will then have to cognitively 'work backwards' to make sense of it while trying to make sense of the sequence of points being made.

Autistic students, on the other hand, will find the 'what' and 'why', 'big picture' context frustrating if discussed first, as their strengths lie in detail, systems, processes, and exploiting local patches of knowledge. The following scenario, for example, can be confusing:

> A discussion with the student concerning the nuances and implications associated with the task before appraising the detail. As we saw in Chapter 1, autistic students feel decidedly less confident working in grey areas or teasing out 'bigger picture' links but are very good at describing detail. As such, work with them in their comfort zone first by praising and evaluating detail before using the diagrams in this chapter to help scaffold what these details mean within their bigger context.

Ultimately, we need to exploit these students' strengths before scaffolding (via the visuals throughout this chapter) what they find more challenging (detail, processes, and sequences in the case of dyslexia and ADHD, and 'big picture' context in the case of autism). In this way of course we are more accurately working with students and scaffolding skills within what Vygotsky (1978) called the 'Zone of Proximal Development'.

'WH' framework for students with dyslexia and ADHD

'WH' question and sequence	Examples
What? By starting with the 'big picture' you can provide a clear overview and sense of orientation. All subsequent information, tutoring, coaching, mentoring, and dialogue are then scaffolded around this core, overarching issue/topic and structure. The open question also starts to orientate the applicability of the topic or issues to the students.	• Start by asking the student what they want to get out of the session, and then write it down or mind map it to provide a clear outline/plan for the session • Discuss, ascertain, or prioritise what the core issues, topics, problems, or barriers might be and plan the session accordingly • Ascertain what the assignment task is asking for, what areas are being assessed or what the student's argument or critical stance is, and scaffold the session around them achieving those aims
Why? Gives a specific orientation conceptually and practically. Learners with dyslexia and ADHD often need to know why something happened, needs to happen, or exists so that they can see how it fits into the 'big picture'.	• Demonstrate why certain aspects of the 'word salad' are problematic • Explain why certain academic conventions or requirements need to be met • Ask the student to explain why they made the decisions they did when writing • Ask the student why they think certain passages are stronger or weaker • Explain why some areas need improvement • Link work to syllabus and assessment requirements, employability etc.
How? This gets more specific and explores the 'meat' of the essay or tutorial. It also acts as a convenient tool for questioning student understanding and providing a revision framework.	• Negotiate how you are going to resolve the issues • Demonstrate or model how to improve the work • Demonstrate, teach, and scaffold the principles of academic writing and literacies, and apply this in respect of how the student can improve • Ask the student to explain to you how they are going to implement changes going forward

'Big picture' to detail

'WH' framework for students with autism:

'WH' question and sequence	Examples
How? This first priority is specific and explores the 'meat' of the essay or tutorial. It also acts as a convenient tool for questioning student understanding and providing a revision framework.	- Negotiate how you are going to resolve the issues - Demonstrate or model how to improve the work - Demonstrate, teach, and scaffold the principles of academic writing and literacies, and apply this in respect of how the student can improve
Why? Gives a specific orientation conceptually and practically. Students with learning differences often need to know why something happened, needs to happen, or exists so that they can see how it fits into the 'big picture'.	- Demonstrate why certain aspects of the 'word salad' are problematic - Ask the student to explain why they made the decisions they did when writing - Ask the student why they think certain passages are stronger or weaker - Explain why some areas need improvement - Link work to syllabus and assessment requirements, employability etc.
What? By ending with the 'big picture' you can provide a clear overview and sense of orientation. The open question also starts to orientate the applicability of the topic or issues to the students.	- Discuss, ascertain, or prioritise what the core issues, topics, problems, and barriers might be, and link the 'how' and 'why' to what needs to be done - Ascertain what the assignment task is asking for, what areas are being assessed, or what the student's argument and critical stance is, and scaffold the 'how' and 'why' around them achieving those aims

Detail to 'big picture'

The shape of the blue triangles here acts as a visual guide or template to help you see the correlation between 'bigger picture' points (the 'what' and 'why') and the broader shape of the triangle, and vice versa, thus helping you to structure the session accordingly. As with all the visuals in compositional pictography, there is a meaningful correlation between the shape of the image and its meaning or pedagogical function.

Note also how we have explained the use of 'WH' question frameworks above via describing the 'what' and 'why' first, before elaborating upon the frameworks ('how') via the tables as a way of modelling the dyslexia and ADHD sequence.

A note about how to use the pictographs in this chapter

- For students with dyslexia and ADHD, start by discussing the 'big picture' elements of the diagrams and templates (e.g. the wide triangles, arrows, and the overall shapes) – all of which are crucial to the pedagogy and have a meaningful correlation with the purpose or principle they are representing.

- For autistic students, the inverse is the case. Start with the detail (the symbols denoting evidence, analysis, evaluation, summarising etc.), all of which again have a meaningful pedagogical correlation with the elements within the assignment, before relating those details to the shape (purpose) of the 'bigger picture' triangles, boxes, arrows, and shapes etc.

- In both cases, the overriding 'big picture' and contextual priority is helping to scaffold students' responses to the assignment question or task.

132 *Academic Writing, Assessment, and Neurodiversity*

Academic reading

Regardless of what type of assessment is being undertaken, reading is a core element of university study (so much so that originally, of course, students were referred to as 'reading' for a degree). However, reading can be not only overwhelming for students with learning differences owing to its quantity and complexity, but often the purpose of reading is misunderstood and reading techniques are either not taught or misinterpreted. Again, given that many students with learning differences need to see how and why what they are reading fits in with the 'bigger picture', a simple visual diagram that can explain the intersections between reading and its role in preparing for assessment can be enormously beneficial. The following diagram can help explain how their work enters into an intellectual conversation with, is informed by, and can even challenge, the work of others:

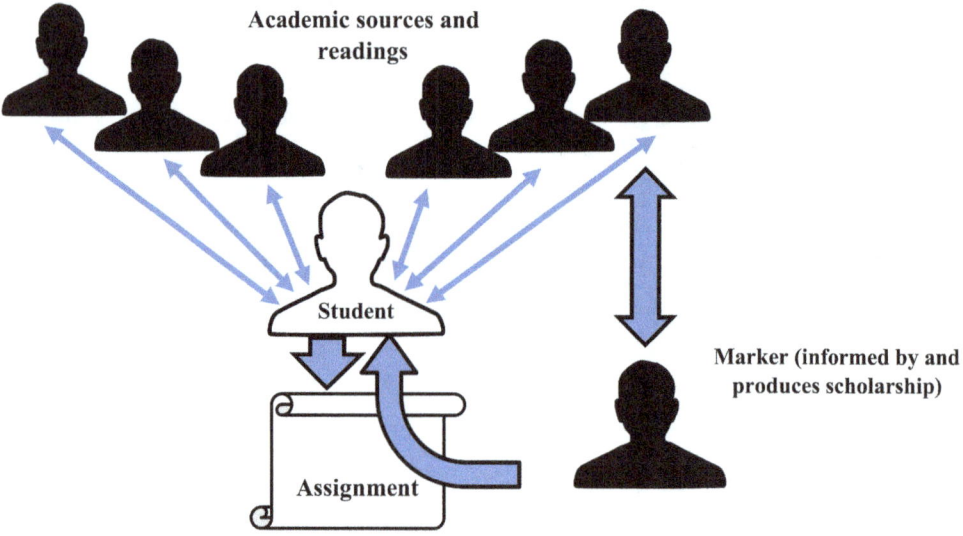

However, many students with learning differences also need to see the strategic purpose of their reading, how it fits into an overarching schema of study, and how other reading strategies such as skimming and scanning (or SQ3R as it is sometimes referred to) fit into their preparation for assignments and where their priorities ought to lie. In what follows, we have a simple diagram that brings all these elements together using various icons to signify the techniques and purpose (e.g. icons to denote skimming and scanning, glasses to indicate detailed reading, and symbols indicating the application of reading materials in assignments in the form of direct quotation, paraphrasing, and summarising).

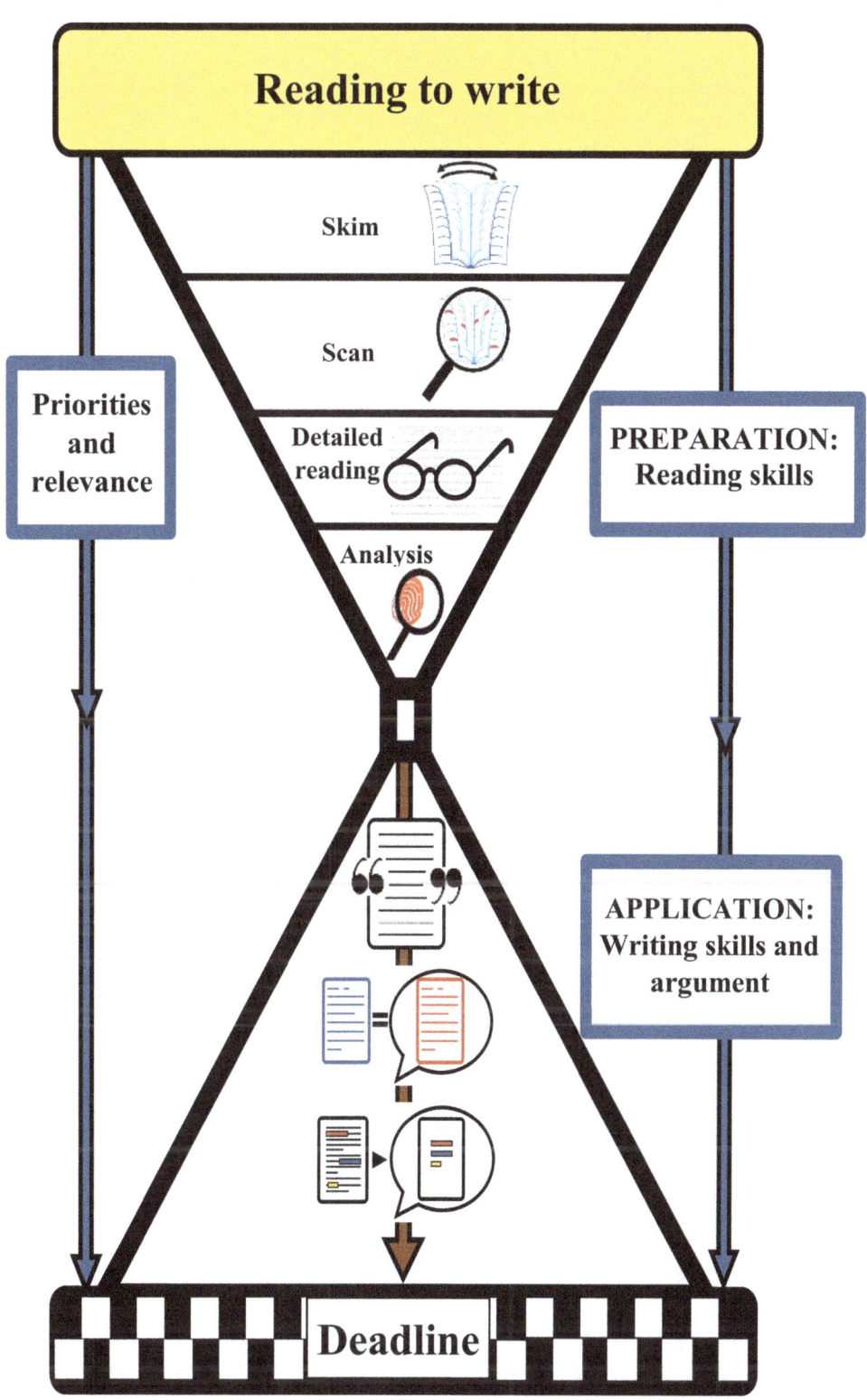

Many students get bogged down with detailed reading. This causes not only fatigue as a result of cognitive overload but does not play to their strengths (in 'big picture' and 'gist' thinking in respect of dyslexia or ADHD) or does not enable them to make connections to the 'bigger picture' (in respect of autism). The overarching map/schema above brings together the purpose of reading, the eventual aim (the assignment in this case), the goals associated with preparation and application, and the various techniques associated with each. The hourglass structure with the narrowing triangles indicates increasing focus and detail and then, in the case of the integration of the literature, decreasing focus (quotation, for example, being more detailed and focused than summarising). Talking through this diagram with students can help them to be more purposeful, strategic, and focused in their reading, as we shall see in the case study below.

As discussed previously in Chapter 3, the idea behind using such a diagram to illustrate the overarching purpose of reading for assessment is to tap into and exploit the affective ('why'), recognition ('what'), and strategic ('how') brain networks, and scaffold the information or purpose of the reading by supplying the background context, big ideas, relationships, critical features, strategy development, and management of information, all of which align with the key tenets of the principles of UDL and enable students to establish and exploit their metacognitive strengths. More importantly, however, by relating (via visually meaningful representations) how such techniques, strategies, and purposes relate to the 'bigger picture', this helps students with dyslexia and ADHD see how detail (while suggesting techniques for getting to that detail) relates to its overarching 'bigger picture' (their strength) while also encouraging students with autism (whose strength is in the fine detail and recollection) to relate detail to the overarching aims and the 'big picture'. In other words, the diagram, like most of the diagrams that follow in this chapter, works both ways – it helps students with learning differences see the wood for the trees and/or the trees for the wood.

Case Study A: Reading to write (Tutor: Mona Khatibshahidi)

Student A: 'A' is a first-year sociology student with dyslexia. The student is making the transition to university and finds it very difficult to adjust to their new life both academically and personally. The student had a set way or habit of studying established during their prior educational studies (where little reading was required) and was reluctant to adopt the new skills required for university-level reading. Specifically, this was problematic when they had to read academic sources in preparation for writing an assignment. The student would persist with reading every word and line in their textbooks, monographs, and journal articles and was getting overwhelmed with details. A's reading tactics, which used to be effective during their A levels, are no longer effective due to the volume of reading required. This issue, coupled with the processing difficulties associated with their dyslexia, created significant problems such as short attention span, tiredness, stress, and decreasing interest in the subject.

Intervention

Given that this was A's first experience of a study skills session, my initial step was to build a rapport by creating a safe environment and asking them open questions. This encouraged the student to openly discuss the challenges they were facing and the techniques they used to overcome these issues. Knowing this gave me the opportunity

From Theory to Practice 135

to diagnose the difficulties. To help the student, I first elaborated on the key issues so that 'A' could understand why they are experiencing difficulties (contextualising the problems) and why the reading tactics are not effective at university. Given that the student's learning preferences seemed to favour visuals, we initially used the 'reading to write' diagram above to assist in diagnosing their challenges and to explain to 'A' why the detailed/analysis reading tactic they were deploying was not effective as a starting point. This helped the student to understand why detailed reading without any purpose in mind is counterproductive. This visual explanation helped 'A' to be more open in adopting alternative and more appropriate methods of reading.

As a result of skipping the two initial stages of reading (skim and scan), the student could not understand the context or the 'bigger picture' of the reading source. I suggested that 'A' should skim their reading materials first without looking into details and find some initial basic information such as the length of the article, the title, what can be understood from it, and how the material is divided into different sections. I then suggested that the student move on to the next level of context reading, which is scanning. So, at this stage, I encouraged 'A' to read the abstract, parts of the introduction, and the topic sentences of the material to find more information, understand the 'bigger picture' and, more importantly, find out whether or how the source is relevant to the topic of the assignment by exploiting A's ability to detect the gist of the article. This helped the student to have some initial questions in mind about the material. Creating key questions encouraged the student to remain focused throughout the detailed reading stage. Furthermore, I suggested that 'A' use a text-mapping technique where they wrote, highlighted, or colour-coded key points, summaries, or notes while they were reading a source next to each section as opposed to separating the notes from the reading text. This allowed the student to not only create a visual mind map of the text but also helped them to remind themselves of the content of the text by referring to their notes without having to read everything again.

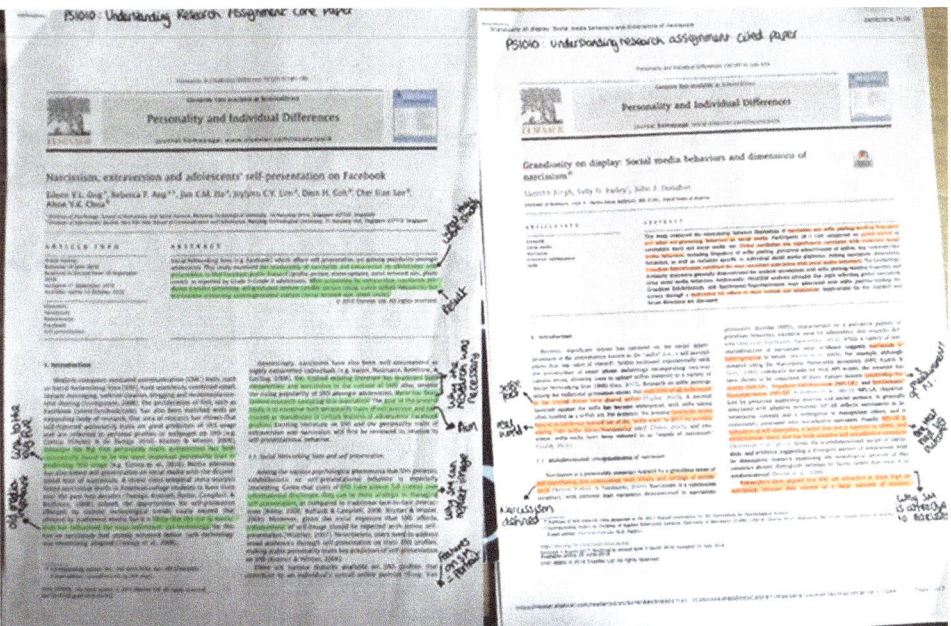

'A' mentioned that they found using the text-mapping technique to be very effective and efficient.

Before this intervention, 'A' stated that a typical journal article would take three hours to read. However, after using this diagram as a strategic framework, 'A' managed to not only increase their confidence in fully comprehending their reading materials but was also able to select the information to be incorporated and referenced in their assignments in under 30 minutes. 'A' also felt that by using this technique they managed to extract more information compared to when they used to spend three hours on each article.

Searching for and managing reading materials online

Understanding the purpose of reading and strategies for locating information is sometimes only the beginning, however. Further problems can arise for students with learning differences when they read and search for texts in today's highly digital and hyperlinked online world. Given the well-documented issues with working memory overload, coupled with organisation issues and difficulties in sequencing and concentration, students with learning differences (especially those with dyslexia and ADHD) often need reminding that navigation needs to be carefully managed. Again, referring to this navigation using a visual icon can help reinforce this idea, especially as it pertains to reading online and the propensity for the online world to be dominated by hyperlinks.

Hyperlinks can obviously be phenomenally useful as signposts to relevant or additional material. They can even support understanding of complex issues if they link to explanations or definitions or if hovering over the hyperlink allows a box to appear with supplementary information or the complete reference. This can enable easy, instant comprehension. However, hyperlinks can be everywhere and in almost every line. This can be very useful as a way of quickly skimming for information and can enable students to quickly delve into other pieces of information and link pieces of information together (thus allowing them, in the case of dyslexia for example, to exploit their 'big picture' thinking, 'gist', and speed reading strengths). However, students could end up in a scenario where they have clicked on so many hyperlinks that the following somewhat disorientating issues arise:

- The original article and focus have disappeared. Often when you follow a link, the browser goes to the new article in either a new tab or a replacement webpage without seeing the original (unless students have the luxury of utilising more than one screen).

- Students can end up having so many tabs open that it is difficult to backtrack to the original focus or article.

- Trying to 'tidy' the browser by closing tabs in an attempt to reorientate can lead to overcompensating and deleting the most important or original tabs. Consequently, the search has to start again (using the browser's 'history' can help, but it all takes time and is a distraction).

It can be helpful to reinforce and remind students that such a plethora of hyperlinks can act like a vortex that can seriously deplete the ability of the working memory to cope. The following diagram can be used to illustrate this.

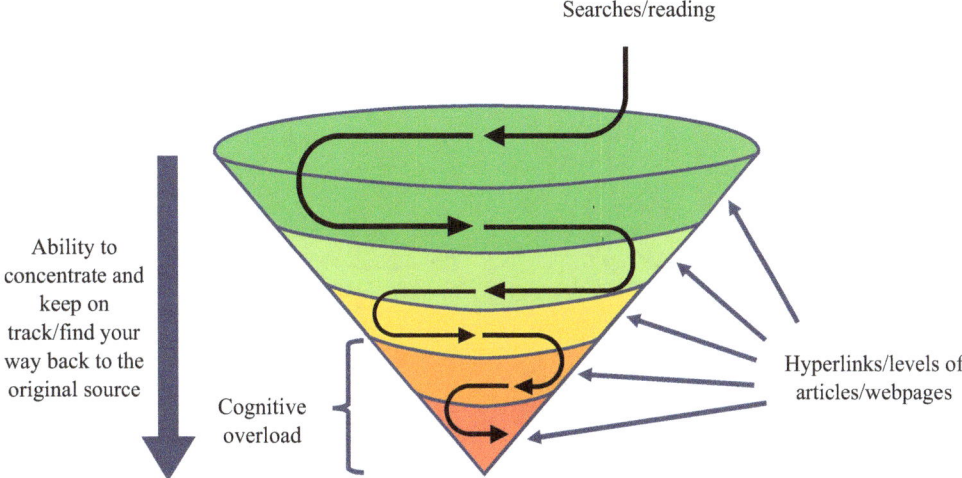

You can ask the students to apply the following three tests to help keep them on track:

1) Is the hyperlinked source or article strictly relevant? If yes, follow it; if not, avoid it.
2) Does it add detail to the original focus, or does it tempt you off onto a tangent?
3) Does it ultimately get you to an academic source or piece of verifiable data/evidence? If yes, follow it. If not, avoid it.

Each time a new link is opened, encourage students to skim for relevant detail by looking for subheadings, imagery, introductions, conclusions, and topic sentences, and only then look at other hyperlinks. Encourage students to refrain from opening further hyperlinks until they have subjected them to the three tests above, and to CLOSE the new tab or link to get back to where they started before continuing.

It can also be helpful to remind students that the internet is literally a worldwide 'web'. But it is crucial to keep in mind the structure of the web – THEIR web of searching and reading and the deliberate tangents scattered around the internet for the purposes of marketing in what amounts to a battle for our attention (the so-called attention economy [Steinhorst, 2024]). This is important because once students start following hyperlinks, the web structure often cannot be seen and they can get lost in a maze of 'clickbait' material. Encourage students to keep in mind how they can backtrack to 'base' or their original starting point, article, or link by showing or reminding them of the following diagram:

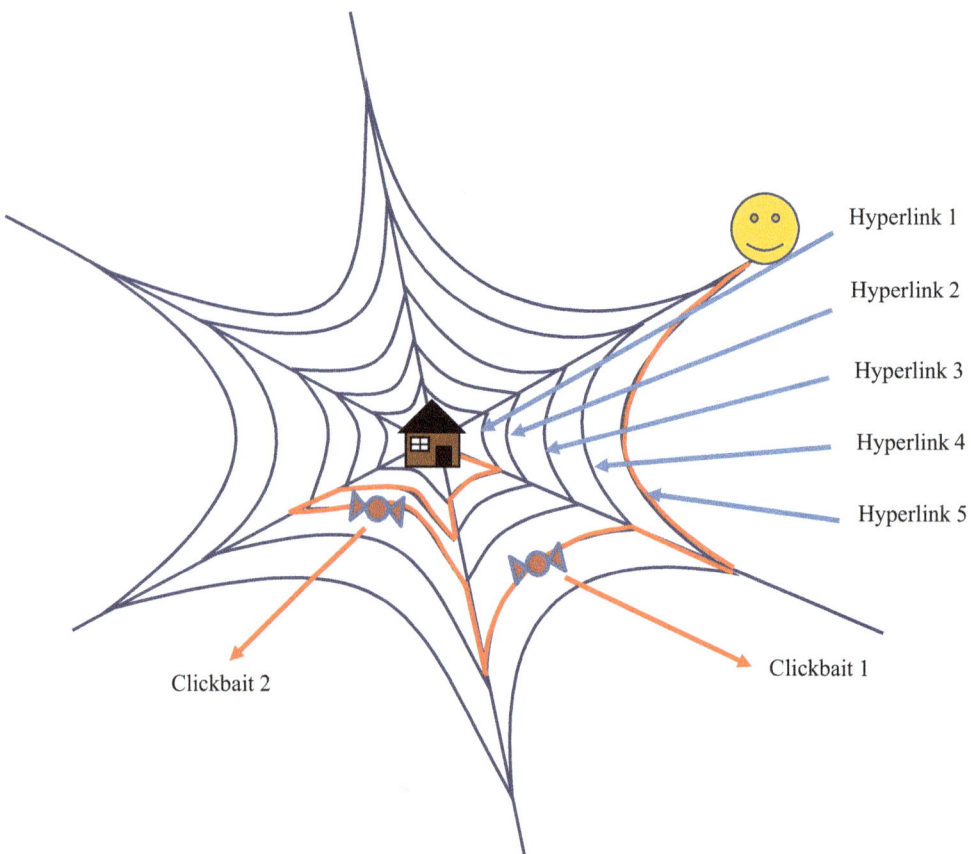

Again, the purpose of these visuals is to provide meaningful prompts and reminders that can help students with learning differences orientate themselves, scaffold sequencing, prioritise information, develop compensatory strategies, and retain valuable mental resources (working memory) while helping them to make meaningful connections to purpose and context. Students with dyslexia, in particular, do not just respond exceptionally well to visual pedagogies but, crucially, visuals which, in alignment with Roberts's (2016, 2018a, 2018b 2019) observations, have a *meaningful* connection to the core message needing to be conveyed are especially effective. These all help students with learning differences build and appreciate the mental structures, architectures, and navigational tools needed to help overcome or compensate for the inherent challenges caused by their learning difference while exploiting and scaffolding their need to make connections to the 'bigger picture'.

Writing: essay and assignment structures

As we saw in Chapter 1, another area in which students with learning differences have issues is in relation to structuring essays and paragraphs, primarily because of their difficulties with sequencing. Not only will the overall essay structure sometimes lack coherence, but paragraphs can be overly lengthy (or even comprise the entire essay), and ideas within the paragraphs themselves can become disjointed, confused, or even repetitive, thus resulting in the sort of 'schizophrenese' or 'word salads' discussed in Chapter 2. In order to address this, again, students with learning differences need to be able to see an overarching, preferably visual 'roadmap' to help scaffold, sequence, and structure their thoughts in a logical manner, and in a manner that intersects with other paragraphs to create a coherent flow of points and argumentation. One of the best ways in which we can support students to do this is by teaching them that all aspects of a body of writing (whether an essay, an exam script response, a case study, or a laboratory report) follow the shape and structure of a Christmas Cracker.

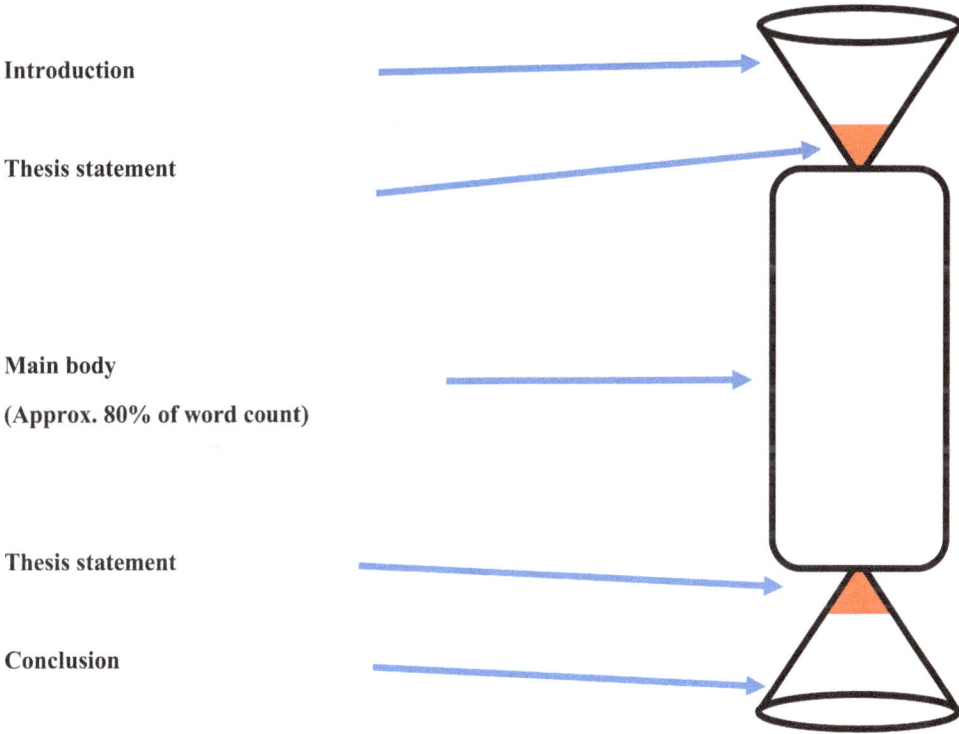

The shapes here are crucial, as they have a meaningful correlation with the structure and purpose of each section of the essay. For example, for the introduction, the cone can be explained and broken down into its four key components as follows, with the shape of the cone indicating the gradual narrowing of focus and specificity into a thesis statement:

Identify broad topic/subject area: The student needs to demonstrate that they have accurately interpreted the essay question or assignment task and what it asks them to do in relation to the topic. Students could provide an interesting 'hook' for the reader by integrating a 'headline-grabbing' fact, quote, or piece of data.

Why is it important and what is the problem? The student needs to ask themselves why this subject or question even matters. Being able to show that they have an appreciation of the significance of the topic in relation to its context, world events, and research developments will gain them marks.

Background: Students should highlight significant events, changes, laws, policies, or research within which they are situating their argument. They should indicate the major issues at stake and their areas of controversy and counter-claims. Students should show the 'gap' in knowledge, especially if the introduction is to a research-based essay or dissertation.

Argument/thesis statement: Students should articulate a clear, concise thesis statement which answers and addresses the key elements of the question or provides a solution while outlining the main structure of their argument.

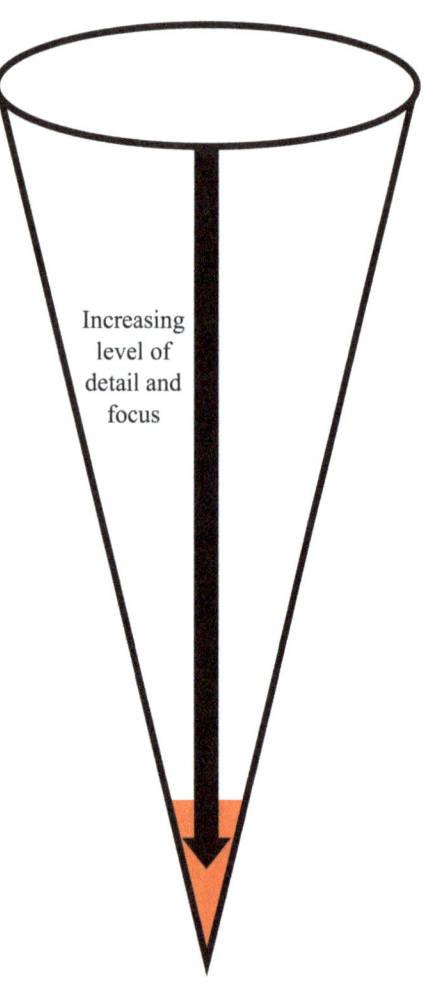

Increasing level of detail and focus

Again, with students with dyslexia and ADHD, it might be best to start with the 'big picture' topic and work with them to identify and express their argument (topic sentence). In contrast, with autistic students start with the detail that pertains to their argument. Use the diagram to help them appreciate how it needs to sit within the broader context of the topic, discipline, world, why it is important, and what constitutes the background information the reader may need to know in order to understand the detail.

Encourage your students to either a) look at exemplars and map onto the exemplars the cone shape at the top of the Christmas Cracker and/or b) use their own draft introductions and talk through with them how (or not) their draft aligns with the shape of the template. An example of how this might look with an exemplar is as follows:

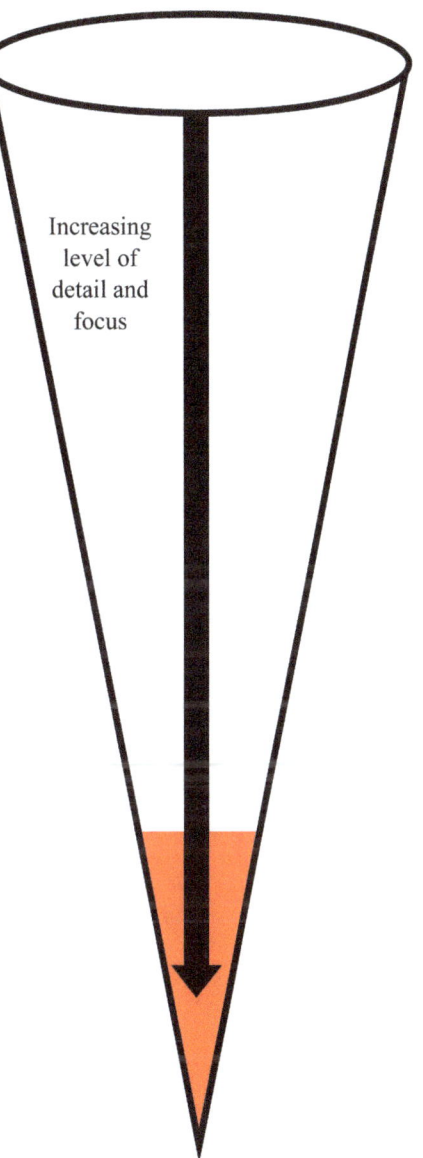

Domestic violence is a major problem in the UK, if not globally, and its prevalence is far from decreasing. National estimates as to the number of women who experience such abuse within the last year range from 7% (Office for National Statistics, 2014, p.1) to up to 10% (Women's Aid, 2006). 77 women were killed by their partners or ex-partners in the UK in 2012–13 (ONS, 2014) and as many as 63.4% of separated women reported experiencing 'violence' from ex-husbands, with 59% experiencing an 'assault' (Painter and Farringdon, 1998, p.263). Equally, data suggesting that 25% to 30% (ONS, 2014) of women suffer domestic violence in their lifetime, with up to one billion experiencing it internationally (United Nations, 2014), back up this trend. These statistics show that the continuing prevalence of domestic violence is incontestable – women are clearly not being protected from abuse in practice. Law and policy relating to domestic violence has running through it an explicit goal – protecting victims of abuse (Home Office, 2014, pp.3–6). Yet if these victims are receiving unsatisfactory protection, the adequacy of the criminal justice response to domestic violence must be called into question. This essay critically examines whether those who experience or are at risk of abuse are actually protected in practice. It argues that despite considerable changes in law and policy in this area, the criminal justice system's response is insufficient, despite there being multiple ideological, patriarchal, and media-driven forces which also contribute to the proliferation of domestic violence, and which are obviously altogether extraneous to the criminal justice system.

Points you could explain and emphasise to the student:

- The gradual transition from the broad topic (domestic violence, UK global situation, and national estimates of abuse) to the specific problem (deaths, violence, and assault), highlighting the key issues at stake, why they are important, and how they relate to the law and policy. The student then specifically addresses the inadequacies of the present system.
- The clear and concise thesis statement which specifically addresses the question or assignment task.
- How the above maps onto the shape of the cone or template.

When it comes to writing the main body of the assignment, articulate to the student that the best way of presenting a logical, compelling argument is to start with principles, definitions, and foundations (much as they would if they were building a house) before moving onto specific details. In trying to prove their argument, then, encourage the student to move from the general to the specific, from the basics to the more advanced, and from what is known to what is new. This can be mapped onto the main body of the Christmas Cracker as follows:

'Big picture':
Foundations, definitions, principles, theories, key background data etc.

Building the argument:
Evidence, discussion, analysis, and consideration of counterarguments.

Argument increasingly specific and proven:
More specific evidence and analysis leading to overall evaluation.

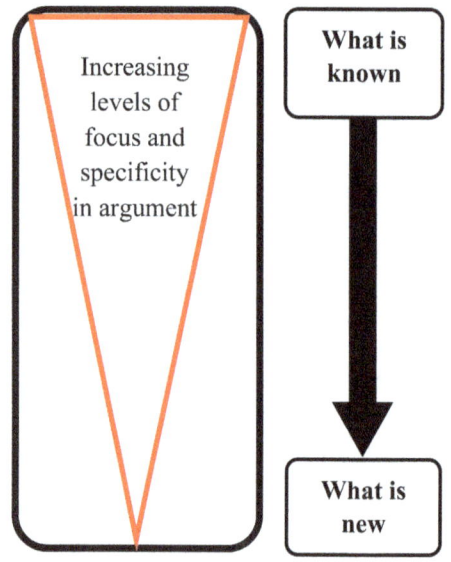

Further to this, it is useful to demonstrate, using exemplars and aligning the flow of ideas to the template, how the ideas mapped across an essay adhere to or deviate from this. Take the following essay question and possible topics as an example:

Assignment task: People respond to trauma in various ways. Discuss and explain why some individuals seem resilient while others develop severe post-traumatic stress disorder (PTSD). Is it possible to predict how people will respond to trauma?

Possible topics for consideration		
Theories concerning biological differences (between men and women)	Theories relating to individual genetics	Type of event
Case studies of victims of 9/11	Theories of psychological vulnerability	Not possible to predict how people will respond to trauma – thesis statement
Competing definitions of trauma	Family and social networks of support	Case studies of rape victims

There are clearly lots of possibilities here in terms of possible topics to cover, and it would be very easy to lose a sense of overall direction and structure. This is precisely what happens in the following essay plan:

Main body	
Paragraph 1:	Theories concerning the type of event (case studies of 9/11 and rape victims).
Paragraph 2:	Critique of studying event type as a predictor of PTSD.
Paragraph 3:	Theories of psychological vulnerability.
Paragraph 4:	Critique of theories of psychological vulnerability.
Paragraph 5:	Theories concerning biological differences (gender).
Paragraph 6:	Critique of theories concerning biological differences.
Paragraph 7:	Role of family and social networks of support.
Paragraph 8:	Not possible to predict how people will respond to trauma.
Paragraph 9:	Competing definitions of trauma.

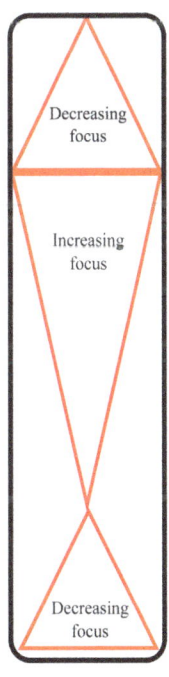

As you can see by the shape of the corresponding red triangles, there are several sequencing and coherence issues here. The student leaps into detailed, specific theory first (as depicted by the narrowness of the red triangle) but then completely separates off the sections which subject the theories to analysis and evaluation. The competing definitions of trauma, meanwhile, is a big, broad, general topic (thus depicted by the broader aspect of the red triangle) and ought to have been considered earlier in the essay, whereas the role of family and social networks of support is more specific and detailed (and hence aligned to the narrow point of the red triangle). This needed incorporating into the paragraphs that discuss the theories more carefully and smoothly. By structuring the essay as above, it appears very 'blocky' and fragmented. The overall sequence of ideas is haphazard and illogical, and what is perhaps more crucial, the argument and its direction remain unclear and insufficiently signposted. Here is how these same ideas can be mapped onto the Christmas Cracker template by moving from 'big picture' foundations to specific details:

Main body	
Paragraph 1:	Competing definitions of trauma = not possible to predict how people will respond to trauma because the definitions themselves are unclear and disputed.
Paragraphs 2–3:	Theories concerning biological differences (gender) and critique/evaluation = not possible to predict how people will respond to trauma.
Paragraphs 4–5:	Theories of psychological vulnerability and critique/evaluation = not possible to predict how people will respond to trauma.
Paragraphs 6–7:	Theories concerning the type of event (case studies of 9/11 and rape victims) and critique/evaluation = not possible to predict how people will respond to trauma.
Paragraphs 8–9:	Role of family and social networks of support = the only plausible theory that can help predict how people will respond to trauma.

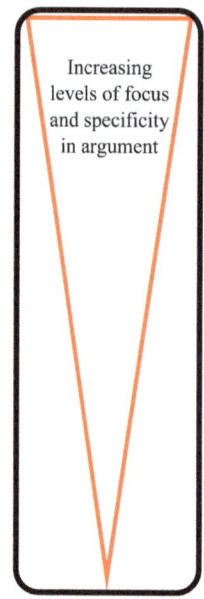

Increasing levels of focus and specificity in argument

In this version, the structure is much clearer because the analysis, evaluation, and argument run throughout each paragraph, building in focus and specificity and moving from the foundations to the specifics. This presents the ideas in a much more logical, less disjointed manner, which slowly adds layers of detail and complexity, thus rendering the argument much more thorough and convincing.

Essentially, when helping students to structure their ideas and the overall sequence of arguments/points through the essay, ask them to align which of them are the most 'big picture' and contextual and which are the most detailed, and align them accordingly with the red triangle above. Those topics that are a little more debatable might need negotiation, but the task then is to place the remaining topics against where they might sit in regard to context/'big picture' vs. specificity/detail as demonstrated above. This will help them to 'map' the terrain of the assignment and the sequence of ideas and is very different, as we have seen, to say Cottrell's suggestion that 'if you have difficulties with paragraphing', try dividing a page into columns comprising 1) arguments, 2) main information, and 3) supporting detail, with each paragraph containing 'one, two or three items from column 2' and 'several items from column 3' (Cottrell, 2013, p.299). With this method, there is no *meaningful* correlation between the columns and the structure or sequencing of ideas, whereas the triangle almost forces students to align the topics according to their purpose and how they align with the shape of the triangle/main body of the assignment.

What can be especially confusing for students with learning differences are comparison essays and assignments. Comparison essays require students to evaluate and synthesise competing or different issues and/or two or more theories or perspectives. As such, they are much trickier to construct and require considerable concentration and planning to get them right. The temptation with a comparison essay is to deal first with one side of the argument, issue, piece of literature, or theory, and then the other, before arriving at a conclusion in which the student presents their overall argument and evaluation. This is called a block structure. While it may appear logical and is a style frequently taught by English for Academic Purposes instructors, this format is fraught with problems. This is how such a structure might look if mapped onto the main body template from the Christmas Cracker.

Assignment task: Psychology and psychiatry differ in several key respects. Compare and evaluate these two forms of treatment from at least two different perspectives.

Possible essay plan for the main body of an essay using a block structure:

Structure	Block
Paragraphs 1–2	**Psychology** in relation to: 1) Origins of thought processes. 2) Patient outcomes.
Paragraphs 3–4	**Psychiatry** in relation to: 1) Origins of thought processes. 2) Patient outcomes.
Paragraph 5	Argument and evaluation – which discipline is the best or most successful?

As you can see, this structure is very logical and clear, but in terms of the overall sequence of ideas and, perhaps more crucially, the argument, it is somewhat repetitive and clumsy. It alternates between disciplines and goes back and forth between 'big picture' ideas and detail, thereby failing to synthesise and evaluate the issues holistically. In other words, the 'flow' of the ideas is repeatedly interrupted. The point-by-point or thematic structure is a much better option.

Possible essay plan for the main body of an essay using a point-by-point thematic structure:

Structure	Point-by-point/thematic
Paragraphs 1–2	**Origins of thought processes** in relation to: 1) Psychology AND psychiatry • Incorporate evaluation, analysis, and argument.
Paragraphs 3–4	**Patient outcomes** in relation to: 1) Psychology AND psychiatry • Incorporate evaluation, analysis, and argument.

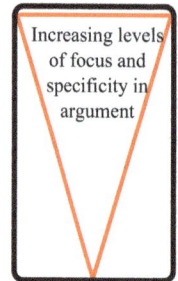

Increasing levels of focus and specificity in argument

The sequence of ideas here 'flows' much more smoothly. Notice that the all-important analysis, argument, and evaluation are integrated throughout because what drives the structure is not a 'one step at a time' block consideration of the two forms of treatment but a thematic appraisal and evaluation through two themes or perspectives. This structure builds a comparative argument into its core, and unlike in the block structure, the direction of travel is always forward. It moves from the 'big picture' (the origins of thought processes) and then gets more specific and detailed in relation to patient outcomes. It also eliminates needless repetition since the block structure would require the student to talk about thought processes and patient outcomes twice (once in relation to each form of treatment) and it eliminates the need for a concluding, evaluative paragraph as the perspectives have been synthesised and evaluated comparatively rather than separated. The point-by-point or thematic structure requires more skill, but it allows for deeper, more incisive analysis and argumentation, the result of which will be higher marks.

Conclusions are often thought of as something which has to be included just because you can't stop an essay randomly and hope for the best – a little like a handshake at the end of a formal conversation. As such, students often perceive the conclusion as fairly pointless in terms of generating marks but something one has to do so as not to appear rude. Consequently, students often pay little attention to conclusions and invariably just summarise what they have previously said. Conclusions will never generate the same amount of marks as a paragraph within the main body of the essay, but they can make them count by demonstrating how what the student has just argued intersects with, challenges, or complements current thinking and trends in the field, the discipline, or even the world.

A good way of helping students with learning differences to understand the purpose of conclusions is to encourage them to think of them as an inversion of the introduction. In other words, rather than moving from the 'big picture' to the details and an argument, encourage students to do the opposite by going from the argument back out into the 'big picture' – hence the cone shape at the bottom of the Christmas Cracker we saw earlier. An ideal conclusion, then, covers the following key points and looks a little like this:

Reiteration of thesis statement:

This does not mean simply copying and pasting the thesis statement from the introduction – students need to reword it from the perspective of the argument having been proven.

Summary of discussion:

Students should not labour this, as the marker has just read the essay. Simply ask your students to remind their readers what they have proven.

Discuss implications:

Here the student should start to broaden out into the 'big picture' and indicate why what they have just discussed matters (to the world or the discipline). Encourage them to ask themselves, who cares? What needs to change and why? Why does any of this matter?

Signal the future:

Point to where things might go next, even if this is merely that more research needs to be done.

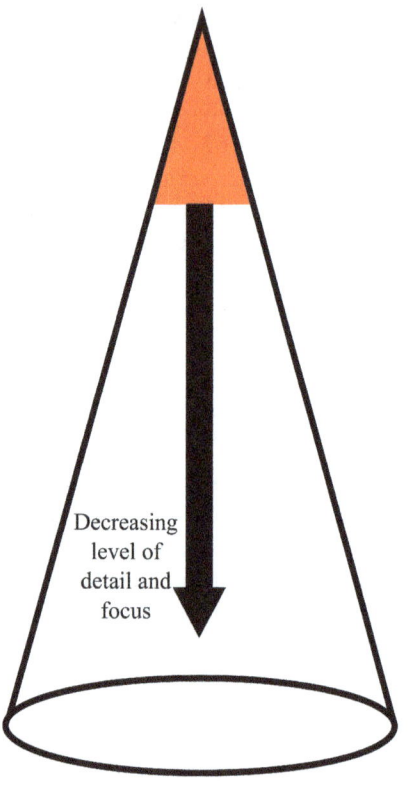

Decreasing level of detail and focus

Individuals with dyslexia and ADHD generally excel at 'big picture' thinking and intuitively spotting links and connections between ideas. In many ways, this is precisely what is required when considering the implications of what they have argued and how it relates to the wider world or the discipline. Encourage these students to harness their 'big picture' thinking abilities to craft insightful and perceptive conclusions, while in the case of autistic students, scaffold their preference for detail by encouraging them to relate detail and precision back out to context using the template as a 'map' of how to do so. Again, utilising exemplars or drafts alongside the templates can help demonstrate to the students how to do this. The following is an example of a good conclusion you could use to illustrate this.

It is clear that in relation to the 'knowledge economy' and its intersection with commodity production, there has been a crisis of mass production and that flexible specialisation is emerging in its place. This essay has argued that a new form of mass market has emerged with 'the fragmentation of style rather than any real "paradigmatic" or fundamental change in consumption which implies a change in production' (Curry 1993, p.108). It appears that mass commodity production and Fordist labour processes are still evident, but production is being relocated to non-western countries to allow advanced economies to concentrate on developing high-technology, knowledge sectors (Giddens 2000). This is a highly contentious issue and has led to suggestions of an international division of labour (Thurow 1997, p.78) which is evidence of capitalist development towards increasing global inequality (May 2000). Thus, the idea that flexible specialisation and the 'knowledge economy' are generalised trends 'obscures the real processes of capitalist development' and, in this instance, commodity production (Curry 1993, p.118). Hence, it seems that theorists supporting shifts in the nature of capitalism are 'merely apologists for the continuing exploitation of the poor in the global capitalist system' (Hull 2000, p.148). In advanced economies, therefore, high technology manufacturing industries constitute 'a declining minority of employment' (Hyman 1991, p.272) and it is evident that these firms 'are capitalist and locked into the imperatives of capitalist accumulation' (Curry 1993, p.119). This phenomenon has been introduced by, and perpetuated by neoliberal politicians, particularly in America, and it can be suggested that globalisation has left many disenfranchised. It is a damning indictment of such processes that many have been left dispossessed and unengaged, and this is largely reflected in recent developments in politics (which is increasingly putting nationalist rhetoric at the fore in response to the perceived threat from the very economic systems neoliberalism has put into place). Understanding this is of paramount importance for global and national security given the rise in rhetoric not seen since the 1930s, and as such clearly more research and understanding is required in the interests of global security and wider economic sustainability.

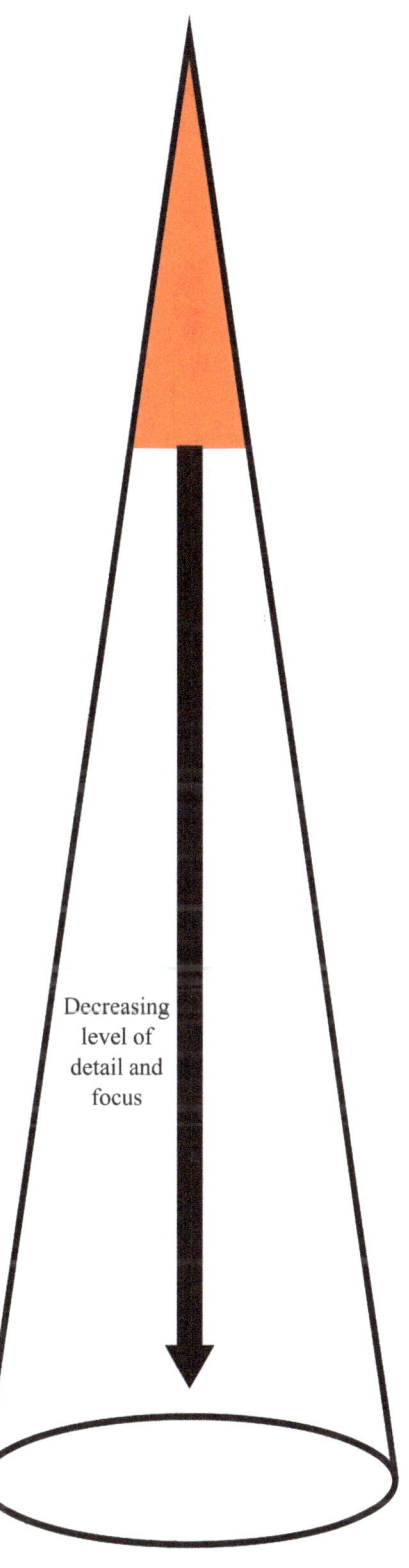

Decreasing level of detail and focus

Things to highlight to the students here are:

- How the student wastes little time summarising what has been discussed and quickly proceeds to highlight how contentious the issue is while linking this to changes in the capitalist economy and the continuing exploitation of the poor.

- The student then broadens out even further to consider the significance of the issue given that globalisation has left many 'dispossessed and unengaged', thereby linking to contemporaneous political changes, nationalism, and global security. In other words, having examined the issues relating to the 'knowledge economy', capitalism, and work, the student has stood back from the argument and asked (and then addressed) the 'big picture' questions mentioned earlier – namely 'who cares?' and 'why does any of this matter?'

- By considering these issues rather than merely summarising what they have already said, the student shows a greater awareness of the implications of what they have argued, and this will be credited.

Paragraphing

In terms of paragraphing, again everything can be understood and taught via the Christmas Cracker template, but this time with the edition of meaningful icons such as a fingerprint to denote evidence, a magnifying glass to indicate analysis of the evidence, and a set of scales to encourage critical evaluation, with the top and bottom cones representing the topic sentence and link to the next paragraph, respectively.

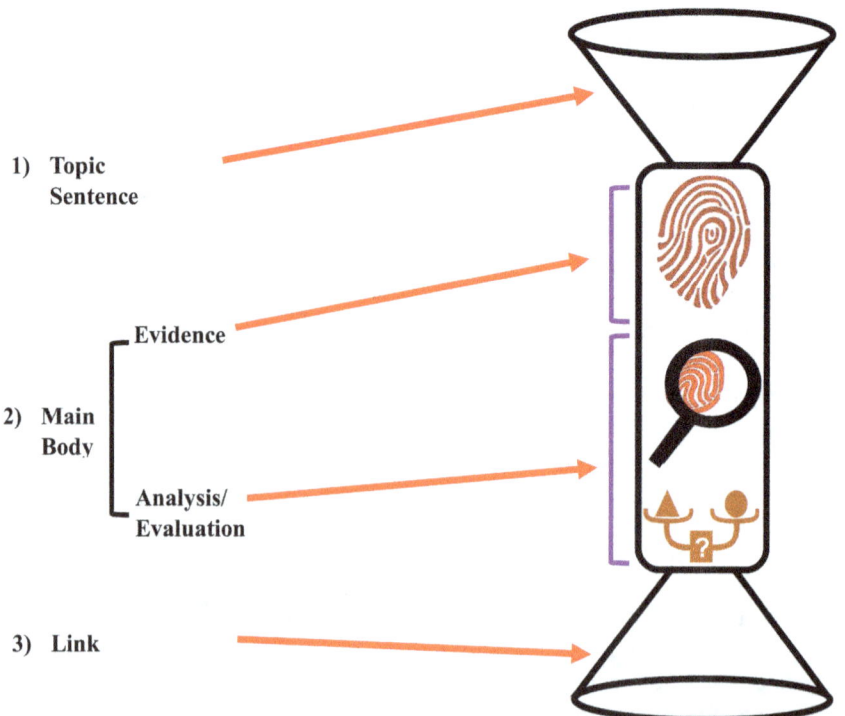

Once again, the shape here is crucial as a means of scaffolding the flow of ideas. Topic sentences, for example, are clearer when observing a topic to a provable opinion or argument sequence because the reader is led, much like in the introduction, from the general to the specific, from the given information to the new. Indeed, it provides the reader with a 'hook' that draws them in and captures their interest. It is for this reason that the topic sentence, again like the introduction, is best conceived as being triangular (as the handle of the Christmas Cracker), with the general point at the beginning of the sentence (as represented by the broad, general, wide opening at the top), followed by a specific argument and detail (as represented by the much narrower, focused section of the handle). A 'big picture' representation of a couple of the topic sentence examples highlighted above, then, can be visualised and mapped onto the Cracker as follows:

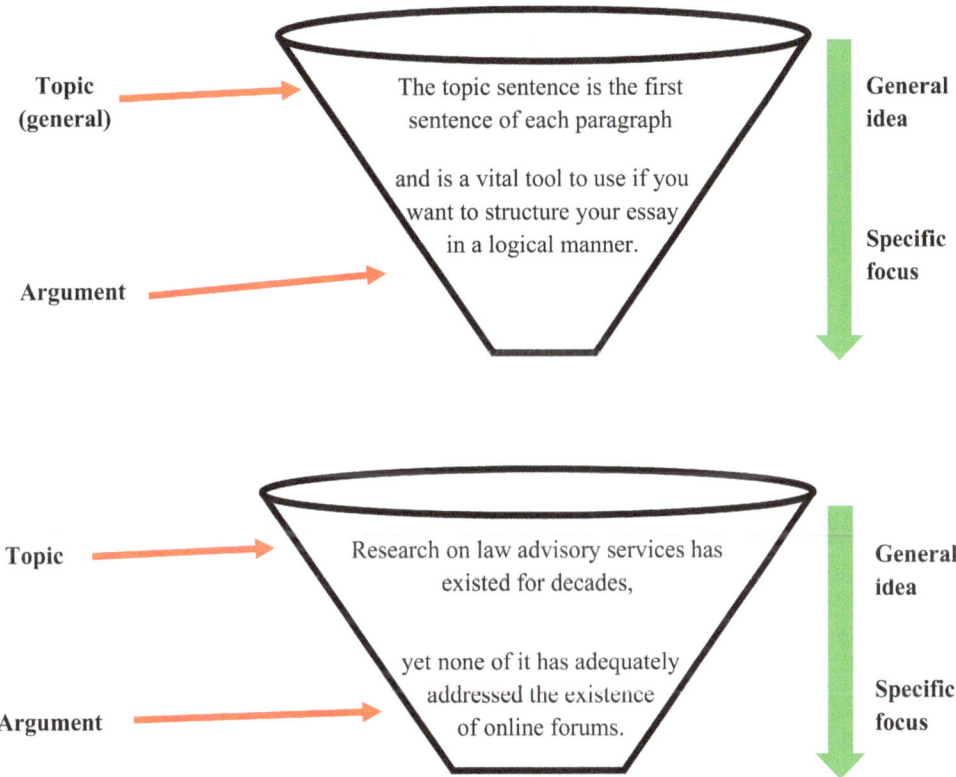

By depicting topic sentences, for instance, diagrammatically as a triangle that moves from a broad opening theme to a provable opinion or argument, and then inserting this triangle within a wider 'Christmas Cracker' roadmap (with accompanying meaningful icons denoting content/focus) of the rest of the paragraph (and indeed the essay as a whole), the student is led to see how the sequence of ideas should follow logically from one another. They are able to see how their arguments fit into the 'big picture' (or not) in a holistic, interlinking, rather than detrimentally sequential way (Cooper, 2019, p.85; Wallbank, 2022, pp.99–101).

Topic sentences are a particularly useful 'anchor' within an essay to help students with learning differences map the overarching structure of the essay but also as a means of checking to see whether each paragraph has an argument. We often suggest to students that in their final editing/proofreading stages, they read just the opening sentence of each paragraph so that they can get a very quick sense of whether each paragraph has an argument, and that it contributes to a forward momentum of ideas which addresses the assignment question. One way of doing this is to use the following diagram as a means of orientating students as to 'what', 'how', and 'why' everything in the essay fits together:

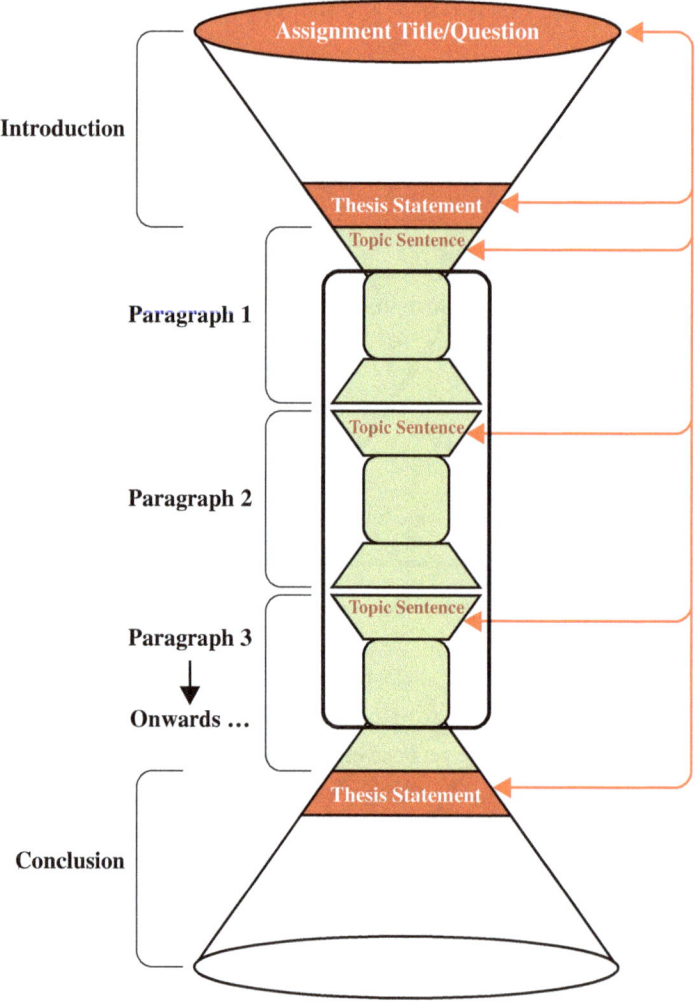

Note here how this visual diagram or template provides a meaningful roadmap to the entire essay or assignment and the various functions associated with each component. This is somewhat different to how GenAI would support this task, for instance. Meechan (2025, p.115), for example, suggests that GenAI tools could be used to suggest 'sentence starters' (topic sentences) for an essay. Take the essay above regarding trauma, for example. If we ask ChatGPT to do precisely this task using the essay planner and the original assignment task, it suggests topic sentences such as:

Paragraph 1: Trauma is a complex and multifaceted concept, often defined in varying and sometimes conflicting ways.

Paragraph 2: Biological theories often highlight gender differences as a key factor in understanding trauma responses.

Paragraph 3: Psychological theories focus on individual vulnerabilities, such as pre-existing mental health conditions or personality traits.

There are two key issues here. Firstly, although all of the topic sentences contain a topic, crucially none of them contain a provable opinion or argument; as such, they do not lend themselves to criticality and do nothing to support the student to be anything other than descriptive rather than analytical (thus resulting in lower marks). Secondly, while the student could use them, there is no sense of how the topic sentences serve to knit the assignment response together as a coherent whole, or how they contribute to a forward, logical progression of ideas (as mapped onto the diagrams/templates above). As such, the pedagogy behind compositional pictography is intended to be meaningful, as it scaffolds the need students have with learning differences have to see the 'big picture' and 'what', 'why', and 'how' everything fits together. GenAI does not and cannot provide this level of meaningful support.

In thinking about the rest of the paragraph, take the following example of a topic sentence and main body of a paragraph as an example, this time with the addition of an internal triangle to indicate the narrowing of focus as the paragraph progresses and the paraphrasing symbol we saw earlier to indicate the type of evidence being used.

Things to highlight to the students here are:

1) The gradual transition in the analysis and evaluation from the general to the specific, from the given to the new (even though the student is discussing several pieces of literature). As such, the sequence of ideas is clear and logical.

2) Following the evidence, the student evaluates current secondary research by stating that none of the recent studies have examined online forums. The student then discusses which issues academic studies have focused upon instead and cites specific research related to the issue in question before providing a critique of their failings and a justification for their unsuitability.

Research on law advisory services has existed for decades, yet none of it has adequately addressed the existence of online forums. Online modes of seeking advice are becoming increasingly popular, and as Jones (2015) has demonstrated, 53% of people seeking legal advice for employment related issues say they acquire advice via the internet following recent cutbacks in face-to-face provision. But none of the most prominent recent examinations of law advisory services (Smith, 2014, Evans, 2013 and Whittaker, 2013) have examined online forums, and have chosen instead to focus upon issues relating to gender, disability and government austerity measures. Evans did consider the implications of what he terms 'the Facebook generation' (p.38), but given that his sample size was only 98 participants, his conclusion that online forums do not present a threat to face-to-face provision is to be treated with caution. Indeed, the research is now significantly out of date given recent changes in government policies, all of which have resulted in further cutbacks to law services, and his focus upon issues pertaining to land law is too restrictive to give us any real sense of the overall picture concerning legal online forums. As a consequence, research on law advisory services needs to shift its attention to online mediums if it is to understand today's service implications.

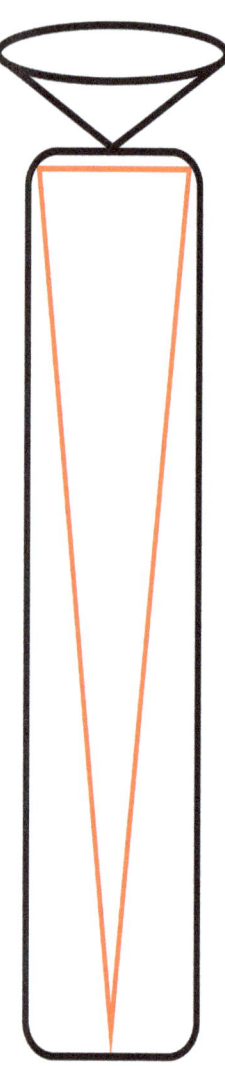

Often, students will need to introduce and incorporate evidence from multiple sources in their paragraphs to demonstrate a thorough knowledge of the subject, their ability to synthesise information, and their engagement with key debates in the field. For students with learning differences, this can be cognitively demanding. To help with this, in *Academic Writing and Dyslexia: A Visual Guide to Writing*, Wallbank developed a suite of symbols which again meaningfully convey the purpose of techniques such as quotation, summarising, and paraphrasing to help students understand their purpose. However, a particular challenge that students with learning differences have here is in terms of sequencing the flow of ideas and sources. The key here is to help students sift through the material to identify points of similarity and contrast and then prioritise and select which are the most relevant and important for their argument. This can be done via a table, 'synthesis' grid, or Venn diagram, for example, but getting the ideas down and into a paragraph can be the main challenge. Again, this is where

From Theory to Practice 155

the Christmas Cracker template and the use of exemplars can help. Take the following extract, for example:

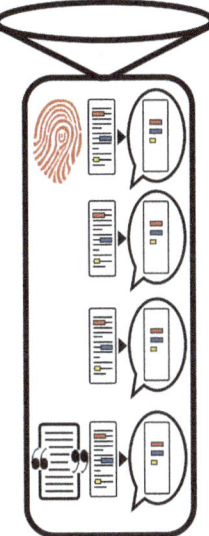

Although somewhat contentious, it is possible that arranging workforces into teams may lead to high levels of employee performance. It has been claimed that when an individual worker is positioned in a team, they can draw on the knowledge and skills of their peers and thus maximise their ability to function effectively (Fenwick 2006; Landri 2014). Organising a workforce into teams may also encourage workers to transcend their own self-interest and prioritise the collective good of the organisation (Guzzo and Ditson 2012). Moreover, as Polanyi (2010) argues, if team members are able to participate in joint decision-making, then task motivation may increase. However, Hockman (1990) suggests that a high level of employee performance is "not inevitable" when a workforce is organised into teams. He claims that there is a tendency to "romanticise" the idea of the team and suggests that there is little empirical evidence to support the widespread belief that team-working is the most effective way of organising a workforce.

Key:

Purple: Summary of two sources for first piece of supporting evidence.

Green: Summary of source for second piece of supporting evidence.

Orange: Summary of source for third piece of supporting evidence.

Blue: Summary of source (with quotation) to introduce counterargument.

In this example, note that only the most important headlines or key ideas have been included (using good summarising skills). However, they have been synthesised and incorporated in a manner that tells a story and outlines the background to the core issue of employee performance in teams and the degree to which the relationship between teamwork and performance is contentious. This sequence is vital, as it lays the foundation for the student's own 'voice', argument, and analysis (which follows). Each source also has a specific function in laying the foundation for the contention expressed in the topic sentence as follows:

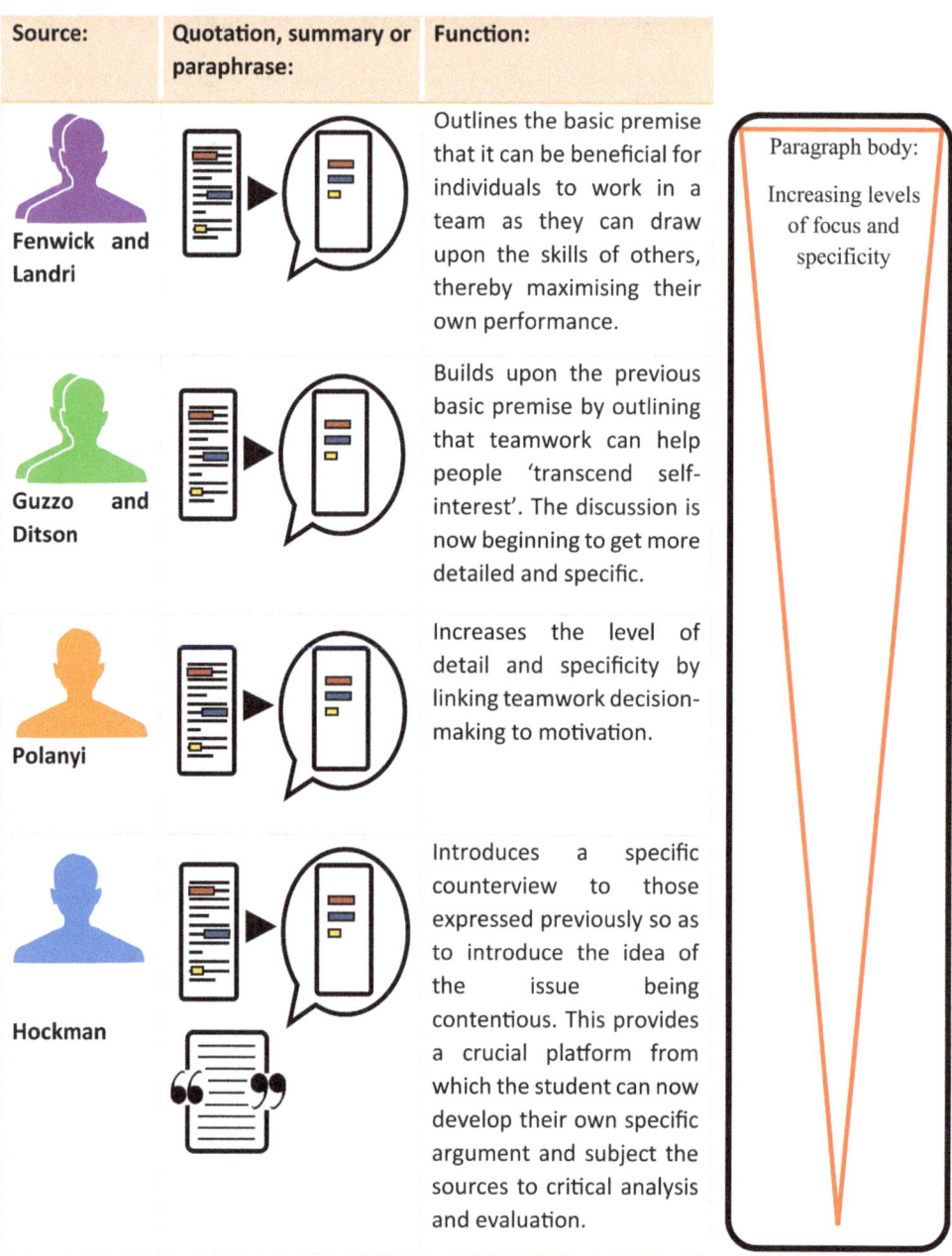

By breaking down the structure of the above example of synthesis and mapping it onto a *meaningful* visual framework that indicates the transition from the 'big picture' to specific details or areas of contention, you can enable the student to see that the sequence of ideas is logical. Without this structure, the synthesis is likely to appear somewhat random and haphazard and will not build a platform from which they can develop their argument and analysis. A lack of direction when synthesising evidence and ideas will also render it unclear with respect to how it is addressing the assignment task or question.

Case Study B: Paragraphing (Tutor: Mona Khatibshahidi)

Student B: 'B' is a postgraduate student who is studying English Literature and is diagnosed with dyslexia and ADHD. At the time of the support commencing, the student was in the process of writing a 20,000-word dissertation. Due to a negative experience during their undergraduate studies, the student was initially reluctant to take up academic literacies support.

Intervention

The key issues that 'B' was facing mainly centred around maintaining attention when writing the dissertation. When speaking, the student was extremely knowledgeable about their topic and could confidently explain the ideas behind their work. However, when writing, the student would lose their flow of thoughts, get distracted very easily, and become unable to write anything. Even though 'B' had a thorough plan for their dissertation, such as a clear outline and the key arguments of each chapter, putting ideas into writing was a huge cognitive challenge for them in terms of their processing and organisational skills, and they found it immensely difficult to articulate their ideas in the logical and coherent manner expected within academic writing. Furthermore, the fear of not achieving a perfect piece of writing resulted in 'B' constantly procrastinating and diverting too much focus to planning rather than composition. This type of perfectionism/hyper-focusing and procrastination can be common symptoms of ADHD, and the focus on planning rather than actual composition illustrates well how they were trying to overcompensate for their difficulties to the point of inertia.

After the initial stage of diagnosing the issues, it was discovered that 'B' preferred visual strategies, as the plan of the dissertation was colour-coded and thoroughly designed. For instance, the key sections of each chapter such as the context/background, main arguments, literature review, and analysis were put into a chart and were colour-coded accordingly so that 'B' could structure them in the writing stage. As such, I used the visual diagrams described above for each section of the dissertation to break down the process into manageable steps. For instance, in the introductory chapter, even though the student clearly colour-coded the key information in their plan, they were not sure where to start, or how to prioritise the ideas. As such, the Christmas Cracker diagrams were used to help them organise their initial thoughts in a coherent way.

When providing the diagrams, the student was able to see how to not only prioritise their thoughts but to express them coherently. To encourage the flow of writing and to avoid 'blank paper syndrome', and given that the student was a strong speaker, I also suggested that 'B' use speech-to-text software to capture ideas without any interruption and without concerning themselves about perfect structures, sentences, and/or grammar. This allowed 'B' to produce the first draft of their dissertation in the duration of a month, a level of productivity that was encouraging for them. Moving to the next stage, I suggested that the student use further visual methods to be able to identify if the information is in the right place and if it is linked effectively throughout. In the paragraph below it is evident that the key argument is unclear, and the student was unsure as to why they got negative feedback from their supervisor. Using a simple colour-coding technique, we clarified the purpose of the different parts of this sample paragraph to identify the location of the key information, which allowed them to see the 'bigger picture' and realise why the main argument within the paragraph was not clear.

> 1) topic sentence/argument 2) evidence 3) analysis/evaluation/discussion 4) link/implications
>
> Before expanding on the fragmentation of the sexed body, it is important to address the experiences of those who are trans – those who were ascribed a gender at birth of which they no longer identify with. Stoller's sex and gender distinction comes into play here as it was created to understand those who desired to transform their gender and bodies (Stoller 1968 cited in Schrock, Reid and Boyd 2005, 319). The distinction was accepted within the community as trans identified individuals can state that no matter the sex of their bodies, their gender identity can exist as separate from this – the two can exist in opposition to one another. Despite this being a used by trans people to articulate and express the way they experience alienation from their body, this distinction plays into the dualistic separation of mind and body. The adoption of Stollers sex and gender distinction by trans people is unwittingly an attempt to expand the cis male dualistic mind to all genders and sexes as one is primarily a mind that inhabits a body – the expansion is that one's mind rather than one's body asserts gender identity. These individuals often regard themselves as having a 'true-self' that is misaligned with their corporeality (Rubin 2013, 12), meaning that the dualistic distinction of mind and body can resonate with them especially as gender is correlated to the mind and sex to the body. In cis people this correlation is not highlighted as gender and sex for them do not feel at odds but within the trans experience gender and the mind are prioritised as the self over the body and its sex; trans embodiment involves the attempt to transcend the body in a similar way to the cis male. However, as their bodies are not perceived as the norm, not catered for in society the way cis male bodies are, they are unable to experience the privilege of being regarded as minds over bodies; they are categorised as dualistic bodies similarly to the female body. Operating with Stoller's sex and gender distinction can be viewed as them seeking to be acknowledged as minds or affirming themselves as minds. This project of expanding the cis male dualistic hierarchy is better replaced by an understanding of Merleau-Ponty's embodiment, where once again the experience of alienated embodiment stems from one's body image being misaligned to corporeality. The body image is influenced by the situated environment and context of embodiment; the way fertility influences cis women's perception of their gender – as either defective or affirmed – is produced by the cultural context of their embodiment, the ways that gender and sex are perceived and treated in society.

Once the passage was colour-coded, it was evident as to why the main argument of the paragraph was unclear as it was in the centre of the paragraph instead of the beginning. Furthermore, the paragraph lacked a clear link to the next argument, which made the passage even more confusing. Using this technique allowed the student to visualise the issue and understand why the argument in this sample was not structured clearly. We then utilised the Christmas Cracker template to help the student refocus their ideas and produce a more coherent draft. By using this visual method of planning the essay, deconstructing draft passages, and aligning them to the Christmas Cracker templates, 'B' also mentioned that they felt they had more control over the writing stage and could elaborate on their ideas more confidently without going off on tangents. Due to this comprehensive and visual planning, the student also stated that 'the writing stage was more efficient and productive' and took them only a few hours with only a brief editing and proofreading time, which was a huge achievement for 'B'.

Grammar, sentences, and rhetoric

Another area where students with learning differences can struggle is with respect to writing effective, logical, compelling sentences. It should be noted from the above that many students with learning differences are extremely able to articulate their thoughts verbally, but struggle to do so in writing, even to the point of experiencing writer's block. This is because of the increased demands on the working memory associated with written, textual composition. Structure, grammar, spelling, and even the task of typing involves considerable multitasking and automaticity which proves problematic, especially for students with dyslexia. As such, grammar and syntax can be seriously impeded.

One way of assisting with this issue is obviously through the use of speech-to-text software; additionally Google Docs auto-predicts sentence fragments and GenAI can reformat draft pieces of writing into more polished final products or compositions. However, these only go so far in terms of scaffolding the development of language and composition. 'Outsourcing' such work completely to GenAI is obviously an easy option but does not develop the skills needed to write autonomously (as in an examination or in the event of an IT outage – at the time of writing the world has just gone through the global computer outage sparked by the Crowdstrike debacle).

Particular issues identified with students with learning differences (especially dyslexia and ADHD) often centre around not only macro sequencing (as we have seen in relation to thought generation and essay and paragraph structure) but also sequencing at a micro level (i.e. grammar and sentence structure). Sentence fragments and run-on sentences are particular problems. To tackle this, it is possible to teach grammar and sentence structure visually, again carefully ensuring that visual representations are a) meaningful and b) have inherent 'followability' (Macbeth, 2010, p.45).

Structuring sentences and understanding the rules of grammar are probably the most difficult challenges students with dyslexia, ADHD, and sometimes autism can face. This is partly because, until recently, grammar was simply not taught in many UK schools. But additionally, it is often very difficult to see and visualise, let alone understand, a direct correlation between grammatical rules and meaning – something that individuals with dyslexia, for example, often need. For instance, the advice in Strunk and White's famous and immensely popular book, *The Elements of Style*, that 'a noun in apposition may come between antecedent and relative' (2003, p.30) means very little, precisely because it is difficult to visualise or conceptualise. In addition, there appears to be little connection between the rule and the meaning. One may well ask, why may a noun in apposition come between antecedent and relative? The answer is that it is less ambiguous, but why is it less ambiguous? Without a visual or material explanation that can be seen or touched, these abstractions will remain abstract, and individuals with dyslexia, for example, are likely to remain entirely confused. One way around this is to view sentences and rhetoric not from the perspective of grammatical rules but from the perspective of visual frameworks, the shape of which again explains the purpose of the sentences and why the sequence of ideas is best in a particular order. Students can then use these templates to help them visualise and see the 'big picture' of their own sentences so that they can understand how to write with confidence, direction, and clarity.

In order to exploit the affective, recognition, and strategic networks of the brain associated with the 'why', 'what', and 'how' elements of UDL, a good starting point is to teach the *purpose* or meaning/logic of and behind sentences. According to the Oxford English Dictionary, a sentence is a 'set of words that is complete in itself and held together with grammatical rules'. The ideal sentence is short and communicates either ONE idea or a closely connected set of ideas. In English, sentences usually fall into four distinct categories: simple, compound, complex, and compound-complex. Each of these sentence categories has its own particular rules in relation to clauses, predicates, subjects, objects, and verbs, but none of this tells us what they are actually for. As we have seen, research has shown that individuals with dyslexia need to understand and see the overarching purpose, aim, or 'big picture' of a sentence before looking at the details. This is a requirement that is opposite to traditional approaches which start with sentence construction (nouns, verbs etc.) and then work towards the purpose and aims (Eide and Eide, 2011, pp.192–193). In order to help students with their composition, then, it is crucial to help them think about what sort of idea they want to express. What is their end goal, and what do they want to achieve? What is the key message they want the reader to take from the sentence (note the emphasis upon 'what' here before thinking about the 'how')? Again, this is where the visuals displayed here have to be meaningful rather than arbitrary and model the logic of sentences and writing in a meaningful way.

A sentence is obviously much more than merely a 'set of words … held together with grammatical rules' – it is a means of communicating ideas, usually new ideas. As such, it is worth starting with Bruce's concept of 'communicative dynamism' (1988), which is the underlying principle all sentences have in common and which ought to be your main priority when teaching writing to students with learning differences. For Bruce, a sentence is a means of guiding the recipient from what they already know to a new piece of information (and 'dynamism' increases in a wave pattern along the way).

One way of making ALL sentences contribute to advancing your argument, then, is to follow the given-to-new pattern. For example:

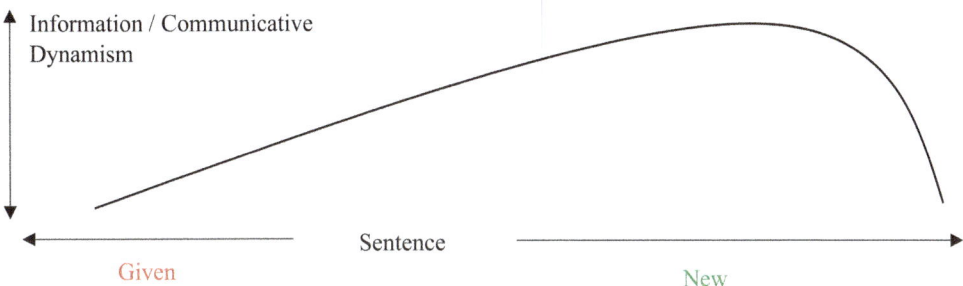

The defendant's claim is clearly inadmissible due to the specifications outlined in Clause 2:1.

Shakespeare's metaphors have been revised given the discovery of the new manuscript.

Ash dieback is increasing, but in laboratory tests, Ye (2017) successfully halted its mutation.

This sequence enables the reader to start with information and topics familiar to them before being guided towards new, detailed information (the argument). The golden rule here is to ensure that the most prominent, important, and detailed information is at the end of each sentence, as in the three examples above. Indeed, by ensuring that students place the most important, new information at the end, they will find they write more concisely.

Once the overarching purpose of a sentence has been taught, tutors can then help students think about narrowing down the focus of sentences into sub-purposes and map these onto visual templates (again, the shape here is crucial in conveying, scaffolding, and mapping or modelling meaning).

For example:

1) Evaluative sentences:

Because evaluation is so important for scoring high marks, the template is green throughout. An evaluative sentence aims to consider two ideas or pieces of evidence. In considering the first idea or piece of evidence, encourage the student to move from the 'big picture' or 'given' information to new information or detail. When introducing the second, alternative idea or piece of evidence, however, the student should pick up from either the same narrow detail (which they usually have in common) or new details (the specifics of the issue at stake), before moving back out into the 'big picture', as can be seen in the shape of the templates below. An evaluative sentence can do this in an even-handed manner, or it can evaluate to demonstrate a preference and concede the strengths of an opposing argument (this can be indicated by the comparative length of the triangles). In both cases, these sentences can be very useful for showing the marker that they have considered all the angles and can skillfully weigh up pros and cons. For example:

Even-handed evaluation:

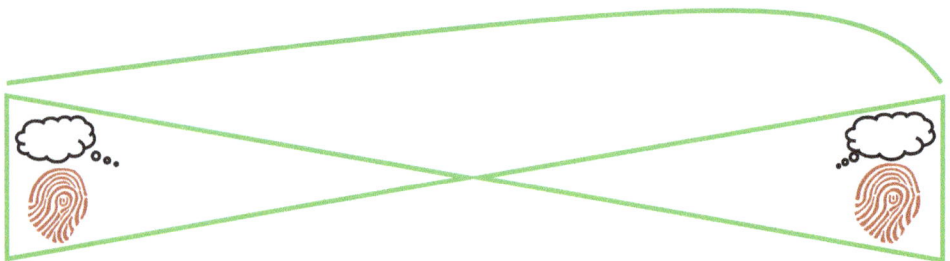

Profitability can derive from strategic risk-taking, but it can also cause financial deficits.

Crop yield was high due to high rainfall, but better pesticide use may also be a factor.

Preferential evaluation/the art of concession:

For preferential evaluation and concession, students should use the template below to briefly summarise, empathise with, highlight, and concede the strengths of the opposing ideas or evidence before outlining their position and evidence, again moving from the specific point of detail, divergence, or principle objection out to the 'big picture'. This demonstrates that they have anticipated possible objections or counter-arguments on the part of the reader and marker but can still forge an argument. As can be seen in the examples below, one of the best ways of doing this is to put concessions in a subordinate clause, thereby putting the most crucial, new parts of the argument at the end:

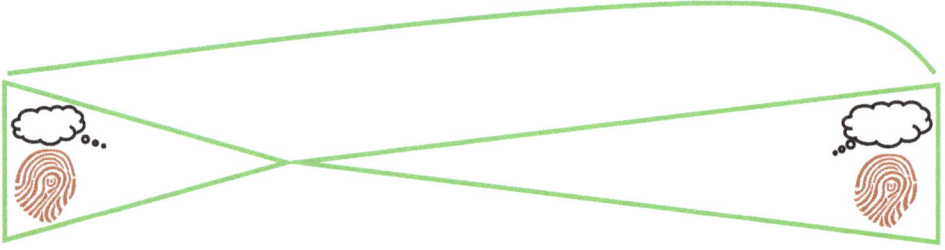

Although CO_2 has increased, it would appear that levels of NO_2 are of greater concern.

Despite Wu's suggestions, it is the authoritarian nature of patriarchy that needs addressing.

Note in all of these examples how the triangle indicates the broad, 'big picture' topic idea at the beginning, followed by an increased focus towards the end, then back out to the new idea. Bruce's 'wave' is mapped on the top to illustrate the 'communicative dynamism', and the use of either fingerprints or thought bubbles denotes either ideas or evidence.

2) Argumentative or analytical sentences:

Argumentative or analytical sentences are probably the most important for students to master, as they directly show the marker that they are answering the question or assignment task, critiquing or evaluating ideas, and proving their point. These sentences often follow descriptive, narrative, evaluative, concessional, refutational, and/or persuasive sentences and justify or provide depth to the views expressed therein. The best way for students to present their analysis in a compelling, confident, and clear manner is to either move from the 'big picture' to specific details or present ideas chronologically. Some examples/extracts from argumentative sentences can be mapped onto the template as follows (again, note the triangle indicating the broad, 'big picture' topic idea at the beginning, followed by an increased focus towards the end, Bruce's 'wave' mapped on the top to illustrate the 'communicative dynamism', and the magnifying glass and fingerprint to denote the critical engagement with evidence).

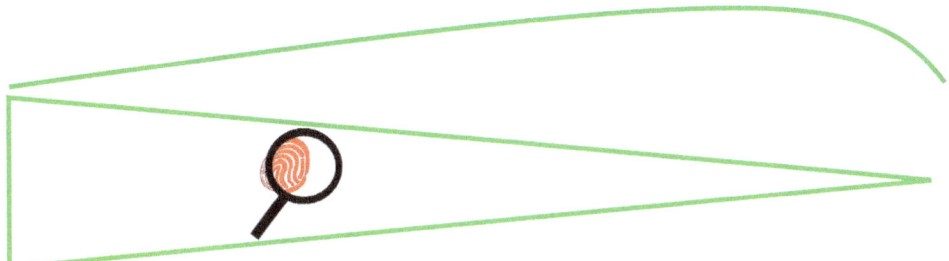

State liability is too arbitrary to have any effect domestically, let alone internationally …

The limitation of synthesising these hypotheses is the failure to implement variables …

Obviously, over the course of an essay, the student will use combinations of the above sentence types to express their argument, and in *Academic Writing and Dyslexia: A Visual Guide to Writing at University*, these are broken down into six academic sentence types with accompanying images and explanations like those above. Together they form the student's analysis and they are the building blocks of their paragraphs. Indeed, if we put to one side for a moment the Christmas Cracker framework and purely focus on the sentences and their purpose, you can show students how the sentences are combined to provide rich and insightful analysis while driving the argument forward from the given to the new as follows using a sample short paragraph like this one from a law essay:

Sentence:	Sentence type / template:
Legal responses to the issue of domestic violence are far from satisfactory.	Topic sentence: 
Although CPS reports suggest that 'highest volumes ever' of domestic violence referrals were charged last year (over 70,000 [CPS 2014b]), there are numerous significant counterarguments which point out inadequacies in the legal framework and its ambiguous definitions.	Preferential evaluation / concession: 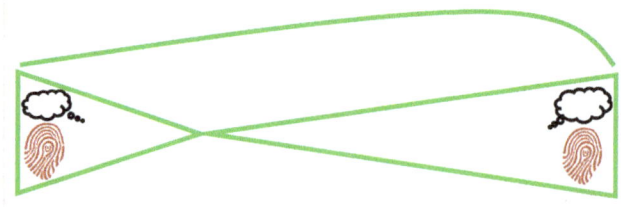
Despite repeated, valid attempts to create a definition of domestic violence which encompasses a wide array of actions (Smith, 1999 and Jones, 2001), the notion of domestic violence as meaning physical beating, remains the 'dominant view' (Stark, 2007, p.84).	Preferential evaluation / concession: 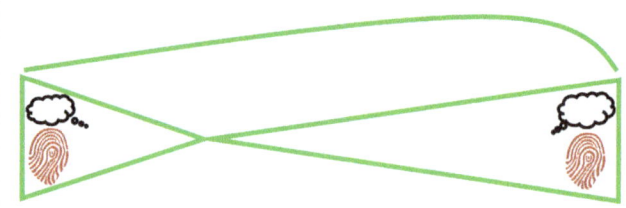
As Stark (2007) has testified, victims are reluctant to acknowledge their situation absent of physical violence (p.111).	Reporting sentence: 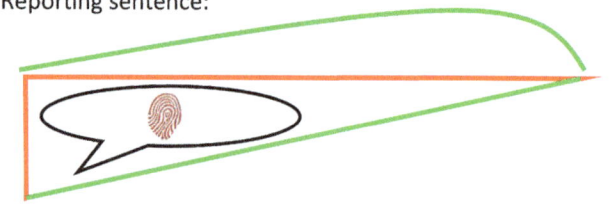

Furthermore, no specific 'domestic violence' offence exists, with instances being artificially categorised as regular offences instead.	Argumentative / analytical: 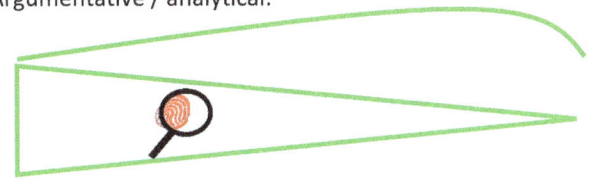
Indeed, they are mostly categorised as 'common assault' which does not accurately reflect the severity of domestic violence (Hester, 2006, p.85).	Argumentative / analytical: 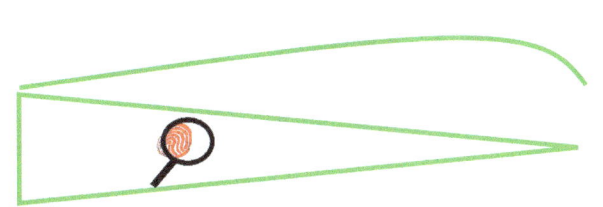
Additionally, state liability for failing to prevent domestic violence, though welcome, is set to a very high threshold (Osman v UK), and as such may not be robust enough to have much effect domestically save in exceptional circumstances (Burton, 2010, p.134).	Argumentative / analytical: 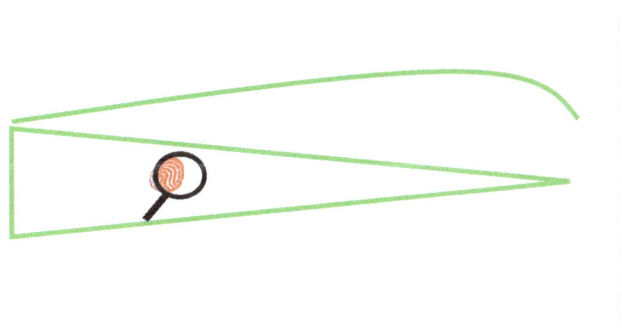

Note here how the student has moved from preferential evaluation/concession sentences and reporting, to more detailed argumentative/analytical sentences, thus adhering to the template of the main body of paragraphs demonstrated via the Christmas Cracker model from earlier (i.e. moving from a topic sentence and evidence though to analysis). Furthermore, notice also how frequently we see signposting (usually at the beginning of the sentences such as 'indeed' and 'additionally') to indicate that arguments build upon each other and intersect. As such, this piece of writing is very compelling.

Once the overarching purpose of a sentence is understood by the students, you can drill down into sentence-level grammar. This requires reframing the traditional model of sentence composition (the transition from subject → verb → object or, much less frequently, subject → object → verb, which forms the basis of over 87% of world languages [Tomlin, 1986, p.22] to thinking of sentences as consisting of TOPIC, ACTION, and DETAIL, or 'TAD'). Fortunately, 'TAD' can be made even more accessible and understandable if we map it visually onto the Christmas Cracker template, again with purposeful, meaningful shapes and icons. For example:

166 *Academic Writing, Assessment, and Neurodiversity*

1) Simple sentences:

'Freud had a huge impact on psychoanalysis'. Here we have a TOPIC (Freud), ACTION in the form of a verb (impact), and a new piece of information or DETAIL (psychoanalysis). This type of sentence can be visualised thus:

Freud   **had a huge impact**   **on psychoanalysis.**

Note here the Christmas Cracker template denoting the three major components of the grammatical construction, the apple to denote the topic/main idea (to align with knowledge and its Biblical and Newtonian connotations), action denoted by a moving wheel, and detail denoted by progressively smaller, interlinking cogs to symbolise increasing levels of detail.

2) Compound sentences:

'Freud had a huge impact on the field and his theory of dreams remains the cornerstone of psychoanalysis'. Both parts of the sentence, either side of the conjunction 'and', can stand alone and still make sense as complete thoughts. This type of sentence can be visualised like this:

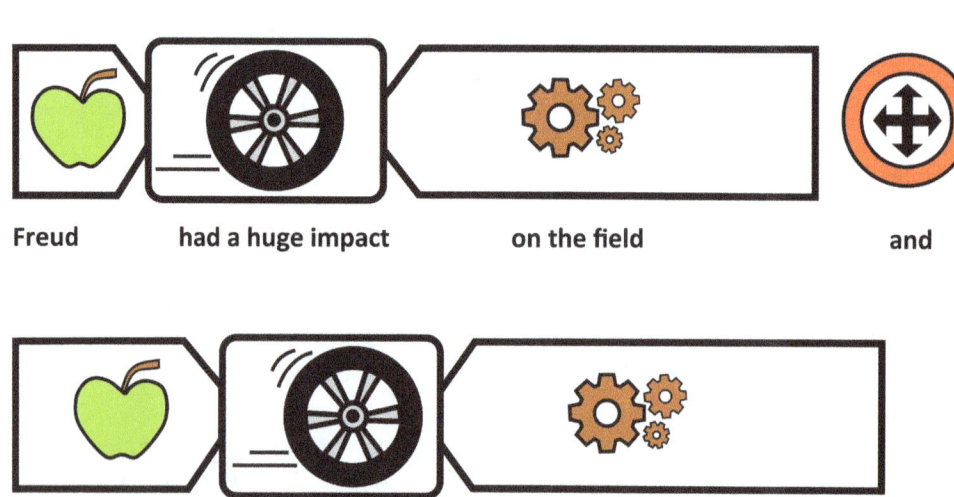

Freud   **had a huge impact**   **on the field**   **and**

his theory of dreams   **remains**   **the cornerstone of psychoanalysis.**

3) Complex sentences:

Here, because this type of sentence expresses an independent, complete thought or clause and a dependent, incomplete thought/subordinate or relative clause, we need a new meaningful icon or symbol. This is owing to the fact that subordinate or relative clauses add supplementary and possibly non-essential detail to the main clause and qualify ideas, act as additional thoughts, and can thus be represented as a thought bubble. Complex sentences, then, can be visualised in the same way as the simple sentence but with the addition of a 'floating', dependent thought (thought bubble), which can appear anywhere within the sentence. For example:

Example a):

Freud's conception of dreams,   despite being superseded,   is   still a valid psychoanalytical tool.

Example b):

Despite being superseded, Freud's conception of dreams   is   still valid psychoanalytical tool.

The principles outlined above work not only for academic writing of course (in whatever guise, be it traditional essays, literature reviews, laboratory reports, methodology recounts, report writing, reflective writing, and writing in examination conditions), but they also work for other forms of assessment such as presentations, as they still require a structured, coherent, language-based response.

Case Study C: Presentations (Tutor: Mona Khatibshahidi)

Student C: 'C' is autistic and is studying second-year Politics and International Relations. 'C' is very confident in discussing key points in history and has a strong long-term memory. In this presentation task, the students were expected to pick a topic from one of the lecture weeks and 'respond to it creatively' in any format they would like. Below is a sample of one of the slides from C's work.

The story of the book.

The introduction and the first two chapters look at the beginnings of the Jewish population from the mass immigration from the Pale to the cities of the Russian Empire along with the increase in territory of the Russian Empire which encompassed modern day Poland among other territories which saw the Jewish population increase considerably. It also look at the beginning of the relationship between the state and the population with the beginning of its categorisation policies through the Internal Passport system and how Jews began to blend in with other population groups in order to avoid this. This was due to the segregation policies followed by the government which saw Jewish people have rights such as the right to join the armed forces of live in certain areas of the country restricted. However, due to the ways Jewish people circumvented this the policies largely failed.

The first two chapters look at how the Russian government to compile data on the Jewish population through census data and the use of birth and death certificates. The use of surnames as a means to identify Jewish people were also used. The Russian government established the Jewish committee which was tasked with fulfilling laws and policies within the Jewish community but also compiling census data and fulfilling data on deaths and births within the community. However, the census taking was largely flowed due to discrepancies in the data and the faking of birth and death certificates. Due to this the power of population information within the population was handed to Crown appointed Rabbis. However, due to continued discrepancies in census data and despite government punishments being promised against people who gave wrong information the government never had reliable data on the Jewish population.

Chapter 2 discusses how a way the government combated this was through fiscal repercussions as without documentation Jewish people would not be able to seek employment or participate within the economy. The chapter discusses how there was a partial relaxation in policies against certain Jews regarding education and employment although compared to other groups impacted in the Great Reforms Jews still remained as second-class citizens.

Within the book on the issue of Jewish Residence and Movement the book discusses how starting in 1890s the Government under Alexander II began to relax restrictions on Jewish immigration and movement across Russia. This along with a new way of fields of work and industry including Finance and Textile saw Jews immigrate to places such as Ladz and Kiev along with other cities across the Russian Empire as the Government began to relax restrictions on Movement toward Jewish People.

Prior to this Jews largely remained in the New Pale within the Western Borderlands. Although despite this Jews were still largely discriminated against with the reforms being limited as Jews could not immigrate into new areas permanently with immigration into Siberia being encouraged due to expansion of Railways across Russia making cross-country travel more accessible. As a result, Jews were only given temporary permission to conduct business and travel in particular areas of the country such as Moscow and St Petersburg. Jewish people were still excessively monitored by Russian interior forces with informers being used to continuously spy on Jewish people of particular interest.

Following the assignation of Alexander II the repressive laws against Jewish People were brought back into effect. This was done through the ordinances on Measures for the prevention of the State Order and the Public Tranquility which was a temporary edict by Alexander III. This was relaxed following a period of disorder by working class and revolutionary movements protesting against the government.

Intervention

As we can see from this sample (also evident in the other slides, 'C' has not been wholly successful in striking 'a balance between being informative and being engaging' (extracted from the assignment description). Instead, the slide is densely packed with text and the student has been very descriptive without raising any specific questions or engaging in any debates or critical thinking around the topic. This amount of description also prevented the student from answering some of the key questions raised in the assignment brief (i.e. 'what are the big debates about the topic (literature review)?' and 'what are the seminal works (books or articles) that have framed or challenged the interpretation of this topic?').

The current format is also problematic in the sense that it can encourage the student to read word by word from the slide without making any eye contact with the audience, which goes against the advice given in the assignment description that requests students to 'show an ability to engage with the audience'. It is evident that the student needs to develop summarising skills and develop bullet points of the main arguments to help prevent them from digressing. Note that one additional factor here may have been not only the tendency of the student to write their slides in great detail owing to the inherent depth-first strengths associated with their autism, but also the possibility of them using the script on the screen so that they need not have to make eye contact with the audience. For this case study though, I focused on the first issue.

In developing an effective summary, 'C' was encouraged to explain the key topic of each section in only one short sentence. This was initially very challenging for 'C' as they feared that they would miss the key details. However, with practice, 'C' managed to develop short bullet points and move a lot of text from the current slides to the notes section. The below step-by-step guide was used to help the student to break down the process of summarising.

Highlight the **main ideas** in the text and **copy** them in this box (separately). To find these check the topic sentences, introduction, abstracts, crucial data, and/or conclusions. Make sure you **do not include any minor details**. Put the list into a logical order.
a.
b.
c.
Read the ideas very carefully and re-write each sentence in your own words (separately). Make sure that you are interpreting the original ideas correctly. **DO NOT** include **your own opinion** or add **any extra information**.
a.
b.
c.
Finally, **combine** the re-written ideas together and put them in a few coherent sentences. Use formal vocabulary different from that in the text (unless you are using quotation marks). Again, **DO NOT** include **your own opinion** or add **any extra information**.
Don't forget to write your **source** using the **correct referencing format**.

As already alluded to, another issue that was addressed in this draft was the lack of analysis or evaluation. As we can see 'the story of the book' has been described heavily in the above slide without any key arguments or analysis. To help the student understand the task, the body paragraph diagram was used in order to emphasise the topic/argument of the slide.

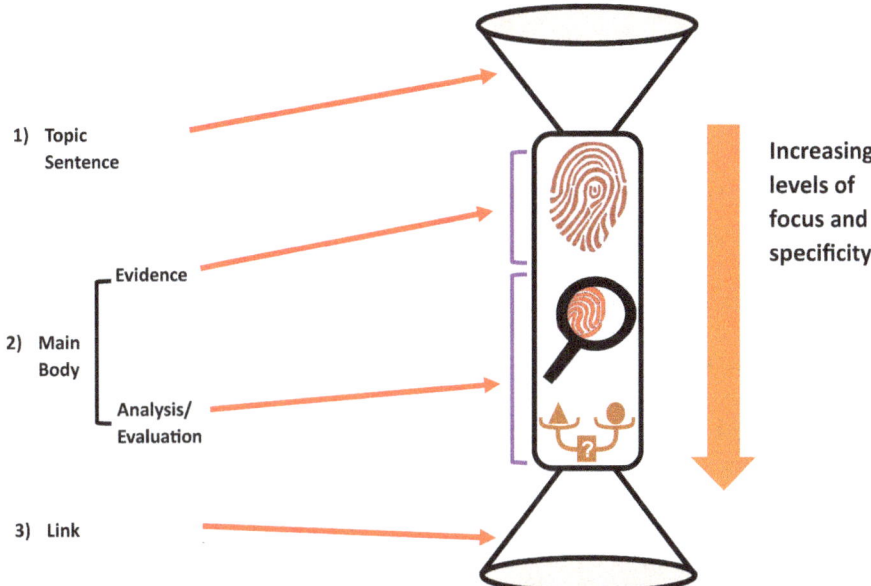

In doing so, I encouraged the student to map the above diagram to the current slide and identify the key elements of topic sentences, evidence, analysis, and links. 'C' was able to successfully identify the evidence and its description; however, they found it confusing to point to a specific argument within the slide. The use of this visual diagram allowed the student to see the 'bigger picture' and the map of a body paragraph (in this case, the main body of the presentation). It also helped the student to focus on articulating an argument in the presentation rather than just describing the evidence. As a result, the student developed a much more focused/concise presentation, and the heavy description was moved to the note section for their own reference or discussion points.

The story of the book.

- The evaluation of the introduction and the first two chapters – Jewish immigration to the Russian Empire
- The way that the Russian government combated this mass immigration – Primarily through fiscal repercussions
- Relaxing the restrictions on Jewish immigration – during 1890s
- Prior to this Jews largely remained in the New Pale within the Western Borderlands. Although despite this Jews were still largely discriminated against with the reforms being limited as Jews could not immigrate into new areas permanently

Although this example has been improved significantly, there is still room for improvement (i.e. the last point is still descriptive). However, the feedback received for the final version of the presentation was more positive and 'C' received an overall mark of 72 on this assignment.

Summary and using supplementary visual techniques

Diagrammatic representations of structure provide both a 'roadmap' or template for the student's perhaps incoherent thoughts, or a template for the tutor to reverse engineer and demonstrably and meaningfully disentangle a student's 'word salads'. Crucially, as Macbeth (2010) suggests, the key to their 'instructional effectiveness' is 'followability' but without imposing too strict a model which would encourage learning almost by rote (p.45). This approach enables students with learning differences to tap into their strengths in identifying connections and visual processing. The visuals allow students with dyslexia, for example, to harness their 'big picture' strengths, while for autistic students, the visual frameworks and 'roadmaps' encourage them to see how their strengths in detail, focus, rationality, and logic map (or not) onto the more complex, ambiguous 'big picture'. Furthermore, one of the key advantages of visual pedagogies, aside from giving students instantaneous access to the 'big picture' context and rendering complex ideas easier to comprehend, is that they reduce or in some cases remove the issues associated with working memory overload so often seen in students with learning differences (Roberts, 2019, p.355). The visual frameworks and icons enable orders, hierarchies, and meanings to be instantaneously established (via their inherent 'followability') without the risk of additional cognitive or working memory overload associated with word word-based decoding and sequencing activities.

Visualising sentences, paragraphs, or even whole essays in a *meaningful*, diagrammatic form is but one medium of representation, however. Elsewhere in your practice, you can deploy flipcharts, mindmaps (either in paper format or via an app such as Mindnode or MindMeister), text scrolls, and text mapping (Wallbank, 2022, pp.34, 172) as a way of offering alternative or complementary visual frameworks for helping students express themselves in multiple ways before mapping those thoughts or arguments into the conventional essay. In respect of how thought generation and prioritisation of ideas can be rendered visible and comprehensible, a particularly effective technique is Oliver West's 'Footnotes' visual multi-layered thinking strategy (West, 2008). By placing thoughts (via visuals) into non-hierarchical grids (especially perspectives, decision-making, and organisational grids), West encourages students to make sense of their ideas in non-linear, non-linguistic, visual, multidimensional ways – precisely the strengths of learners with dyslexia and ADHD (West, 2008; Schneps, 2014; Cooper, 2019; Eide and Eide, 2023). The ability to both map and see one's thoughts mapped out simultaneously and instantaneously without any initial ordering, coherence, or word-based mental processing lessens additional cognitive demands and allows the student to see how everything sits within the 'big picture' in readiness for the next task of imposing order (structural or linguistic). As such, it allows students to see the wood for the trees, whereas making a list in the manner advocated by Cottrell, for example, places too much demand on the working memory and can lead to overload, stress, and confusion.

The effectiveness of compositional pictography

At this point, the question might reasonably be asked, do any of these techniques and pedagogies work? Do they have an impact, and have they been evaluated? The above techniques have been trialled extensively across two studies over the course of one academic year (2019/20) at Royal Holloway, University of London, UK. Ethical clearance was certified via the College's Research Ethics Review process and the impact of the Covid-19 pandemic was judged to be minimal as the pivot to online learning as a result of lockdowns only happened in the final two weeks of the final terms, so most of the contact with students was face-to-face. The first study was with 40 undergraduate students registered as having a SpLD (in receipt of DSA-funded support) in one-to-one academic writing study skills sessions (from a range of disciplines), and the second study was with 158 Integrated Foundation Year (IFY) students, which consisted of a diverse range of students (49% BAME, 43% WP, and 22% disabled/specific learning difficulty) across two core strands (humanities and sciences) in a mix of academic writing workshops and one-to-one interventions – all of which centred around utilising the above visual frameworks and pedagogies and which were embedded into a core module named Global Perspectives and Academic Practice 1 and 2 (GP&AP). The results were then compared with the centralised, open-to-all one-to-one writing tutorials in which the above visual, inclusive pedagogies were not used, and which relied upon conventional teaching methods. Feedback was gathered using a questionnaire with optional feedback comments. It is notoriously difficult to measure the impact of academic writing interventions owing to the multitude of factors and educational interventions elsewhere in their courses. For this reason, the primary measure utilised was student confidence (as self-reported via questionnaires), followed by written feedback comments.

The students were asked to rate their confidence in a range of academic literacy skills at the start of the academic year and at the end on a scale of 1–6 (1 being very unconfident and 6 being very confident) and again at the end of the academic year. The comparative results for the students diagnosed with SpLDs taught in one-to-one sessions are as follows.

Questions:

Q1 Planning and organisational skills
Q2 Revision techniques
Q3 Note-taking
Q4 Reading academic books and journal articles
Q5 Understanding assessment questions
Q6 Academic writing and structure
Q7 Critical thinking and analysis
Q8 Referencing
Q9 Summarising and paraphrasing academic sources
Q10 Teamwork
Q11 Oral presentation
Q12 Using assistive technology
Q13 Your overall view of your ability to study on your course

At the start of the academic year, the average confidence for the students with SpLDs was 3.08. By the end of the year, overall student confidence had risen to 4.52 – an increase of 46.75%. Overall, 74.1% of students said that they had found the sessions 'useful' for developing their confidence in academic writing.

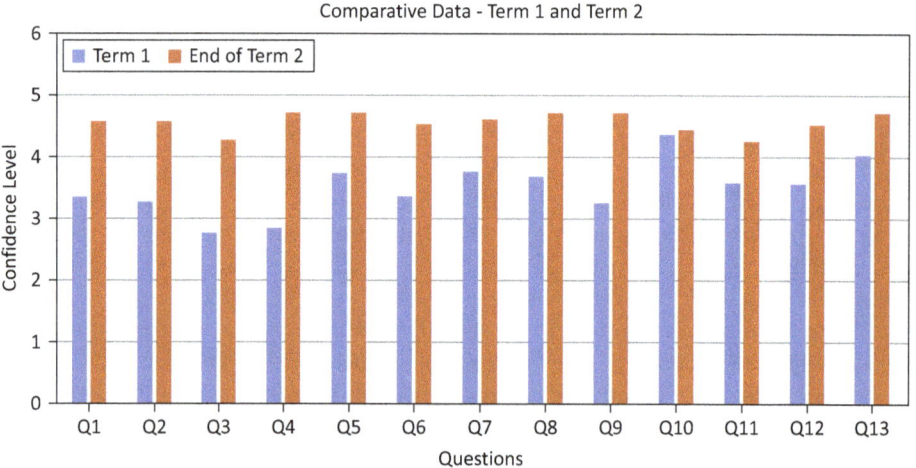

The above data contrasts favourably with the 'open to all', generic academic skills provision in which 66% of students (126 students, 24 responses) found the sessions 'useful' in developing their academic writing confidence – a difference of 8%.

For the IFY cohort, the methodology was slightly different. We measured and evaluated the students through the four lenses of the Kirkpatrick and Kirkpatrick model (2006, 2016) while also utilising elements of the University of Bolton's Learning Excellence Achievement Pathway (LEAP) framework (McIntosh and Barden, 2019) and the Conley Readiness Index. We conducted a mixed methods survey to assess four parameters: student engagement, learning, behaviour, and results.

A diagnostic questionnaire, which gauged the students' perceptions of factors that could impact their learning development and engagement, was opened in Term 1. Students rated the extent to which they agreed or disagreed with statements covering academic writing skills and academic oral skills. A five-point Likert scale was used, from 'completely agree' to 'completely disagree', including a neutral 'neither agree nor disagree' option. They could also write a longer response on their motivations for undertaking a foundation year. 74 students completed this questionnaire (50% response rate). The second questionnaire opened at the end of Term 2. Only 38 students completed the questionnaire (26% response rate); this may have been due to the rapid transition to remote learning during the first lockdown of the Covid-19 pandemic and its associated upheavals. The students could also write longer comments about their positive and negative experiences on the programme. Student success was measured based on a) overall results on the IFY and b) their results for Year 1 in comparison with the College's direct-entry Year 1 students. Student engagement was measured via attendance data. All data gathered was anonymous.

Results

Students felt that both their academic writing and academic oral skills had improved across the year, notably the ability to construct an argument (Figure 1) and the ability to share views in small groups (Figure 4).

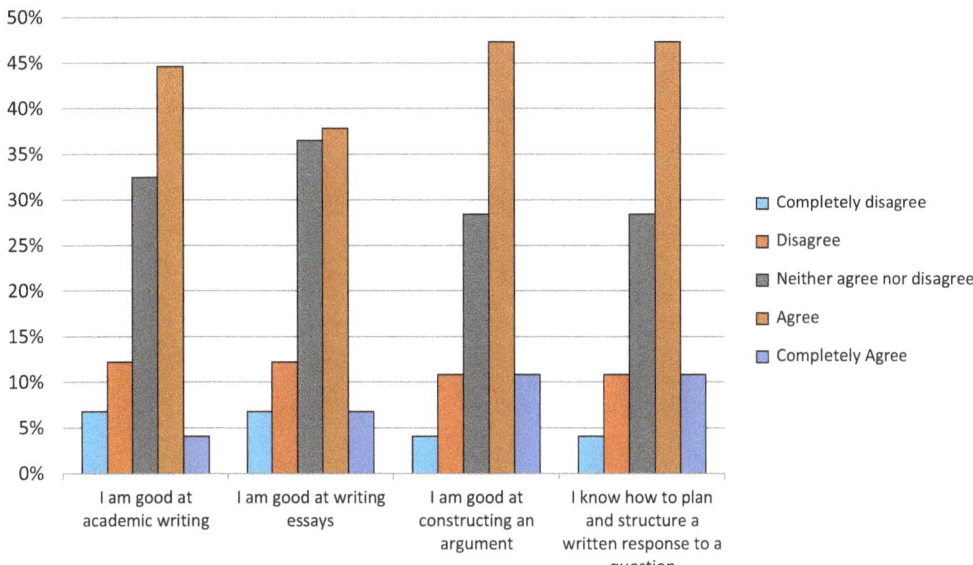

Figure 1 Academic writing skills (Questionnaire 1)

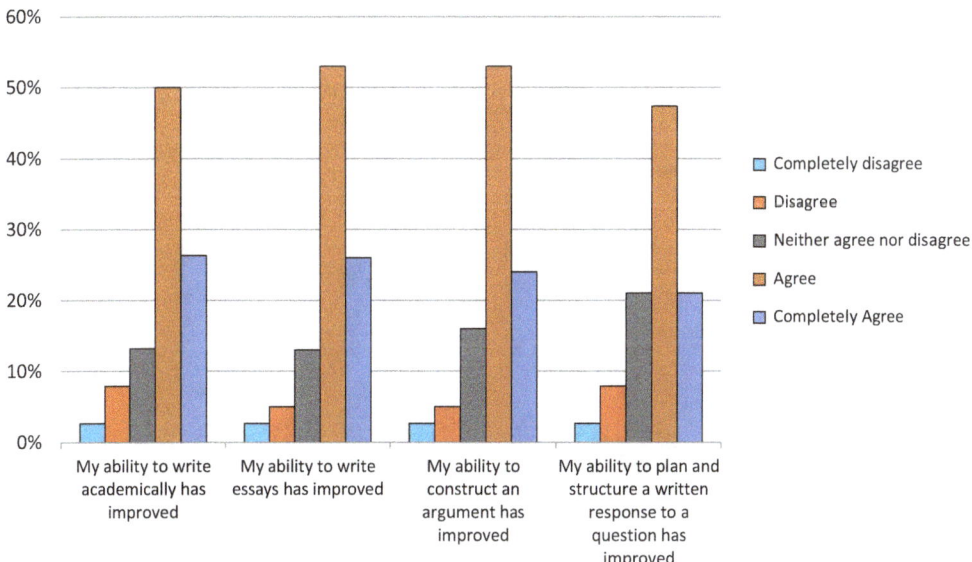

Figure 2 Academic writing skills (Questionnaire 2)

176 *Academic Writing, Assessment, and Neurodiversity*

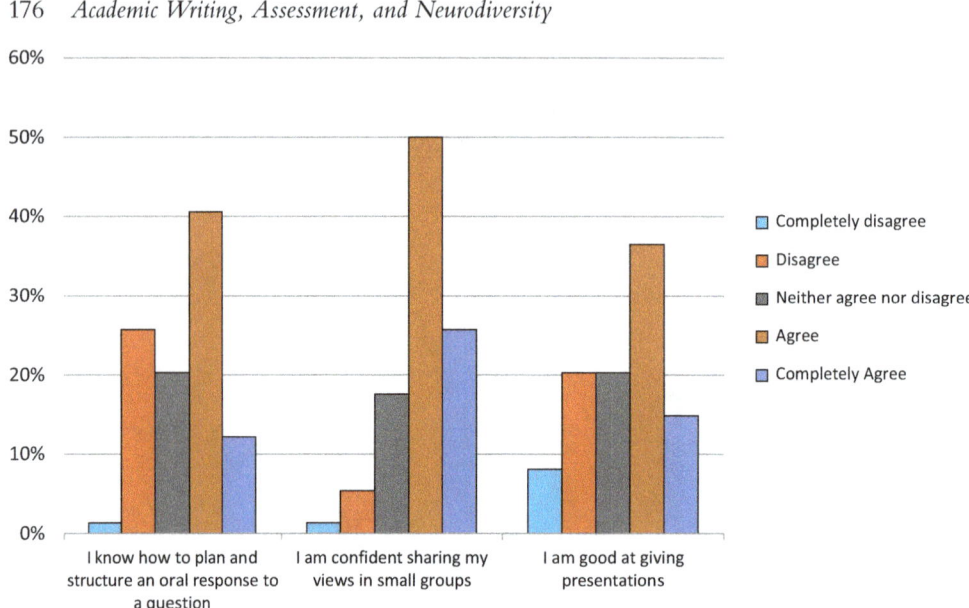

Figure 3 Academic oral skills (Questionnaire 1)

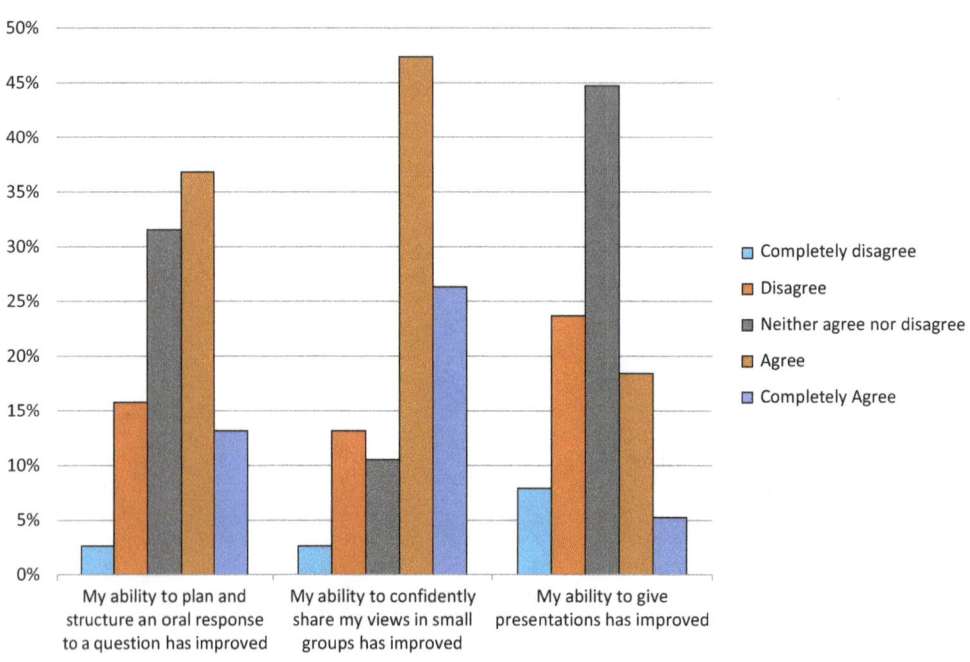

Figure 4 Academic oral skills (Questionnaire 2)

Average confidence levels in academic writing had risen from 3.3 to 4.0 – an increase of 21%. Additionally, 76% of the IFY (across both strands) either 'agreed' or 'strongly agreed' that the interventions had helped improve their confidence in academic writing (10% higher than for the open-to-all provision). Although beset with difficulties and extraneous factors, it is also worth noting that in terms of attainment, by the end of the Foundation Year programme, no statistically significant gap existed between disabled and non-disabled students (students attaining overall marks in either the upper second or first-class categories was 62%). Even more striking is the fact that progression into first-year study was 75.32% for non-disabled and 80% for disabled students. In essence, our research suggests that adopting inclusive, visual frameworks and pedagogies can increase student confidence levels in academic writing by 21–46% (depending upon the cohort and mode of delivery), increases student satisfaction by 8–10%, close the attainment gap between students with learning differences and those without, and has the potential to assist in closing BAME attainment gaps.

Written feedback provided by students in receipt of the inclusive, visual pedagogies also attests to their efficacy, especially in relation to structuring writing and thoughts. Of the 20 students who wrote comments, 10 students highlighted that the methods deployed in the sessions helped them with their academic writing, and recurring comments centred around the fact that the visual, pedagogical methods 'helped me with planning my work and structuring my essays in a coherent way' and helped improve 'the flow of my thoughts ... and work'. Others commented specifically that 'the visual and verbal explanation of the paragraphs and colour-coding each part helped me a lot to understand the structure of paragraphs'. On a related note, a further three students commented that they would frequently attend the sessions 'as confused as anything', but leave having either a 'good' or 'clear idea of what I'm supposed to be doing'. A further six students also praised the way in which the methods used were not only 'varied' but 'focused around the student' and 'individual issues', which once again attests to the inclusive, student-centred application of UDL and the adaptability of visual pedagogies/compositional pictography to students with learning differences.

Similar feedback was received for the sessions run with the IFY students. Comments such as 'really helpful and interesting sessions, certainly helped in explaining essay writing techniques and structure', 'helped me to improve my essay writing skills', and 'extremely helpful for me in terms of feedback and helping me to improve my essays in future' were typical. The inclusive, visual mode of delivery received particular praise and garnered comments such as 'easily accessible', 'extremely engaging and interactive ... I felt challenged each time to achieve better', 'really interesting and enjoyable teaching methods', and 'subject was made interesting and good at explaining'.

Year 0 IFY results

The table below shows the average marks for the GP&AP modules and progression results overall. The best 90 credits were used as part of the no-detriment policy brought in because of the pandemic.

Average marks and progression results

Stream	Average marks for GP&AP 1/ GP&AP 2	Average marks for all courses	Best 90 credits	Average progression	Progression (students with SpLD)	Offered resits
Humanities	61%/58%	54%	60%	71%	87.5%	29%
Sciences	62%/49%	61%	67%	78.2%	90%	21.8%

We were particularly interested in investigating whether students with a diagnosed specific learning difficulty continued to perform well after their foundation year. We wanted to ascertain this because, while the UDL framework is, by definition, inclusive, it has been recommended as specifically useful for the development of students with SpLDs (Burgstahler, 2017; Layer, 2017; CAST, 2018, Norman and Newham, 2018; Krčmář, 2019; Wallbank, 2022). While we saw that progression for students with a declared disability was superior to those without, the average grade for the eight students diagnosed with a SpLD in their first year was 65.6% – significantly above the first-year direct-entry average of 60% and even higher than the IFY average. This attests to the efficacy of utilising an UDL framework to help transition students with diagnosed SpLDs into their studies and reinforces the point that inclusive pedagogies are a 'route to excellence' (Layer, 2017). This clearly indicates that the self-reported increases in academic literacies and skills confidence translates into better performance on their main courses.

Even more intriguing, however, is the extent to which the UDL framework we deployed helped students with lower entry grades. This was not a result we necessarily expected, but in terms of progression, we compared those students on the IFY and direct entry in terms of entry grades (A levels). Of those students entering with grades CCD–EEE and below, 73% who entered via the IFY progressed, as opposed to 65% who were direct entry. Overall, the IFY Humanities cohort consisted of a high percentage of BAME (35%), WP (30%), and disabled (26%) students, while the Sciences strand comprised 61% BAME, 29% WP, and 26% disabled students.

Our approach was further vindicated not only by the positive student results but by the external examiner reports, which described the programme as 'innovative'. As one of the external examiners put it:

> I was impressed with the progression of skills, the depth and breadth of understanding and conceptual engagement, and the levels of achievement reached by the best students. Success for the programme as a whole will lie in how many students progress. I hope RHUL will continue its institutional commitment to this 'TEF Gold' offering … The comparatively low dropout rate for this Foundation year in comparison with the sector average is telling evidence of its quality and the efforts of the RHUL team as well as the commitment of your recruits.

The second external examiner concurred, stating that:

> I was very impressed with the programme that has been put together. In particular, I like the coherence of the programme. It is evident that the courses were not developed in isolation, but by the course teams working together.

Concluding thoughts

In essence, the main message here and throughout this book is that the principles of academic writing and approaching assignments can be broken down into meaningful (not arbitrary) visual images, icons, templates, and even metaphors so as to help scaffold the underlying purpose of the principle under consideration in a way that makes it:

a) accessible to students with learning differences (often owing to their visual learning preferences);

b) taps into their need for developing mental structures or metacognition via their affective networks (the 'why' of learning), recognition networks (the 'what' of learning), and strategic networks (the 'how' of learning);

c) helps students see the wood for the trees (in the case of students with dyslexia and ADHD helping harness their 'big picture' thinking strengths to enable them to understand and appreciate detail, rules, logic, and the need for sequencing, and in the case of autistic students it harnesses their abilities in detailed thinking to help them understand and apply it to the 'bigger picture');

d) proven to be successful, especially when compared with traditional approaches to supporting students.

Furthermore, the aim throughout is to help minimise cognitive load and working memory by providing meaningful workarounds and scaffolding. One of the core issues at stake here is the need for support. This book has been at pains to try and refute the disability model, but there is no getting away from the fact that dyslexia, ADHD, and autism present students with considerable academic challenges, much in the same way as a disabled person faces challenges and requires accommodations. ADHD, dyslexia, and autism are incurable (and bring many benefits anyway), and as such it is a case of either making 'reasonable adjustments' for these students or supporting them to be autonomous learners by equipping them with strategies to enable them to compete on a level playing field with their 'neurotypical' peers (preferably both). The inclusive UDL pedagogic strategies contained in this book, it is hoped, go some way to providing some of these techniques and strategies, and as the 'neurodiversity' in the title of this book suggests, are a pedagogical 'route to excellence' (Layer, 2017) which is good for *everyone*. However, as we shall see in the next chapter, there is much lecturers can do without adopting such techniques to make assessment design more inclusive and accessible.

References

Bruce, N. J., (1988) 'Communicative Dynamism in Expository Academic English: Some Strategies in Teaching the Pragmatics of Writing', *Working Papers in Linguistics and Language Teaching*, 11, pp.42–53. Available from: https://eric.ed.gov/?id=ED331300 (Accessed: 12 August 2022).

Burgstahler, S., (2017) 'Universal Design in Education: Principles and Applications', *Do-It*. Available from: https://files.eric.ed.gov/fulltext/ED506545.pdf (Accessed: 14 September 2023).

CAST, (2018) *Universal Design for Learning Guidelines, Version 2.2.* Available from: http://udlguidelines.cast.org (Accessed: 16 July 2023).

Cooper, R., (2019) 'Specific Learning Difficulties', in Krčmář, K. (ed.), *The Inclusivity Gap*. Aberdeen: Inspired by Learning, pp.80–95.

Cottrell, S., (2013) *The Study Skills Handbook*. Fourth Edition. Basingstoke: Palgrave Macmillan.
Eide, B. L, and Eide, F. F., (2011) *The Dyslexic Advantage: Unlocking the Hidden Potential of the Dyslexic Brain*. First Edition. London: Hay House.
Eide, B. L, and Eide, F. F., (2023) *The Dyslexic Advantage: Unlocking the Hidden Potential of the Dyslexic Brain*. Second Edition. London: Hay House.
Kirkpatrick, D. L., and Kirkpatrick, J. D., (2006) *Evaluating Training Programs: The Four Levels*. Third Edition. San Francisco, CA: Berrett-Koehler Publishers, Inc.
Kirkpatrick, D. L., and Kirkpatrick, J. D., (2016) *Kirkpatrick's Four Levels of Training Evaluation*. Alexandria, VA: ATD Press.
Krčmář, M., (2019) 'Social Cognitive Theory', in Oliver, M. B., Raney, A. A., and Bryant, J. (eds), *Media Effects: Advances in Theory and Research*. Fourth Edition. New York: Routledge, pp.100–114.
Layer, G., (2017) *Inclusive Teaching and Learning in Higher Education as a Route to Excellence*. London: Department for Education. Available from: www.gov.uk/government/publications/inclusive-teaching-and-learning-in-higher-education (Accessed: 16 July 2023).
Macbeth, K. P., (2010) 'Deliberate False Provisions: The Use and Usefulness of Models in Learning Academic Writing', *Journal of Second Language Writing*, 19:1, pp.33–48. Available from: www.sciencedirect.com/science/article/pii/S1060374309000393 (Accessed: 1 December 2024).
McIntosh, E., and Barden, M. E., (2019) 'The LEAP (Learning Excellence Achievement Pathway) Framework: A Model for Student Learning Development in Higher Education', *Journal of Learning Development in Higher Education*, 14, pp.1–21. Available from: https://journal.aldinhe.ac.uk/index.php/jldhe/article/view/466 (Accessed: 11 December 2023).
Meechan, D., (2025) *Generative AI for Students: The Essential Guide to Using Artificial Intelligence for Study at University*. London: Sage.
Norman, E., and Newham, E., (2018) 'The Role of Learning Advisors and Support Staff within an Increasingly Differentiated Student Community', *Journal of Academic Language and Learning*, 12:1, pp.128–140. Available from: https://journal.aall.org.au/index.php/jall/article/download/545/291/0 (Accessed: 2 August 2024).
Roberts, D., (2016) 'Visual Feasts of the Mind: Matching How We Teach to How We Learn', *TEDxLoughboroughU*. Available from: www.youtube.com/watch?v=FJyhTg26w-A (Accessed: 15 November 2020).
Roberts, D., (2018a) 'The Engagement Agenda, Multimedia Learning and the Use of Images in Higher Education Learning: or, How to End Death by Powerpoint', *Journal of Further and Higher Education*, 47:7, pp.969–984. Available from: www.tandfonline.com/doi/full/10.1080/0309877X.2017.1332356 (Accessed: 14 August 2023).
Roberts, D., (2018b) *The Ultimate Guide to Visual Lectures*. Amazon: David Roberts.
Roberts, D., (2019) 'Visual Lectures', in Krčmář, K. (ed.), *The Inclusivity Gap*. Aberdeen: Inspired by Learning, pp.350–364.
Schneps, M., (2014) 'The Advantages of Dyslexia: With Reading Difficulties Can Come Other Cognitive Strengths', *Scientific American*. Available from: www.scientificamerican.com/article/the-advantages-of-dyslexia (Accessed: 20 August 2019).
Steinhorst, C., (2024) 'Lost in the Scroll: The Hidden Impact of the Attention Economy', *Forbes*, 6 February 2024. Available from: www.forbes.com/sites/curtsteinhorst/2024/02/06/lost-in-the-scroll-the-hidden-impact-of-the-attention-economy/ (Accessed: 20 December 2024).
Strunk, W., and White, E. B., (2003) *The Elements of Style*. Fourth Edition. Boston, MA: Allyn and Bacon.
Tomlin, R., (1986) *Basic Word Order: Functional Principles*. London: Croom Helm.
Vygotsky, L. S., (1978) *Mind in Society: The Development of Higher Psychological Processes*. Cambridge, MA: Harvard University Press.
Wallbank, A. J., (2022) *Academic Writing and Dyslexia: A Visual Guide to Writing at University*. Second Edition. London: Routledge.
West, O., (2008) *In Search of Words: Footnotes Visual Thinking Techniques*. Oliver P.B. West.

6 Designing Assessment Tasks to Be Inclusive and the Future of Assessment in an Age of GenAI

Adrian J. Wallbank

Hitherto we have considered how we can support students with learning differences in their approaches to assessment and writing, but at this point, it is worth taking a step back to consider how we might make the design and wording of assessments themselves more inclusive. This chapter offers practical considerations and principles for making assessment tasks more accessible and inclusive.

Constructive alignment

The first element to consider is whether or not you are assessing what has actually been taught or what has been outlined in the programme or module intended learning outcomes. Ideally, this should be clear through a process called constructive alignment (Biggs and Tang, 2011). Constructive alignment is where there is a clear synergy between 1) the intended learning outcomes, 2) the teaching and learning activities, and 3) the assessment tasks. This alignment ought to be clearly threaded throughout these three elements, but often they are not (often as a result of programme teams changing, new ideas, and revalidations that can result in unintentional 'mission drift'), which can have a negative impact not only on the coherence of the module but its inclusiveness. Take the following as an example. Here we have the intended learning outcomes for a module on Research Methods:

1) Remember and understand research knowledge.
2) Understand and critically evaluate research processes to ensure the quality of evidence.
3) Critically evaluate research methods and papers and create new solutions to the papers.
4) Understand and critically evaluate participant recruitment, data collection, and methods of data analysis.
5) Understand the ethics and governance principles involved in research.

The first problem here is the fact that the word 'understand' is not measurable or indeed 'SMART' (the first principle of designing good learning outcomes is to ensure they are **S**pecific, **M**easurable, **A**chievable, **R**elevant, and **T**ime-bound [SMART]). The verb 'understand' is impossible to quantify or measure, and as such not only allows for considerable 'mission drift' but can be vague for students. However, more concerning is the type of assessment used to measure the above learning outcomes in this particular module.

The assessment is 100% examination via multiple-choice questions (MCQs). The task is to read four research papers prior to the examination, and then answer the MCQs under timed conditions. For example:

Vaiva et al. (2006) estimated that 600 participants were needed for the trial to reach statistical significance. This is called: a) A Type 2 error   b) A Type 1 error   c) The standard error   d) A power analysis   1 mark
Glencorse et al. (2014) compare the results of their survey with a similar survey done with GPs. Is it valid to compare the studies in this way?   a) Yes, because the aim of the study was to compare the two groups   b) Yes, because this enhances the external validity of the paramedic study   c) No, because there were 142 respondents to the paramedic study and 282 to the GP survey so the sample sizes are not equal   d) No, because the survey of GPs was carried out in the East Midlands and it is not stated if this region has a comparable rate of excessive drinking to the north-east   5 marks

Note here that while the mark allocation is quite different, the questions are mostly testing knowledge, recalling information, and application. In other words, they test primarily the first learning outcome, 'remember and understand research knowledge'. In large part, throughout the entire exam paper, the MCQs do not test the remainder of the learning outcomes, especially concerning critical evaluation. Here we have a classic example of how constructive alignment has either fallen apart or was not in place from the outset (perhaps because two modules were folded into one and the best bits were taken from each without much thought given to the cohesion or constructive alignment). This is pedagogically unsound for all students, but especially students with learning differences because if they try to make connections between the 'big picture'/context (in this case the overarching learning outcomes and the teaching) and the detail (what they will get marks for and what they need to do in the assignment), the two do not align. This renders the module's clarity, cohesion, and accessibility (and thus inclusiveness) highly problematic and unclear. As such, always ensure that your intended learning outcomes, the teaching and learning, and the assessment, align.

Constructive alignment and the wording of assignment tasks

We have seen how there can be a mismatch between intended learning outcomes and what is assessed, but there can also be a lack of alignment between the marking rubric and the assignment task.

A problem lots of students seem to encounter, irrespective of whether they have a learning difference or not, is difficulty accurately decoding the question or assignment task. This may sound straightforward, but many students tend to either misunderstand or even ignore key directions in the task instructions, particularly in the assignment question. While this is a key academic skill that can be taught, when designing your assignment task or question, break it down into three main components as a way of scaffolding precisely what the students are required to do. The three main components are as follows:

1) **Content/topic keywords**

These are the non-negotiable parameters of the subject and are key topics or themes that the students simply have to include. Typical content/topic keywords might be terms such as 'the Data Protection Act', 'global warming', 'the European Union', 'gravity', 'urban planning', 1956, 'feminism', 'Shakespeare', or 'the Suffragette Movement'.

2) **Activity keywords**

Put very simply, this is what the students have to do. Below is a table of common activity keywords and their meanings for guidance.

Keyword	*Meaning*	*Position on Bloom's taxonomy (1956)*
Analyse	Subject the topic(s) to scrutiny, identify strengths, weaknesses, and flaws and possibly gaps in knowledge. Construct an argument based on the analysis.	Analysis/synthesis/evaluation
Argue	Make a persuasive case for or against something.	Analysis/synthesis/evaluation
Comment on	Identify and write about salient points and possibly criticise or evaluate.	Analysis/synthesis/evaluation
Compare/ contrast	Identify important points and highlight their similarities and differences through analysis. Construct an argument based on your observations.	Analysis/synthesis/evaluation

(Continued)

Critique	Analyse, subject the topic(s) to scrutiny, identify strengths, weaknesses, and flaws and possibly gaps in knowledge. Construct an argument based on the analysis.	Analysis/synthesis/evaluation
Define	Identify and express the meaning of something, including the limitations of such definitions (be concise).	Knowledge/comprehension/application
Describe	Identify and outline the key points.	Knowledge
Discuss	Examine and analyse the issues, evaluate them, and construct an argument which is critically perceptive.	Analysis/synthesis/evaluation
Evaluate	Examine and discuss the pros and cons of something with a view to coming to a verdict, position, and argument.	Analysis/synthesis/evaluation
Examine	Subject the topic(s) to scrutiny, identify strengths, weaknesses, and flaws and possibly gaps in knowledge. Construct an argument based on the analysis.	Analysis/synthesis/evaluation
Explain	Describe and give reasons for something.	Knowledge/comprehension/application
Illustrate	Find and use examples to explain something.	Knowledge/comprehension/application
Indicate	Identify and explain the important points and signal likely outcomes, reasons, conclusions, or arguments.	Knowledge/comprehension/application
Justify	Provide reasons or evidence for a proposition or argument.	Knowledge/comprehension/application
Outline	Identify and describe the main features of something.	Knowledge
Review	Critically examine something, usually something which has been done before, to appraise its strengths, weaknesses, limitations, and arguments. Possibly recommend actions.	Analysis/synthesis/evaluation
State	Describe the main points.	Knowledge
Summarise	Identify and describe the main ideas.	Knowledge/comprehension/application

However, all is not as simple as it might seem here. Many of these keywords are either vague, do not seem to indicate what the students are required to do accurately, or even overlap. More problematically, often the activity keyword does not align with the intended learning outcomes and/or the correct position on Bloom's taxonomy. For example, essay questions can lack an activity keyword, such as 'should the Olympic games ever be cancelled owing to the threat of a terrorist attack?' Such a question does not specifically indicate whether a simple 'yes' or 'no' answer is required, if the student is required to present an argument, if they are intended to critically evaluate arguments, or even if they are to simply describe key theories or facts. In other words, it is not clear where on Bloom's taxonomy (or perhaps on the marking rubric/criteria) the student is being tested, thus creating unnecessary confusion. In other scenarios, it could be that there is a clear activity keyword, but it is incorrectly aligned with what is required from the intended learning outcomes and the mark scheme. If we take the task 'compare and contrast qualitative and quantitative research methods', for example, the student could quite literally (especially in the case of students with autism) 'compare and contrast' the methodologies with no consideration given to critical analysis and evaluation. Yet, the mark scheme or intended learning outcomes, as we saw a moment ago, might be distinctly weighted towards critical analysis and evaluation. In other words, the student can quite literally do what the activity keywords suggest but not fulfil the requirements of the marking rubric or learning outcomes, simply because incorrect or misleading activity keywords were used. To render your assignment tasks as inclusive and accessible as possible, always ensure that activity keywords correctly align with what it is you are aiming to examine to avoid confusion, not least as students with dyslexia, ADHD, and autism will be trying to either look for connections to the 'bigger picture' when that might not be required (as in the case of dyslexia and ADHD) or take the instructions literally (as in the case of autism). In both cases, the students will be unable to submit an assignment that truly reflects their potential as the wording has inadvertently provided a stumbling block to their processing and learning preferences.

3) **Focus or limitation keywords**

These restrict the students' options and tighten the focus of the assignment. Typical focus or limitation keywords or phrases might include things like 'contemporary', '1940–80', 'two poems', 'any three plays of your choice', 'recent developments', 'North America', or 'studied on this course'. It is relatively easy for students with learning differences to gloss over these words in favour of the activity or content keywords (owing to inattention and speed reading [looking for the 'bigger picture', connections, or gist]), so it is vital to ensure they are prominent, clear, precise, and preferably scaffolded via explanations in any accompanying classes that explain or scaffold the assignment.

To illustrate how this can be problematic, compare and contrast the following essay tasks:

1) Critically evaluate the contention that cities are central to development
2) Critically evaluate the contention that cities are central to sustainable forms of development

In green we have a clear activity keyword(s) and in red a clear content keyword, but in the first example the focus or limitation keyword (in blue) is too vague (although at least there is some focus). In the second example, this is narrowed down to 'sustainable' development, which makes all the difference. In the second version, the student will not only need to define both 'development' and 'sustainability', but they will also need to decide what forms of sustainable development are the most important or sustainable. This is testing their ability to prioritise information and make judicious selections which can be subjected to analysis, evaluation, and argumentation. Without this prompt, focus, or limitation keyword, the student could rightly focus not only on any form of development but become confused or cognitively overloaded owing to the vagueness of the assignment parameters. Remember, students with dyslexia and ADHD are looking for the 'bigger picture' (often via making gist connections), but sometimes the 'bigger picture' is so big that it can become overwhelming, thus resulting in cognitive overload or missing the detail entirely. Autistic students, meanwhile, are inclined to look for detail and focus, but here not only is none forthcoming or directed, but any attempt to relate detail to the 'bigger picture' will be that much harder.

In summary, then, you can help students with learning differences (and thus all students) enormously simply by making sure that you have

a) constructive alignment between the intended learning outcomes, what is taught, and what is assessed;

b) clear alignment between what is being asked and the marking rubric or learning outcomes;

c) clarity in all content, activity, and focus/limitation keywords.

All three of these align with UDL approaches to assessment in so far as students are given clarity in terms of assessment goals and strategy, and in particular how they will be assessed. It negates any elements of 'surprise' which can erode trust (Padden and O'Neill, 2021), 'communicates meaningfully', and helps develop assessment literacies – key planks of the Quality Assurance Agency's *Embedding Inclusive Assessment: A Reflective Toolkit* (2022). It also helps render explicit the *why*, *what*, and *how* elements of UDL, thus helping students to comprehend the task through exploiting their affective, recognition, and strategic brain networks.

Utilise authentic modes of assessment

Incorporating a broad range of assessment types can contribute to not only mitigating against or recognising the potential applications of GenAI in assessments but also helps promote the idea of assessment *as* learning, as it helps students to develop a broader range of skills. In addition, a rich diet of assessment modes enables different learning outcomes to be assessed and from multidimensional angles, enriching the learning experience and promoting deeper, more inclusive engagement.

To be an authentic assessment activity, the task must be realistic and meaningful, leading to an artefact, product, or performance which is – or could be – useful in its own right (Villarroel et al., 2018) in work, study, or social life. McArthur (2021) states that authentic assessment is 'that which contributes to the nurturing of students as independent members of the social whole'. Authentic assessments promote the use of higher-order cognitive skills such as problem-solving, creativity, analysis, and decision-making, and they promote evaluation – both at the level of assessing information and of the self to encourage self-regulation (Villarroel et al., 2018) – and inclusion. In this way, authentic assessment can meaningfully support inclusion and diversity while remaining relevant to many other real-world challenges.

An authentic assessment task should be relevant to students. For example, does it meaningfully connect with the rest of the discipline and/or their lived experiences? Will it be the kind of task they might have to perform in their future lives? (Rust, 2022). Such activities are likely to involve students working with 'abstract concepts, facts, and formulae inside a realistic—and highly social—context', in ways that replicate the activities of a professional or disciplinary community (Lombardi, 2007, p.3). Realistic contexts for assessment allow students to choose their own paths through the task and reach their own, contextually informed conclusions rather than mechanistically applying procedures to arrive at a correct solution. Diversity of approach and response is encouraged (Lombardi, 2007) and can be used in contexts that either embed and embrace GenAI, or try to find ways to minimise its use to facilitate the development of other skills while remaining inclusive and accessible.

Embed support into a holistic assessment strategy

Clarity in writing clear assessment tasks, outlining expectations and providing instructions can only go so far. It is the nature of authentic assessments to mirror the real world in all its complexity and as such requires the development of enhanced critical thinking skills to decipher truth from fiction, especially in an age of GenAI 'hallucinations'. 'Hallucinations' are when GenAI presents fabricated information as facts with confidence and authority (Keary, 2023). GenAI is flooding the internet with misinformation or 'deeper deep-fakes' (Miao and Holmes, 2023, pp.16–17), so the ability of students to critically evaluate information and distinguish between truth and fiction is becoming increasingly important. This work may be challenging for students who have come from educational environments that value certainty and will require careful support from staff to overcome these challenges (Rust, 2022).

TIPS:

- Scaffold academic and assignment support by offering clear instructions and assignment briefings within classes, forums, or drop-in hours.

- Encourage students to self-evaluate and prepare for and understand assignments through peer activities, or even co-create assignments with students.

- Enlist the support of writing centres, academic skills centres, and learning developers. Research recently undertaken across five UK higher education institutions strongly supports the idea that this kind of support translates into higher achievement, better outcomes, and increased inclusivity (University Alliance, 2023).

- Construct a programme-level assessment map or strategy. Research has shown that programme-level assessment strategies are effective in helping to scaffold academic literacies development and foster sustainable, inclusive student support (University Alliance, 2023). Programme-wide constructive alignment (Biggs and Tang, 2011) and assessment scheduling considers the students' learning journeys in a holistic way (Jessop and El Hakim, 2010; Elkington, 2020, p.7), can eliminate unnecessary duplication, and encourages students to achieve intended programme outcomes (Price et al., 2010). The map allows you to identify duplications, 'pinch points', and areas where feedback cannot be effectively implemented.

Examinations

Historically, examinations have been considered to be one of the most effective means of evaluating and verifying student learning, aptitude, skills, knowledge, and competence, especially in disciplines where key competencies need to be certified or accredited (Bearman et al., 2017). During the Covid-19 lockdown, new approaches to exams (e.g. online, flexible timings) emerged that worked effectively for students under duress or requiring flexibility (Brown and Sambell, 2020), but concerns have been raised about their validity given the relatively unsupervised online examination window. More recently, interest in exams has had a resurgence in response to wider concerns about academic integrity (Jisc, 2023); timed, controlled conditions negate opportunities for students to look up information (in closed-book examinations), use 'essay mills', or harness GenAI.

However, examinations are not necessarily inclusive to a diverse student body (Nieminen, 2022); they can disadvantage students with learning differences; cause undue anxiety in a context where mental health issues amongst the student population are increasing (Lipson et al., 2022); judge students inequitably (owing to personal circumstances, illness, or learning differences); focus too narrowly (depending on rote memory, which may be an inherent weakness in cognitive processing for students with learning differences [Taylor and Vestergaard, 2022]); and are time constrained (disadvantaging students with different processing speeds or working memory overload [e.g. dyslexia, ADHD, and autism]). In addition, there is often the argument that examinations encourage 'teaching to the test' (or 'washback' [Green, 2020]) over deeper understanding and critical thinking. Other scholars, however, have pointed to the fact that memorisation is not only useful for employment but also strengthens key memory pathways (Van Bergen and Lane, 2014; Plé, 2024).

The literature on designing inclusive assessments is 'sparse' (Tai et al., 2022). However, this section sets out and synthesises the core pedagogical, literature-informed principles for designing inclusive examinations.

1) **Use exams within the context of a holistic, varied assessment strategy**

Examinations should be used within the context of an integrated, constructively aligned programme and assessment strategy which provides students with a diverse and holistic range of assessments. Exams can be inherently exclusive, and there are limitations in terms of the ability of timed examinations to accurately assess deeper understanding. The default position of assessment design should be the use of authentic and meaningful assessment modes. The literature on this tends to recommend offering choice and/or diversifying assessment. A recent University Alliance project (2023) describes offering a choice of assessment as an inclusive assessment practice, and in the UK, the AdvanceHE Disabled Students' Commission (DSC) is developing a Disabled Student Commitment which asks higher education providers to ensure 'there is choice in the form of assessment for each module where possible and appropriate' (DSC, 2022). The Disabled Students' Commission, in their 2021–22 annual report, conclude that 'anticipatory reasonable adjustments and a more flexible approach to teaching, learning and assessment provides disabled students with the choice to learn and be assessed in a way that supports, rather than impacts on, their disability' (AdvanceHE DSC, 2022). Thus, assessment variety and choice are integral to assessment *for*, *as*, and *of* learning, and exams are a key and valuable part of this approach, especially as we shall see later in the current context of GenAI use in assessments.

TIPS:

- Exams are especially useful when required by Professional, Statutory, and Regulatory Bodies (PSRBs) or for the testing and validation of key competencies, but always consider the extent to which examinations may fit (or not) into a wider assessment strategy that incorporates choice and diversity.
- Use examinations to test primarily knowledge, skills, and competencies (e.g. knowledge recall and application) as aligned to the lower-order skills (see Bloom's taxonomy [1956]) within the module or programme learning outcomes.
- Avoid unnecessarily duplicating the testing of different skills or learning outcomes across a programme or module so as to streamline assessment and reduce assessment load.

2) **Ensure support is in place and implemented correctly**

Examinations can be made more inclusive by embedding support and appropriate scaffolding. Such support is often primarily aimed at students with Individual Support Plans (ISPs), but many of the recommendations here ought to be implemented as part of our anticipatory duty or anticipatory 'reasonable adjustments' to be as inclusive as possible. Although sparse, the available literature on inclusive examination arrangements (such as additional time, breaks, separate rooms, oral formats, scribes, or the use of assistive technologies) indicates that such adjustments are helpful (Tai et al., 2022). However, recent research has shown that variabilities in the organisation or deployment of such support can be detrimental, especially when such support is not in place, disrupted, poorly organised, or even ignored. Students often report 'feeling like an inconvenience' (Tai et al., 2022, p.394), which can further entrench the idea of assessment being exclusionary rather than inclusive (Nieminen, 2022), and can perpetuate, reinforce, or further problematise prior traumatic experiences during earlier education (possibly before formal diagnosis and support).

TIPS:

- Ensure students' individual support requirements or reasonable adjustments are catered for effectively and efficiently – delays can cause additional stress and cognitive burdens.
- Rather than putting students with ISPs in separate rooms, it can be better to place them with students who have similar requirements. This can have the benefit of the students having 'fewer distractions but still a sense of inclusion' (Tai et al., 2022, p.396).
- Ensure familiarity with any institutional-specific marking arrangements or 'reasonable adjustments' such as not penalising for grammar and spelling issues.
- Assistive technologies have been shown to make examinations more inclusive for students with ISPs, but not if the technology is unreliable, there is poor or unreliable internet connectivity, or students are used to certain interfaces (e.g. Microsoft Word) but are then required to use different tools with different or unfamiliar functionalities. Have your institution's information technology services/support phone number to hand in examinations so that problems can be remedied swiftly.
- Allow backup internet devices and accommodate student preferences in terms of technological platforms to enable the examination to progress smoothly with minimal additional cognitive burdens or stressors.
- Allow flexibility for students with ISPs or alter the format so that they can undertake their examination at some point over 24 or 48 hours (either within a set window or over a longer period). This allows students to choose a time that suits them and/or allows for breaks to prevent cognitive overload.
- Ensure any of the above arrangements are clear and organised in advance to avoid last-minute stressors and confusion.

3) **Scaffold the examination tasks or questions**

Like any other assessment activity, examinations should be scaffolded, not least because they are known to cause high levels of anxiety for significant numbers of students (Robotham and Julian, 2006; Păduraru, 2019). Scaffolding simply means 1) building activities into your programmes that enable students to develop the skills they need; and 2) rendering expectations, parameters, instructions, and marking rubrics clear, consistent, and understandable. Familiarity with the format and demands of the task can help to reduce levels of anxiety (Tai et al., 2022).

TIPS:

- Use 'open book' examinations, which can significantly reduce stress and reduce the chances of cognitive overload. The availability of materials within the examination acts as a key scaffolding device as it can assist students to critically engage with the material rather than expending too much mental energy on rote memorisation and recall.
- Fully align what is being tested with the intended learning outcomes.
- Use, share, and model the use of assessment rubrics (such as via peer assessment, sessions on exam preparation, and expectations). This enables the goals and expectations to become transparent, socialised, and thus accessible. The clear communication of expectations and marking criteria helps to scaffold the acquisition of examination and assessment literacies (CAST, 2024 while building opportunities for creating feedback-centric assessment.
- List what intended learning outcomes are being tested and, if necessary, rank them in terms of importance.
- Write examination questions in clear English, avoiding unnecessarily distracting, lengthy, or extraneous text (such as prefacing simple questions with overly complex quotations). Extraneous complexities act as a barrier to success for students with either cognitive overload issues (such as those with learning differences) or those for whom English is a second language. Reduce any prefaces to only the information or context that is relevant to the question or intended learning outcomes to not overcomplicate the task or send students on unnecessary tangents.
- Consider the use of sub-questions for complex or lengthy responses (such as essay responses) to scaffold the task. In cases where students struggle with cognitive overload, this can be invaluable in enabling them to demonstrate their knowledge independently from the cognitive challenges associated with their learning difference, thus helping to level the playing field.
- If using MCQs, avoid the use of double negatives, unnecessary narration, or irrelevant detail. Use plausible but not overlapping or equally valid alternative answers. See below for more details.

4) **Make your examinations as authentic as possible**

One of the key aspects of the QAA's *Embedding Inclusive Assessment: A Reflective Toolkit* (2022) is that 'the assessment tasks are relevant to students' subject areas, employment sectors and contexts of further study to which students will progress'. Ensure what is tested is authentic by relating content and question types to disciplinary requirements, conventions, and employment. If students can see the relevance, applicability, and usefulness ('why', 'what', and 'how') of what is being tested, it can help scaffold not only motivation but sense-making (CAST, 2009; Tai et al., 2022).

TIPS:

- Ensure material, content, and questions are fully and accurately aligned with the intended learning outcomes. This ensures students are tested equitably and fairly on what they have been taught and are expected to achieve.

- Align subject content to both the discipline and the world/employability. This ensures students can see the direct, authentic relevance, applicability, and importance of the exam content.

- Build in opportunities for students to draw upon prior knowledge or educational experiences. We should never assume students arrive at university (or even progress through university) with highly developed assessment literacies. Scrutinise what students in your discipline have been taught or tested on before (e.g. in the UK, at A level, BTEC, Access, Year 1, undergraduate level etc.) and design examinations that build upon that prior knowledge or approach to assessment or assessment competence.

- Provide authentic feedback. Ensure that feedback authentically scaffolds towards success in future assignments across the full spectrum of an integrated programme assessment strategy.

- If possible, utilise examination formats and approaches that authentically align with future employment. Many professions rely upon examinations (e.g. law, accounting, healthcare, and safety-critical industries such as rail and aviation), so familiarising students with examination techniques, etiquette, and approaches authentically prepares them for employability. However, do bear in mind that these assessment literacies need to be scaffolded and 'reasonable adjustments' put in place if appropriate to remain as inclusive as possible.

Writing effective, inclusive multiple-choice questions (MCQs)

MCQs can be an effective way of testing some learning outcomes, especially those at the lower end of Bloom's taxonomy (e.g. knowledge, understanding, and application). Particular benefits of using MCQs include:

1) Reliability: Scoring is reliable and not susceptible to marker variability and interpretation. Reliability is enhanced when questions are focused on one learning objective. Scoring can reflect difficulty.

2) Efficiency: Less marking time once set up; student time on test is less than with coursework or conventional essays. MCQs can cover a broad range of topics and materials quite quickly and efficiently.

3) Versatility: Can be designed to home in on specific types of learning (e.g. recall, knowledge, application).

4) Variety: Can effectively mix up the assessment diet and can be used effectively as a diagnostic tool.

5) Can be a good way of ascertaining thresholds (minimum levels, competency etc.).

However, as discussed in Chapter 1, their simplicity belies the fact that MCQs are not particularly inclusive from the perspective of students with learning differences, especially those with dyslexia and ADHD. This is because the 'big picture', holistic, and divergent thinking strengths associated with these individuals mean that they tend to approach the options provided from the point of view of looking for connections and implications that do not necessarily exist or are beyond the remit of the assessment. In other words, when presented with various options to choose from, students with dyslexia or ADHD overthink the topic and often find that either none of the suggested answers are wholly satisfactory because they have rapidly identified nuances, ambiguities, and implications that do not 'fit', or that all of the answers are potentially right depending on the circumstance, but the question or task constrains them into choosing just one option. This either leads to cognitive overload, paralysis (in the sense that the student is unable to select any of the suggested answers because they do not necessarily agree with any of them), or the student chooses the incorrect option purely because in some circumstances that *might* be the correct answer or because they cannot select which of the options is the most viable. MCQs tend to be more suitable for autistic students owing to their strengths in precision and detail, rules, and 'correct' answers. In essence, then, the recommendation here is to not use MCQs if at all possible. However, as a practitioner or lecturer, you might not be in that position. As such, here are some general tips that can help remove some of the barriers inherent within MCQs and render them more inclusive than might otherwise be the case:

1) **The initial question or proposition ought to be clear, meaningful, definite, and focus on the learning outcome**

The initial statement or 'stem', as it is known, should represent a clear problem rather than merely asking which of the following is true or false. For example:

Not meaningful: 'Which of the following is a true statement?'
Meaningful: 'The dependent variables in this study by Vaiva et al. (2006) are:'

In the first circumstance, there is more likelihood of students with dyslexia or ADHD considering the extent to which none of the statements are wholly true or pondering that the situation is not quite so clear-cut owing to their divergent thinking and cognitive search abilities. With the second option, however, such possibilities are closed off owing to the specificity and precision of the 'stem'.

2) **The 'stem' should not contain any irrelevant material, narration, unnecessary detail, or ambiguity**

'Waffle', unnecessary narration, or detail encroaches on working memory capacity unnecessarily and can lead students with learning differences to misinterpret what is being asked. It also decreases the reliability and validity of the responses or scores. For example:

Irrelevant material: 'Vaiva et al. (2006) used a specific form of random allocation called block randomisation. This is often used to ensure equal numbers of similar participants in each arm of the trial and is an alternative to:'

More concise stem: 'Block randomisation is an alternative to:'

For the purposes of inclusion, ensure the 'stem' is clear and not inadvertently designed to trip students up or create working memory overload by adding in the task of deciphering. For example:

- Avoid mixing instruction words or asking questions within questions, which can lead to confusion, anxiety, and increased queries.

- Avoid words like 'not', 'no', and 'none', as well as prefixes such as 'a', 'un', and 'dis', which change the meaning of the question or assignment tasks, and double negatives such as 'not atypical' and 'not false', which can obscure meaning, increase student confusion, and place unnecessary cognitive burdens on the working memory for students with learning differences.

3) **The 'stem' should be a question or partial sentence**

Partial sentences or questions allow students to hold the sentence or question in their working memory and try to complete it using the possibilities provided in a sequential manner (Statman, 1988).

4) **Alternative answers need to be plausible but not overlapping or equally valid**

The purpose of incorrect answers is to serve as distractors – they may be selected by those students who have not achieved the desired learning outcome and ignored by those who have. Implausible answers do not serve as functional distractors and need to be avoided. Equally, do not use answers that overlap and may be considered as a 'trick' by students. This not only erodes trust in the testing process but severely hinders working memory and cognitive processing, especially for students with dyslexia and ADHD. For example:

Distractors: 'The dependent variables in this study are:

a) Beck Hopelessness Scale

b) Symptom Checklist-90-Revised

c) All deaths by suicide

d) The defined adverse outcomes

e) The Russian invasion of Ukraine'

Equally valid alternatives: 'The study was flawed owing to the fact that:

a) The respondents were all female

b) The study was only conducted in and around Oxford

c) The authors did not declare that their research was privately funded

d) The tests only looked for candida as a source of the symptoms'

In this case, ALL of the above options are to some extent valid, so while students without a learning difference may choose the correct answer, the 'big picture' and divergent thinking skills of students with, say, ADHD or dyslexia mean that they will immediately think either 'all of these are relevant' or 'it depends', and thus overcomplicate the responses or question, often resulting in cognitive overload.

- It does not really matter how many alternatives you have provided they are all plausible.
- Avoid using alternatives such as 'all of the above' or 'none of the above' – this encourages partial knowledge.

5) **Alternatives should be stated clearly, concisely, free from clues, and in a homogenous manner**

Again, avoid wordy, excessively detailed options that distract students and take up valuable processing skills that can become dedicated to deciphering meaning rather than attaining the learning outcome. Be concise.

To avoid giving students too many clues, ensure your alternatives are expressed in similar ways. Alternatives that are expressed in varied ways make it easier for students to sift out glaring 'false flags' or trick alternatives. Make sure your alternatives:

a) Are similar in grammar and language and are consistent with the stem

b) Are parallel in form (avoid bias towards certain positions)

c) Are of a similar length

d) Use similar language

e) Avoid multiple-choice answers (e.g. 'A and B').

6) **Ensure the MCQs are aligned with your intended learning outcomes, match up with the intended level of Bloom's taxonomy, and are allocated appropriate marks**

When designing MCQs, always ensure that they:

a) Align with a specific, SMART learning outcome. For more information and a useful guide on creating SMART learning outcomes, see: www.ctl.ox.ac.uk/effective-learning-outcomes

b) Align with a specific level of Bloom's taxonomy

c) Are allocated marks according to degree of difficulty and the extent to which 'higher-order' skills on Bloom's taxonomy are utilised.

For example:

MCQ	Learning outcome	Bloom's taxonomy
Vaiva et al. (2006) estimated that 600 participants were needed for the trial to reach statistical significance. This is called: a) A Type 2 error b) A Type 1 error c) The standard error d) A power analysis 1 mark	Select appropriate research designs to inform evidence-based practice Select the research process required in order to ensure the quality of evidence Application of participant recruitment, data collection, and methods of data analysis	Knowledge, comprehension, application
The initial method used to distribute the questionnaire to prospective respondents was open to selection bias because: a) Divisional managers distributed the addressed envelopes to their paramedic staff b) All paramedics in the north-east region were selected to take part in the survey c) Respondents were invited twice, once by paper and again via email d) Social media was used to conduct the survey 3 marks	Select appropriate research designs to inform evidence-based practice Select the research process required in order to ensure the quality of evidence Application of participant recruitment, data collection, and methods of data analysis	Knowledge, comprehension, application
Glencorse et al. (2014) compare the results of their survey with a similar survey done with GPs. Is it valid to compare the studies in this way? a) Yes, because the aim of the study was to compare the two groups b) Yes, because this enhances the external validity of the paramedic study c) No, because there were 142 respondents to the paramedic study and 282 to the GP survey so the sample sizes are not equal d) No, because the survey of GPs was carried out in the East Midlands and it was not stated if this region has a comparable rate of excessive drinking to the north-east 5 marks	Demonstrate an awareness of the trustworthiness, rigour, reliability, and validity of the research process	Knowledge, comprehension, application, evaluation

Finally, remember that in addition to presenting problems for students with learning differences, MCQs come with the following inherent flaws:

- They are primarily suited to testing lower-order thinking on Bloom's taxonomy – testing higher-order skills is doable but is more challenging owing to the restrictions associated with the format.

- Students can often work 'backwards' from the least plausible options to ascertain the correct answer rather than deploying their knowledge or understanding. As such they can be an inaccurate way of measuring learning.

- Any MCQ with four options always presents even the least prepared learner with a 25% chance of choosing the correct answer. If they remove one distractor the odds increase to 33%. Given that the correct answer is literally on the page it can inadvertently encourage a guessing game rather than testing or encouraging learning.

- MCQs bypass the process of learning inherent within the process of writing (writing to learn pedagogy).

Oral presentations and vivas

Oral presentations have been around for centuries in one form or another, but interest in them seems to be increasing since the advent of GenAI as they present a means of assessing students more reliably. Indeed, mini vivas have been touted as one possible way of examining students who have submitted traditional essays but are accused of using GenAI in unethical ways. As such, oral presentations and vivas are not only here to stay but likely to see further expansion into the assessment strategies of modules and programmes, as well as diversification into subgenres such as pitches, Pecha Kuchas, gobbits, and vlogs.

Oral presentations and vivas can present particular problems for students with learning differences. The main issues pertain to structuring ideas, flow, and cohesion, much as in the case of written work, but the oral, 'live' dynamics of the presentation can cause significant additional anxieties (and thus further reducing working memory capacity). Challenges often revolve around problems remembering what is said and asked, challenges associated with holding questions in the mind and then answering after referring to information stored in the long term-memory (for some students the task of coming up with a response is so effortful that they end up responding to a question that has not even been asked), difficulties remembering key dates, names etc., problems keeping track of ideas when listening and speaking (multitasking), and challenges in generating full and coherent responses to questions when under pressure.

In terms of inclusion, designing and setting up presentations and vivas can be subdivided into two areas: 1) making the conditions and arrangements for the presentation or viva more inclusive, and 2) making the use of questioning and cross-examination within the presentation or viva more inclusive and empathetic. Many of the core principles above – such as making tasks clear, precise, explicit, and constructively aligned – still apply when supporting students to structure their presentations and articulate their ideas (see Chapter 5).

TIPS:

1) **Conditions and arrangements**
   - Provide all written information in an accessible format.
   - Ensure clear timetable information and written instructions are provided in a timely way to allow candidates sufficient time to prepare.
   - Give advance notification of and access to the venue so the student can familiarise themselves with the route and the environment (if on campus). If held online, be sure that the student is comfortable with the technology being used.
   - Clearly explain the procedure and method of the examination at the outset.
   - Break down information into manageable chunks.
   - Allow the use of a whiteboard, mind maps, diagrams, and prompt cards/notes to help the student present their ideas in multidimensional ways. Prior to the presentation or viva, discuss with the student their needs and how their learning difference affects them, and agree on the 'reasonable adjustment' or support required.
   - Provide a clear written summary of any formal feedback, corrections, and action points as part of the feedback.
   - Consider alternatives such as offering one-to-one presentations, or offer this early in the course to help build skills and confidence, allow students to record their presentations in advance, or change the format into a one-to-one question-and-answer discussion.

2) **Questioning and cross-examination**
   - Provide opportunities for the student to write down questions and to repeat the questions back to ensure understanding.
   - Keep questions short and clear. Avoid questions within questions (this can exacerbate cognitive or working memory overload and can inadvertently encourage tangents owing to divergent thinking abilities).
   - Present one question at a time (avoiding multifaceted questions).

- Where possible (that is, when this does not compromise academic standards), provide extra clarification or early redirection of questions towards the topic intended.

- Use unambiguous language (where possible, remembering that students should be aware of technical terminology).

- Allow the candidate brief pauses to compose answers.

- Where possible (that is, when this does not compromise academic standards), provide the broad areas of questioning half an hour before the presentation or viva. Being able to consider the questions in advance would reduce the pressure on working memory and would avoid information overload.

- Allow for poor fluency (e.g. word finding, rambling, irregular speed and flow of response).

Specific adjustments for students with autism

Owing to the fact that autism can affect the ability of individuals to 'read' social situations and they can experience sensory overload, the following additional tips ought to be borne in mind:

- Where possible, provide an opportunity to meet the examiners or marker beforehand (e.g. online) if there are anxieties about meeting new people; it should be made clear this is not part of the examination and the conversation would not address academic matters but be limited to an introduction to personnel and the likely conduct of the viva or presentation.

- Provide a more detailed explanation of the process and structure of the presentation or viva in advance, particularly in terms of any social conventions (the student may find it helpful to rehearse greetings, requests for clarification of a question, etc.).

- Be aware of the student's particular requirements, such as their need to have adequate personal space (when in person).

- Be aware of sensory overload, such as bright overhead lights or background noises (where viva is in person).

- Be prepared to rephrase/ask questions in more explicit concrete terms if the student is having difficulty interpreting what is being asked or expressing their knowledge clearly, and redirect/prompt the student if they stray off topic or have difficulty judging how much information is required.

- Ensure markers are aware of the potential for unusual behaviour or social communication and greater anxiety than might typically be expected (suggest short breaks if necessary).

Final thoughts

Remember, assessment is not simply a means of testing knowledge and providing a grade or feedback – assessment ought to facilitate learning in and of itself as well. Designing assessments that are not just a method for testing knowledge but with a focus on encouraging multidimensional learning and the development of higher-order cognitive skills can foster a more comprehensive, inclusive educational experience.

FINAL TIPS:

- Aligning activity keywords with Bloom's taxonomy can help retain clarity and assist with sense-making. Assessments that focus on ethical issues, self-management, social intelligence, and innovation may appear vague to some students or need unpacking/ scaffolding.

- Provide context. If students can see *why*, *what*, and *how* they will be assessed (the three pillars of UDL [CAST, 2024]), it can help them link what they need to do with the affective, recognition and strategic networks of learning. This renders the task more accessible, easily assimilated, inclusive, and scaffolded. It can also help them see assessment as an integral part of learning (assessment *as* learning) rather than something that is 'done to them' (Evans, 1995, p.2).

- Always scaffold assignments both backwards and forwards. In other words, familiarise yourself with the types of assessments and students encountered prior to enrolling on your course (e.g. in the UK, at A level or BTEC/Access) to support student transition into the more rigorous demands of higher education while also thinking ahead to what sorts of assignments students will have to take later on in their modules, courses, or programmes (again, have a programme-level assessment strategy). This ensures that the process of transition is smoother. We should never assume that any student comes onto our courses knowing how to write essays or approach assessment tasks.

The future of assessment in an age of GenAI

At the time of writing, assessment within higher education and beyond is under immense scrutiny and pressure owing to the sheer pace of change being brought in by the emerging technologies associated with GenAI. In terms of options going forward, firstly, it would be almost impossible to impose a ban or restriction on students using GenAI for their assessments, as it is very hard to reliably detect its use (except in the most obvious cases). In a recent blogpost, Compton (2023) proposed four visions of assessment for 2033, the first of which is a nightmarish vision he calls 'panopticopia' (exams complete with 'micro-drones buzz(ing) overhead, scanning for unauthorised augmentations and communications'), which by 2033 might be the only way of assessing students to ensure GenAI is effectively restricted but is deemed highly undesirable. Compton's other options include either the status quo, a form of multimodal, 'stackable' degrees, or a blending of human and GenAI in a way that approximates with the Perkins et al. (2024) 'Artificial Intelligence Assessment Scale' (discussed in Chapter 3).

Fundamentally, it is not in the best interests of students or universities to ban GenAI entirely, as digital and information literacies are not only a key plank of university education policies (and even wider policies and frameworks are being developed such as the draft UNESCO Competency Frameworks for Teachers and School Students [2024]), but the use of GenAI and skills in prompt engineering are increasingly becoming essential employability skills. In terms of restricting the use of GenAI, however, this may be desirable in cases where there are no other ways in which to assess the learning outcomes (e.g. demonstrating knowledge of or competencies in accurate translation or professional practice) or in cases where you want to develop independent thinking, critical analysis, or distinctly 'human' skills. Hitherto, this entailed devising either 'authentic' assessments that purposely try to engineer out ways in which GenAI could be used or facilitating the deployment of GenAI as a platform for students to critically engage with its outputs. For the former option (devised and proposed by myself and a colleague at Oxford Brookes in 2022), for example, assessments could be aligned with discussion topics and debates within seminars. It was originally thought that this would simultaneously render the assessment immediately relevant and 'authentic' to the students' context while bypassing information that could be easily 'scraped' from the internet, thereby limiting the usefulness of GenAI. However, such ideas have quickly become outdated, as GenAI tools such as NotebookLM from Google can now turn information that occurred within a non-public space such as a classroom or course information and turn it into an assignment. Similarly, having tested ChatGPT's ability to respond to MCQs, it was previously only possible for it to help the student if the question and options were fairly generic (e.g. if the question was about the appropriacy of research methodologies to a specific piece of research, even if the GenAI tool was unable to access the original study, the student could input a specific prompt about research methodologies and easily extrapolate the response to what is being asked in the MCQ). However, we now have GenAI tool such as QuizMate, which can read quizzes off the screen and answer the question for the student.

Attempts to tackle GenAI with AI detecting tools such as Turnitin's AI writing detection tool are similarly becoming futile, as many GenAI tools such as HumanizeAI transforms text generated by, say, ChatGPT into text that is largely undetectable by AI detectors. There are many other similar tools emerging every day and the pace of innovation is simply outstripping the ability of assessment modes and higher education institutions to respond, despite Jisc (2020) calling for the sector (admittedly before GenAI tools such as ChatGPT burst onto the scene) to make assessment 'smarter, faster, fairer and more effective – we will need to increase the current pace of innovation in the sector'. The Jisc report believed that setting five targets for 2025 would help the sector 'achieve this transformation', the targets being 'to progress assessment towards being more authentic, accessible, appropriately automated, continuous and secure'. Not only has this arguably not happened, but the sheer pace of developments in GenAI has made such targets redundant. Criticality and evaluation have often been cited as the last bastion of assessment that GenAI is less able to handle well, but again, most experts in the field of GenAI believe that it is only a matter of time before this will be performed competently by GenAI as well.

If we go back to the idea that assessment ought to be *of, for*, and *as* learning, we can see that GenAI has rendered the idea of assessment as and of learning (in particular) highly unreliable, if not increasingly unachievable (except if we deploy in-person examinations). GenAI has rendered the reliability of testing knowledge acquisition almost impossible (according to the latest and now outdated data on this topic, over 53% of students use GenAI to help them with their assignments [Freeman, 2024]). One option could be to change our learning outcomes to test not knowledge, understanding, and critical evaluation but the ability of the student to curate knowledge and develop or test skills in prompt engineering. However, as we have argued previously, this would be true learning per se, and they are largely the skills of curating and organising rather than knowledge, analysis, and synthesis (the higher elements of Bloom's taxonomy).

On the face of it, GenAI appears to hold some promise for facilitating assessment *for* learning, especially in the form of feedback assistants or quasi-private tutors (Freeman, 2024; Meechan, 2025). This form of immediate advice, modelling, and 'writing buddy' guidance is likely to be of some value, but the more pressing issue we need to be mindful of going forward is the idea of AI-generated marking and feedback. The idea of utilising GenAI itself to provide students with feedback is increasingly gaining traction (e.g. MarkingAI, Graide, or the University of Surrey's KEATH.ai). Many of these tools confidently claim that, for instance, they 'rapidly grade and provide feedback on students' work and assessments, helping to improve student learning outcomes while also freeing time for educators to devote to more student contact time and additional time for research' (University of Surrey, 2024). However, there are two issues with this approach.

Firstly, as I have argued elsewhere, students often struggle to find a 'voice' or express and forge a sense of 'agency' through academic writing and assessment in its traditional forms, and they can frequently feel a sense of 'powerlessness' and 'alienation' (Wallbank, 2022), often because of the content of higher education being increasingly consumer oriented and focused on attainment in a massified, neoliberal, performative environment. This is likely to be exacerbated if, by virtue of writing being an 'act of identity' (Ivanic, 1998), and having laid 'an element of oneself on the line' through their writing, they find that their grade and feedback have been outsourced to a 'bot'. Writing an assessment is human labour and students need to see their labour and emotional investment acknowledged, affirmed, and validated by another human. The likely corollary of students receiving automated or GenAI feedback is a further entrenchment of surface learning owing to the increasing dehumanisation and commodification of their educational experience (Wallbank, 2022; Coldwell, 2024).

Secondly, note that there is no mention throughout the press releases or websites that marking tools such as KEATH, MarkingAI, or Graide are in any way inclusive or able to render feedback bespoke to the needs of students with learning differences. The focus, rather, is on faster turnaround times for marking, possible improved NSS scores (note again the focus on performativity and metrics creeping into the rhetoric here), and freeing up academic time for research. At the time of writing at least, it is hard to see how such tools can a) identify student learning differences within assessments (as we noted in Chapter 1), or b) provide bespoke, scaffolded feedback tailored to such needs and differences. As such, in an era of increasing financial pressures and cost-cutting exercises, it is difficult to see how the notion of assessment *for* learning as a productive, educative process can be wholly effective (notwithstanding the argument, of course, that in an age of performativity, metrics, and attainment, and often surface learning, many students do not even read their feedback in the first place, whether human or otherwise [Murtagh and Baker, 2009]). So where does this leave us in terms of the future of assessment and, in particular, how students with learning differences experience and engage with assessment, given that seemingly no corner of assessment remains wholly 'secure'?

One option of course is traditional, in-person, timed, supervised exams (whether we get to Compton's vision of 'micro-drones buzz(ing) overhead' is another matter and seems a little far-fetched), but for many institutions, this remains unpalatable, often because of concerns about exam stress and accessibility/inclusion, especially in the wake of the *Abrahart* case in the UK. What I propose is a dual way forward that on the one hand completely revises the notion of assessment (as it pertains to formative work), and on the other attempts to sure up academic integrity by reasserting the crucial role of 'open book' exams as part of a balanced, holistic assessment strategy in a way which, by being appropriately scaffolded, can still be inclusive.

1) Dialogic formative assessment as learning

What I propose is that we reassert the central role of formative assessment but in a way that focuses purely on assessment *as* and *for* learning. This requires going back to the original meaning and etymology of the word *assessment*, which derives from the Latin *assessus* 'sitting by', past participle of *assidere/adsidere* 'to sit beside'. One starting point, as I have argued elsewhere, is the need to abandon the almost sacred adherence to polished argumentation as a key indicator of a good assignment, but here I would also like to argue for the abandonment of grading. A more inclusive, accessible way of writing and assessment (and, by extension, student support) ought to be adopted which allows for debate, critical thinking, academic freedom, the cultivation of humanity, and the fostering of key skills. If we abandon argumentation and grades, we make way for dialogue – a dialogue with one's self and, perhaps more importantly, with others (either within the writing or as part and parcel of the process of writing, which could be supported more through dialogue rather than 'enculturation' and be augmented by GenAI as a 'guide on the side'). What appears to have happened is that we have strayed away from the original Socratic notion of argument, learning, and student support as dialogue towards the type of discourse Socrates identified in *Gorgias* as belonging to the sophists. The sophists utilised language not for discovering truth, Socrates complained, but in the service of individual agendas. The marking criteria of most universities seek to test attainment of knowledge, evaluation, and argumentative skills, but we seem to have interpreted this (as have centuries of scholars) as meaning presenting a persuasive, convincing argument and, in more recent times, the need to acquire a grade as though it were a commodity. This is not necessarily true evaluation or learning, and often evaluation is sacrificed at the altar of rhetorical 'intent'. Indeed, it is even a betrayal of the natural processes of human cognition. As discussed in Chapter 3, and as Game and Metcalfe (1996) have identified, 'everything about writing is deliberately fabricated'. Its 'linearity', which of course is particularly important for coherent, convincing argumentation, is especially problematic because 'neither experience nor contemplative thought comes naturally in linear form' (p.109). Such a situation, of course, is not just artificial but specifically exclusive (students with specific learning difficulties such as dyslexia or ADHD, for example, have profound difficulties trying to force their thoughts into conventional form), and as Mann (2001) has rightly observed, silencing, repression, and alienation inevitably occurs when something is sacrificed at the altar of unity inscribed within academic practices (p.11).

While Bakhtin (1981) was right in his work on 'heteroglossia' that populating language with meaning and intention is troublesome, my proposal here invites us (and thereby our students) to challenge the apparent necessity of trying to force language to convey one's own intent for the purposes of a grade at all. When it comes to formative assessment, why not merely allow our students to revel in the fact that their language is not their own? Why not *support* our students dialogically rather than attempt to 'enculturate' them via didactic, impersonal academic writing classes that focus on the product rather than the process? Why not let students engage with GenAI with no regard for worries about cheating? Such a stance would certainly eliminate some of the anxieties surrounding plagiarism and 'performativity' for a start. Why not allow students to merely play with intellectual dialogue, either with themselves, others, or indeed GenAI tools?

In many respects, what I am advocating for here is a reconfiguration of Shaftesbury's eighteenth-century 'Advice to an Author' in respect of dialogism and argumentation. Shaftesbury argued that it is the 'peculiarity of philosophers and wise men to be able to hold themselves in talk' (1999, p.77) and saw this as a remedy for unsound argumentation. Shaftesbury advocated extensive dialogue within oneself as a means of self-criticism – a process he called the 'gymnastic method of soliloquy' (p.84). Such a method, Shaftesbury contended, allows for a more convincing and persuasive performance because one's argument has been 'taken to pieces, compared together and examined from head to foot' and thus one's ideas have 'been used to sound correction by themselves ... before they are brought into the field' (p.76). Being a 'thorough-paced dialogist in this solitary way' makes one a 'good thinker', Shaftesbury contended, and he has a valid point. However, his overall agenda was to make writing more convincing, persuasive, and argumentative via an 'anticipatory remedy' (p.72). The dialogue is a means to an end, rather than the journey being the end in itself. When put into the service of persuasion (or attaining a grade in our context), what results from Shaftesbury's dialogising is thus not necessarily truth, proper argument, or evaluation but 'performative' rhetoric. What I propose is that students be encouraged to submit written or verbal, 'solitary', group, or AI-augmented dialogues with no necessity to present a persuasive argument with a view to attaining a grade. In other words, what is submitted and assessed is a record or portfolio of the student's personal but academically justified reflections, arguments, philosophising, negotiations, and 'gymnastic ... soliloquising' (with oneself or others). This is a genuine 'warts and all' record of the process of learning and the 'processes' of 'reading and thought' which 'challenge' the student (Haggis, 2006, p.3), rather than the submission of a 'performative' product or 'right argument', as one of the students in my original study so aptly put it (Wallbank, 2022). This, as Shaftesbury himself confessed, would enable our students to become better thinkers, not least because, as Rancière (1991) insists, 'reason begins when discourses organised with the goal of being right cease' (p.72).

Such an approach would be inclusive, flexible (its adaptability would make it perfect for aligning with UDL principles), and encourage our students to become 'good thinkers' along the lines of the original Socratic model of humanist education (Nussbaum, 1997) without doing away with the kind of critical thinking and evaluation skills we often tout as being key employability skills. Indeed, such a mode of writing arguably strengthens such skills more than conventional modes of writing and argumentative essays. It would help eliminate some of the anxieties students face, as what is communicated is an ongoing, developmental intellectual process rather than a polished yet somewhat 'artificial' record of oneself. It also puts agency right back where it belongs – in the thick of evaluative, deliberative, self-reflective, truth-seeking dialogue rather than at the service of argument – and firmly reorientates assessment into the realms of assessment *as* and *for* learning. It also brings the genre of academic writing, and its concomitant student support apparatuses, more in step with the dynamic, diverse student bodies we now recruit. While we openly acknowledge that the student body has become diverse (Haggis, 2006, p.6) – and GenAI has now seriously undermined previous centuries-old models of assessment – academic writing, assessment models and genres, and academic writing support has not diversified or kept pace to reflect such changes. Dialogic formative assessment, which emphasises thought processes rather than rhetoric and prioritises the journey over the grade, would enable students with learning differences to chart their own path through the assignments more authentically and enable them to play to their strengths.

The move away from the notion of assessment *of* learning in favour of dialogue would not only allow our students to articulate themselves in a more authentically human way (Schiller noted that man is only fully human 'when he is playing' [2004, p.80] and Winnicott [1971] has suggested that 'only in playing' is the human being 'free to be creative' [p.53]), but would help encourage a less instrumentalist, 'deeper' approach to learning which may help alleviate the concomitant alienation associated with being perpetually in the 'double bind' discussed earlier and the necessity of 'performativity' (Barnett, 1994; Mann, 2001) and surface approaches to learning and assessment (Säljö, 1982; Mann, 2001). As such, the support provided by writing centres and tutors could focus far more specifically on the 'personalised' dialogic development of writing and its associated processes (critical thinking, evaluation, and analysis) rather than on the end product.

What is being proposed here is undoubtedly imperfect but surely in the face of the challenges being presented to traditional models of assessment by the advent of GenAI, it is a better way forward than adhering, with almost religious fervour in some quarters, to the conventional argumentative essay and the preoccupation we have with grades? In an age of more and more 'conformity' (Williams, 2016), increasingly suspicious attitudes towards truth and increasingly polarised, entrenched politics (as epitomised in the rise of the right, Trump, Le Pen, Brexit, and a return to propaganda and 'fake news' not seen since the 1930s), surely we need dialogue now more than ever? Surely a new mode of student writing and assessment which encompasses such dialogue can only be a good thing, however unconventional it may seem? These debates and a fundamental rethink of assessment urgently need to be had given that existing models of assessment are now so vulnerable to GenAI, and the legitimacy of the status quo is under threat.

We are no longer in an era where universities and markers can fully say that standards have been met. As such, a radical and urgent rethink of assessment is required, and the approach advocated above at least proposes a model that is more inclusive for students with learning differences than the path of increasing automatisation and outsourcing to GenAI seems to be promising.

2) **Reasserting the role of examinations**

Having rethought the role of formative assessment, we are still left with the dilemma of how we can reliably and accurately test students' skills and knowledge in ways that satisfy the need for rigour in academic standards and ensure that degrees have a worth that students, governments, industry, and society demand. This is where summative exams have their place. As discussed at the start of this chapter, exams can be made more accessible and inclusive, but what I propose here is that one of the roles of the dialogic formative assessment is to a) help hone and scaffold students' academic writing and literacies to such an extent that they feel more confidence when entering into an examination, and b) the exams be 'open book', so that students can take into the examination their notes, learning journals, and other resources to draw upon. This would further scaffold the content and format of the examination and help test not only knowledge recall but critical thinking and evaluation, but without access to either their tutor or GenAI, thereby ensuring integrity.

Unfortunately, in recent years examinations have fallen out of favour and become almost a dirty word owing to the perception that they are not inclusive, put too much pressure on students, and only test knowledge recall (thereby perpetuating 'surface-level' approaches to learning). But as we have seen, there are many common-sense and 'reasonable adjustments' that can be put in place to support students, and when combined with dialogic formative work, students would be well able and prepared to content with them. Such an assessment regime is bound to have its detractors, but again we come back to the same questions posed above, namely that GenAI has presented such an upheaval to assessment protocols that a fundamental rethink is required if degrees and university learning and assessment are to retain their value in the face of mounting critiques of the use value of university degrees (Lambert, 2022; Turnbull, Wilson, and Agoston, 2024).

References

AdvanceHE, (2023) Disabled Students' Commission, *Annual Report 2022–23*. Available from: www.advance-he.ac.uk/equality-diversity-inclusion/disability-equality-higher-education/disabled-students-commission (Accessed: 5 July 2024).

Bakhtin, M. M., (1981) *The Dialogic Imagination: Four Essays*, ed. Holquist, M. Austin, TX and London: University of Texas Press.

Barnett, R., (1994) *The Limits of Competence – Knowledge, Higher Education and Society*. Buckingham: Society for Research into Higher Education/The Open University Press.

Bearman, M., Dawson, P., Bennett, S., Hall, M., Molloy, E., Boud, D., and Joughin, G., (2017) 'How University Teachers Design Assessments: A Cross-Disciplinary Study', *Higher Education*, 74:1, pp.49–64. Available from: https://link.springer.com/article/10.1007/s10734-016-0027-7 (Accessed: 5 July 2024).

Biggs, J., and Tang, C., (2011) *Teaching for Quality Learning at University: What the Student Does*. Fourth Edition. Maidenhead: McGraw-Hill Education.

Bloom, B. S. (ed.), Engelhart, M. D., Furst, E. J., Hill, W. H., and Krathwohl, D. R., (1956) *Taxonomy of Educational Objectives*. New York: David McKay.

Brown, S., and Sambell, K., (2020) 'Making Assessment Future Fit: Ensuring Authentic Assessment Approaches in the Light of Coronavirus Changes to HE Practice', *IEECOnline*. Available from: https://ieec.co.uk/wp-content/uploads/2020/09/Brown-and-Sambell-no-voiceover.pdf (Accessed: 5 July 2024).

CAST, (2024) 'The UDL Guidelines'. Available from: https://udlguidelines.cast.org/ (Accessed: 5 November 2024).

CAST, (n.d.) 'UDL Tips for Assessment'. Available from: www.cast.org/binaries/content/assets/common/publications/downloads/cast-udltipsforassessment-20200920-a11y.pdf (Accessed: 1 July 2024).

Coldwell, W., (2024) '"I Received a First but It Felt Tainted and Underserved": Inside the University AI Cheating Crisis', *The Guardian*, 15 December, 2024. Available from: www.theguardian.com/technology/2024/dec/15/i-received-a-first-but-it-felt-tainted-and-undeserved-inside-the-university-ai-cheating-crisis (Accessed: 16 December 2024).

Compton, M., (2023) 'Assessment 2033', *HEducationist*, 12 December, 2023. Available from: https://mcompton.uk/2023/12/12/assessment-2033/ (Accessed: 23 November 2024).

Disabled Students Commitment, (2022) *AdvanceHE*. Available from: www.advance-he.ac.uk/equality-diversity-inclusion/disabled-student-commitment (Accessed: 9 June 2025).

Elkington, S., (2020) 'Essential Frameworks for Enhancing Student Success: Transforming Assessment in Higher Education', *AdvanceHE*. Available from: www.advance-he.ac.uk/knowledge-hub/essential-frameworks-enhancing-student-success-transforming-assessment (Accessed: 23 November 2023).

Evans, C., (1995) 'Enhancing Assessment Feedback Practice in Higher Education: The EAT Framework', *EAT*. Available from: www.southampton.ac.uk/assets/imported/transforms/content-block/UsefulDownloads_Download/A0999D3AF2AF4C5AA24B5BEA08C61D8E/EAT%20Guide%20April%20FINAL1%20ALL.pdf (Accessed: 12 November 2023).

Freeman, J., (2024) 'Provide or Punish: Students' Views on Generative AI in Higher Education', HEPI Policy Note 51. Available from: www.hepi.ac.uk/2024/02/01/provide-or-punish-students-views-on-generative-ai-in-higher-education/ (Accessed: 17 December 2024).

Game, A., and Metcalfe, A., (1996) *Passionate Sociology*. London: Sage.

Green, A., (2020) 'Washback in Language Assessment', *The Encyclopedia of Applied Linguistics*. Available from: www.semanticscholar.org/paper/Washback-in-Language-Assessment-Green/a22677c55f348657034df46d95c4cfb86a3e2384 (Accessed: 5 July 2024).

Haggis, T., (2006) 'Pedagogies for Diversity: Retaining Critical Challenge Amidst Fears of "Dumbing Down"', *Studies in Higher Education*, 31:5, pp.521–535. Available from: www.tandfonline.com/doi/full/10.1080/03075070600922709 (Accessed: 12 December 2024).

Ivanic, R., (1998) *Writing and Identity: The Discoursal Construction of Identity in Academic Writing*. Amsterdam and Philadelphia, PA: John Benjamins Publishing Company.

Jessop, T., and El Hakim, Y., (2010) 'Nine Ideas for Feedback Week: An Evidence-based Guide', *Transforming the Experience of Students through Assessment (TESTA)* National Teaching Fellowship Project. Available from: www.testa.ac.uk (Accessed: 23 November 2023).

Jisc, (2020) 'The Future of Assessment: Five Principles, Five Targets for 2025'. Available from: www.jisc.ac.uk/reports/the-future-of-assessment-five-principles-five-targets-for-2025 (Accessed: 23 November 2024).

Jisc, (2023) 'Generative AI – A Primer'. Available from: https://beta.jisc.ac.uk/reports/generative-ai-a-primer (Accessed: 12 August 2023).

Keary, T., (2023) 'AI Hallucination', *Techopedia*. Available from: www.techopedia.com/definition/ai-hallucination. (Accessed: 5 December 2023).

Lambert, H., (2022) 'The Great University Con: How the British Degree Lots Its Value', *The New Statesman*. Available from: www.newstatesman.com/politics/2019/08/the-great-university-con-how-the-british-degree-lost-its-value (Accessed: 14 December 2024).

Lipson, S. K., Zhou, S., Abelson, S., Heinze, J., Jirsa, M., Morigney, J., et al., (2022) 'Trends in College Student Mental Health and Help-seeking by Race/Ethnicity: Findings from the National Healthy Minds Study, 2013–2021', *Journal of Affective Disorders*, 306, pp.138–147. Available from: https://doi.org/10.1016/j.jad.2022.03.038 (Accessed: 2 July 2024).

Lombardi, M. M., (2007) 'Authentic Learning for the 21st Century: An Overview. ELI paper 1', *Educause Learning Initiative*. Available from: www.researchgate.net/publication/220040581_Authentic_Learning_for_the_21st_Century_An_Overview (Accessed: 10 October 2022).

Mann, S. J., (2001) 'Alternative Perspectives on the Student Experience: Alienation and Engagement', *Studies in Higher Education*, 26:1, pp.7–19. Available from: www.tandfonline.com/doi/abs/10.1080/03075070020030689 (Accessed: 12 December 2024).

McArthur, J., (2021) 'QAA Annual Conference Blog – Rethinking Authentic Assessment in a Post-Covid World: Is it Right to Hope for Change?' *QAA Blog*. Available from: www.qaa.ac.uk/news-events/blog/qaa-annual-conference-blog-rethinking-authentic-assessment-in-a-post-covid-world (Accessed: 5 November 2023).

Meechan, D., (2025) *Generative AI for Students*. London: Sage.

Miao, F., and Holmes, W., (2023) 'Guidance for Generative AI in Education and Research', *UNESCO*. Available from: https://unesdoc.unesco.org/ark:/48223/pf0000386693 (Accessed: 5 November 2023).

Murtagh, L., and Baker, N., (2009) 'Feedback to Feed Forward: Student Response to Tutors' Written Comments on Assignments', *Practitioner Research in Higher Education*, 3:1, pp.20–28. Available from: https://core.ac.uk/download/pdf/96590615.pdf (Accessed: 2 August 2022).

Nieminen, J. H., (2022) 'Assessment for Inclusion: Rethinking Inclusive Assessment in Higher Education', *Teaching in Higher Education*, 29:4, pp.841–859. Available from: https://doi.org/10.1080/13562517.2021.2021395 (Accessed: 29 June 2024).

Nussbaum, M., (1997) *Cultivating Humanity: A Classical Defence of Reform in Liberal Education*. Cambridge, MA: Harvard University Press.

Padden, L., and O'Neill, G., (2021) 'Embedding Equity and Inclusion in Higher Education Assessment Strategies: Creating and Sustaining Positive Change in the Post-Pandemic Era', in Baughan, P. (ed.), *Assessment and Feedback in a Post-Pandemic Era: A Time for Learning and Inclusion. AdvanceHE*, pp.138–147. Available from: www.advance-he.ac.uk/knowledge-hub/assessment-and-feedback-post-pandemic-era-time-learning-and-inclusion (Accessed: 23 August 2024).

Păduraru, M. E., (2019) 'Coping Strategies for Exam Stress', *Mental Health: Global Challenges Journal*, 1:1, pp.64–66. Available from: https://doi.org/10.32437/mhgcj.v1i1.26 (Accessed: 25 June 2024).

Perkins, M., Furze, L., Roe, J., and MacVaugh, J., (2024) 'The Artificial Intelligence Assessment Scale (AIAS): A Framework for Ethical Integration of Generative AI in Educational Assessment', *Journal of University Teaching and Learning Practice*, 21:6. Available from: https://doi.org/10.53761/q3azde36 (Accessed: 12 December 2024).

Plé, L., (2024) 'The Rise of AI Doesn't Mean We Should Forget about Memorisation', *Times Higher Education*. Available from: www.timeshighereducation.com/opinion/rise-ai-doesnt-mean-we-should-forget-about-memorisation (Accessed: 5 July 2024).

Price, M., Carroll, J., O'Donovan, B., and Rust, C., (2010) 'If I Was Going There I Wouldn't Start from Here: A Critical Commentary on Current Assessment Practices', *Assessment and Evaluation in Higher Education*, 36:4, pp.479–492.

QAA, (2022) 'Embedding Inclusive Assessment: A Reflective Toolkit'. Available from: www.qaa.ac.uk/docs/qaa/members/embedding-inclusive-assessment-reflective-toolkit.pdf?sfvrsn=7369a281_8 (Accessed: 24 February 2024).

Rancière, J., (1991) *The Ignorant Schoolmaster: Five Lessons in Intellectual Emancipation*. Translated by Kristin Ross. Palo Alto, CA: Stanford University Press.

Robotham, D., and Julian, C., (2006) 'Stress and the Higher Education Student: A Critical Review of the Literature', *Journal of Further and Higher Education*, 30:2, pp.107–117. Available from: https://doi.org/10.1080/03098770600617513 (Accessed: 3 July 2024).

Rust, C., (2022). 'Meaningful Assessment: What Is It and Why Does It Matter?' *Teaching Insights*. Available from: https://teachinginsights.ocsld.org/meaningful-assessment-what-is-it-and-why-does-it-matter/ (Accessed: 10 October 2022).

Säljö, R., (1982) *Learning and Understanding*. Gothenburg: Acta Universitatis Gothenburgensis.

Schiller, F., (2004) *On the Aesthetic Education of Man*. Trans. R. Snell. New York: Dover Publications Inc.

Shaftesbury, A., (1999) *Characteristics of Men, Manners, Opinions, Times*, ed. Klein, L. E. Cambridge: Cambridge University Press.

Statman, S., (1988) 'Ask a Clear Question and Get a Clear Answer: An Enquiry into the Question/Answer and Sentence Completion Formats of Multiple Choice Items', *System*, 16:3, pp.367–376.

Tai, J., Mahoney, P., Ajjawi, R., Bearman, M., Dargusch, J., Dracup, M., and Harris, L., (2022) 'How Are Examinations Inclusive for Students with Disabilities in Higher Education? A Sociomaterial Analysis', *Assessment and Evaluation in Higher Education*, 48:3, pp.390–402. Available from: https://doi.org/10.1080/02602938.2022.2077910 (Accessed: 3 July 2024).

Taylor, H., and Vestergaard, M. D., (2022) 'Developmental Dyslexia: Disorder or Specialisation in Exploration?' *Frontiers in Psychology*. Available from: https://pubmed.ncbi.nlm.nih.gov/35814102/ (Accessed: 4 July 2024).

Turnbull, N., Wilson, S., and Agoston, G., (2024) 'Revaluing and Devaluing Higher Education Beyond Neoliberalism: Elitist, Productivist, and Populist Policy and Rhetoric in a Field of Conflict', *European Educational Research Journal*, 23:5, pp.631–654. Available from: https://journals.sagepub.com/doi/10.1177/14749041241272627 (Accessed: 11 November 2024).

UNESCO, (2024) 'AI Competency Framework for Students'. Available from: www.unesco.org/en/articles/ai-competency-framework-students (Accessed: 11 December 2024).

University Alliance, (2023) 'Supporting Student Progression and Attainment Through Sustainable Inclusive Assessment Practices: What Works?' Available from: www.unialliance.ac.uk/our-work-2/university-alliance-inclusive-assessment-research-project/ (Accessed: 13 November 2023).

University of Surrey, (2024) 'AI-driven Academic Marking Tool Unveiled'. Available from: www.surrey.ac.uk/news/ai-driven-academic-marking-tool-unveiled-offering-potential-enhance-student-learning-outcomes-and (Accessed: 13 December 2024).

Van Bergen, P., and Lane, R., (2014) 'Exams Might Be Stressful, but They Improve Learning', *The Conversation*. Available from: https://theconversation.com/exams-might-be-stressful-but-they-improve-learning-35614 (Accessed: 5 July 2024).

Villarroel, V., Bloxham, S., Bruna, D., Bruna, C., and Herrera-Seda, C. (2018) 'Authentic Assessment: Creating a Blueprint for Course Design', *Assessment and Evaluation in Higher Education*, 43:5, pp.840–854. Available from: www.tandfonline.com/doi/abs/10.1080/02602938.2017.1412396 (Accessed 5 November 2023).

Wallbank, A. J., (2022) 'Writing Support and Student Identity – Can We Help Learners Write in an Age of Massification and Consumerism?' in Padró, F. F., Kek, M., and Huijser, H. (eds), *Student Support Services: Exploring Impact on Student Engagement, Experience and Learning*. Singapore: Springer, pp. 203–222.

Williams, J., (2016) *Academic Freedom in an Age of Conformity: Confronting the Fear of Knowledge*. Basingstoke: Palgrave Macmillan.

Winnicott, D. W., (1971) *Playing and Reality*. London: Routledge.

7 Conclusion

Chris Rust

I have long been a proponent of academic literacies as central to providing a framework for essential graduate attributes (Rust and Froud, 2016), and advocate for inclusive pedagogy (e.g. Rust, 2013) and, especially, valid and authentic assessment (e.g. Rust, 2020 revised), as well as the development of assessment literacy (Price et al., 2012). Therefore, I was both pleased and extremely interested when invited to write the conclusion to this timely and important book.

For both the specialist and non-specialist reader alike, Chapter 1 provides an extremely detailed, useful, comprehensive exploration and explanation of neurodiversity – especially in separating out the fundamental characteristics and challenges of three distinct groups – ADHD, dyslexia, and autism. The examples of how the different traits might manifest themselves in student writing are very welcome and enormously helpful illustrations. But possibly the most powerful take-away message is the extreme shorthand, aide memoire summary that for autism it's about seeing the wood for the trees, while for ADHD/dyslexia it's about seeing the trees for the wood.

I was also struck by the incredible irony that in coining the term neurodiversity in 1998 – with an intended similarity to ecodiversity to argue that we are all actually neurodiverse and to attempt to balance the negative medical deficit model – Judy Singer actually provided the label that is now so widely used to identify and separate these particular groups of students. But from what we know about students and learning, the notion that as individuals we all learn differently (and therefore are part of a neurodiverse landscape) should surely be uncontested? The literature is clear that how we learn is affected by many things – our feelings, our epistemological development, our beliefs about learning, our study skills ability, our motivation, and (although the theory has come in for, I believe, some exaggerated and unfounded criticism) by our preferred learning styles (Rust, 2013) – and our pedagogy should reflect this.

A salutary message, in Chapter 2, is the dramatic recent rise in numbers of students with learning differences, with no concomitant increase in funding for specialist support. This evidence alone provides a prima facie case for the importance of this book, and the need for all university educators to engage with this issue and to embed appropriate support in the curriculum. But the chapter goes much further in making the case for inclusivity, rightly foregrounding the need for inclusive pedagogy to facilitate the development of academic literacies – beginning with the fact that it overcomes the 'deficit model' of student support. A further powerful argument, supported by research evidence, is that such support for the development of academic literacies has been shown to drive up the achievement and attainment of all students.

The point is also well made that simply devising an inclusive curriculum is insufficient, as if it is then delivered in a non-inclusive way, it achieves nothing. This, along with the weaknesses of attempts to make intended compensatory adjustments, such as giving extra time, provides two important take-home messages.

DOI: 10.4324/9781003398974-7

The section on one-to-one tutorials is a thought-provoking and detailed exploration of the tension between what should be their potential, contrasted with the many problems and barriers regarding meeting the reality of different individual students' needs. Different approaches and ways to resolve this dilemma are thankfully provided later, in Chapter 5. In concluding the chapter, there is a useful brief consideration of the relative in/effectiveness of bolt-on generic support versus embedded support, reinforcing the importance of this book, which aims to help tutors involved in either form of support.

In Chapter 3, we come to the all-important issue of how to support students with learning differences when it comes to assessment. It starts by identifying the major problem caused by the prevalence of writing as the main medium for assessment – even where courses have moved to more innovative and varied forms of assessment than traditional essays and written exams – the problem being the 'need for sequencing, coherence, and linearity' in articulating thoughts in this form. There is then a useful consideration of the three different purposes of assessment – *as* learning, *for* learning (formative), and *of* learning (summative) – arguing that although a core tenet of the book is the importance of assessment *as* learning, this element has been increasingly overlooked while there has been an increase in both summative and formative assessment and a concomitant increase in workload. I have long argued that a fundamental problem with assessment practices is that we do not distinguish the three purposes (e.g. Brown, Rust, and Gibbs, 1994) but try to do all three at the same time, with the net result being that because the task is summative it raises the stakes and the pressure, so students do not take risks and therefore do not learn from the potential to experiment and make mistakes. They also do not learn from the feedback because they do not engage with it since it has come at the end of the module and they are moving on to something else (for an excellent summary critique of the problems with assessment practice, I recommend the PASS Project Position Paper, available from: www.brad.ac.uk/pass/resources/position-paper.pdf).

One of the reasons for the increase in summative assessment is the notion that essentially students just will not do work if it is not assessed – an issue identified over 20 years ago by Gibbs and Simpson (2005). Leaving aside idealist thoughts that they would if the work/subject was interesting and they could see its relevance and be intrinsically motivated, I would argue we need to be cleverer and more strategic in what we do. For example, setting two formative pieces of work that would receive feedback but not count for marks, which could be taken into the final summative module exam as a resource, could provide sufficient motivation to do the work well and be interested in the feedback, but without the high-stakes pressure. Along with the problem of too much, and increasing, summative assessment is that it is not done very well, lacks rigour, and is of questionable validity, failing to assess what it purports to assess. Less, but more rigorous and valid, summative assessment focused on the course programme outcomes is the inescapable answer (Rust, 2020 revised).

The practical help and advice in Chapter 3 continues with the introduction of the principles of Universal Design for Learning (UDL), linked to the fundamental point that for all three identified neurodiverse groups there is the need for inclusive 'scaffolding' to support their learning with provision of 'roadmaps' and 'meaningful orientations' and, most importantly, their individual conceptual frameworks with the ultimate goal of reaching a 'core, coherent framework'. As part of this, there is consideration of the importance of images and the potential of multimedia learning. But as I have said already, given what we know about learning and the importance of context and relevance in creating motivation, as well as affecting learning intentions (Marton et al, 1984) – along with the possibility that some students will have visual, aural, or kinesthetic preferences in their learning styles (e.g. see https://vark-learn.com/) – these pedagogical approaches are going to benefit a far wider group of students than those who have been identified as having learning differences. In the final section of the chapter, there is an interesting and timely, speculative consideration of what role ever increasingly powerful AI might play and whether it could be helpful in supporting students – with the conclusion, as I read it, that the jury's out on the matter at the moment, but the answer is probably not. It could possibly offer some potential help but probably more harm.

I like Chapter 4 a lot because it brings together the concepts of metacognition and metaphor (including simile), and the potentially powerful use of the latter. It provides a detailed consideration as to why they can be so useful for students with learning differences – whether in creating their own metaphors or trying to interpret metaphors presented to them. And of course, metaphors can be presented as pictures, as well as in words. Most usefully, as well as providing a detailed consideration of the theoretical underpinning, the chapter also has a lengthy, illustrative example of a pedagogical intervention based on the preceding theory.

In Chapter 5 we return to consider Universal Design for Learning (UDL) in more detail, along with visual pedagogies and guidance on structuring tutorials and feedback sessions, in what is possibly the most practical chapter in the book. It provides excellent detailed, practical advice, along with research evidence of the efficacy of these approaches/practices. And again, the argument is clear that these practices will help and support all students.

I was reminded while reading the section on academic reading of two examples from my distant past. Firstly, I remember Dai Hounsell giving a presentation in which he pointed out that there is a group of students who had done very well at A level by going to their school library, finding the only three books on the subject at hand, and paraphrasing key sections and probably getting at least a B+ for their efforts, if not an A. But at university, even in the most impoverished library, when confronted by more books on the subject than they could possibly read in the time available, they still try to do what had worked for them in the past and do not understand why they are now only getting 2:1 grades at best. The second memory that stirred was of the William Perry experiment at Harvard (detailed in Graham Gibbs' seminal book, *Teaching Students to Learn*, 1981) where 1,500 freshmen were given a 30-page chapter, told to make notes for a test on the important details, and that they would be stopped after 20 minutes to be questioned on how they had approached the task. After the time had elapsed, virtually all the students had simply tried the impossible task of reading it all straight from the beginning. Only 150 (10%) of the students had looked through to the end where there was a summary paragraph entitled 'recapitulation'. The point of both these stories is that even successful students (in the second example, some of the most successful in the world) can have seriously deficient approaches to study and would benefit from the kind of structured support offered in this chapter.

Chapter 6 is very much my area of interest, looking in depth at assessment design and inclusivity. It provides a rich mixture of practical advice and detailed critique of many aspects of common practice. The case for authenticity in assessment is well made, and especially the positive link to student motivation that comes from seeing the relevance of the task (although I would argue that validity is even more important, and some tasks can be valid without being authentic). I also totally concur with the assertion that we need to reconsider assessment by examination. While traditional examinations rewarding regurgitation and memory have rightly been criticised for their lack of validity, and hence moved away from, exams clearly do not need to be like that – 'open book' exams, for example, have of course existed for many years. The fundamental thing is that the task should involve the student doing something that involves putting into practice their learning, thus demonstrating their understanding. And with the rapidly growing power and ability of AI, which is considered in detail at the end of the chapter, I think the conclusion must be that examinations, be they written or oral, are now the only way of knowing that the work is truly the student's own and therefore the only form of summative assessment. And if this is the case, they need to be part of a holistic assessment strategy with appropriate scaffolding, as detailed in this chapter.

One aspect of assessment not specifically covered in the book is that of how to ensure assessment feedback is inclusive. Clearly the most important aspect of feedback is that the students have to engage with it, and the most useful and succinct advice on how to achieve this that I know comes from Val Shute. She says you need MOM! (Shute, 2008), which is an acronym for Motive, Opportunity, and Means. There needs to be a reason why the students should want to engage with the feedback (motive), so they need to think it will be useful. And that links very much with knowing they will have an opportunity to apply the feedback (soon) in a future piece of work (which could be a revision of the original). But alone those two conditions are not enough to improve the student's subsequent work if they do not have the means to understand and address and put into practice what the feedback says. For example, being told that your analysis is not very good is no help at all if you are not actually sure what analysis is or would look like. The student will need help with that – such as a tutorial or exemplars – if they are to have any chance of gaining from this feedback.

Between 2005 and 2010, the Assessment Standards Knowledge Exchange Centre for Excellence (ASKe CETL) produced a range of leaflets on different aspects of assessment, especially feedback, all based on assessment-related research, and focused on improving the students' assessment literacy (see https://radar.brookes.ac.uk/radar/hierarchy.do?topic=3468b1d5-ec7e-4094-a116-e6b15b4cab8f&page=1).

Regarding inclusive feedback practice, we reduced it to three main pieces of advice:

1) Prepare the students to receive feedback:
    - Align their expectations with yours, so that you agree the purpose of the feedback prior to the assessment. When handing in work, you could get students to identify what they would specifically like feedback on. And certainly specify when delivering the feedback that 'this feedback is focused on …'.
    - Encourage the application of feedback by asking students to use their previous feedback to improve their current assignments, and to say how they have tried to do this when handing the work in.
    - Support processes of self-assessment by asking students to submit evaluations of their work along with their assignments.
    - Identify all channels of feedback, especially oral (in class), as well as that written on assignments. Research has shown that many students do not recognise oral feedback as feedback – for example, tutors walking round making comments during a science practical, or even students at Oxford with their weekly tutorials – seeing it as just 'chat'.
    - Model the application of feedback by using previous students' anonymised work to look at a previously marked assignment and a later assignment to consider how feedback was used to improve the quality of the second assignment.

2) Reduce emphasis on written feedback:
    - Explicit, written feedback is important when correcting errors, explaining technical points, and giving positive encouragement.
    - However, written feedback (i.e. without dialogue) rarely communicates tacit understandings about disciplinary content and academic literacy skills.
    - Student engagement is enhanced if written feedback is supplemented with dialogue. Technology offers many ways of doing this (e.g. recorded onto a memory stick; using embedded sound files; or a video-recorded commentary while you indicate the relevant passage, using software like Camtasia), or you can use in-class discussions of exemplars, peer-review discussions supported by tutors, or the use of 'learning sets', for example.

3) Provide timely feedback:
    - Feedback on draft assignments may engage students more effectively than feedback on final work, which is returned at the beginning of the next semester.
    - Consider giving generic feedback as soon as a general picture emerges of the quality of all assignments.
    - Remember Val Shute and MOM.

(Revised ASKe leaflet, *How to Make your Feedback Work in Three Easy Steps*, available from: https://radar.brookes.ac.uk/radar/items/b07e70a4-89bc-6c32-554e-33dd6862df41/2/)

So, in summary, inclusive feedback needs to be a cyclical process with preparation beforehand provided as part of a dialogue in time for the students to be interested in engaging with it, preferably seeing how and where they can put it into practice and with the means to address their weaknesses. And it is clear that it is especially important to emphasise and scaffold feedback in this way for students with learning differences because they need to see the 'what', 'why', and 'how' of things (the 'bigger picture'/the wood for the trees/trees for the wood).

Fundamentally, I believe our aim should be to develop the students' assessment literacy to the point that they do not need feedback from others. And to do this, I would argue that the simplest yet most important change we can make is to recognise that the ability to judge the quality of one's own work and the work of others (self and peer assessment) should be seen as essential programme/graduate outcomes. Therefore, the development of these abilities should be fundamental to our assessment practices and permeate course and programme design. And as with everything else in this book, while this and pedagogies of inclusion may be especially helpful for particular groups of students such as those with learning differences, ultimately they improve learning and are of benefit to all students. Here we find ourselves returning to Layer's (2017) suggestion back in Chapter 1 that inclusive (and in light of the *Abrahart* case in the UK), anticipatory 'reasonable adjustments' and pedagogies should be seen as a 'route to excellence' and not just a bolt-on mechanism to help specific groups of students. This book, in relation to assessment at least, helps us move ever closer to that goal.

References

Brown, S., Rust, C., and Gibbs, G., (1994) *Strategies for Diversifying Assessment*. Oxford: Oxford Centre for Staff Development.

Gibbs, G., and Simpson, C., (2005) 'Conditions Under Which Assessment Supports Students' Learning', *Learning and Teaching in Higher Education*, 1, pp.3–31.

Layer, G., (2017) *Inclusive Teaching and Learning in Higher education as a Route to Excellence*. London: Department for Education. Available from: www.gov.uk/government/publications/inclusive-teaching-and-learning-in-higher-education (Accessed: 24 September 2023).

Marton, F., Hounsell, D., and Entwistle, N., (1984) *The Experience of Learning*. Edinburgh: Scottish Academic Press. Available from: www.docs.hss.ed.ac.uk/iad/Learning_teaching/Academic_teaching/Resources/Experience_of_learning/EoLChapter3.pdf (Accessed: 13 January 2025).

Price, M., Rust, C., O'Donovan, B., Handley, K., with Bryant, R., (2012) *Assessment Literacy: The Foundation for Improving Student Learning*. Oxford: Oxford Centre for Staff and Learning Development.

Rust, C., (2013) 'What Do We Think We Know about Student Learning, and What Are the Implications for Improving That Learning?', *Improving Student Learning Through Research and Scholarship: 20 Years of ISL*. Oxford: Oxford Centre for Staff and Learning Development. Available from: www.academia.edu/2522500/What_do_we_think_we_know_about_student_learning_and_what_are_the_implications_for_improving_that_learning (Accessed: 13 January 2025).

Rust, C., (2020, Revised) *Re-thinking Assessment – A Programme Leader's Guide*. Available from: https://www.researchgate.net/publication/322291901_Re-thinking_assessment_-_a_programme_leader's_guide (Accessed: 13 January 2025).

Rust, C., and Froud, L., (2016) 'Shifting the Focus from Skills to "Graduateness"', *Phoenix*, Issue 148, June, pp.8–9. Available from: https://www.researchgate.net/publication/303975538_Shifting_the_focus_from_skills_to_%27graduateness%27 (Accessed: 13 January 2025).

Shute, V., (2008) 'Focus on Formative Feedback', *Review of Educational Research*, 78:1, pp.153–189.

Index

Abrahart case 47, 49
academic map making 117
academic reading 132–136
academic socialisation 63–64
activity keywords 183–185
ADHD: and dyslexia: paragraphing (case study) 157–159; and exploration learning strategy 18–22; prevalence and characteristics 3; rise of, and emergence of co-occurrence (AuDHD) 29–33; WH question framework 128, 129, 131; working memory 28
AdvanceHE (DSC) 49–50, 74, 189
AI *see* GenAI and digital technologies
Aiyar, Y. 51
American College Health Association, US 50
analogical reasoning/metaphorisation 101–102, 108, 109
analogy and metaphor, compared 101–102
Anthony, P. 76
anticipatory 'reasonable adjustments' 47, 49, 189–190
argumentative or analytical sentences 163–165
'Artificial Intelligence Assessment Scale' (AIAS) 87
Asher, G. 54
assistive technology, GenAI as 92–94
authentic assessment/examinations 187, 191–192
autism: co-occurrence (AuDHD) 31–32; and exploitation: local, depth-first search strategies 22–27; and metaphors 107–109; oral presentations and vivas 199; presentations (case study) 167–172; prevalence and characteristics 4; visual pedagogical techniques 82; WH question framework 128, 130, 131; working memory 28, 29
autism-specific textbooks 62

Bakhtin, M. M. 91, 204
bi-directional digital media 29–31
'big picture': dyslexia 9, 82; right hemisphere function 11; *see also* compositional pictography

Bloom's taxonomy 64, 88, 185, 195–197
Brabazon, T. 46, 56, 62
brain structures and functions: minicolumn circuitry 12, 23, 24; networks and UDL 80–82, 83; right and left hemisphere 11–12, 73
Brown, E. N. and Brown, D. L. 83–84

cabinetmaker metaphor 88–89
Caldwell, E. et al. 48, 58, 59
Carlsson, A. 78
ChatGPT 76, 88, 91, 92, 93
Chomsky, N. 76
Christmas Cracker template 139–159, 165–167
Clark, A. 91–92; and Chalmers, D. 91
'clickbait' material 137–138
Clouder, L. et al. 54, 121
Clughen, L. and Connell, M. 56–57, 60, 92
co-occurrence (AuDHD) 31–33
cognition: and assessments 71–73; complementary 5–6; embodied 104–106
cognitive load/overload 28, 72, 84–85, 92, 93
cognitive maps: and conceptual frameworks in inclusive pedagogy 77–82; *see also* internal models
cognitive offloading, GenAI 87–91
cognitive strengths: and challenges in academic study and assessment (summary) 33–34; exploration learning strategy 12–13; *see also* Universal Design for Learning (UDL)
colour-coding technique 157–159
comparison in essays and assignments 145–147
complementary cognition 5–6
complex sentences 167
compositional pictography 83–85
compositional pictography (tutorial/feedback session) 127–131; academic reading 132–136; effectiveness of 173–179; essay and assignment structures 139–150; grammar, sentences, and rhetoric 159–172; paragraphing 150–159; searching and managing reading materials online 136–138; summary and conclusion 179

compound sentences 166
concept mapping 117
conceptual metaphors *see* metaphors
conclusions, purpose and structure of 147–150
conducting representations 122
conductor meta-role 120–122
constructive alignment 181–186
content/topic keywords 183
context: 'context blindness' 108; *see also* meaning
control tower feedback exchange 119
Cooper, R. 84–85, 127
Cottrell, S. 61, 145, 172
Covid-19 pandemic 51, 52–53, 59, 74, 86; examinations 188
Cremin, L. A. 77
Critchley, M. and Critchley, E. A. 7
culture and metaphors 106

Damasio, A. R. 107; and Carvalho, G. B. 107
Davies, S. et al. 56
DeCaro, M. S. et al. 28
'deeper deep-fakes', GenAI 187–188
deficit model/discourse 3–4, 56, 91–92, 108, 210
designing assessment tasks: authentic modes 187, 191–192; constructive alignment 181–186; embed support into holistic strategy 187–188; multiple-choice questions (MCQs) 192–197; oral presentations and vivas 197–199; summary 200; use of GenAI 200–206; *see also* examinations
diagnosis: at university 51; rise in 29–33
dialogic formative assessment 203–206
dialogue, role in tutorials 59–61
Dickinson, J. 87–88, 91
digital technologies *see* GenAI and digital technologies
disabilities: learning difficulties/differences or neurodiversity 1–4; legal perspective 1, 47, 49; medical model vs social model 3–5
Disabled Student Allowances (DSAs) 48, 50
Disabled Students' Commission/Commitment (DSC) 49–50, 74, 189
divergent thinking 10, 28, 29
Dyllick, T. H. et al. 106–107, 110, 120–121
dyslexia: and ADHD: paragraphing (case study) 157–159; and autism, comparative strategies 22–23, 24; co-occurrence (AuDHD) 31–33; and exploration learning strategy 7–18; and metaphor 109; MIND strengths 81–82; prevalence and characteristics 3; reading to write (case study) 134–136; WH question framework 128, 129, 131; working memory 27–29
dyslexia-specific writing guides 61–62

education budgets and spending demands 51, 53–54
Eide, B. L. and Eide, F. F. 11–12, 15, 28–29, 32, 61, 81–82, 85, 160
embedded and generic provision 63–64
Embedding Inclusive Assessment (QAA) 186, 191
embodied cognition and metaphors 104–106
Emmers, E. et al. 19, 20
employability 205; and authentic examinations 192; GenAI skills 201
episodic buffer 72–73
episodic memory 10
'equality, diversity and inclusion' initiatives 46, 54
Equality Act (2010) 47, 49
Equality and Human Rights Commission (EHRC) 47
essay and assignment structures 139–150
evaluative sentences 161–162
examinations 188–189; authentic 191–192; holistic, varied assessment strategy 189; 'open book' 191, 213; reasserting role of 206; scaffolding tasks or questions 190–191; support and implementation 189–190
exploration–exploitation continuum 6–7; ADHD 18–22; autism 22–27; dyslexia 7–18
extended mind, GenAI as 91–92

face-to-face vs online learning 86
facts, context and meaning, synthesis of 78, 89
feedback: authentic 192; conferencing 58; GenAI 92–93, 202–203; inclusive 213–215; marking and 55–56; types of 59; *see also* compositional pictography (tutorial/feedback session)
Flavell, J. H. 103, 105
flight plan creation 119
focus or limitation keywords 185–186
'Footnotes' visual strategy 172
formative assessment: dialogic 203–206; and summative assessment 211
Freire, P. 90
French, A. 46, 55, 56, 58, 62
Fulwiler, T. and Young, A. 77
fuzzy-trace theory (FTT) 10–11

Game, A. and Metcalfe, A. 57, 72, 203
Geither, E. and Meeks, L. 62
GenAI and digital technologies 29–31; academic misconduct and understanding 75–76; assignment types 71–72; assistive technology 92–94; cognitive offloading 87–91; examinations 188; extended mind 91–92; future of assessment and use of 200–206; institutional policies 87; pedagogical effectiveness 85–87; tutor's role 59

generic and embedded provision 63–64
Geschwind, N. 7–8; and Galaburda, A. M. 12
Gibbs, R. W. 103–104, 105, 110, 117; et al. 101, 103–104
'giftedness', ADHD 19
gist and verbatim memory traces 10–11
global exploration *see* exploration–exploitation continuum
global and local representations *see* internal models
Gordon, J. 57, 58, 59
Graham, S. and Harris, K. R. 62–63
grammar, sentences, and rhetoric 159–172
Greenfield, S. 29, 78, 89
Gribben, M. 61

'hallucinations', GenAI 93, 187–188
Hargreaves, S. 61
Heidegger, M. 88–89, 90
Hern, A. 30
Higher Education Statistics Agency 50
Hockings, C. 46
holistic assessment strategy 187–188, 189–190
hyperlexia 23
hyperlinks 136–138

inclusive examinations 188–189
inclusive feedback 213–215
inclusive pedagogies: cognitive maps and conceptual frameworks in 77–82; concept and case for 45–54; models of embedded and generic provision 63–64; one-to-one support 54–58; 'schizophrenic' tutorial and quest for 58–63
Individual Support Plans (ISPs) 189–190
insight-based reasoning 28, 29
intended learning outcomes: constructive alignment 181–186; multiple-choice questions (MCQs) 195–197
internal models 8–10; *see also* cognitive maps
International Monetary Fund 51

Jisc 188, 201

keywords, assignment tasks 183–186
Kolb, D. A. 89
Kovecses, Z. 100

Lakoff, G. and Johnson, M. 100, 101, 105–106, 109
Langford, A-M. and Kimberley, E. 54
language and visual functions of working memory 72–73
language-based assessment literacies, centrality of 73–77
Lawrence, J. 49
Layer, G. 49

learning: assessment *as*, *of*, and *for* 73–77, 104, 202–203, 205, 211; defining 6–7
learning approaches and assessment: ADHD 19–22; autism 24–27; dyslexia 13–18
learning difficulties/differences or neurodiversity 1–4
legal perspective 1, 47, 49
Leki, I. 59
limitation or focus keywords 185–186
linearity of conventional writing 57, 72, 203–204
Lombardi, M. M. 187

McArthur, J. 187
Maple Hayes Hall Dyslexia School and Research Centre 83
mapping: navigator meta-role 116–117; 'roadmap' 84–85, 127–128, 139–140, 172; text-mapping technique 135–136
marking: and feedback 55–56; GenAI 202; and intended learning outcomes 182, 195–197
meaning: facts and context, synthesis of 78, 89; 'roadmap' for 84–85, 127–128, 139–140, 172
medical model and social model of neurodiversity 3–5
memory 10–11; *see also* working memory
meta-representations 9, 78, 84
meta-roles 109–111; conductor 120–122; navigator 114–117; pilot 118–119; Stage One 111, 112–114; Stage Two 111–112, 114–122; Stage Three 112
metacognition 102–104
metaphors: conceptual metaphor theory (CMT) 100–102; in education 109–110; and embodied cognition 104–106; and learning differences 107–109; and metacognition 102–104; and motivation 106–107; use and etymology 84
MIND strengths 81–82
minicolumn circuitry of neocortex 12, 23, 24
mistakes/misinformation, GenAI 93, 187–188
motivation and metaphors 106–107
multi-modal learning approaches 62
multiple-choice questions (MCQs) 182, 192–197; dyslexia 17–18; GenAI 201

National Forum for the Enhancement of Teaching and Learning in Higher Education 73, 74
National Tutoring Programme 53
navigator meta-role 114–117
neurodiversity 1–4; social model 4–5; term 4, 5, 210
Nguyen, T. 86

one-to-one support: inclusive pedagogies 54–58; *see also* compositional pictography (tutorial/feedback session); tutorials
online learning, positive claims and negative effects 85–87
online searching and managing reading materials 136–138
'open book' examinations 191, 213
oral presentations and vivas 197–199
orchestral manoeuvres: synthesising sources 121
outsourcing/cognitive offloading, GenAI 87–91
Oxford Brookes Inclusive Curriculum Model (IDEAS) 46–47

paragraph structure 61, 145, 150–159
Paul, J. and Jefferson, F. 86
Perkins, M. et al. 87
personal conceptual frameworks 78, 79, 84
Phillips, J. and Fok, H. 58, 59
pictography *see* compositional pictography
pilot meta-role 118–119
plagiarism, GenAI 76
poiesis 88, 90
procedural memory 10
Professional Standards Framework (UKPSF) 49–50
progress tracking dashboard 119
prompts and prompt engineering, GenAI 92–93, 201

Quality Assurance Agency (QAA): *Embedding Inclusive Assessment* 186, 191; 'equality, diversity and inclusion' initiative 46; Teaching Excellence Framework (TEF) 52
questions/questionnaires: dyslexia and MIND strengths 82; effectiveness of compositional pictography 173–179; oral presentations and vivas 198–199; *see also* multiple-choice questions; Universal Design for Learning (UDL)

reading: academic 132–136; online materials 136–138; 'slow reading' 90
'reasonable adjustments' 47, 49, 189–190
reasoning, MIND strengths 81–82
Richards, K. and Pilcher, N. 63–64
'roadmap' 84–85, 127–128, 139–140, 172
Roberts, D. 85, 138, 172
Roseneil, S. 52–53
Rowsell, J. 47
Royal Holloway, University of London 50, 51, 52, 173

scaffolding: in embedded provision 63–64; examination tasks or questions 190–191; learning technologies and GenAI 85–94; metaphors 103–104, 105, 110; trade-offs 79, 81, 82, 84, 85; in tutorials 60, 61; *see also* compositional pictography (tutorial/feedback session)
'schizophrenese'/'word salad' 56–57, 92
'schizophrenic' tutorial and quest for inclusive pedagogies 58–63
searching and managing reading materials online 136–138
Self, W. 29
self-diagnostic monitoring 103–104
self-reflection 105
self-regulated learning (SRL) 103
Self-Regulated Strategy Development (SRSD) 62–63
SEND, education budgets and spending demands 51
Seneca 91
sensory–motor/embodied approach *see* metaphors
sentences, grammar, and rhetoric 159–172
Shaftesbury, A. 204
simple sentences 166
Singer, J. 4, 5, 210
skim and scan stage of reading 135
'slow learning'/'slow reading' 90
SMART principle of designing good learning outcomes 181–182
social interaction skills 32
social justice movement 5
social media 29–30
social model of neurodiversity 4–5
Solomon, M. et al. 23
stress and ADHD 18
student achievement, case for inclusive pedagogies 51–52
summative assessment 211
support, in holistic assessment strategy 187–188, 189–190
synthesis of facts, context and meaning 78, 89
systems thinking 13

Taylor, H. et al. 8; and Vestergaard, M. D. 9, 10, 33–34, 72, 104
Teaching Excellence Framework (TEF) (QAA) 52
text-mapping technique 135–136
time issues: examinations 190; GenAI 90–91
topic/content keywords 183
trade-offs: exploration–exploitation 10–11, 12; scaffolding 79, 81, 82, 84, 85
Tuck, J. 55–56
tuning sources 122
tutorials: 'schizophrenic' 58–63; *see also* compositional pictography (tutorial/feedback session); one-to-one support

UNESCO: definition of inclusion 48–49; *Technology in Education* report 86–87
Universal Design for Learning (UDL) 79–82, 128–131, 186, 211–212; and compositional pictography 83–85; and sentences 160; vs GenAI 89–90
University Alliance 52, 188, 189
unpleasant obligations 106–107, 114
'unrealised potential' 57–58, 59

value lines 117
verbatim and gist memory traces 10–11
visual and language functions of working memory 72–73
visual pedagogical techniques *see* compositional pictography; mapping
visual processing 9–10
visual representation, metaphor as 100, 101
visual and verbal association, metaphor as 106–107
vivas, oral presentations and 197–199
Vygotsky, L. 60, 128

Walker, M. B. 89, 90
Walker, N. 5

West, O. 172
West, T. G. 12, 13
Weyandt, L. L. and Dupaul, G. J. 19–20
'why'/'what'/'how' (WH question framework) *see* Universal Design for Learning (UDL)
Williams, E. L. and Casanova, M. F. 12, 23, 24
Woodward-Kron, R. 60, 61
wording: of assignment tasks 183–186; of multiple-choice questions (MCQs) 193–195
working memory: and cognitive load/overload 84–85, 92; episodic buffer 72–73; role in learning differences 27–29; and technological tools 89
workload, assessment 74–75
Writing Across the Curriculum (WAC) 63, 77
Writing in the Discipline (WID) 63, 77
writing generators and 'assistants', GenAI 90–94
Writing to Learn (WTL) 76–77

Zinsser, W. 77, 94
'Zone of Proximal Development' 60, 128
Zurich Resource Model (ZRM) 106–107

For Product Safety Concerns and Information please contact our EU representative GPSR@taylorandfrancis.com
Taylor & Francis Verlag GmbH, Kaufingerstraße 24, 80331 München, Germany

www.ingramcontent.com/pod-product-compliance
Lightning Source LLC
Chambersburg PA
CBHW080613230426
43664CB00019B/2875